Unwin Education Books: 10

THE SOCIOLOGY OF EDUCATION: AN INTRODUCTION

Books by Ivor Morrish

Disciplines of Education
Education Since 1800
The Background of Immigrant Children
The Sociology of Education: an Introduction

Unwin Education Books

Series Editor: Ivor Morrish, B.D., B.A., Dip.Ed. (London), B.A. (Bristol).

Unwin Education Books: 10
Series Editor: Ivor Morrish

The Sociology of Education

An Introduction

IVOR MORRISH
Principal Lecturer in Education
La Sainte Union College of Education, Southampton

London
GEORGE ALLEN AND UNWIN LTD
RUSKIN HOUSE   MUSEUM STREET

ISBN 0 04 301045 8 Cased
     0 04 301046 6 Paper

Printed in Great Britain
in 10 point Times Roman
by Cox & Wyman Ltd.
London, Fakenham and Reading

To Keith

The Gospel of Mark

When casually asked what he liked best about his
nursery school Mark, aged four, replied:
'Everything best is each other.' In a work on the
sociology of education the moral hardly needs
pointing.

Contents

Author's Preface

This book is an attempt to provide a guide to the sociology of education for students pursuing courses in colleges and departments of education. The general method adopted is an approach from the larger society to the institution of the school and the individuals who make up the institution, and finally outward to the society once more. The coverage has been as wide as possible within the compass of a brief book; it must inevitably, therefore, lack something in depth. The author hopes that the fairly full bibliographies may do something towards providing the basic material for the further study of each particular topic. No attempt has been made here to produce a *catalogue raisonné*; this would have been an impossible task in a book of this length. Anyone who has taught in a college of education will have experienced the difficulty, as well as the frustration, involved in recommending a few standard works to perhaps two hundred or more students pursuing the same course at the same time. The incredible inadequacy of our college libraries – particularly in the field of education – is too well-known, and too painful a subject, for me to elaborate here. It is hoped that the bibliographies will fulfil, *under some specialist tutorial guidance*, a felt need for a wide variety of titles which have some bearing upon the particular subjects considered.

I must thank my wife once again for her care and patience in typing my manuscript, and also my many colleagues and students for their helpful criticism of various parts of the book. As always I am indebted to all the authors whom I have quoted or to whom I have referred.

Southampton　　　　　　　　　　　　　　　　　　IVOR MORRISH
Hants

Chapter 1

The Nature of Sociology

The word 'sociology' first appeared in one of the volumes by Auguste Comte (1798–1857), entitled *Cours de Philosophie Positive* (1). Comte considered that one could discern the natural development of society in accordance with some law within the history of mankind. He further believed that there was some form of progress attendant upon this natural development of society, and that the main task of sociology was concerned with the reconstruction and progress of social forms and structures. According to Comte there were three definite stages in the law which governed such progress:

(*a*) the theological or fictive;
(*b*) the metaphysical or abstract;
(*c*) the scientific or positive.

This third stage, the phase of science, included sociology which was, to Comte, the very crown of science and of intellectual achievement.

Comte undoubtedly saw sociology as a humanizing science. It would react upon the other sciences and show their true function in the fabric of man's intellectual achievement; and, in consequence, sociology as a discipline and study was of pre-eminent importance. Moreover, it was a *positive* science; it was a science in its own right and not simply as a specialized application of one or more of the other sciences. Comte was looking for the laws which governed the actual observed phenomena, and not for any absolute or ultimate inner essences of a metaphysical order. He considered that these latter were neither knowable nor useful; but the regulating laws behind and in observable phenomena were facts both discoverable and socially helpful.

As one reads Comte on the spirit of social science and the possibilities of 'rational prevision' or prediction based upon the precise observation of social phenomena (2), one feels how remarkably 'modern' he is, and that many of the current attacks on sociology as a sort of *parvenu* science are wide of the mark. Nearly a century and a half have passed since Comte first began to write on sociological matters, and first sought to separate the disciplines of philosophy and sociology. In the judgement of Professor E. A. Tiryakian of Princeton University the consequences of this divorce have been twofold:

'On the positive side, one may mention that it has enabled sociology to become an academic discipline in its own right, free from the shackles of subordination. In divorcing itself from metaphysics and social philosophy, sociology became an empirical science' (3).

On the more negative side, however, Tiryakian feels that sociology has tended to concentrate on 'problems at the microscopic level' (4), and that, in consequence, research projects tend to accumulate rather than to be cumulative.

Any relatively new discipline – if sociology can really be so called – is certain to be the object of considerable scrutiny and criticism; at any rate, sociology has been no exception to this. Like some great octopus sociology seems to have extended its tentacles in every direction, missing nothing that even remotely resembles a social fact or relationship, whether it be in the bedchamber or the council-chamber. There are the natural prudes, and even the naturally reluctant who are not necessarily prudes, who feel that there is something vaguely indecent about the detailed inquiries into their sex life, whilst others equally resent the probing of their religious and political persuasions. It remains true, however, that the steady, thorough, unremitting march of the sociologist will leave no observable social fact unrecorded. A glance at the 'Index of Research' of *The British Sociological Association Register* (5) will reveal that at the time of writing over two hundred social questions of a general nature, or branches of sociology, or constellations of social facts are being investigated. Topics range from consumer behaviour and cybernetics to bereavement and social ecology; and there is in evidence a very wide interest in every conceivable facet of social life and activity.

It is, perhaps, partly because of this catholic interest that sociology has been attacked as being a 'non-subject', or a depository of all subjects. But attacks of this sort, when they are not motivated merely by vested interests, are mistaken with regard to the nature of sociology itself. Sociology is concerned with social facts: this means, more specifically, that it is the province of sociology to examine both the structural aspects of human society and every type of social relationship that occurs within those structures. And all this information must be investigated and tabulated as objective facts. Indeed, the sociologists' increasingly cold, statistical and scientific assessment of such social fact has often been a matter of discomfort to many in society. 'Instead of being content just to state it, describe it and analyse it, why don't they do something about it?' This represents the cry of concern of those who feel strongly about social abnormality and pathology. The answer is simple, and it has been made by Professor P. L. Berger in the following terms: 'Social work, whatever its theoretical rationalization, is a certain *practice* in society. Sociology is not a practice, but an attempt to understand' (6).

This does not mean, of course, that sociologists are not interested in corrective or compensatory action in society, or that they have no philosophy of life, or that they are determinists, or are all immoral, or humanists, or atheists. They may, in fact, fall into any of these categories; but, primarily, sociologists are just people serving society in a variety of capacities as teachers, lecturers, researchers, journalists, workers in industry, personnel officers, social workers or administrators, town planners, parsons, criminologists, probation officers and so forth. As sociologists they are interested in establishing the facts of society and of social relationships in as objective and scientific a manner as possible; as people living and working in society, with its multifarious problems, they are – most of them – also interested in passing some judgement upon the facts and in seeking some solution to social problems. In doing so they are changing their role from that of sociologist *qua* sociologist to that of (say) moralist, philosopher, reformer, or just a member of society with a concern for people and their social relationships – particularly, perhaps, where those social relationships have somehow gone astray, or where weak relationships require reinforcing.

Naturally, the abnormal has its fascination; there is nothing more intriguing than social pathology. But, again, it would be quite a mistake to imagine that this is the prime interest of the sociologist. Social facts, whatever their nature, are the raw material of the sociologist; and his concern is to establish what those facts really are when divested of personal prejudice and opinion in recording and in observation. Equally, of course, he is concerned to delineate social aspects of opinion and prejudice. In it all, however, he is involved not in the making of value-judgements but of factual-judgements. That is, if he is investigating the sexual behaviour of a particular society, as a sociologist he neither approves of nor condemns any particular form of sexual activity; he notes it as accurately as he possibly can and seeks, at the same time, to establish whether it is normal or abnormal for that particular society, or for the observed section of a particular society. Later, when he has doffed his role as an objective investigator, that is, as a sociologist, he may wish to praise or express his abhorrence of such behaviour. In doing so he may take on the role of a social philosopher, or he may speak as one who adheres to a particular religious and moral code, or simply as one who accepts or objects to certain forms of behaviour on aesthetic grounds.

Or, again, the sociologist may take the very tolerant view that all things are relative. The 'realities' of society as we know them are expressed in very limited historical contexts; and if

'sociological laws, structures, types and classifications have no absolute character and are general only in a partial sense . . . All analyses in the social sciences are relative to a certain moment in a historical period and to a certain geographical area' (7),

then we must be doubly wary of any value-judgements made at a different point in time or from a different location in space.

It is important to establish norms of behaviour in all sorts of social relations, even in order that the abnormal may be fully understood. Thus we find sociologists researching into 'the role of the beerhalls', 'the employment of married women', 'the social effects of redundancy', 'the structure of solidarity', 'the social and economic position of widows in Australia', 'living accommodation for young people', 'the sociology of popular music', 'the social consequences of shift working', and a thousand and one other intriguing social topics. And not only intriguing – some of them at first glance may appear to be almost bizarre. One sometimes gets the impression that a particular sociologist has gone out of his way to find a topic that no one else could possibly have dreamed up, and has then set to in order to research it and become the world's authority on some isolated piece of social interaction.

This, however, is not quite fair or true. The old gibe about knowing more and more concerning less and less has some validity; but it is also true that the researcher – if his research is to be of any value at all – must first of all, in the present context, have had a thorough grounding in general sociology, its organization, and its methods of inquiry. Even then, however, his detailed research may still be of little value in isolation: it must be seen in the perspective of the totality of all similar or related research (8). There is a lot of 'dead wood' in the archives of the universities; and many a researcher must have felt a pang of disappointment and regret that several years of his labour have never received even a mention in relation to other, or perhaps similar, inquiries. This is, of course, true to some extent of all forms of research which are being tackled at the somewhat abstract academic level. Seen, however, in proper relation to other and similar research most sociological inquiries, although apparently isolated and microscopic, have some value and significance at the more global level. It is often just a question of the general availability of the material and its proper documentation for reference purposes.

Thus the 'oyster' of sociology is a large one, and all human activity involving social relationships is the subject-matter for its consideration and research. Emile Durkheim remarked: 'there are, in reality, as many branches of sociology, as many particular social sciences, as there are varieties of social facts' (9). It is this richness and variety of contexts for social activity and interaction which have led to the inevitable division of sociology into a large number of sub-sections. In addition to general sociology there are such offspring as comparative sociology, economic sociology, sociology of education, historical sociology, industrial sociology, sociology of culture, sociology of knowledge, sociology of law, mathematical sociology, political sociology, sociology of morals, sociology of science, sociology of art and literature, sociology of music, sociology of language, rural sociology, urban sociology, sociology of migration, and so on.

The ramifications of sociology, or of the social sciences for those who prefer the term (10), are virtually limitless, and it is because of this that many have suggested that 'sociology' is more of a collation of subjects than a subject *per se*. One might, however, take many other 'subjects' and perform a similar analytical exercise in order to consider the component parts, as it were, of the discipline. The fact is that almost all disciplines, and 'subjects', are somewhat like voracious monsters ever seeking fresh fodder for consumption. In the past, for example, metaphysics sought to provide a global view, or *Weltanschauung*, of the whole of our knowledge. In the process there developed the philosophy of science, the philosophy of history, the philosophy of religion, the philosophy of art, the philosophy of politics, the philosophy of morals, the philosophy of education, and so on. To date philosophy appears to be the only universe of discourse wherein the 'voracious monster' has ultimately sought to devour itself by a process of reductionism to pure logic. But when man has eventually found that he cannot live by logic alone, and that logical positivism is, to say the least, a trifle cold and barren, there seems little doubt that a new metaphysic will arise, which may well add to its many branches a fully-fledged meta-sociology.

One of the reasons for the sub-division of sociology into an increasingly large number of specialisms is the basic human fact of our own personal limitations. One cannot be an 'expert' in sociology any more than one can be an 'expert' in physics. One has to choose a particular area of interest, once the general groundwork has been covered, and concentrate upon that, or some part of it, if one is to 'drink deep' of the 'Pierian spring'. Durkheim, for example, would not have agreed that comparative sociology was a separate branch of sociology; he held that 'it is sociology itself, in so far as it ceases to be purely descriptive and aspires to account for facts' (11).

But Durkheim's was a counsel of perfection since, so far as he was concerned, one could not explain any social fact of any complexity *'except by following its complete development through all social species'* (12). This represents a formidable task which can be accomplished only by the principle of 'divide and conquer'. The study of education has similarly accepted, in recent years, that its many problems may best be considered through a variety of disciplines, including philosophy, psychology, sociology, history and the comparative method (13). The important thing is that none of the sub-divisions of a subject, whether that subject be sociology or education, should consider itself self-sufficient and go off into orbit. There must always be that referral to the centre in order that the various parts may make some ultimate synoptic sense, and that the main branch may be enriched and expanded by their contributions, however 'microscopic' they may be.

Perhaps this is one of the gravest dangers that face sociology as it comes of age. It is the old pride of being a 'pure' man as opposed to 'applied' in science or mathematics – indeed, these terms have already appeared in the divisions of sociology. To some extent it is the old fallacy of the 'economic man' as opposed to 'religious man', or 'political man', or some other sort of man. Society is a complex interweaving of all the intricate patterns of human social relationships; a man may act in an economic way, or in a religious way, or in a political way – but he remains a man in relation with other men, and his activities have this common focal point. We may study these social relationships in isolation, to some extent, in order to produce our neat statistical tables and sociological data. Any final judgements made upon them, however, with regard to cause and effect must have an eye to the totality of relationships and not to just one order of them. Durkheim himself tended to disregard individual motives and intentions in his study of the 'social' phenomenon of suicide; he was concerned simply with the *social* logic of the situation (14).

Any synthesis in sociological study must obviously do more than collect facts and utilize statistical and scientific methods of analysis. The study of social psychology, whether as a branch of psychology or of sociology, has made it clear that such concepts as the 'collective representations' of Durkheim (15), or the 'group mind' or 'collective mind' of McDougall (16), require very careful analysis and examination. At the end of an interesting paper on 'The Sociological Nature of Human Valuations', Karl Mannheim discusses the difference between the psychological and the sociological approach. He suggests that one can observe and define any human action in terms of the psychological, that is the purely subjective, intentions or motivations implied in it; or one can define its meaning in terms of the social functions which it fulfils, either consciously or unconsciously. These two approaches supplement each other; but there is at the same time 'a series of interesting problems implied in the continuous transmutation of subjective motivation into objective functionally determined behaviour' (17). Thus, one cannot ignore the 'subjective motivation' even though it may go through the process of transmutation into socially determined behaviour.

Behind the cold statistical data of the sociologist as to 'who?', 'how many?', 'when?', 'how often?' and 'where?', there lie the thoughts, motivations, purposes, hopes and fears of living, warm people who have relationships, who change their minds and habits – sometimes quite suddenly and dramatically, who undergo stresses and who suffer insupportable ugliness and tragedy. These are facts, personal and social facts, that the statistics do not, and cannot convey by mere numbers. Nor, of course, can they possibly reveal the incredible beauty and laughter that people also experience. Sociology is a science, using scientific techniques and methodology; but it is a science that needs, perhaps more than most, to consider the importance of human variables whilst dealing with norms and averages. P. L. Berger has admirably put the point when he says:

'Sociology will be especially well advised not to fixate itself in an attitude of humourless scientism that is blind and deaf to the buffoonery of the social spectacle. If sociology does that, it may find that it has acquired a foolproof methodology, only to lose the world of phenomena that it originally set out to explore ...' (18).

The writer believes that Berger is right in his insistence that sociology, whilst using scientific procedures and methods, has a humanistic affinity with philosophy and history; and that it is not *just* a descriptive science, or one simply involved in intriguing questions of methodology and statistical analysis. One of the great difficulties concerning the establishment of a 'science' of society is that we frequently reach the point where the collection of mere data becomes almost an end in itself, and the reliable knowledge acquired is carefully filed away and never used to increase man's capacity for happiness and a fuller life, or his awareness of his need for reconstituted relationships with his fellows.

Even if we accept that the sociologist *qua* sociologist does not make value-judgements about his data, or that he 'ought' not to introduce the word 'ought' into his final analysis, we may still accept that sociology is a science which, like others, may be *predictive* on the basis of statistical information but that, unlike many other sciences, it may also be *teleological* in that it provides information which may be used prescriptively. This means, briefly, that if we can accurately describe man's social ailments, and can predict the effects of his social activity, we can increasingly direct research towards those things which belong to man's peace, and towards his personal and social betterment.

No analogy, of course, is perfect; but there is something analogical between medical and sociological science here. We would, I suspect, think very little of medical sciences which carefully investigated and tabulated the nature of our diseases, and made predictions about their incidence and mortality rates, but made no attempt whatsoever to suggest or provide suitable prophylactic treatment. It is precisely at this point that we come close to the main purpose of this book, namely, a discussion of the sociology of education.

In a paper which he presented at a conference in London in 1936, held under the auspices of the Institute of Sociology and World University Service, Karl Mannheim discussed 'The Place of Sociology' (19), and he distinguished between static and dynamic sociology. In *dynamic* sociology, he said:

> 'we concentrate on those factors which are antagonistic in their respective tendencies. Here we stress the working of those principles which in the long run tend to a disequilibrium and thus bring about changes which transform the social structure' (20).

It is this dynamic sociology that Mannheim again deals with in his *Man and Society*. He believed very strongly that if one could plan, as Hitler did, for the submission and enslavement of a society, one could equally plan for freedom in society; but he also accepted that this would involve at the same time the whole problem of 'transforming man' (21). We are not concerned here with the precise terms of Mannheim's argument, but rather with the fact that Mannheim himself had experienced the collapse of democratic culture under Nazi totalitarianism. He saw the uselessness of merely analysing a situation without attempting to make some positive contribution towards its amelioration or change in one way or another. This, to him, was dynamic sociology, and it involved an examination of social techniques and forms of social control whereby man and society might be transformed for the better.

It is here that sociology differs most from the exact sciences. The purpose of the exact sciences is to give some precise description and explanation of physical facts. The German philosopher and sociologist, Wilhelm Dilthey, distinguished between this exact explanation (*Erklärung*) of the natural sciences and the understanding (*Verstehen*) which is characteristic of the humanistic sciences, including sociology (22). Dilthey insisted that social facts were comprehensible 'from the inside'; they involved the life of the human psyche which was not amenable to the exact analysis required in the mathematical and empirical sciences.

Few have been more rigorous or objective in their search for social causation than Max Weber (23); and yet Weber, like Dilthey, also emphasized the importance of a total understanding (*Verstehen*) of any social situation to the extent of probing motives and subjective meanings of human behaviour, whether of the individual or of the group, before attempting to establish correlations or social causation. The term *Verstehen* is now used as a technical term for sociological understanding and interpretation, although one cannot pretend that the majority of contemporary sociologists accept this concept. Professor Morris Ginsberg suggested the phrase 'sympathetic intuition' as a reasonably adequate English equivalent of the word, and as representing that penetration into the inner aspects of any situation which no natural science claimed to do (24).

Weber saw the necessity of relating sociology and its investigations to other studies such as psychology and history (25); and the importance of this view is further emphasized by the total unpredictability of the 'charismatic' element in social development. Charisma is 'a gift that inheres in an object or person simply by virtue of natural endowment' (26). By means of this natural gift the individual develops a social, political, or religious authority which may be expressed in a way completely contrary to accepted tradition and loyalties. Such figures as the Buddha, the Christ, Muhammad, and Gandhi, and in a different sphere Alexander, Napoleon, and Hitler, all had charismatic personality and power. It was said of the Christ that people were astonished at his teaching 'for he taught them as one who had authority, and not as the scribes' (27). The Greek word used for 'authority' here is ἐξουσία (exousia), which means 'out of (his) being, essence or substance'. Jesus, according to the gospel writer, possessed a charismatic power to the extent that when he said, 'Your leaders and authorities, your scriptures, scribes and priests say this and that, but *I* say unto you . . .', he in reality put himself above tradition, authority and the law, and staked a claim for new leadership, for change and even revolution.

This intangible, impalpable element of charisma is something that cannot be weighed or measured, whether one is thinking in terms of its origin or its effects. It may arise in the barren, desert waste of a defeated and subdued theocratic society, or in the social and economic ferment of an industrialized community. But, however it arises, it not only goes in the face of all possible prediction, it frequently changes the face of the world as well as the inner springs of individual and group activity. Throughout Weber's *The Sociology of Religion*, which was first published in Germany between 1920–2, this theme recurs along with many other analyses of individual and group phenomena which are more amenable to description (and *Verstehen*) than to precise statistical correlation or prediction.

Sociological predictions are, at best, statements of probability accompanied by an estimated margin of error. But, as Professor Duverger points out, there are special difficulties in prediction when one is concerned with the social sciences, and measurement of the factors involved in the physical universe is easier than of those involved in the realm of social phenomena. Therefore prediction is easier in the physical than in the social sciences. But even more important is the rapidity of the modifications of the social context – modifications which are also more 'profound and complex' than those of the physical context (28). The whole question obviously requires a more detailed investigation than can be afforded here but, as Duverger emphasizes, there are in the social context so many and varied chain reactions and 'feedback' effects that they are impossible to define, accurately measure or predict.

It is these chain reactions and feedback effects which make society and social relationships the complex and unpredictable elements that they are. And we, as individuals, are located in society. If, as Professor Berger suggests, 'society is the walls of our imprisonment in history' (29), it is very important for us to understand the nature of our imprisonment as well as the possibilities of extending those limiting walls which make us history's captives. Indeed, as Berger would agree, not only is man in society: society is also in man. Man internalizes the cultural heritage and the expanding perspectives of his own society. He may, in Berger's terms, push out the walls in order to extend the area of social activity; indeed, he may repair the walls where the ravages of time have eroded something of that imprisonment and so co-operate in his own captivity. But, as long as society exists for him, he is involved in its structures, its *mores*, its laws and its sanctions; he cannot escape its control and its interpenetration of his very consciousness.

It is because of this saturation of the self by society that it becomes increasingly important for the individual to study his society at depth. There is a very real sense in which through studying society, we are studying ourselves. According to George Herbert Mead:

> 'the self is not a metaphysical entity, it is a process of behaviour and response realized in time. It is not innate or given from birth, it is built up from experience and it gains its definition in response to and in opposition to the social process in which it is set' (30).

For Mead education was a question of the development of unity within the self, and the ever-growing development of the self through social interaction. Without attempting to develop Mead's theme here it becomes increasingly clear that a detailed study of social interaction is of some considerable importance for the educationist.

In conclusion, then, sociology is the general science of society. From the data collated by sociologists an attempt is made to develop a theory, or rather theories, concerning any particular society, or concerning societies in general. By means of comparative analysis, whether comparative sociology is regarded as a separate division of sociology or not, theories concerning the macro-society and its evolution may be developed. In particular, sociology is concerned with social institutions, such as class structure, the family, kinship, law, religion and so forth. Any science develops precision as it constructs a grammar or language with terms which provide shorthand statements of descriptive accounts of social institutions, relationships and events. It is clearly important that words, which may have a more popular connotation, should have limited meanings in the context of any particular science.

In its development of a specialist vocabulary it seems true, as Professor

Berger contends, that much of the 'contemporary "sociologese" can be understood as a self-conscious mystification' (31). Granted the necessity for a specialist grammar or vocabulary which has to be understood, there is still no reason why the large percentage of sociological writing should be unintelligible except to an elite. This is certainly not intended as an attack on sociology as a discipline, or on its need to become as clear, precise and objective as possible; indeed, quite the contrary. The writer is acutely aware of the many dangers that accompany any over-popularization of a subject such as sociology. But he is equally aware of the almost total exclusion that can occur through the development of an 'in-group' mystique by the deliberate cultivation of what is often nothing more than an ugly jargon, which may well prove ultimately to be sterile and self-destructive through its very obscurity of expression. Esotericism, whether in theology, psychology or sociology, can lead in the end merely to the complete obfuscation of sometimes invaluable material for individual and social improvement and development.

REFERENCES

1 *Vide* Comte, A., *Cours de Philosophie Positive*, 6 vols (Bachelier, Paris, 1830–42), in particular Vol. IV, Lesson 47 (published in 1839), where he names the new science 'sociology'. *Vide* also Martineau, Harriet, *The Positive Philosophy of Auguste Comte* (George Bell and Sons, 1896), in particular Vol. II, Book VI, Chapter 3, pp. 218–32.

2 *Vide* Parsons, T. *et al.* (eds), *Theories of Society* (Free Press, Collier-Macmillan, 1965), pp. 125–36.

3 Tiryakian, E. A., *Sociologism and Existentialism* (Prentice-Hall, 1962), p. 4.

4 Ibid., p. 4.

5 *Vide The British Sociological Association Register,* available from The British Sociological Association, Skepper House, 13 Endsleigh Street, London, W.C.1.

6 Berger, P. L., *Invitation to Sociology* (Penguin, 1966), p. 15.

7 Duverger, M., *Introduction to the Social Sciences* (Allen and Unwin, 1964), p. 33.

8 *Vide* notes 3 and 4, and the comment that 'research projects tend to accumulate rather than to be cumulative'.

9 Durkheim, E., *De la Méthode dans les Sciences* (Alcan, Paris, 1902), p. 242; quoted by Inkeles, A., *What is Sociology?* (Prentice-Hall, 1964), pp. 5–6.

10 Duverger, M., op. cit., pp. 17 and 43.

11 Durkheim, E., *The Rules of Sociological Method* (Free Press, Glencoe, 1964), p. 139.

12 Ibid., p. 139. Durkheim's italics.

13 *Vide* Morrish, I., *Disciplines of Education* (Allen and Unwin, 2nd

impression 1968); and Lynch, J., 'Comparative Education and Colleges of Education' in *Education for Teaching*, No. 82, Summer 1970.

14 *Vide* Durkheim, E., *Suicide: A Study in Sociology* (Free Press, Glencoe, 1951; Routledge, 1952), *passim*.

15 *Vide* Durkheim, E., *Sociology and Philosophy* (Cohen and West, 1965), Chapter I on 'Individual and Collective Representations', pp. 1–34.

16 *Vide* McDougall, W., *The Group Mind* (Putnam, 1920), *passim*.

17 Mannheim, K., *Essays on Sociology and Social Psychology* (Routledge, 1953), Chapter VII, pp. 241–2.

18 Berger, P. L., op. cit., pp. 187–8.

19 Mannheim, K., op. cit. Chapter V, pp. 195–208.

20 Ibid., p. 207.

21 *Vide* Mannheim, K., *Man and Society: In an Age of Reconstruction* (Routledge, 1940; reprinted 1960), particularly Parts IV and V.

22 *Vide* Hodges, H. A., *The Philosophy of Wilhelm Dilthey* (Routledge, 1952), and Duverger, M., *Introduction to the Social Sciences*, pp. 30–1.

23 *Vide* Gerth, H. and Mills, C. W. (eds), *From Max Weber: Essays in Sociology* (Routledge, 1948; 5th impression 1964).

24 *Vide* Mannheim, K., *Essays on Sociology and Social Psychology*, p. 216.

25 *Vide* Mitchell, G. D., *Sociology: The Study of Social Systems* (U.T.P., 1959; reprinted 1963), pp. 24–5; and Berger, P. L., op. cit., pp. 146–7.

26 Weber, Max, *The Sociology of Religion* (Social Science Paperbacks, Methuen, 1966), p. 2.

27 Mark 1: 22.

28 Duverger, M., op. cit., p. 228.

29 Berger, P. L., op. cit., p. 109.

30 Mannheim, K. and Stewart, W. A. C., *An Introduction to the Sociology of Education* (Routledge, 1962), p. 97. *Vide* also Mead, G. H., *Mind, Self and Society* (Univ. of Chicago Press, 1934; 13th impression 1965), in particular Part III, 'The Self'.

31 Berger, P. L., op. cit., p. 25.

BIBLIOGRAPHY

A. *General and Introductory*

AUBERT, V., *Elements of Sociology* (Heinemann, 1968).

BARNES, H. E. (ed.), *An Introduction to the History of Sociology* (Univ. of Chicago Press, abridged edition 1966).

BERGER, P. L., *Invitation to Sociology* (Penguin, 1966).

BOTTOMORE, T. B., *Sociology* (Allen and Unwin, 1962; 2nd edition 1971).

CHINOY, E., *Society: An Introduction to Sociology* (Random House, N.Y., 2nd edition 1967).

COHEN, P., *Modern Social Theory* (Heinemann, 1968).

COLE, W. E., *Introductory Sociology* (David McKay Co. Inc., N.Y., 1962).

COTGROVE, S., *The Science of Society* (Allen and Unwin, 1967).

DAHRENDORF, R., *Essays in the Theory of Society* (Routledge, 1968).

FYVEL, T. R. (ed.), *The Frontiers of Sociology* (Cohen and West, 1964).

GINSBERG, M., *Sociology* (O.U.P., 1934).

GOLDTHORPE, J. E., *An Introduction to Sociology* (C.U.P., 1968).

GOULD, J. and KOLB, W. (eds), *A Dictionary of the Social Sciences* (Tavistock Publications, 1964).

GOULDNER, A. and H., *Modern Sociology* (Harcourt, Brace and World, 1963).

GREEN, B. S. R. and JOHNS, E. A., *An Introduction to Sociology* (Pergamon Press, 1966; reprinted 1968).

INKELES, A., *What is Sociology?* (Prentice-Hall, 1964).

JOHNSON, H. M., *Sociology: A Systematic Introduction* (Routledge, 1961; 4th impression 1964).

LOWIE, R. H., *Social Organization* (Routledge 1950; 3rd impression 1962).

MACIVER, R. M. and PAGE, C. H., *Society* (Macmillan, 1950).

MARTINDALE, D., *The Nature and Types of Sociological Theory* (Routledge, 1961; 2nd impression 1965).

MAUS, H., *A Short History of Sociology* (Routledge, 1962; 2nd impression 1965).

MERTON, R. K., *Social Theory and Social Structure* (Free Press, Glencoe, 1951; revised edition 1957).

MERTON, R. K. *et al.* (eds), *Sociology Today: Problems and Prospects* (Basic Books, N. Y., 1959).

MITCHELL, G. D., *Sociology: The Study of Social Systems* (U.T.P., 1959; reprinted 1963).

MITCHELL, G. D., *A Hundred Years of Sociology* (Duckworth, 1968).

MITCHELL, G. D. (ed.), *A Dictionary of Sociology* (Routledge, 1968).

OGBURN, W. F. and NIMKOFF, M. F., *A Handbook of Sociology* (Routledge, 5th edition 1964).

PARSONS, T., *et al.* (eds), *Theories of Society* (Free Press, Glencoe, 1965).

SOROKIN, P. A., *Contemporary Sociological Theories* (Harper, 1928).

WEBER, M., *Basic Concepts in Sociology* (Peter Owen, 1962).

WINCH, P., *The Idea of a Social Science* (Routledge, 1958; 3rd impression 1963).

B. *Methodology*

BLALOCK, H. M., *Social Statistics* (McGraw-Hill, 1960).

BLALOCK, H. M., and E., *Methodology in Social Research* (McGraw-Hill, 1968).

BROWN, R., *Explanation in Social Science* (Routledge, 1963; 2nd impression 1964).

CICOUREL, A. V., *Method and Measurement in Sociology* (Free Press, Glencoe, 1964).

COLEMAN, J. S., *Introduction to Mathematical Sociology* (Free Press, Glencoe, 1964).

DURKHEIM, E., *Suicide: A Study in Sociology* (Routledge, 1952; 2nd impression 1963).

DURKHEIM, E., *The Rules of Sociological Method* (Free Press, Glencoe, 1964).

DUVERGER, M., *Introduction to the Social Sciences* (Allen and Unwin, 1964).

GALTUNG, J., *Theory and Methods of Social Research* (Allen and Unwin, 1967).
GIBSON, Q., *The Logic of Social Enquiry* (Routledge, 1960; 2nd impression 1964).
KAUFMANN, F., *Methodology of the Social Sciences* (O.U.P., 1944).
MADGE, J., *The Tools of Social Science* (Longmans, 1953).
MANN, P. H., *Methods of Sociological Enquiry* (Blackwell, 1968).
MORENO, J. L. (ed.), *The Sociometry Reader* (Free Press, Glencoe, 1960).
MYRDAL, G., *Value in Social Theory: A Collection of Essays on Methodology* (Routledge, 1958; 2nd impression 1962).
REX, J., *Key Problems of Sociological Theory* (Routledge, 1961; 3rd impression 1965).
SELLITZ, G. *et al., Research Methods in Social Relations* (Holt and Co., 1959).
STACEY, M., *Methods of Social Research* (Pergamon Press, 1969).
WEBER, M., *The Methodology of the Social Sciences* (Free Press, Glencoe, 1949).

Chapter 2

The Sociology of Education

A. ITS ORIGIN AND DEVELOPMENT

Of the more recent educationists, John Dewey (1859–1952), writing at the turn of the century, was one of the first to appreciate the essential relationship between the school and society. He had observed that the old simple life and the village community were inevitably breaking down, and that social structures generally were changing. Yet, Dewey felt, the institutions of school and church had done little or nothing to make the child aware of the new society growing up around him, and of which he was an essential member. There were tensions developing between village and town life of which both pupils and adults were quite unconscious.

In addition, whilst the village child was close to the earth and was fully aware of the context of his daily and social life, the town child, in a much more complex fabric of relationships, was making use of amenities that he had never seen constructed and that he could never really internalize. For example, the clothes he wore were manufactured in a way that he knew little or nothing about; he lit the gas, but he was quite ignorant concerning its preparation and also of the principles of combustion.

It was Dewey's purpose to help promote, through his experimental school at Chicago, a social spirit of co-operation and mutual aid, and to provide within the classroom itself the sort of living situations in which such co-operation might be elicited. In order to achieve this aim Dewey realized that something must be done to bring the school into closer relation with both the individual homes of the children and with the more general life of their neighbourhood. He saw the school virtually as a second home for the child; but it must be essentially a *good* home in which there existed a real sense of community and of common interests and pursuits. For Dewey the school was a community in miniature, a micro-society which both reflected the larger society outside and also sought, in the long run, to improve upon that society. In this way Dewey sought to make the importance of the home and environment explicit in the educational process (1).

Emile Durkheim (1858–1917) was born a year before John Dewey, and when the latter was developing his educational theories at the universities of Chicago and Columbia, New York, Durkheim held the Chair at the Sorbonne, Paris, in the Science of Education, which became in 1913 the

Chair in the Science of Education and Sociology. Not unnaturally, as a result of his training and his primary interest in sociology, Durkheim saw education as a 'social thing', and he argued:

'it is society as a whole and each particular social *milieu* that determine the ideal that education realizes. Society can survive only if there exists among its members a sufficient degree of homogeneity; education perpetuates and reinforces this homogeneity by fixing in the child, from the beginning, the essential similarities that collective life demands. But on the other hand, without a certain diversity all co-operation would be impossible; education assures the persistence of this necessary diversity by being itself diversified and specialized' (2).

It was this view of education as an eminently social thing that led Durkheim to argue that there was not just one form of education, ideal or actual, but many forms; indeed, there were as many different forms of education as there were different *milieux* in a given society (3). Thus society as a whole, and each particular *milieu*, would determine the type of education that was realized.

It is not our purpose here to develop or analyse Durkheim's themes in any detail, but merely to emphasize the really important part that Durkheim played in the development of the sociological view of education. For him education was a means of organizing the individual self and the social self, the *I* and the *We*, or the *homo duplex*, into a disciplined, stable and meaningful unity (4). The 'interiorization' or 'internalization' of values and discipline represented for Durkheim the child's initiation into his society. It was, therefore, vitally important to understand and analyse that society in a methodical and scientific way. When in 1902 Durkheim gave his inaugural lecture at the Sorbonne, he urged that the profound transformations which contemporary societies were then undergoing necessitated corresponding changes in the national education. He concluded his lecture with the words: 'I do not believe that I am following a mere prejudice or yielding to an immoderate love for a science which I have cultivated all my life, in saying that never was a sociological approach more necessary for the educator' (5).

During the next forty years the development of what was at first termed 'educational sociology' was slow but steady; a number of textbooks appeared (6), and in 1927 the *Journal of Educational Sociology* was founded by E. Payne. But as far as England was concerned the real development of the subject began with the appointment of Sir Fred Clarke as the Director of the London University Institute of Education in 1937. Clarke was very conscious of the contribution which sociology might and could make to the development of educational thought. In particular, he believed very strongly that there should be planning in education, and in his book

Education and Social Change, which was published in 1940, Clarke stated that 'we propose to accept unreservedly what may be called the socio-logical standpoint and to exhibit as well as we can its concrete application to the field of English education' (7).

Although not all educationists supported Clarke's unreserved acceptance of the sociological standpoint then – and many still have their reservations – there was behind him the dominating figure of the refugee from Nazi totalitarianism, Karl Mannheim (1893–1947). Mannheim settled in London and became a lecturer in sociology at the London School of Economics, and he was a prominent figure at the annual conferences of the Institute of Sociology. From 1940 onwards he was invited to lecture part-time at the Institute of Education of London University, and in 1946 he was appointed to the Chair of Education. Like Durkheim, Mannheim was interested primarily in sociology, and he came to education as a sociologist. But, in effect, he saw education as one of the dynamic elements in sociology; it was a social technique in itself and a means of social control. In *Man and Society*, Mannheim stated:

'Sociologists do not regard education solely as a means of realizing abstract ideals of culture, such as humanism or technical specialization, but as part of the process of influencing men and women. Education can only be understood when we know for what society and for what social position the pupils are being educated' (8).

It was because he felt strongly that we could not educate in a vacuum that Mannheim anxiously sought to diagnose the sort of society in which we were living. By analysing the society, and categorizing its ills, we might be able to plan our educational programme for a new and better society. Mannheim's *Diagnosis of Our Time*, which was first published in 1943, was an attempt to demonstrate the possibility of a Third Way between the extremes of *laissez-faire* and totalitarianism (9). The planned democracy that Mannheim envisaged meant that there was a need for a consensus of values. The democracies must surrender their complete in-difference to valuations, for democracy could function only if democratic self-discipline was strong enough to make people agree on concrete issues for the sake of common action, even if they disagreed on details.

But consensus was more than agreement on specific issues – consensus was common life. Mannheim believed, for example, that if a democratic society were to invest as much energy and time in the mitigation of race and group hatred as the totalitarian societies did in fostering it, important achievements in the elimination of conflicts would thereby be accom-plished. What we needed, he argued, was a moral substitute for war; and one of the lessons we could derive from the Second World War was the extent to which psychological and institutional forces could become operative in society, if integration were really desired. We are now living in the midst of an evolving multi-cultural society, in which consensus becomes increasingly problematic and integration a question of organized planning. Education must surely have something to offer in the amelioration of interracial clash and strife.

Mannheim saw the sociological approach to educational problems as one which could ultimately provide some positive aims in education itself, as well as helping to establish both content and method. His Third Way was a way of consciously directed planning in order to preserve freedom and the democratic way of life. But planning inevitably meant planners, and this immediately laid emphasis upon an elite and the possibility of making the centralization of power and minority rule much easier. Planning was not to be envisaged as utopian; rather, it accepted as its datum the present determined state of society. But though it was not 'totalitarian', the planning conceived by Mannheim would be *total*.

Mannheim was, in fact, advocating the planned guidance of the lives of the people on a sociological basis, with the assistance of both individual and social psychology. Social education was the planned use of a wide variety of social forces and institutions in order to create the democratic personality-type necessary to guarantee social integration in a reconstituted society. As a discipline, sociology taught us how to find out; it taught us not to take for granted any of the social influences, but rather to regard the social environment as a set of patterns to be explored for their educational significance; we might then exploit them for our educational purposes. Since the prime need of our society was for consensus, the first task of a really social education was to achieve this. Mannheim saw education as a part of the totality of the conscious processes which were rapidly replacing unconscious techniques. With the fading of tradition in the most important spheres of life, Mannheim maintained:

'The principal contribution of the sociological approach to the history and the theory of education is to draw attention to the fact that neither educational aims nor educational techniques can be conceived without a context, but rather, that they are to a very large extent socially directed. Who teaches whom for what society, when and how, as the sociological questions were once framed' (10).

Mannheim's commitment to this sociological approach did not mean that he was blind to other important aspects of education; education for social integration did not, in itself, imply the elimination of other concepts such as 'self-realization'. But there can be no self-realization *in vacuo*. Man is a social and political animal, and he must ultimately realize himself in and through other people. There are not isolated selves, only (as John Macmurray would have it) 'persons in relation' (11); and this concept is an inter-disciplinary one. Education, it is true, is mainly a social business but it is not static, it is a *dynamic* process concerned with both social and personal experiences, which require analysis, selection, reflection and evaluation. Thus it is that philosophic reflection, psychology and sociology have become, with history and comparative analysis, the fundamental studies which collectively provide a corpus of knowledge for a deeper understanding of education as a whole (12). But it is always dangerous to view the self in isolation from society. How well this has been expressed for all time in the words of the Jewish sage Hillel:

'If I am not for myself, who will be for me?
If I am only for myself, then what am I for?'

During the years 1943–5, the Institute of Sociology held conferences on the subject of 'Sociology and Education', and both Mannheim and Clarke contributed to these (13). During the remainder of the decade an ever-increasing number of books on education, written from a sociological point of view, were published. In 1948, the year after Mannheim died, Clarke published his *Freedom in the Educative Society*. In this book he developed further the theme of planning for freedom in an English society, which he likened to the Platonic educative society. An 'educative society' was one which accepted as its master-purpose the production of a given type of citizen:

'The type itself may be defined with varying degrees of precision and detail. But, whatever the type may be, that society may be called educative which consciously directs its activities and organizes every department of its life with a view to the emergence of citizens bearing the characters of the preferred type' (14).

Clarke, nevertheless, agreed with Professor W. E. Hocking that, whilst education should be geared to the production of a certain type, it should also make possible development 'beyond the type' (15). Clarke maintained that a true culture would emerge from the common life and experience of a healthy society; a common purpose of that society would define itself, and this should be heeded both within the school and outside. The content of education should be relevant to this common purpose, and the teachers chosen should be its especially sensitive representatives. There should be in education deliberate training for 'citizen consciousness', and this fact reinforced the claims of sociology to take a place in the field of studies covered by education.

In 1950 W. A. C. Stewart wrote an important article for the *Sociological Review*, entitled 'Philosophy and Sociology in the Training of Teachers' (16). This article still has a lot to offer in a consideration of the content of, and the difficulties involved in, a course for training teachers. Right from

c

the start Professor Stewart made the point that 'one of the main problems of the whole training course is to avoid overlapping in any wasteful degree. Another is to avoid discreteness, or, put another way, to give some coherence to the many aspects of study' (17). Professor Stewart spoke of the 'traditionally cautious scrutiny' which the study of sociology had received in Britain, but he also emphasized that both teachers and teachers-in-training should be aware of the critique brought to bear by sociology. He then went on to outline the three courses proposed by Karl Mannheim for the teacher-in-training, which were as follows:

A. *Sociology for the Educator*
    I Human Nature and the Social Order
    II The Impact of Social Groups upon the Individual
    III Social Structure

B. *The Sociology of Education*
    I School and Society
    II Sociology of Education in its Historical Aspects
    III School and the Social Order

C. *The Sociology of Teaching*
    I Sociological Interpretation of Life in School
    II The Teacher–Pupil Relationship
    III Problems of School Organization (18)

This outline is reproduced here in order to indicate the depth at which Mannheim considered the discipline should be studied in teacher-training centres. It is clear from the foregoing that Mannheim felt very strongly that any approach to the sociology of education, as a separate discipline within the total framework of educational study, must be preceded by an introduction to the discipline of sociology itself, including some knowledge of the social order and structure, and some understanding of group dynamics. In his article, however, whilst showing considerable sympathy with Mannheim's approach, Professor Stewart felt that *because of the limitations of time alone* the proposed course, in initial teacher-training, would have to keep close to education and would have to omit most, and abridge the remainder, of the course in 'Sociology for the Educator'. At the same time, Stewart accepted that it would be essential 'in any advanced work in education' (19).

Stewart's own suggested shorter course began with a necessary consideration of 'what sociology is about'; and this would involve a study of social structure, social function and control, and social change. There was also a need to provide a sociologist's taxonomy, that is, his classification and definition of various groups, systems and terms, such as 'society', 'community', 'association', 'institution', 'mores' and so forth. There must, in addition, be some examination of the 'field work' of the social scientist and of the general evidence of sociological inquiry, with some emphasis upon the fact that any conclusions from such study might, and usually would, 'lead towards considerations of social philosophy' (20). Professor Stewart was obviously interested in the sociological approach as one involving stringent, scientific methodology; but equally he saw that its application in the realm of education must ultimately lead to the discussion and establishment of values.

His proposed programme went on to an examination of such items as the institutions of society, sociology and the curriculum, 'education for culture', the classroom sociologically considered, discipline and order, the teacher in society; and, finally, sociology and values. With regard to the latter, Stewart argued that 'relativism' was by no means the only course open to a consistent sociologist. For him, the important function of sociology, particularly in relation to values in education, was

> 'not to explain away the basis of ideals as merely a form of social convenience, but rather to show the situation in which certain acts of educational policy or adjustment took place at any given time, and to admit also the influence of the life-view which made only certain kinds of adjustment possible' (21).

At the time of writing most, if not all, colleges and departments of education have their own schemes and syllabuses for a study of the sociology of education, within the framework of the principles and practice of education. A rapidly increasing number of colleges of education are also developing sociology as a main, subsidiary or basic subject; some have even adopted the sociology of education (or educational sociology) as a main academic study. Certainly there is, in the colleges of education, an increasing realization and awareness of the importance of an objective and analytical approach towards the study of the society in which we live, before we can begin to consider, with any accuracy or sense of confidence, the aims and purposes of our educational system.

B. EDUCATIONAL SOCIOLOGY AND SOCIOLOGY OF EDUCATION

The reader will note that, in our discussion of the origin and development of the sociology of education, both of the terms 'educational sociology' and 'sociology of education' have been used to classify this particular discipline. When W. A. C. Stewart wrote his article in 1950 (22), he used the terms 'sociological approach to education', 'educational sociology' and 'the sociology of education'. When, in 1962, he published the fruits of Mannheim's work in relation to education he entitled it *An Introduction to the Sociology of Education*. In the text itself the terms 'sociology of education' and 'a sociological approach to education' are used, but not 'educational sociology' (23).

There was certainly, at first, a tendency in the various university departments of education to refer to the discipline as 'educational sociology', although there is now an increasing preference for the use of the term 'sociology of education'. It has been suggested by Professor W. Taylor (24) that it might be useful to keep both terms with, however, quite distinctive meanings. Educational sociology would imply an emphasis upon educational and social questions; the sociology of education would emphasize sociological problems. A similar sort of distinction is maintained by R. J. Stalcup in his *Sociology and Education*, where he also uses the term 'the social foundations of education' (25). Stalcup's definition of these three terms is as follows:

> '*Educational Sociology*. The application of general principles and findings of sociology to the administration and/or processes of education. This approach attempts to apply principles of sociology to the institution of education as a separate societal unit.
>
> *Sociology of Education*. An analysis of the sociological processes involved in the educational institution. This area of study evolved out of the field of Educational Sociology and emphasizes the study *within* the institution of education.
>
> *Social Foundations of Education*. A field of study which usually includes history, philosophy and sociology of education and comparative education. Obviously the field is broader than either Sociology of Education or Educational Sociology' (26).

In his *Educational Sociology*, G. E. Jensen discusses the distinction at some length and argues that the problems of educational sociology are derived from the field of education, whereas the problems of the sociology of education are derived from the field of sociology (27). For Jensen sociology is a practical field of study, concerned with both sociological and socio-psychological types of knowledge which have relevance for, or logical connections with, problems of educational practice (28). It is the primary concern of the sociology of education, however, to investigate the sociological aspects of educational phenomena and institutions, and the problems here examined are regarded as essentially problems of sociology and not problems of educational practice (29).

Despite the clear logic of some of these pleas for such precise diversification of disciplinary approach, the general movement in this country has been towards the establishment of the one discipline, the sociology of education. As Dr Olive Banks remarks:

'It is now becoming customary to refer to the sociology of education rather than the old and now suspect terminology of educational sociology. On the whole, too, this new emphasis has come about because sociologists themselves have started to take an interest in education as a field of study' (30).

Dr Banks goes on to suggest that the future of the subject will be as a branch of sociology rather than of education (31). The present writer feels, however, that the future of the subject will depend far more on the close co-operation of sociologists in education (particularly those with some practical experience in the classroom or in some aspect of the educational system), and educationists interested in the sociological approach (particularly those with some basic training in the discipline of sociology). And this is, of course, already happening: some lecturers and professors in sociology began as humble assistants in the school classroom, whilst some lecturers and professors in education began their careers as qualified sociologists.

It is this sort of professional mobility and cross-fertilization of educationists and sociologists that is increasingly needed – for the good of both branches of study. To reiterate the words of Professor W. A. C. Stewart, 'if ever any study was inter-disciplinary it is education' (32); and the sociology of education is no more the private or special preserve of sociology than the philosophy of education is a special branch of philosophy, or educational psychology is the province only of the psychologist. And, if we are going to be particularly difficult, who has a prior claim to social psychology, or ethics and social philosophy, or comparative religion?

Increasingly in the academic world we are faced with inter-disciplinary forms of inquiry; and once the question of prerogative is raised we are back where we started – with fragmented subjects and isolated pieces of research. The footballer may well leave the 'sociology of football' to the sociologists; the gamblers will be well content to remain completely ignorant of the 'sociology of gambling'; the bucolic rustic is not likely to dispute the sociologist's claim to sole competence in the study of rural sociology; but the sociology of education is as much the concern of the educator or educationist as it is of the sociologist. Mannheim and Stewart were, of course, right to warn of the dangers of dilettantism in this field, which could 'spoil the reputation both of the subject and of the profession of the educator' (33); but this applies no more to the sphere of the sociology of education than it does to any other discipline connected with educational study.

The sociology of education is a discipline with which both sociologists and educationists are concerned, and to which both have something valuable to contribute. Some of the contemplated research in this field is undoubtedly best conducted by professional sociologists; other areas of research are better conducted by educators or practising teachers, particularly where the reactions, relationships and activities of the child in the classroom are concerned. But in all instances the important thing is that the research should be properly controlled and directed, and with generally sound methodology.

The whole study is one in which sociologists and educationists can, and indeed do, amicably co-operate. In fact, it is not particularly profitable to discuss any more whether the sociology of education is a branch of sociology or of education; it is much more vital to decide which questions it is important to ask, and to discover those sociologists and educationists who are in the best position to answer them. Dr D. F. Swift, who was himself trained in both education and sociology, has summed up the matter in these words:

'The development of the discipline (and hence its value in society) follows from a mutually stimulating relationship between theorizing and information-gathering, each of which is dependent upon the other for its meaning. There is no point in distinguishing between the motives for doing the research. What matters is the candlepower of the theories which illuminate the information, and the rigour with which it is collected. Consequently sociology and education have a great deal to offer each other' (34).

C. THE CONTENT OF THE SOCIOLOGY OF EDUCATION

In any consideration of the aims, content and techniques of education we are concerned with the immediate context of the particular educational process that we are discussing. Thus, in order to understand the situation as fully as possible, we become inevitably involved in a comparative study of contextuality both *within* our own society, and between our own society and others. Comparative education is a discipline in its own right (35); but it is also clear that in any deep study of the sociology of education there must be cross-societal analysis, that is, some comparative analysis of educational situations in a variety of geographical and ethnological contexts. Educational methods which are fully applicable in one society are not necessarily so in another, and educationists must be fully aware of the dangers of 'cultural transplantation' referred to by James Lynch in his article on 'Comparative Education and Colleges of Education' (36). Thus, the comparative method is implicit in the study of the sociology of education, just as the study of comparative education demands some cognizance of, and training in, the methodology of the social sciences.

In the study of the various relations between education and society, the sociology of education is concerned with such general concepts as society itself, culture, community, class, environment, socialization, internalization, accommodation, assimilation, cultural lag, sub-culture, status, role and so forth. It is further involved in such considerations as the effect of the economy upon the sort of education provided by the state; the social forces and determinants that effect educational and cultural change; the social institutions involved in the educational process, such as the family, the school and the church; various problems of role structure and role analysis in relation to the total social system and the micro-society of the school; the school viewed as a formal organization, involving such problems as authority, selection, the organization of learning, and streaming; questions of curriculum building and the development of sub-cultures; the relationship between social class, culture and language, and between education and occupation; and problems of embourgeoisement, democratization and elitism.

In an introductory volume of this sort we can obviously do little more than acquaint the student, in the college or department of education, with the main areas in which socio-educational problems arise, and introduce him to some of the more important literature and research relevant to each topic. In general terms, the approach of the book is to work from the larger society inwards to the pupil in the school context and the classroom situation. It is hoped throughout, however, that everything that we consider will have some ultimate, if not immediate and direct, relation to the teacher and his problems.

REFERENCES

1 *Vide* Dewey, J., *The School and Society* (Univ. of Chicago Press, 1900), and *Democracy and Education* (Macmillan, 1916; reprinted 1955).

2 Durkheim, E., *Education and Sociology* (Free Press, Glencoe, 1956), pp. 70–1. This passage is from the article, 'Education: Its Nature and Its Role', which first appeared in the *New Dictionary of Pedagogy and Primary Education*, published under the direction of Professor F. Buisson (Hachette, Paris, 1911). The collection of Durkheim's writings, now translated as *Education and Sociology*, was first published as *Education et Sociologie* (Alcan, Paris, 1922) five years after the author's death.

3 Ibid., p. 67.

4 Cf. also the ideas expressed by Mead, George H. in *Mind, Self and Society* (Univ. of Chicago Press, 1934; 13th impression 1965).

5 Durkheim, E., op. cit., p. 134.

6 E.g. Smith, W. R., *An Introduction to Educational Sociology* (Houghton Mifflin, 1917; revised edition 1929); Peters, C. C., *Foundations of Educational Sociology* (Macmillan, N.Y., 1924; revised edition 1930); Waller, W., *The Sociology of Teaching* (J. Wiley, N.Y., 1932; reprinted, Russell and

Russell, 1961); Kilpatrick, W. H. (ed.), *The Teacher and Society* (Appleton-Century, 1937).

7 Clarke, F., *Education and Social Change* (Sheldon Press, 1940), p. 1.

8 Mannheim, K., *Man and Society: In an Age of Reconstruction* (Routledge, 1940), p. 271.

9 Mannheim, K., *Diagnosis of Our Time* (Routledge, 1943; 7th impression 1962), pp. 4–11, 49–53, 71–2 *et passim*.

10 Mannheim, K. and Stewart, W. A. C., *An Introduction to the Sociology of Education* (Routledge, 1962), p. 159.

11 *Vide* Macmurray, J., *Persons in Relation* (Faber, 1957).

12 Cf. Professor W. A. C. Stewart's prefatory remarks to *An Introduction to the Sociology of Education*, p. ix: 'At the risk of being cloven by a sociological spade or a psychological pick, I would say that if ever any study was inter-disciplinary it is education. It is liable to serious distortion if any particular scholar gets his magnifying glass on just a part of it.'

13 *Vide* 1943 Conference Papers on *Sociology and Education*, published in 1944 by the Le Play House Press, and edited by Miss D. M. E. Dymes; 1944 Conference Papers on *Synthesis in Education*, published in 1946; and 1945 Conference Papers on *School and Society*, published in 1949.

14 Clarke, F., *Freedom in the Educative Society* (Univ. of London Press, 1948), p. 13.

15 *Vide* Hocking, W. E., *Man and State* (Yale Univ. Press, 1926).

16 Later published with the same title, in booklet form, by the Le Play House Press, Ledbury, Herefs (1950).

17 Ibid., p. 2.

18 Ibid., pp. 23–4. This is further developed in Chapter XIV of Mannheim, K. and Stewart, W. A. C., *An Introduction to the Sociology of Education*, pp. 143–55.

19 Ibid., p. 25.

20 *Vide* ibid., pp. 25–7.

21 Ibid., p. 34.

22 *Vide* note 16 *supra*.

23 *Vide* Manheimm, K. and Stewart, W. A. C., op. cit., p. 159.

24 *Vide* article by Taylor, W., entitled 'The Sociology of Education' in Tibble, J. W. (ed.), *The Study of Education* (Routledge, 1967).

25 Cf. also Mannheim, K. and Stewart, W. A. C., op. cit., p. 160 where the term 'sociological foundations of education' is used.

26 Stalcup, R. J., *Sociology and Education* (C. E. Merrill Pub. Co., Columbus, Ohio, 1968), p. 5.

27 *Vide* Jensen, G. E., *Educational Sociology* (Center for Applied Research in Education, Inc., Prentice-Hall, 1965; 2nd printing 1967), Chapter I *passim*. In his Foreword, Jensen refers to an early American Herbartian, Henry Suzzalo, who offered a course in 'educational sociology' in 1907. Jensen says, 'Apparently he was in revolt against the largely metaphysical educational philosophy current in his time' (p. ix).

28 Ibid., p. 1.

29 Ibid., p. 4.

30 Banks, Olive, *The Sociology of Education* (Batsford, 1968; 2nd impression 1969), p. 8.
31 Ibid., p. 9.
32 *Vide* note 12 *supra*.
33 Mannheim, K. and Stewart, W. A. C., op. cit., p. 155.
34 Swift, D. F., *The Sociology of Education* (Routledge, 1969), pp. 5–6.
35 *Vide* Lynch, J., 'Comparative Education and Colleges of Education' in *Education for Teaching*, No. 82, Summer 1970, pp. 42–8 (Journal of the A.T.C.D.E., 151 Gower Street, London, W.C.1).
36 Ibid., p. 43.

BIBLIOGRAPHY

ASHLEY, B. J. *et al., An Introduction to the Sociology of Education* (Macmillan, 1969).
BANKS, O., *The Sociology of Education* (Batsford, 1968; 2nd impression 1969).
BEAR, R. M., *The Social Functions of Education* (Macmillan, 1937).
BROOKOVER, W. B. and GOTTLIEB, D., *A Sociology of Education* (American Book Co., 2nd edition 1964).
BROWN, F. J., *Educational Sociology* (Prentice-Hall, 1947).
COLLIER, K. G., *The Social Purposes of Education* (Routledge, 1959; 2nd impression 1962).
COOK, L. A. and E. F., *A Sociological Approach to Education* (McGraw-Hill, 1950; 3rd edition 1960).
CORWIN, R. G., *A Sociology of Education* (Appleton-Century-Crofts, 1965).
DURKHEIM, E., *Education and Sociology* (Free Press, Glencoe, 1956).
EGGLESTON, S. J., *The Social Context of the School* (Routledge, 1967).
HALSEY, A. H. *et al.* (eds), *Education, Economy and Society* (Free Press, Glencoe, 1961).
HAVIGHURST, R. J. and NEUGARTEN, B. L., *Society and Education* (Allyn and Bacon, 1957).
JENSEN, G. E., *Educational Sociology* (Prentice-Hall, 1965; 2nd printing 1967).
KING, R. A., *Education* (Longmans, 1969).
MANNHEIM, K. and STEWART, W. A. C., *An Introduction to the Sociology of Education* (Routledge, 1962).
MUSGRAVE, P. W., *The Sociology of Education* (Methuen, 1965).
OTTAWAY, A. K. C., *Education and Society: An Introduction to the Sociology of Education* (Routledge, 1953; 4th impression 1960).
STALCUP, R. J., *Sociology and Education* (C. E. Merrill, Columbus, Ohio, 1968).
SWIFT, D. F., *The Sociology of Education* (Routledge, 1969).
WALLER, W., *The Sociology of Teaching* (J. Wiley, 1932; reprinted, Russell and Russell, 1961).

Chapter 3

Society and Culture

A. SOCIETY

Definitions, certainly those of the dictionary and glossary variety, can be very misleading unless they are further expanded by illustration and exemplification. In the consideration of a concept such as that of 'society' it is salutary to remember that the introductory analysis of the topic by R. M. MacIver and C. H. Page extends to nearly seven hundred pages (1).

In her discussion of the structure of society, Marion Levy argued that there were four criteria which had to be fulfilled before any group could be considered as constituting a society (2). These criteria were as follows:

1. The group must be capable of existing longer than the life-span of the individual.
2. The group must recruit its new members, at least in part, by means of sexual reproduction.
3. The group must be united in giving allegiance to a common complex, general system of action.
4. That system of action should be self-sufficient.

These criteria were taken up in the definition of society previously provided by Marion Levy and others in a paper contributed to *Ethics* in January 1950. There a society was defined as 'a group of human beings sharing a self-sufficient system of action which is capable of existing longer than the life-span of an individual, the group being recruited at least in part by the sexual reproduction of its members' (3). It will be seen from the foregoing that the definition of a society is given in terms of the criteria for its existence, so that the concept under discussion is, in fact, a structure fulfilling certain functions and meeting specified prerequisites.

D. F. Aberle and his co-authors have emphasized, in 'The Functional Prerequisites of a Society', that a society's identity and continuity persist and inhere in the 'system of action in which the actors participate' rather than in the actors, or set of actors themselves. A society could disintegrate, and yet the individuals comprising that society could conceivably survive. They might join other societies or, of course, they might create a number of new societies for themselves.

A society, in terms of a self-sufficient structure or system of action, would cease to exist if most of its members became extinct or were dispersed; or if the members became unmotivated and apathetic; or if within the society there is 'the war of all against all', involving the exploitation or annihilation of one group by others. Where one society becomes absorbed into another the members may continue to exist, but there is an inevitable loss of integrity and identity. In consequence, the original self-sufficiency of the system of action has gone, and the individual has to accommodate to a new action-system (4).

The functional approach of D. F. Aberle *et al.* is, in the main, a very valuable point of reference in any consideration of educational aims, content and method; and whilst their analysis of society may not be acceptable to all sociologists, it at least presents a positive functional structure for development, consideration and criticism. The authors of the article emphasized that they were concerned with *what* must get done in a society, not with *how* it was done. The educationist is, of course, concerned with both matter and method; but he recognizes that in education, at least, the *what* and the *how* cannot be absolutely segregated.

It is the writer's intention in this section to look at the functional prerequisites of society delineated in the article already mentioned (5), but to apply them specifically to the process of education in so far as this analysis has relevance. This can, of course, be done only in outline at this stage, but elaboration of these prerequisites and their implications for education will be examined in greater detail in the chapters that follow.

1. *A society must make the necessary provision for adequate relationship to the environment and for sexual recruitment*: there can be little doubt that the first part of this statement has implications for education which have been recognized, in one form or another, for a long time. The present emphasis upon local, environmental and social studies alone indicates that those most closely involved in education are aware of this prerequisite of provision for as full a relationship to the environment as possible. If the members of a society are to function at an adequate level, as well as in adequate numbers, it is clear that they must understand what their society is all about, and how they can best fulfil their role in that society.

This was obviously one of the main concerns of the Newsom Report when it suggested that the school programme, in the final year at least, should be deliberately outgoing; that it should, in fact, constitute an initiation into the adult world of work and leisure (6). But it is obviously insufficient to consider that relationships with the environment should be built up only during the final year of school attendance. The Plowden Report considered that the use of, and acquaintanceship with, the environment of the child had to begin as early as possible (7). Not only was this a way of learning, of 'integrating the curriculum', it was also an essential feature of the socialization of the child.

It must be emphasized that 'adequate relationship to the environment' means far more than just *learning about* the environment. It implies the fullest possible participation in the world around, both urban and rural, both immediate and more remote. It implies, further, the development of attitudes towards other individuals, towards the environment, and towards the complexity of social relationships which constitute a society. In a society which is becoming increasingly multi-racial this apprehension of people, places and relationships is becoming, *pari passu*, more problematic.

The patterning of heterosexual relationships may not at first sight seem to be an educational problem at all; people have always somehow managed to find sex and/or marriage partners. But this is, of course, an over-simplification of the situation. Every society, however simple and however complex, has its sex mores which cover the relations of men and women to each other before marriage and in marriage. These mores include also the rights and duties of both married and unmarried in relation to the rest of society (8).

In our own society this problem of socialization with regard to sex mores is not just a question of whether or not there shall be co-education, although this is one of the basic problems. It is also a question of the manner in which co-education should be conducted. There are still, for example, those classrooms in which boys are made to sit in areas separate from the girls, and in which heterosexual contact and relationships are kept as minimal as possible. There is an ever-narrowing gap between the school-leaving age and the age of majority, namely eighteen years. As a result there is an increasing recognition that the school is, in fact, the training ground where one becomes educated not simply in things or in factual knowledge, but also in basic human relationships. It is certainly no longer a question of mere instruction in human biology, nor of 'sex instruction'; it is the development of natural situations in which children of the opposite sex learn about one another, and in discussion can help to resolve some of their most urgent and fundamental problems.

The Newsom Report epitomizes the problem, in its discussion of the school community, in the following way:

'Positive and realistic guidance to adolescent boys and girls on sexual behaviour is essential. This should include the biological, moral, social and personal aspects. Advice to parents on the physical and emotional problems of adolescents should be easily available. Schools of whatever type should contrive to provide opportunities for boys and girls to mix socially in a helpful and educative environment' (9).

If with some reluctance, the Plowden Report also considered the problem of 'Sex Education' in the context of the primary school curriculum (10). It held that children's questions about sex should be answered plainly and truthfully whenever they were asked, according always, of course, to the ability of the child to understand. The Report, however, went further than the mere purveyance of information about sex. Human sex involves relationships; these relationships involve ethics. In the primary school this side of the matter will directly affect the children only rarely, but in many of their questionings it will be there implicitly or explicitly. But, in the words of the Report:

'The foundation for good sexual ethics can be laid in a school in which the children learn to respect and appreciate each other as personalities, to treat everyone with consideration and never to make use of human beings or treat them callously or contemptuously and where they find in adults the same attitude towards each other and towards themselves' (11).

At first blush, it does not appear likely that our society will 'suffer biological extinction' because of the lack of provisions for sexual recruitment (12). But life is never quite as simple as the *what* of life in these terms; the *how* is also involved. Indeed, a society may have adequate provision for sexual recruitment, in the bio-sociological terms of Aberle, and yet it may destroy itself *as a society*. The changes in the patterns of heterosexual relationships which are occurring in our own time must inevitably cause us to consider whether, ultimately, they will make not only for man's happiness, but also for his survival.

2. *A society must provide adequate role-differentiation and assignment*: the stability and continuance of any society depend to a very large extent upon the persistent performance of particular activities by different groups in that society. Without these habitual and orderly activities the society would very quickly collapse. Nor is it sufficient for just *anyone* to attempt to perform such activities; there must be a division of labour based upon training, ability and expertise, as well as upon motivation. This applies to any society, however simple or complex, although there will generally be less role-differentiation in a primitive society than in a more developed one.

Role-assignment has, in the past, depended very much upon birth and the status of the individual in the social stratification. In the Hindu society of India, at least formerly, the caste system almost entirely decided both role-differentiation and role-assignment (13). The *brahmin*, at the head of the caste system, was destined in the main for the role of priest, the *kshatriya* was born to rule, the *vaishya* was the merchantman, the lawyer, the doctor or teacher, and the *shudra*, at the lower end of the caste system, was destined to work as a labourer. Despite the fact that caste still persists, India is breaking down the equation between caste and role-assignment.

In our own society role-assignment is ultimately a question of the development of inborn intelligence in the most favourable sort of environment, and through the organized processes of education and training. Leaving on one side, for the moment, questions of nepotism, 'the old school tie', and various forms of patronage, role-assignment must finally depend upon some socially accepted system of selection. Even in some of the simpler societies, in which the individual may be initiated into virtually all the techniques involved in his society, there will still be selection for certain offices, based partly upon birth and partly upon training and expertise.

In the modern technological society the complex system of role-differentiation gives rise to a variety of problems related to educational selection and elitism. Moreover, in a society which is changing, and changing rapidly, there must also arise the problem of the modification of role-differentiation within the society. Schools are faced with the task of educating and training children not merely for existing roles but also for roles which are likely to exist in the near future. There are obviously social determinants with which every educator in our society must be concerned and of which they must be fully cognizant.

It is because of these problems of role-differentiation and role-assignment that there must be some clear educational, as well as economic, planning. We have already mentioned Karl Mannheim's insistence upon the rejection of *laissez-faire* as well as the ideological type of planning involved in Nazism and Communism (14); but there must be *some* planning. As D. F. Aberle *et al.* remark: 'A system of role-differentiation alone is useless without a system of selection for assigning individuals to those roles' (15). The principle of selection, and not just the means, which so many egalitarians seek to oppose on utopian criteria, would seem to be inevitable in any society which has a total view of its economic and social requirements. Indeed, Professor H. J. Eysenck has argued both vigorously and cogently that, without certain methods of selection, advancement into the better educated and higher paid groups of society would inevitably be barred to a large number of able, working-class children. This, he argues, would bring to the top many people of mediocre ability, whilst many others of superior ability would remain submerged. Thus, without some form of selection there would occur greater injustice in the 'rise of a new mediocracy' (16).

Education can provide a part of the machinery for selection. By this we mean that *formal* education within the school, college and university is one of the means of deciding what the future role of each pupil or student will be. It is therefore clear that any selection process within the framework of education should be as accurate and as just as possible. But complete *absence* of selection, as Eysenck and others have indicated, may well lead to greater injustice; in fact, one headmaster has claimed that 'the greatest inequality of the present age is the equal treatment of unequals' (17). We shall need to consider in somewhat greater detail later on the various processes of selection at work in our society for the purposes of role-assignment, including those processes which are not so much designed and applied techniques as passive or active, and frequently inherited, social determinants. Social stratification is both cause and effect in the selection process; but irrespective of the type of stratification or system of authority, the role-differentiation depends very much on the sort of values, and their order of priority in the society.

3. *A society must provide a means of communication for its members:* one of the essential elements for living in a society, in community with others, is a means of communication. Communication, or language, provides the society with a means of socializing its members and a mechanism for role-taking. George H. Mead has emphasized the importance of language in understanding and taking the roles of others (18). In the development of the self it is essential to take up the attitudes of those around us, says Mead, and

> 'Language in its significant sense is that vocal gesture which tends to arouse in the individual the attitude which it arouses in others, and it is this perfecting of the self by the gesture which mediates the social activities that gives rise to the process of taking the role of the other' (19).

In a developed and sophisticated society the means of communication is naturally a spoken and written language, which will differentiate into a variety of forms according to the level of any particular group or individual. The differences in syntax, vocabulary and pronunciation of the language spoken by these various social elements are facts which the education process cannot afford to ignore. It is in this particular area of social function that children can experience considerable deprivation, through inarticulateness, illiteracy or the inability to go beyond a very limited vocabulary or 'restricted code' of language (20). It is not intended to elaborate in any detail here upon this question since we shall discuss the whole problem of social class, language and learning later on. It should, however, be noted that the current study of socio-linguistics is not just another academic extension of linguistics: it is the sort of vital study with which every practising teacher is concerned. P. K. Millins is undoubtedly right when he says:

> 'In this re-assessment of courses, the study and practice of language should be given top priority. All students should leave their institutions with a firm grasp of the underlying principles of modern linguistic theory and practice, and they should be able to adopt a carefully planned oral approach to teaching geared to the intellectual and emotional needs of children and adolescents. Sound language teaching should be closely linked with an understanding of the social and cultural factors as they affect individual children' (21).

It is true that Mr Millins was specifically concerned, in his article on 'The Preparation of Teachers', with the linguistic problems of immigrants, but what he has to say has a far more general application. An understanding of the social and cultural factors affecting the children in our classrooms could well provide the clue to their linguistic limitations and learning deficiencies.

4. *A society must afford shared cognitive experiences and orientations:* in their article, D. F. Aberle *et al.* emphasize the need for a society to develop a corpus of cognitive orientations which will provide meaningfulness to social situations, as well as a sense of stability derived from an identity of experiences (22). In this way motivation is sustained in individual and group activity.

This has considerable implications for the processes of socialization and education. All individuals require norms of behaviour – even in order to depart from them; and these norms are the 'shared cognitive orientations' referred to above. Society must, through its various institutions, mediate these norms and orientations to its members and future citizens. It is one of the functions of education to assist pupils to be 'at home' in their world; this can be achieved only by establishing an awareness not merely of common experiences but also of common 'meanings'. But it is also a function of education to help individuals to manipulate and create life situations. If it is important to develop agreement and consensus upon material and social identities, it is equally important to provide opportunities and possibilities for dissensus. A society of citizens who never go beyond 'shared cognitive orientations' may survive biologically but may never have an original thought between them.

A structured world or society, with established values, mores and sanctions, makes for stability and a sense of security. But, as we shall see in the next chapter, change and development are inevitable dimensions of social process; so that our future citizens must be educated and prepared for change as well as for stability. This can be achieved, ultimately, only through increasing the individual's total awareness, his sense of self-assurance and self-confidence, and developing in him a fluidity of mind and reference so that he can tackle new situations with interest and lack of fear. Thus, at least two of the functions of education are here elicited by the prerequisite of society for shared cognitive orientations: they are the establishment of norms and values, and the development of critical approaches to those accepted norms. Survival, whether biological or psychological, depends on more than the mere acceptance of the *status quo*: it involves an active participation in the developing social process.

5. *A society must establish a shared and articulated set of goals:* it is clear that, although there may be a variety of goals within the total society,

these goals must be meaningful to at least the majority within the society. Karl Mannheim sought to emphasize that:

> 'Awareness means both in the life of the individual and in that of the community the readiness to see the whole situation in which one finds oneself, and not only to orientate one's action on immediate tasks and purposes but to base them on a more comprehensive vision' (23).

It was this 'comprehensive vision' which Mannheim identified with the 'articulated set of goals' referred to by D. F. Aberle. Society, with its aims and objectives, needs to be explained to its members; and its structures and ramifications must be internalized.

This is very much the function of the educator; indeed, the main tenor of the Newsom Report (24) was that, by 'going out into the world' as a deliberate part of the school programme, the individual pupil would be initiated into the adult world of work and of leisure, as well as into the total society with its aims, goals and purposes. More recently, the Schools Council has published a report on 'The Educational Implications of Social and Economic Change', in which Professor W. J. H. Sprott emphasizes that in reality a society is 'a figment of the imagination', or a sort of mental fiction (25). Sprott's own definition of society is both interesting and revealing in the present context of the articulation of social goals:

> 'A society consists of a collection of individuals whose patterned inter-action takes place more frequently amongst themselves than with members of other collections, who share a belief that they are co-members of the society, who also share beliefs about the structure of the society, the different activities that have to be carried out for the benefit of at least some, if not all, members of the collection, who also share beliefs about the standards of appropriate behaviour, and who interact in terms of these beliefs' (26).

Figment of the imagination or not, this sort of development of the concept of society has already involved the thinker, who seeks to make the idea explicit, in the articulation of a set of goals – at least in general terms. It is a part of the function of the educational process to work out some of those goals in greater detail, at least to the extent of some sort of discussion as to what they might possibly be – even though there might not be complete consensus on the matter.

6. *A society must prescribe the normative regulation of means*: once a society has established its goals it must prescribe the means for the attainment of those goals. This is where role-differentiation and role-assignment come in, since it is in this area that those who are responsible for the regulation of society must be specified. Further, in defining the goals, and in determining those who are specifically responsible for attaining them,

D

society must also prescribe the means. The means adopted and employed represent the way society is governed politically, controlled and organized administratively, and sanctioned ethically and socially.

Any rejection of the means by groups within a society will develop into states of open rebellion, civil war or *anomie*. The French word *anomie* is derived from the Greek ἀνομία (anomia), meaning 'lawlessness' or 'normlessness'. The English equivalent 'anomy' is also used, with the adjective 'anomic', meaning 'lawless' or 'normless'. Emile Durkheim maintained that anomy resulted from a breakdown in the regulation of goals, and the means to their end, such that, as a result, men's ambitions and aspirations create a constant pressure for deviant behaviour. In such conditions social norms of behaviour no longer control men's actions, and society has failed to regulate the behaviour of individuals. In Durkheim's terms:

'Anomy indeed springs from the lack of collective forces at certain points in society; that is, of groups established for the regulation of social life. Anomy therefore partially results from the same state of disaggregation from which the egoistic current also springs' (27).

The egoistic current of behaviour to which Durkheim refers is found mostly among individuals who have no strong group attachments, and who, therefore, lack integration with their society. We shall consider the effective control of delinquent and disruptive forms of behaviour presently.

In a consideration of the role-differentiation that will decide who will govern and who are to be governed, who are to be the administrators, the executives, the judiciary and so forth, we find ourselves at once involved in the whole process of education, socialization and initiation, and with the difficult question of the selection of individuals and elites to fulfil certain roles and to become role incumbents. In a simple society initiation will involve certain *rites de passage* (28), or ceremonial rituals through which the initiate has to pass before he can take on an adult role in his society. Among the Murngin, a North Australian aboriginal tribe, the life crises of its members, such as birth, maturity and death, are all commemorated by elaborated rituals (29). Max Weber refers to the 'charismatic education' of novitiates in all societies which have experienced warfare, and to the 'vestigial initiation ceremonies' in those societies in which the original concept of rebirth as a hero or magician has been replaced by the simple decoration of the individual with the insignia of manhood (30).

In our own society, once christening, confirmation and/or baptism, and marriage are rejected as religious rituals, there is little left in the way of initiation rites, or occasions set apart for the involvement of the individual in a new level of society. In consequence, there is a sense in which the whole process of education may be looked upon as a form of initiation (31). There may be no awe-inspiring, terror-filling mystiques of mock burials, bull-roarers and sub-incision; but the passage from puberty and adolescence to the full responsibilities of adulthood must be marked at least by an increasingly greater awareness of the goals of society, the variety of roles and their relationships within society, and the means and sanctions which society adopts in order to ensure its own stability and the attainment of its purposes. This is something that the Crowther Report, published in 1959, strongly emphasized, particularly in relation to the curriculum of county colleges. There is need for:

> 'an appreciation of the adult world in which young workers suddenly find themselves; guidance for them in working out their problems of human relations and moral standards; and a continuance of their basic education, with vocational bias where appropriate' (32).

But, sound as this suggestion is, the social awareness implied in this and in other sections of the Crowther Report, as well as in the Newsom Report, is something that should begin on the day that a child enters his first school, and should continue throughout his school career. Social attitudes are not imbibed suddenly on a course, nor yet naturally during the years of adolescence; they have to be inculcated and acquired in actual social and community living. And if the school is just another large factory, through which pupils pass as quickly and as uninvolvedly as possible, they may never become initiated into their society; in fact many will become drop-outs before they enter it. It is not merely during the last year at school that the programme has to be outgoing – the process should be going on all the time. Civics, current affairs, modern and local history, and social studies should, in one form or another, feature in the school curriculum from earliest days. Only in this way can youth begin to visualize its own role and function in our society.

Whilst a society must prescribe the regulation of means to attain its goals in a *positive* way, as far as possible, the necessity for *negative* precepts and controls has been recognized from the Code of Hammurabi onwards. It is an unfortunate fact of social life – but a fact nevertheless – that many individuals can comprehend the limits of acceptable behaviour only through the enumeration of the unacceptable and their accompanying sanctions. The exhortation, 'All we need is love', would certainly work with perfect human beings, but it would also be unnecessary.

The 'rules of the game', which are absorbed in the school playground (33), set a pattern for the laws of society which the child gradually assimilates through his relationships with others. Juvenile deviancy and delinquency are certainly social problems but they are also educational ones, and in a consideration of some of their classroom problems many teachers are brought into contact with both the causes and effects of juvenile delinquency. There is a sense in which pathology often proves more interesting than normality; but any analysis of society and social relationships must accept today, with Durkheim, that there is a certain 'normalcy of crime' (34) which demands our attention as educators if we are to understand many of our pupils.

The existence of criminality in a society is normal, provided that it does not exceed a certain level for each social type in society, which Durkheim felt might well be fixed in conformity with the rules he had laid down in *The Rules of Sociological Method*. Durkheim hastened to add that, whilst crime may be regarded as a phenomenon of normal sociology, it does not follow that the criminal may be regarded, from a biological or psychological point of view, as an individual normally constituted (35). According to Durkheim crime is necessary; it is bound up with the fundamental conditions of our social life, and 'by that very fact it is useful, because these conditions of which it is a part are themselves indispensable to the normal evolution of morality and law' (36).

Whilst society provides its own sanctions and machinery for the effective control of delinquent, deviant and disruptive behaviour, it is clear that education has its own part to play through initial socialization and remedial work. This is not to suggest that 'society' and 'education' are separate entities – quite the contrary. The need, however, is increasingly to look upon the processes of education as a very vital and important part of society's 'normative regulation of means'.

7. *A society must regulate affective expression:* if society were to fail in some way to regulate the expression of love, lust, anger, aggression, and similar affective states, there would exist a state of 'permissiveness' or *anomie*, in which no one would be held responsible for the end result of his lust, or his violent aggressive propensities. Social order and control involve, initially, the development of individuals able to regulate their own affective expressions, and to understand fully what is involved in self-control and their ultimate responsibility for it.

Many of the catch-phrases of our current would-be reformers ignore this essential need for the regulation of affective expression. 'Make love not war' sounds a very reasonable and desirable imperative; but if the balance and stability of society are to be maintained, 'making love' requires as much regulation as making war; indeed, in the event, it may prove to require even more. It may be the regulation of a different and more desirable affective element, but it is an affective state which, when entirely unregulated, would be capable of destroying just as assuredly as war and aggression can. Plato, in *The Republic*, has drawn a very vivid picture of both the individual ('the tyrannical man') and of the society in which there is no longer any regulation of the passions, but in which one monster passion takes control (37). This is the perversion of freedom; it is that unregulated liberty of indifference which leads ultimately to self-destruction, and, in the words of D. F. Aberle, 'the ungoverned expression of lust and rage leads to the disruption of relationships and ultimately to the war of all against all' (38).

In both the theory and practice of education we are vitally concerned with the emotional development of the child, and it is one of the fundamental problems of the educator to assist the child to come to terms with his emotions, to understand them, and to deal with them in a manner which is acceptable to the rest of society. It is the child's contact and experiences with the other children in his class and school which ultimately help him to handle relationships and to regulate his emotions. The Plowden Report was keenly alive to the crises, encountered by the child, which stem from the demands made upon him by society. In his frustration the child frequently becomes aggressive; and his social education should assist him to direct his aggressiveness away from destructive activity and towards creativity and innovation (39).

Quite apart from the more 'normal' emotional development of the child, which presents its own problems with its own 'abnormalities' (40), there is the *abnormal* emotional development which results from a variety of forms of social deprivation including, in particular, maternal deprivation (41). Whilst there is still much to be done by way of prevention of such deprivation, and Dr John Bowlby considers a variety of measures in his *Child Care and the Growth of Love* (42), much of the adverse effects of emotional deviance must be dealt with by the institution of the school.

8. *A society must socialize its members:* this is, in effect, stating in bold letters what we have been attempting to say throughout the whole of this section. The system of norms and behavioural regulators in any society must be mediated to its new members, and this is called socialization. Socialization is a total concept; it is not merely a physical process, although there are undoubtedly physical elements in it. A child who is being socialized must know how to behave in certain social situations; he must develop a sense of the occasion. But socialization goes much deeper than this, into the very consciousness of the child's personality. He is involved in the attitudes and aspirations of the total society of which he is a member, and in the selection and maintenance for himself of some particular role in that society. George H. Mead has referred to this process of socialization as the development of the 'generalized other'; and it is through this generalized other, through taking on the role of others, that the social process can influence and control the behaviour of the individuals involved in it (43).

It is only through such socialization processes that any particular society can continue to exist; and should such processes fail on a large scale, the society would, at worst, become extinct; at best, it would become a very different society. It is just conceivable that it might become a better society.

In our own society the child must be made aware of the social structures that exist, of the accepted relationships within those social structures, and of the sort of behaviour that is quite unaccceptable to society as a whole. To leave a child unaware of the sort of behaviour that is rejected by his society is to leave him uneducated and unsocialized. Even though he does not have to learn the skills of all groups in his community – as he might well do in a simpler society – he should, nevertheless, become *aware* of the roles and attitudes of others. Professor P. L. Berger has well described the process of socialization and internalization of the culture of the child's society in the following terms:

'What happens in socialization is that the social world is internalized within the child. The same process, though perhaps weaker in quality, occurs every time the adult is initiated into a new social context or a new social group. Society, then, is not only something "out there", in the Durkheimian sense, but it is also "in here", part of our innermost being. Only an understanding of internalization makes sense of the incredible fact that most external controls work most of the time for most of the people in a society. Society not only controls our movements, but shapes our identity, our thought and our emotions. The structures of society become the structures of our own consciousness. Society does not stop at the surface of our skins. Society penetrates us as much as it envelops us' (44).

We have seen, with D. F. Aberle *et al.*, that one of the most fruitful ways of viewing society – in fact, of defining that 'figment of imagination' of Professor Sprott – is through its functional prerequisites. Whilst we may not be able to agree theoretically upon exactly what a society is, we can agree to a large extent upon what we expect it to *do*, or rather upon what is required before it can be said to exist. Society is 'the web of social relationships' which is perpetually changing; it exists, as R. M. MacIver and C. H. Page point out, where social beings 'behave' towards one another in ways to a very large extent predetermined by their recognition of one another (45).

It is this web of social relationships that the schools and the educators, or teachers, are trying to mediate to their pupils in a critical as well as constructive way. This is largely what education is all about; it is a fact accepted without much thought or argument in simpler societies, since their means of education are mostly informal and incidental to life itself. But in a complex society such as our own it is very important that, in the more formal aspects of our academic approach to questions of learning, we should not forget that we are educating our youth to live in a society; and that means that they are being educated for life, for living, for a large variety of relationships and for the fulfilment of particular roles.

B. CULTURE

When we ask for a definition of 'culture' we are faced with all the problems that one can meet in a word which has popular, literary and educational, as well as more scientific connotations. Our own universe of discourse here is, initially, anthropological and sociological, and E. B. Tylor provided one of the first definitions of culture from this point of view. Culture, he said, is 'that complex whole which includes knowledge, belief, art, morals, law, custom and any other capabilities and habits acquired by man as a member of society' (46). This, once more, is an attempt to give concretion to what is 'a mental fiction'. It is a shorthand expression, a symbol, for something that is not strictly in itself tangible, although it will inevitably, except in complete decay, find some tangible form of expression.

Kaspar D. Naegele has referred to the view that culture is a collective term for 'patterns of existential and normative assertions' (47). These 'assertions' may take the form of words in literature, language or drama, of sounds in music, of symbols in sculpture and art, of movement in dance and ballet, of fashion in clothes, and so forth. This particular 'existential' view of culture may not, in the long run, change anything, but it does give life and movement to a concept which otherwise might be viewed in a particularly static or sterile sort of way. The difference of viewpoint, when applied to education itself, is seen in the further concept of the transmission of culture which we must analyse later on.

For the present it is sufficient to point out that if culture is viewed as a certain corpus of ideas and knowledge to be 'handed on', then the resultant view of education must inevitably be one in which the accurate assimilation of that corpus becomes of paramount importance. On the other hand, if one views culture as an existential dimension of certain patterns of living and behaviour, then the educational process in relation to culture unavoidably becomes something more than the mere absorption of data or knowledge; it becomes an existential means and mode of patterning human relationships and activities (48). Our cultural 'assertions' are no longer limited to particular forms of learning.

There has been a tendency to think of culture as something which has been built up by the generations of people existing in the past, and which has been 'passed on', like some ritual object, to the generations of the present. It would, however, be quite wrong to go to the opposite extreme and attempt, by some novel means, to eliminate the history of a cultural situation, and to suggest that here we have something which is self-sufficient and which must be understood simply in some existential way. This, as A. L. Kroeber has emphasized, is to cut off its largest component or dimension (49). He argues that the transmission of culture is neither the handing on, nor the discovery of, isolated fragments of knowledge or information, which may or may not fit into some general pattern. Rather 'patterns or configurations or Gestalts are what it seems most profitable and productive to distinguish and formulate in culture' (50). In a consideration of the methodological efficiency, or otherwise of heurism (finding out or discovery methods) it is criteria such as these that one might consider.

Kroeber recognizes that values constitute an essential ingredient of culture, and that these values, however subjectively held, may also be objectively described and analysed. They are an integral part of culture itself and cannot be omitted in any serious sociological study. It is, therefore, important for us to realize that however relativistic the study of values between one culture and another may seem, these are part of the stuff of sociological inquiry. And it is also inevitable that value-judgements should at some point be made between the values of different cultures. As Kroeber points out, there may not be any absolute value-judgements passed to which all will give assent: the result is likely to be a pluralistic view rather than a complete consensus.

The three main anthropological approaches to the whole question of culture have been termed the historicist, the functional and the configurational. The American anthropologist, Franz Boas (51), adopted the historicist or historical view of culture, and considered also the geographical extent of any particular culture, that is, the culture area. Bronislaw Malinowski, who studied the Trobriand islanders, Australian aboriginies and Western Pacific islanders generally (52), and A. R. Radcliffe-Brown, who did some similar work among the Andaman islanders (53), provided a functional approach towards culture and its development. Culture was that integrating function or dimension in society which provided it with equilibrium or, if it failed, with disequilibrium. An integrated society, in which the culture contributed in a positive way towards the maintenance of its structure, was a *eunomic* one; a society which was characterized by some form of dysfunction and disequilibrium, was *dysnomic*. This functional approach has in mind, primarily, the actual causative elements and resultant effects of a culture upon the particular society under consideration.

The configurational approach perhaps owes most to Ruth Benedict (54). In broad terms, she delineated two main types or patterns of culture, the Apollonian and the Dionysian – terms borrowed from the philosophy of Nietzsche (55). The Apollonian type of culture was orientated towards the group: it was conformist and ritualistic, with extrovert forms of behaviour. On the other hand, the Dionysian form of culture was orientated towards the self, and was self-motivated; it was aggressive, individualistic and nonconformist. That cultures may be reduced to such patterns and configurations no one would deny, but a thorough-going view of culture, and therefore of its transmission, cannot afford to ignore the historical, culture area and functional approaches. It is also clear that the means of transmission of culture, or in more advanced societies the general educational system, will differ with each type of culture and with the forms of behaviour which any particular group may regard as desirable.

Increasingly we are faced in our own society with a variety of groups with their own cultures, or sub-cultures. A multi-racial society, a heterogeneous society, may well ask the question, 'What is it that it is desirable for the next generation to know and to be taught?' Culture is not a static *thing*, it is an active *process*; it accumulates and it becomes diffused; and through increasing contact with other societies, the culture of any particular society changes. In an amusing passage in *The Study of Man*, Ralph Linton describes some of the ways in which the diffusion of many cultures has helped to create the 'American culture' (56). Whether it be the bed he lies on, the bedclothes that cover him, the pyjamas and slippers he wears, the soap with which he washes himself, the orange or watermelon on which he breakfasts, the newspaper he reads, the language and print he uses, or the God he worships – for all these things the American is dependent upon the accumulation within his society of other cultures.

It was this awareness of one's historical debt to other societies as well as an understanding of the processes of enculturation and acculturation, that John Dewey sought to develop in his students and pupils through his own instrumental and pragmatic approach to education. But one cannot answer the problems of curriculum and methodology simply by the development of a total philosophy of education – whether it be pragmatic or anything else. They require that sort of analysis applied by the Schools Council in their *Working Paper No. 12*, in which the writers examine the nature of society: the way in which it changes both in its form and in the status of its social principles and objectives; the development of the child in that society; the past, present and future function of the school; and, bearing in mind all these things, the nature and content of the curricula as well as methods of 'enculturation' to be employed (57). The aims of education are no more static than society or culture, they are interdependent. As A. K. C. Ottaway remarks, 'culture is not an impersonal force existing outside the minds and actions of human beings. The outside forces of society are also human forces, and are exercised by individuals or groups of individuals' (58).

In consequence, it is the living activities and the thoughts of members of society which must be analysed in order to fully elicit the culture of any society. It is a living thing, not a dead thing. And education, viewed as the transmission of culture, is for action, for life, for living – not just something to be assessed or examined as a cognitive element in an individual's total personality. Just as animals are enabled, largely by instinct but also by imitation, to cope with their environment, including their relationships with other living creatures, so man is equipped to live in his society through the transmission of culture, through the educative process. It is not being suggested here that the school is the sole element in the educative process – far from it, as we shall see in our discussion of the family and the local environment of the child. But in a complex society such as our own, with the increasing limitation on the size and even duration of each nuclear family, the school has become the chief socializing agency and means of enculturation. It becomes, therefore, more and more vital that the organizers of the educational system, and the teachers directly responsible for the education of the children, should know what they are about.

The object of education, in very general terms, is to provide pupils and students with the means for understanding their society and its structures, and to open up for them a way of creating 'meaning' out of their environment and their relationships (59). This is certainly a part of what culture implies, and from an educational point of view it will mean, in specific terms, that the child is assisted both in language and thought to classify and provide meaning and relationships to things, ideas and events. To proceed from 'this is an apple' to 'this green apple will give me a pain' is a big step for the child. He has advanced beyond mere symbols or signs of identification to concepts of causation and meaning – at least in a simple sense. He has also developed ideas of relationship between himself and a part of his environment.

When Confucius stated that, when the meanings of the father were no longer meaningful to the son, there was danger, he was simply expressing the fact that the transmission of culture is more than the passing on of artefacts and rituals. Unless there is some identity of meaning in the various symbols of our society, culture becomes a dead, ossified thing. Unfortunately, words have a way of decaying, so that their very meanings change and even die. This alone might be a justification for the minimum of explanatory annotations on the plays of Shakespeare or the Authorized Version of the Bible. But culture works in two directions. Of course Confucius was right; but he might equally have said in the context of an evolving, accumulative culture, 'When the meanings of the son remain unmeaningful to the father, there is danger.'

A virile use of symbolism will involve the creation of new symbols for new expressions of meaning in an environment which is not only changing, but is being understood at different levels and at different depths. To remain 'uptight' and inflexible in an era of rapid change is to lose an opportunity for understanding society and its relationships in the very process of transformation. Culture is not merely transmitted, it is made; it is not simply historical and related to the past, it is functional and vitally concerned with the present; it is not the collective catalogue of discrete objects, ideas, mores and pieces of knowledge, it is a configuration of the total social inheritance and way of life. It is the function of education not merely to preserve and transmit the best of the past; it must demonstrate its function in the present as well as its possibilities for the future; and ultimately it must seek to provide a total view of society and its purposes.

REFERENCES

1 MacIver, R. M. and Page, C. H., *Society: An Introductory Analysis* (Macmillan, 1950; reprinted 1957).
2 Levy, Marion, *The Structure of Society* (Princeton Univ. Press, 1952), p. 113.
3 Aberle, D. F., Cohen, A. K., Davis, A. K., Levy, M. J. and Sutton, F. X., 'The Functional Prerequisites of a Society' in *Ethics*, Vol. 60, January 1950 (Bobbs-Merrill Reprint Series in the Social Sciences, S-1), p. 101.
4 *Vide* ibid., pp. 103–4.
5 *Vide* ibid., pp. 104–11.
6 *Vide* Ministry of Education, *Half Our Future* (Newsom Report) (H.M.S.O., 1963), pp. 72–9, 'Going out into the World'.
7 *Vide* D. E. S., *Children and their Primary Schools* (Plowden Report) (H.M.S.O., 1967), paras 543–8, 'Use of the Environment'.
8 *Vide* Sumner, W. G., *Folkways* (1906; Mentor, New English Lib., 1960), Chapter IX, 'Sex Mores', pp. 294–336.
9 Newsom Report, p. 71, recommendation (e).
10 Plowden Report, paras 714–21, 'Sex Education'.
11 Ibid., para. 719.
12 Aberle, D. F. *et al.*, op. cit., p. 104.
13 *Vide* Hutton, J. H., *Caste in India* (O.U.P., 4th edition 1963); Srinivas, M. N., *Caste in Modern India* (Asia Pub. House, 1962); Zinkin, T., *Caste Today* (O.U.P., 1962).
14 *Vide* Mannheim, K., *Diagnosis of Our Time* (Routledge 1943; 7th impression 1962), pp. 4–11, 49–53, 71–2 *et passim*.
15 Aberle, D. F. *et al.*, pp. 105–6.
16 *Vide* Eysenck, H. J., 'The Rise of the Mediocracy' in Cox, C. B. and Dyson, A. E. (eds), *Black Paper Two: The Crisis in Education* (The Critical Quarterly Society, 1969), pp. 34–40.
17 Stubbs, S., Headmaster, The Perse School, Cambridge, quoted in Cox, C. B. and Dyson, A. E. (eds), *Fight for Education: A Black Paper* (The Critical Quarterly Society, March 1969), p. 26.
18 Mead, G. H., *Mind, Self and Society* (Univ. of Chicago Press, 1934; 13th impression 1965), pp. 160–1.
19 Ibid., pp. 160–1.

20 *Vide* the important work of Professor B. B. Bernstein in this field of social class, language and learning. This will be considered later, but the interested reader will find a critique of his work in Lawton, D., *Social Class, Language and Education* (Routledge, 1968).

21 Millins, P. K. C., 'The Preparation of Teachers' in N.C.C.I., *Towards a Multi-Racial Society* (National Committee for Commonwealth Immigrants, 1966), p. 14.

22 Aberle, D. F. *et al.*, p. 107.

23 Mannheim, K., *Diagnosis of Our Time* (Routledge, 1943; 2nd edition 1943), p. 61.

24 *Vide* Newsom Report, particularly Chapter 4, 'Objectives', and Chapter 9, 'Going out into the World', pp. 72–9.

25 Cf. Vaihinger, H., *The Philosophy of 'As If'* (Routledge, 1924; reprinted 1965). Vaihinger holds that in the final analysis fictions derive from comparative apperception. Sprott similarly argues that, in some sense of the word, models of and beliefs about a society are *shared*. He states that:

> 'This makes all the difference to the status of these images, models and schemes that we have in our head, because, being shared, they do achieve a certain quasi-independence of the individual. It was this which made the sociologist Durkheim take the line that what he called social facts confront and constrain the individuals who act in their context. If you say, "Is society real?" in the sense that there is some entity over and above interacting individuals I would say definitely: no. If you ask whether the shared beliefs and models are real, I would say – and the cliché is extremely appropriate – that to all intents and purposes they are, because our intents and purposes are determined by these shared beliefs.' *Vide* The Schools Council, *Working Paper No. 12*, p. 22.

26 The Schools Council, *The Educational Implications of Social and Economic Change* (*Working Paper No. 12*) (H.M.S.O., 1967; 2nd impression 1968), p. 22.

27 Durkheim, E., *Suicide* (Routledge, 1952; reprinted 1963), p. 382.

28 *Vide* van Gennep, A., *The Rites of Passage* (Univ. of Chicago Press, 1960).

29 *Vide* Wach, J., *Sociology of Religion* (Univ. of Chicago Press, 1944; 11th impression 1967), p. 219.

30 Weber, Max, *The Sociology of Religion* (Social Science Paperbacks and Methuen, 1966), pp. 68 and 157.

31 *Vide* Peters, R. S., *Education as Initiation* (Evans Bros, 1964), particularly pp. 33–48.

32 Ministry of Education, *15 to 18* (Crowther Report) (H.M.S.O., 1959), p. 195.

33 *Vide* Mead, G. H., op. cit., p. 152.

34 Durkheim, E., *The Rules of Sociological Method* (Free Press, Glencoe, 1964), p. 66.

35 Ibid., p. 66, note 10.

36 Ibid., p. 70.

37 *Vide* Plato, *The Republic* (translated by B. Jowett) (O.U.P., 1928), sections 562–579E.
38 Aberle, D. F. *et al.*, op. cit., p. 109.
39 *Vide* D. E. S., *Children and their Primary Schools* (Plowden Report) (H.M.S.O., 1967), paras 65–74.
40 *Vide* Valentine, C. W., *The Normal Child and Some of His Abnormalities* (Penguin Books, 1956; reprinted 1962), for a discussion of the meaning of 'normality'.
41 *Vide* Bowlby, J., *Child Care and the Growth of Love* (Penguin Books, 1953; 2nd edition 1965).
42 Ibid., Part II, 'Prevention of Maternal Deprivation', pp. 75–187.
43 Mead, G. H., op. cit., pp. 154–6.
44 Berger, P. L., *Invitation to Sociology* (Penguin Books, 1966), p. 140.
45 MacIver, R. M. and Page, C. H., op. cit., pp. 5–6.
46 Tylor, E. B., *Primitive Culture* (J. Murray, 1891).
47 Naegele, K. D., in his Introduction to 'Social Change' in Parsons, T. *et al.* (eds), *Theories of Society* (Free Press, Glencoe, 1965), p. 1218.
48 For the development of the existential approach to education *vide* Kneller, G. F., *Existentialism and Education* (Phil. Lib. Inc., N.Y., 1958); Jeffreys, M. V. C., 'Existentialism' in Judges, A. V. (ed.), *Education and the Philosophic Mind* (Harrap, 1957); and Niblett, W. R., 'On Existentialism and Education' in *British Journal of Educational Studies*, Vol. II, No. 2, May 1954, Faber.
49 Kroeber, A. L., *The Nature of Culture* (Univ. of Chicago Press, 1952), pp. 4–10.
50 Ibid., p. 5. *Vide* also Kroeber, A. L., *Configurations of Cultural Growth* (Univ. of California Press, Berkeley, 1944).
51 *Vide* Boas, F., *Race, Language and Culture* (Macmillan, N.Y., 1940).
52 *Vide* Malinowski, B., *The Family Among the Australian Aborigines* (Univ. of London Press, 1913); *Argonauts of the Western Pacific* (Routledge, 1922); *Crime and Custom in Savage Society* (Routledge, 1926; 7th impression 1961); *A Scientific Theory of Culture* (Univ. of N. Carolina Press, 1944).
53 *Vide* Radcliffe-Brown, A. R., *A Natural Science of Society* (Free Press, Glencoe, 1957); *The Andaman Islanders* (C.U.P., 1922); *Structure and Function in Primitive Society* (Free Press, Glencoe, 1952).
54 *Vide* Benedict, Ruth, *Patterns of Culture* (Routledge, 1935; 7th impression 1961).
55 *Vide* Nietzsche, F., *The Birth of Tragedy* (1872); and Danto, A. C., *Nietzsche as Philosopher* (Macmillan, 1968), Chapter 1 on 'Philosophical Nihilism', pp. 19–35.
56 Linton, R., *The Study of Man* (Appleton-Century-Crofts, N.Y., 1936), pp. 326–7.
57 *Vide* The Schools Council, op. cit.
58 Ottaway, A. K. C., *Education and Society: An Introduction to the Sociology of Education* (Routledge, 1953; 2nd edition (revised) 1962; reprinted 1968), p. 8.

59 *Vide* Jaeger, G. and Selznick, P., 'A Normative Theory of Culture' in *American Sociological Review*, No. 29, October 1964, 653.

BIBLIOGRAPHY

ARNOLD, MATTHEW, *Culture and Anarchy* (C.U.P., 1932).
BARNETT, H. G., *Innovation: the Basis of Cultural Change* (McGraw-Hill, 1953).
BENEDICT, RUTH, *Patterns of Culture* (Routledge, 1935; 7th impression 1961).
BOAS, F., *Race, Language and Culture* (Macmillan, N.Y., 1940).
BRAMELD, T., *Cultural Foundations of Education* (Harper and Row, 1957).
BUTTS, R. F., *A Cultural History of Western Education* (McGraw-Hill, 1955).
ELIOT, T. S., *Notes Towards the Definition of Culture* (Faber, 1948).
ERIKSON, E. H., *Childhood and Society* (Penguin, 1957; reprinted 1965).
JAEGER, G. and SELZNICK, P., 'A Normative Theory of Culture' in *American Sociological Review*, No. 29, October 1964.
KLUCKHOHN, C., *Mirror for Man* (Harrap, 1950).
KROEBER, A. L., *Configurations of Cultural Growth* (Univ. of California Press, Berkeley, 1944).
KROEBER, A. L., *The Nature of Culture* (Univ. of Chicago Press, 1952).
KROEBER, A. L., and PARSONS, T., 'The Concept of Culture and Social System' in *American Sociological Review*, No. 23, October 1958.
LEE, DOROTHY, *Freedom and Culture* (Prentice-Hall, 1959).
LEVY, MARION, *The Structure of Society* (Princeton Univ. Press, 1952).
LINTON, R., *The Study of Man: An Introduction* (Appleton-Century-Crofts, 1936).
LINTON, R., *The Tree of Culture* (Knopf, 1955; reprinted 1961).
LINTON, R., *The Cultural Background of Personality* (Routledge, 1947; 5th impression 1965).
LOWIE, R. H., *Culture and Ethnology* (McMurtie, N.Y., 1917).
MACIVER, R. M., and PAGE, C. H., *Society: An Introductory Analysis* (Macmillan, 1950; reprinted 1957).
MALINOWSKI, B., *A Scientific Theory of Culture and Other Essays* (Univ. of N. Carolina Press, 1944).
MANNHEIM, K., *Essays on the Sociology of Culture* (Routledge, 1956; 2nd impression 1962).
MEAD, M. (ed.), *Cultural Patterns and Technical Change* (Mentor, New English Lib., 1955).
MERRILL, F. E., *Society and Culture* (Prentice-Hall, 1965).
MERTON, R. K., *Social Theory and Social Structure* (Free Press, Glencoe, 1957).
MONTAGU, M. F. A. (ed.), *Culture and the Evolution of Man* (O.U.P., 1962).
NICHOLSON, C. K., *Anthropology and Education* (C. E. Merrill, Columbus, Ohio, 1968).
PARK, R. E., *Race and Culture* (Free Press, Glencoe, 1950).
PARK, R. E., *Society* (Free Press, Glencoe, 1955).
PARSONS, T. et al. (eds), *Theories of Society* (Free Press, Glencoe, 1965).
RADCLIFFE-BROWN, A. R., *The Andaman Islanders: A Study In Social Anthropology* (C.U.P., 1922).

RADCLIFFE-BROWN, A. R., *Structure and Function in Primitive Society* (Cohen and West, 1952; 2nd impression 1963).

RADCLIFFE-BROWN, A. R., *A Natural Science of Society* (Free Press, Glencoe, 1957).

SHAPIRO, H. L. (ed.), *Man, Culture and Society* (O.U.P., 1956).

SMITH, A. G., *Communication and Culture* (Rinehart and Winston Inc., 1966).

SNOW, C. P., *The Two Cultures and the Scientific Revolution* (C.U.P., 1958).

SOROKIN, P. A., *Society, Culture and Personality* (Harper, 1947).

SOROKIN, P. A., *Social and Cultural Dynamics* (Porter Sargent, Boston, 1957).

STALCUP, R. J., *Sociology and Education* (C. E. Merrill, Columbus, Ohio, 1968).

STENHOUSE, L., *Culture and Education* (Nelson, 1967).

SUMNER, W. G., *Folkways* (Ginn and Co., Boston, 1906; Mentor, New English Lib., 1960).

TYLOR, E. B. *Primitive Culture* (J. Murray, 1891).

VAN GENNEP, A., *The Rites of Passage* (Routledge, 1960; 2nd impression 1965).

WILLIAMS, R., *Culture and Society: 1780–1950* (Chatto and Windus, 1958).

ZNANIECKI, F., *Cultural Reality* (Univ. of Chicago Press, 1919).

Chapter 4

Social Change and Education

A. SOME FACTS AND THEORIES OF SOCIAL CHANGE

In the popular mind everything that changes within society constitutes 'social change', from variations in the patterns of fashion to movements in population and general scientific advance. Some thinkers would distinguish, *ab initio*, at least three types of change, thereby giving to 'social change' itself a greater degree of speciality. There is, for example, *civilizational* change which involves the more physical elements in society, such as its inventions, its technology and science, and its improved forms of communication. There is *cultural* change which is concerned with the changes in knowledge, in ritual and religion, in artefacts and in art forms such as painting, architecture, dancing, drama and literature. *Social* change is then limited to social relationships and their balance or equilibrium. This analysis of change undoubtedly has certain advantages: it gives a seemingly clear-cut reference to a specific type of change, and this makes the investigation of its 'properties' a little more scientific.

But, admirable as such an idea may seem at first sight, the more one considers social change, the relationships between people, their equilibrium and disequilibrium, the more one becomes involved in the change and vicissitudes of civilization and culture. The web of social relationships which we call society is reticulated and intersected by every technical invention, every vagary in fashion or art form, every new technique of birth control, and every increase of efficiency in the means of production or social control. Life is one, and the change experienced in social relationships is both cause and effect. Max Weber recognized this complex nature of social relationships, and the concomitance of social, civilizational and cultural change (1). The problems associated with causation are considerable, and David Hume pointed out a long time ago the difficulty of the whole philosophical concept; he preferred to speak in terms of the 'constant conjunction' of certain events, and of their contiguity and succession rather than of a rigid, however undemonstrable, causation (2).

We shall discuss some of the theories of social change presently; for the moment it is important to note how the rate and nature of change have themselves altered in society. In the simpler societies change has been rare and usually slow: tradition, ritual, *rites de passage*, social hierarchies – these are some of the basic elements that have held such societies together.

These elements, however, are destroyed or changed only by culture contact or by such disasters as wars, disease and famine. The development, sometimes catastrophic, of 'cargo' cults in Melanesia has literally revolutionized religious beliefs as well as life-styles and social activity among many island groups (3).

Under the strong influence of common expectations of cargo and supplies arriving in ships or planes, and of united messianic hopes, many such groups have experienced trance states, convulsions and collective seizure or hysteria. The 'John Frum' cult, which found a stronghold in many Pacific islands during the 1940s and the early 1950s, represented very much a recrudescence of indigenous 'pagan' culture, which had been stifled by missionary culture contact. Behind much of this revolutionary change, supported by fervent and 'possessed' prophets bordering upon the schizophrenic, has been the sense of suppression by alien cultures and the desire by the native population to express itself in and through indigenous cults.

There is a certain ambivalence, however, in the attitudes of many of these island peoples. They are not all looking to the past; many are looking to the present and the future in that they accept the new affluence afforded by their white invaders whilst rejecting the latter themselves and their culture. The presence of the white man undoubtedly evokes a certain sense of guilt: without him they would attach their new-found wealth to traditional cultures, and develop along their own lines. Whilst the white man is there the new hopes are depreciated and embittered by nostalgic yearnings for the continuity of their native culture. There is an aching void which only 'John Frum' and his ilk can fill.

In a somewhat more sophisticated way the citizen of the more complex societies of Europe and the West is looking equally anxiously for his 'cargo' and his 'saviour'. The cargo may be more certain and definable, and the saviours more educated and politically trained; and, in the main, the latter are perhaps less likely to be arrested and placed in jails or mental homes. The cargo is represented by the computers, synthetic fibres, plastic materials and labour-saving devices; the saviours are the inventors, the scientists, the technologists, the industrialists and the economists. One of the citizen's greatest problems is that of keeping up with the speed of social and civilizational change. His television set and his car very quickly become obsolete. Indeed, his 'saviours' have so carefully planned the obsolescence of his purchases that, before he has finished paying for them, they are either worn out or obsolete (4). It was Willy Loman, in Arthur Miller's *Death of a Salesman*, who sadly lamented, 'I'm always in a race with the junkyard! I just finish paying for the car and it's on its last legs' (5).

Thus, the rapidity of social change is something that may be affected by sudden and drastic culture contact as in Oceania, by internal revolution and civil strife as in Russia, by emancipation and the advent of self-government as in some of the new African states, by increased inventiveness through the discovery of something like atomic energy, or by greed interacting with self-gratification as in the 'planned obsolescence of desirability' (6), and in the 'hedonism for the masses' (7).

In discussing all this social movement and interaction, we are tempted to use words such as 'progress', 'evolution', 'process', and so forth. R. M. MacIver and C. H. Page have discussed and distinguished terms signifying modes of change, and the ensuing outline largely follows their analysis (8). The word 'process' implies the idea of continuity, and social change is certainly something that is perpetually happening, and in a variety of ways. But, 'all that is meant by process is the definite step-by-step manner through which one state or stage merges into another' (9). Nothing is said here about the quality, good or bad, of the process: it is simply a way of describing how things happen in society; and also the way in which people adapt to certain elements in their society, or are assimilated to certain forms of activity, or adjust themselves to specific modes of behaviour. But, in describing the total process and these related processes, no judgement is being made of an evaluative nature. Indeed, one can accommodate to or integrate with an evil, disharmonious society, just as one can integrate with a eunomic, harmonious one. One state of society can merge into another with good or bad results – but however it is evaluated, it is a *process*.

The word 'evolution' implies a scientific concept of development and change, an 'unrolling' or unfolding, a movement in some particular direction. MacIver and Page consider that societies may be classified as more or less highly 'evolved' according to the complexity of their differentiation. Thus, they state that 'a civilized society is more highly evolved than that of the Eskimos' (10). This does not mean that the 'civilized' society is necessarily a better one viewed from a moral or idealistic point of view. Indeed, even the word 'civilized' has its overtones and undertones. 'More highly evolved' simply implies a greater complexity and differentiation within the society; but, again, evolution is not a merely quantitative process. One may have complexity without, in fact, having an evolutionary process: on the contrary, it may represent a diseased and disharmonious outcrop. For MacIver and Page, 'wherever in the history of society we find an increasing specialization of organs or units within the system or serving the life of the whole, we can speak of *social evolution*' (11). Thus, although these writers hesitate to impute any standard of valuation by terms such as 'higher' or 'lower' upon the evolutionary scale, or such as 'more advanced' or 'less advanced', it is clear that the term 'social evolution' implies for them some dimension of survival value.

The word 'progress' indicates not merely process, but process towards some pre-established and evaluated goal. The words progress and process are frequently used in popular discussion as interchangeable words, but in the context of social change, at least, 'progress' implies a value-judgement whereas 'process' is simply descriptive of continuity, good, bad or indifferent, without any further judgement. Value-judgements are relative, and what may constitute social progress for one may represent retrogression, decay or stagnation for another. Everything depends upon the sort of ideal one has of society itself and the goal at which one is aiming. Thus 'progress' is, in essence, an ethical concept.

There are currently a variety of descriptions of social change and theoretical analyses of its causation and predictability. No one would pretend that this was in any way a simple matter for analysis or description – as Professor W. J. H. Sprott has pointed out, a full discussion of the problem would require a book some 700 or 800 pages long. He nevertheless presents a clear and simplified scheme of social change within a very small compass (12). According to him there is, firstly, *exogenous* change which is caused by agencies external to society itself. Such factors as invasion, colonization, settlement, culture contact and disease are all highly unpredictable and capable of effecting social disequilibrium and change.

Secondly, there is *endogenous* change which occurs within the society. Sprott divides endogenous change into two main types according to their degree of predictability. There is *episodic* change which is brought about within a society by some event which could not have been predicted from our own personal knowledge of the state of our society. This applies particularly within the realm of inventions which have, sometimes, quite devastating effects upon the whole fabric and life-style of society. This can clearly work for good or ill; indeed, the invention in itself (e.g. radar, atomic energy, laser beams) is neutral – it is the use to which one puts such inventions that will decide whether society will progress or retrogress; but it will certainly change.

There is, however, also *patterned* change within the society which permits of more precise prediction. Such prediction is of a short-term order; it depends upon the increase in a society of mutual concern, planning, rationality and an organized programme of social welfare, as well as political and economic consensus (13).

In an article on 'Social Change', Morris Ginsberg has discussed both causation and teleology (14). He recognizes that change may be effected by the desires and decisions of individuals in such matters as birth control, supported of course by improved techniques and discovery. Changes in social conditions may be brought about by economic fluctuations and structural modification, thereby producing a new sort of equilibrium. The role of war in the causation of social change is largely in the realm of culture contact and increased invention.

Ginsberg goes on to mention such outstanding personalities as Lenin, as well as groups, who have contributed in a very positive and sometimes violent way to social change. They are involved in that causation which can be described only as a collocation or confluence of elements derived from a variety of sources, but which all converge at a given point (15). This is particularly noticeable in times of difficulty or stress, such as war, when many groups are working in different areas of investigation but with, nevertheless, a common purpose. Such change is in a real sense 'teleological' – it has eventuated out of a common purpose of immediate, designed survival. Ginsberg emphasizes that if there were only the accidental in life we would have no history, but merely annals. On the other hand, if there were not the fortuitous and the accidental, we would have science but no history (16). There is, in social change, an element of the scientific as well as both history and annals. It is not always possible to delineate precisely what is fortuitous and what is planned, but in all social life and change there is an interplay of causation, teleology and the purely accidental.

Most of what has been said here can be reduced to a consideration of change under three main types of factor or condition: (*a*) physical and biological; (*b*) technological; (*c*) cultural (17). A consideration of physical and biological factors involves such problems as the changing size and average age of a population, the varying balance between deaths and births, and the variations in the race, colour and culture in the differing elements of the population. Geographical factors, environment, habitats and ecological modifications may also affect society, its distribution and its occupations. Biological factors are only partly predictive along the lines of certain trends in scientific and technological advance and discovery; but all predictions may be modified or made even completely nonsensical by either human will or counter-invention.

Our present technological era is very much involved in the creation of *things*, of objects which sometimes threaten to control our lives and our activities. It is often said that 'things are in the saddle and ride mankind'. However that may be, the ever-increasing creation of amenities and utilitarian objects has made the individual citizen more and more dependent upon man's inventiveness. One of the most interesting revolutions of our time has been in the area of agriculture and in the development of new techniques, and the firm establishment of an agricultural technology. This is an evolving technology, with its vast improvements in mechanical devices, in fertilizers and seeds, and in the acceptance of the vital importance of management, economics, accountancy and genetics – not as extras or sidelines, but as intrinsic dimensions of agriculture itself. The social effects and changes of such a development are reflected in the sort of person taking up farming today, and in the qualifications required to run a farm successfully. Other technological advances have included the development of physical transportation by means of rail, aeroplane and automobile, and the discovery and harnessing of atomic energy.

In any attempt to explain the causation of social change it is, of course, possible to select one particular factor and to over-emphasize this. Thus, E. Huntington (18) held that the determining environment of geography and climate was responsible for social change; for Karl Marx (19) the determining factors which were of paramount importance were economic. For Marx the determinant of primary economic relationships was the power of economic production and the class struggle between the *bourgeoisie* and the proletariat. All this was based upon the Hegelian dialectic – the philosophico-historicist triad of thesis, antithesis and synthesis. The historicist view, in its many forms, cannot be elaborated here: for this the reader should turn to the critical works of Karl Popper (20). Another thinker, Thorstein Veblen, has been referred to as a technological determinist: he argued that technological advance is reflected in the process of our social systems. According to him the variety of our working environment explains the variety of social structure, and the new technologies create new habits in industry and commerce and, ultimately, are responsible for overthrowing the old institutions of society (21).

But man is not only created and determined by his environment: he criticizes and re-creates it. I have argued elsewhere, in relation to Skinnerian conditioning (22), that any thorough-going theory of behaviour and determinism forgets one thing, namely, that even the environment which conditions man's activity and response is freely constructed and reconstituted by man himself. Moreover, he is perpetually adapting that environment in order to condition his prisoners (himself and his associates) in the way he conceives best. Man is himself the conditioner as well as the conditioned; man initiates activity, he creates his technological world, and he modifies his society accordingly.

Some simple societies, which are at the same level of technological, or technical, development, seem to have developed very different cultures. This would suggest that culture is not absolutely correlated with technological advance (23). Moreover, societies which are developing new inventions and new technologies do not necessarily apply them in the same way. Culture is, however, a determinant and basic condition of social change; it may cause one society to use a particular invention and another to reject it. The complex nature of the culture-social relationship has led to a variety of theories. For example, S. N. Eisenstadt (24) has argued that the potentialities for social change may, through the various processes of institutionalization, be transformed into historical realities.

But not all processes of social change necessarily give rise to changes in overall institutional systems. Eisenstadt goes on to suggest that whilst there exist, in all societies, the potentialities for systemic changes, 'the tempo and direction of such changes vary'. Systemic changes which do increase the scope of differentiation within the major spheres of society do not necessarily ensure the institutionalization of a more differentiated social system. Even, however, when some structural differentiation has been institutionalized, each fresh institutional system evinces different potentialities for further change, for stagnation, for breakdown or for further development (25).

Oswald Spengler developed the cyclical theory of cultures in *The Decline of the West* (26). In brief, his view was that all cultures went through regular stages of rise and fall, advance and decay, resembling somewhat the alpha rhythm of the brain or the cycle of alternating current. A. J. Toynbee (27) has argued similarly in favour of a cycle of response after some initial challenge, followed by a period of intense struggle, with an ultimate conquest or final downfall. Any reduction of Toynbee's metahistorical thesis must inevitably be a caricature, and the reader should look at it a little more closely in D. C. Somervell's excellent abridgement. Karl Popper has attacked the theories of both Spengler and Toynbee in his *The Open Society and its Enemies* (28), and Toynbee in *The Poverty of Historicism* (29). Popper makes the point that Toynbee appears to be unaware of the fact that his approach is Hegelian; although he (Popper) recognizes in Toynbee's 'criterion of the growth of civilizations', which is 'progress towards self-determination', the Hegelian law of progress (30).

B. SOCIAL CHANGE AND EDUCATION

The process of institutionalization, says Eisenstadt, helps to transform the general potentialities for change into historical realities (31), and one of the institutions involved in this process is that of education. Education is a conserving institution, seeking to mediate and to maintain the cultural heritage of the society. But, whilst seeking to conserve, education must also try and ensure that as little 'cultural lag' as possible occurs within the society (32). This means that there must be some attempt to adjust the old culture to new conditions in order that individuals within society may keep up with technological change. Patterns of culture and of institutions change rapidly even though the average member of society may be virtually unaware of the transformations taking place around him. Ogburn and Nimkoff have summed up this situation in the following words:

'When culture begins to change, the modifications do not occur evenly in all parts of the social heritage. Some parts change faster than others.

When the different parts are interrelated, the varying rates of change produce a strain between the unequally moving parts. The part that is moving at the slowest rate of speed constitutes the cultural lag. Since the other part of culture has already changed, as a rule the most practicable method of effecting a better integration between the two parts is to make some adjustment in the part that is lagging. Modern technology is changing at a rapid rate and creating important changes, with which our social institutions have not yet caught up. Analysis of important modern social problems, such as unemployment, poverty, and family disorganization, shows that much of our contemporary social disorganization issues from the irregular changes of our culture' (33).

Culture, however, should through the processes of education be dynamic and should perform a directional role. To this end education is, in a real sense, teleological, that is, it provides a common purpose in and for society, which must be intelligently thought out and constructed. Such teleology must carefully consider the technological advances of the particular society concerned, the ways in which those advances may be mediated to the citizens of the future as social facts (34), and also the way in which the pupils in schools and the students in colleges and universities may make use of those advances in their day-to-day work and study. Education may certainly in some ways be regarded as a preparation for the future, but it also exists in its own right and for itself, and to that extent the techniques of the present society must be fully employed within the institution of education. We are, of course, seeing something of the application of those techniques in such areas as audio-visual aids, computers, tape-recorders, ciné projectors, and in the development of resource centres and the methods of storage of information.

In a discussion of the 'cultural lag', which is apparent in the curricula being taught in the schools, Karl Mannheim considers *inter alia* the participation of the pupil in the learning process. This 'lag' he regards as an inevitable result of the general inability to depend as strongly as formerly upon authority. Mannheim goes on to say that as the student increasingly participates in the learning process, so 'the incentives upon which learning is built will tend to move from constraints, external rewards like marks, prizes, ranking, towards mobilizing interest' (35).

The logic of all this is simply that the way in which teachers are educated and prepared for their profession must also change. Such methods can no longer remain at the level of the impartation of 'tricks of the trade', but must be centred upon a social education which demands the development of an 'all-round approach to the pupil'. In this all-round approach the intellectual progress of the pupils is regarded as of less importance than the broadening of their horizons and interests generally, and the development of their awareness and understanding of other human persons. Indeed, the present emphasis, according to Mannheim, should no longer be upon 'instruction and learning but rather on development of living' (36). In consequence, there is a need for schools and colleges to become true societies, and any realistic teacher-training must take this factor into account.

Today, generally speaking, the process of *learning* receives a greater emphasis than that of *teaching*, although it is not easy to see how the two processes can, in fact, be divorced. In both we are concerned with more than mechanical training or rote learning. Current social change indicates a vast increase in innovation and adaptability, and all forms of education must clearly have these things in mind. Sir Ronald Gould has warned that 'Mechanical and industrial changes make greater and greater demands on individuals, and education needs to pull itself together and make quite sure that it meets the needs of modern society' (37). In a rapidly changing society, education has to be keenly aware of change, but it must not just go along with it. Change must be evaluated, and education must encourage the right sort of innovation and help to direct it.

Schools exist not merely to reflect and mediate the cultural inheritance of a society and current change; they exist also to assist in the promotion of social change and reform. One need only look at such countries as Germany, Russia, India and Pakistan, and the evolving societies of the continents of Africa and South America, to see that education has been, and is being, used as an agent of social change. A great deal, of course, depends here upon the nature of the political system of any particular society, and we shall be considering some of the political aspects more fully in the next chapter. Nicholas Hans has remarked that:

'Whereas in England the policy of *laissez-faire* permitted the educational system to lag behind the economic needs for more than a century, the Soviet decentralization and planning made the educational system one of the vital movers of the economic change' (38).

In this respect it is interesting to note that Durkheim held a deterministic view of society and that, in critically examining the various definitions of education and descriptions of its nature, he argued that it was not the aim of education to present some picture of an ideal society to the child. Nor was it the object of the educationist to consider some ideal form of education for such a society. To inquire what such an ideal form of education must be, when abstracted from conditions of both time and place, was 'to admit implicitly that a system of education has no reality in itself' (39). Durkheim argued that there was not just one form of education, ideal or actual, but many forms: there were, in fact, as many different forms of education as there were different *milieux* in any given society (40). And so society as a whole, and each particular *milieu*, would determine the type of education that was realized or realizable.

Durkheim argued, however, that it was vital through education to preserve a degree of 'homogeneity', and to establish in the child from the very beginning the 'essential similarities' of collective life. But he felt that it was also very important to ensure that there was a certain amount of 'diversity' in society, without which all forms of co-operation would be impossible. Durkheim suggested that this diversity was assured by the very diversification of education itself (41).

There are, however, apparent contradictions in Durkheim's writings. It would seem, according to some passages, that the educational system can change neither society nor itself. In *Suicide* he states that 'To the extent that real life increasingly takes possession of him [the child], it will come to destroy the work of the teacher. Education, therefore, can be reformed only if society itself is reformed' (42). But how can society reform itself, or attack the evil from which it suffers 'at its sources', except through some means, agent or institution such as education? It would seem a reasonable assumption that any group or nation which has a vision of some more desirable society will seek to realize that vision partly, at least, through its educational system. Indeed, both fascist and communist societies have accepted this principle.

In the same section of *Suicide* Durkheim remarks that education is only 'the image and reflection of society'; it imitates and reproduces the latter in an abbreviated form, but it does not *create* it (43). This, once more, reflects a very deterministic view; and according to it all educators and teachers are simply the passive servants of the state, carrying out its decrees. As J. Barron Mays comments:

'To ignore the creative and moral significance of the individual altogether is, in the last analysis, untenable. Not only is it true that the net result of innovations within the educational field, by virtue of the fact that they work towards greater equality of opportunity, assists large numbers of people to rise in the socio-economic scale with important (sometimes perhaps unforeseen) consequences for social structure, but it is further clear that individuals within the system may elect to facilitate or obstruct the attainment of ultimate objectives' (44).

There is, and must be, an interaction between education and society. It is not just a one-way process, as Durkheim appears to imply, in which education is wholly determined by the state or by the demands of society; but the institution and structure of education can, in turn, change and modify the social structure. Society at large may dictate the change, through the free election of political parties to power; and in turn the programme of education, its forms and structure will be to a large extent directed and controlled by the political and social aims of society at any particular time. A study of comparative education will adequately reveal the fact that the ideologies, the political ideals, and the social aims of such a variety of countries as China, U.S.A., U.S.S.R., France, Germany and England, are reflected in their educational systems (45). Education, however, does not merely reflect society: it co-operates with society to change it.

Karl Mannheim also considered the problem of social change and social progress in relation to education. He considered that there was a lack of awareness in social affairs as well as a lack of comprehensive sociological orientation. The leaders of the nation, including teachers, should be educated in a way which would enable them to understand the meaning of change. Mannheim argued that in the present situation no teaching was sound unless it trained a man to be aware of the whole situation in which he found himself, and to be able after careful deliberation to make his choice and come to a decision. For him the aim of social progress was not an imaginary society without a governing elite; it was 'the improvement of the economic, social, political, and educational opportunities for the people to train themselves for leadership, and an improvement of the method of the selection of the best in the various fields of social life' (46). The development of new educational techniques would lead to the emergence of new elites, not the deadly dull equalization of all.

Mannheim considered also the bipolarity of education, by which he implied that we must educate for both conformity and originality. By conformity he meant the willingness to submerge one's aggressiveness and individuality in the interests of the group and social 'belongingness'; it was the adjustment of the self for common effort, and a desire to be obedient and subservient to the common will. But, at the same time, we must educate also for originality, for creativeness, for responsibility and for spontaneity. Mannheim warns, however, that these things should help us to realize more and more that we are members one of another, and that failing such a realization the result could be 'neurosis and psychosis' (47).

With all this in mind Mannheim suggested that we must seek in education to provide curricula which have sound cultural justifications; that is, they must be firmly based on the social situation of the learner in which there is involved the pattern of inherited culture, the unique content of contemporary culture, and the culture of the foreseeable future. The whole complex of social relationships is a part of this intricate cultural pattern, and only a full awareness of what this implies will ensure a society and a world in which individuals accept their responsibility for others (48).

In a consideration of the ways in which education can assist social progress, it is necessary to think in terms of the many investigations by commissions, councils and committees into the state of education in our society, and their recommendations. Increasingly there is a recognition, in education, that there is a need in the classroom and in the school generally to *compensate* for individual, or group, social deprivation. Both the Newsom Report (49) and the Plowden Report (50) were concerned to show that many children were socially deprived and that education, through its various media, must compensate for this deprivation in cultural background, in language development and in general environmental amenities.

The school is involved increasingly with the ever-mounting problems of urbanization, of the faceless, anonymous members of dense factory and tower-flat populations. The changes that have occurred in the composition of families, in their social and economic security, and in their attitudes, have all affected the educational approach to children within the social context. We are fast moving through various phases of the new industrial revolution, which have been termed biotechnic, nucleotechnic and cybernetic (51). Automation, calculating machines, electronic brains, self-guiding missiles and programmed-learning machines are all here. Automatic machines will all help to reduce the number of brains as well as hands required for any particular operation, and they will reduce man's drudgery and increase the leisure time at his disposal. It is obvious that the education of the future, and the teacher-training of the present, cannot afford to ignore these facts.

In particular, those who do not possess sufficient intelligence or capacity to have a real, active and useful part in this cybernetic revolution must, nevertheless, be educated for the emergent society and for living in it. This means that we must not be too surprised if our youth try out a great variety of jobs before they finally settle; indeed, this may prove to be a good thing in a world of change in which adaptability holds a premium. But whilst educating for adaptability we must also educate for *leisure* (52). Ultimately we are educating people *to be*, that is, to live the fullest and most integrated life possible within their society. And in order to accomplish this they must first understand both society and themselves.

Mannheim has stressed the importance of developing, or eliciting, a sense of common purpose between the home, the school and society. For so many 'education' ends when school ends: it is the end of a period of compulsion which, for many, may appear quite purposeless. But we must seek to eradicate this concept of 'compulsory' education for a particular period of our lives, and accept much more freely the 'compulsive' quality of education during the whole of life. Mannheim suggested that, in this sense of common, continuous purpose and through emphasizing the educative fabric of the whole of society, educators must seek to harmonize the *apparently* antagonistic elements in that society – school and life, work and leisure, action and reflection, self-control and self-expression, individuality and co-operation, change and tradition (53).

Education in our society is increasingly concerned with the indigenous regional differences, with urban and rural variety, and with the rapidly developing multi-racial and multi-cultural elements. There is also the additional problem of the fragmented and fragmentary sub-cultures, which arise suddenly and almost as suddenly die, change or become transformed or subsumed in the main cultural stream.

Change of any sort is very painful to many people who have established their own norms, standards and concepts of stability. For some social change can be an unnerving, disorientating, even neurotic experience, with sometimes a violently changing scale of values and morals. New techniques and technologies require some sort of adaptation or accommodation by everyone, but, in the words of Professor P. H. Taylor, '"The enemy" is not only – and perhaps, not significantly – social change but our own perceptions' (54).

This is very deeply true in the sense that 'the enemy' is within ourselves, in our very attitudes towards change itself. Our rejection of change, our inability to adapt to it, our fear of the novel and unfamiliar – these are very often the things that make real social *progress* difficult, if not impossible. Education must therefore be for mobility, for flexibility of thought and action, for the production of individuals with a high general level of culture calculated to make them 'adaptable to changing economic and social conditions' (55).

REFERENCES

1 *Vide* Weber, Max, *The Sociology of Religion* (Methuen, Social Science Paperbacks, 1966), in particular Chapter XIII, 'Religious Ethics, the World Order, and Culture'.

2 *Vide* Hume, D., *Essays, Literary, Moral and Political* (Ward, Lock and Co., n.d.), Essay XXXIX, 'An Inquiry Concerning Human Understanding', Section VII, 'Of the Idea of Necessary Connection', pp. 343–55.

3 *Vide* Firth, R., *Tikopia Ritual and Belief* (Allen and Unwin, 1967); Worsley, P., *The Trumpet Shall Sound: A Study of 'Cargo' Cults in Melanesia* (London, 1957); Lanternari, V., *The Religions of the Oppressed* (Mentor Book, New American Library, 1963), pp. 166–90.

4 *Vide* Packard, Vance, *The Waste Makers* (Penguin, 1963), Chapters 6 and 7.

5 Ibid., quoted on p. 57.

6 Ibid., Chapter 7.

7 Ibid., Chapter 15.

8 *Vide* MacIver, R. M., and Page, C. H., *Society: An Introductory Analysis*, pp. 521–30.

9 Ibid., p. 522.

10 Ibid., p. 528.
11 Ibid., p. 527.
12 *Vide* Sprott, W. J. H., 'Society: What is it and how does it change?' in The Schools Council, *The Educational Implications of Social and Economic Change* (*Working Paper No. 12*) (H.M.S.O., 1967), pp. 21–7. Cf. also Bottomore, T. B., *Sociology: A Guide to Problems and Literature* (Allen and Unwin, 1962; 2nd edition 1971), pp. 286–8.
13 Sprott, W. J. H., ibid., p. 24.
14 *Vide* Ginsberg, M., 'Social Change' in *British Journal of Sociology*, Vol. IX, No. 3, September 1958, pp. 205–29.
15 Ibid., pp. 217–18.
16 Ibid., p. 218.
17 *Vide* MacIver, R. M. and Page, C. H., op. cit., pp. 512–18, 'The Permanent Conditions of Social Change'.
18 *Vide* Huntington, E., *World Power and Evolution* (Yale Univ. Press, 1919); *Civilization and Climate* (Yale Univ. Press, 3rd edition 1924); *Mainsprings of Civilization* (Mentor Books, New American Library, 1959; 3rd printing 1964).
19 *Vide* Marx, Karl, *Capital*, 2 vols (Everyman Lib., Dent, 1930).
20 *Vide* Popper, Karl, *The Open Society and its Enemies, Vol. II – Hegel and Marx* (Routledge, 1962; 5th edition 1966); *The Poverty of Historicism* (Routledge, 2nd edition 1960).
21 *Vide* Veblen, Thorstein, *The Theory of the Leisure Class* (Macmillan, 1899; Mentor Books, New American Library, 1953); *Essays in our Changing Order* (Viking Press, N.Y., 1934).
22 *Vide* Morrish, I., *Disciplines of Education* (Allen and Unwin, 1967), pp. 223–4.
23 *Vide* Benedict, R., *Patterns of Culture* (Routledge, 1935; 7th impression 1961); Mead, M. (ed.), *Cultural Patterns and Technical Change* (UNESCO, 1953).
24 *Vide* Eisenstadt, S. N., 'Institutionalization and Change' in *American Sociological Review*, Vol. 29, April 1964, pp. 49–59.
25 *Vide* Eisenstadt, S. N., 'Social Change, Differentiation and Evolution' in *American Sociological Review*, Vol. 29, No. 3, June 1964, pp. 385–6.
26 *Vide* Spengler, O., *The Decline of the West*, 2 vols (Knopf, N.Y., 1926–8).
27 *Vide* Toynbee, A. J., *A Study of History* (A one-volume abridgement by D. C. Somervell, O.U.P., 1946).
28 Op. cit., Vol. I, pp. 231–2.
29 Op. cit., pp. 110 ff.
30 *Vide The Open Society and its Enemies*, Vol. I., p. 232.
31 *Vide* Eisenstadt, S. N., 'Institutionalization and Change', pp. 49–59 (quoted in note 24).
32 For the 'cultural lag' theory, *vide* Ogburn, W. F., *Social Change* (Viking Press, N.Y., 1922; reprinted 1932), pp. 200–13, 'The Hypothesis of Cultural Lag'. There is a brief criticism of this view in Ottaway, A. K. C., *Education and Society* (Routledge, 2nd edition 1962; reprinted 1968), pp. 43–5.

33 Ogburn, W. F. and Nimkoff, M. F., *A Handbook of Sociology* (Routledge, 4th revised edition 1960), p. 547.
34 Cf. Durkheim, E., *The Rules of Sociological Method* (Free Press, Glencoe, 1964), Chapter I, 'What is a Social Fact?'
35 Mannheim, K. and Stewart, W. A. C., *An Introduction to the Sociology of Education* (Routledge, 1962), p. 32.
36 Ibid., p. 32.
37 The Schools Council, *The Educational Implications of Social and Economic Change*, in the 'Opening Address' by Sir Ronald Gould, p. 8.
38 Hans, N., *Comparative Education: A Study of Educational Factors and Traditions* (Routledge, 1949; 3rd edition (revised) 1958), p. 79.
39 Durkheim, E., *Education and Sociology* (Free Press, Glencoe, 1956), pp. 64–5.
40 Ibid., p. 67.
41 Ibid., pp. 70–1.
42 Durkheim, E., *Suicide* (Routledge, 1952; reprinted 1963), p. 373.
43 Ibid., p. 372. The reader should refer to the excellent article on Durkheim by Ottaway, A. K. C., 'Durkheim on Education', in *British Journal of Educational Studies*, Vol. XVI, No. 1, February 1968, pp. 5–16.
44 Mays, J. B., *Education and the Urban Child* (Liverpool Univ. Press, 1962), p. 9.
45 *Vide* Hans, N., op. cit.; King, E. J., *Other Schools and Ours* (Holt, Rinehart, 3rd edition 1967); King, E. J., *Education and Social Change* (Pergamon Press, 1966).
46 Mannheim, K., *Diagnosis of Our Time* (Routledge, 1943), p. 72.
47 Mannheim, K., and Stewart, W. A. C., op. cit., p. 113.
48 Ibid., pp. 107–13.
49 *Vide* Ministry of Education, *Half Our Future* (Newsom Report) (H.M.S.O., 1963), paras 50–74, 204, 290–2.
50 *Vide* D. E. S., *Children and their Primary Schools* (Plowden Report) (H.M.S.O., 1967), paras 53–5, 70, 131–73, 178–99, 301–2.
51 *Vide* Ottaway, A. K. C., op. cit., pp. 78–80.
52 *Vide* Carter, M. P., *Education, Employment and Leisure* (Pergamon Press, 1963).
53 *Vide* Mannheim, K. and Stewart, W. A. C., op. cit., pp. 131–3, 149.
54 *Vide* Taylor, P. H., 'Towards a Strategy for Education' in The Schools Council, *The Educational Implications of Social and Economic Change* (*Working Paper No. 12*), p. 3.
55 John Vaizey, quoted by Sir Ronald Gould in his 'Opening Address', The Schools Council, op. cit., p. 11.

BIBLIOGRAPHY

BARNETT, H. G., *Innovation: the Basis of Cultural Change* (C.U.P., 1932).
BARNETT, H. G., 'Invention and Cultural Change' in *American Anthropologist*, 1942, pp. 14–30.
BERNBAUM, G., *Social Change and the Schools, 1918–1944* (Routledge, 1967).

BOTTOMORE, T. B., *Sociology: A Guide to Problems and Literature* (Allen and Unwin, 1962; 2nd edition 1971), Part V, 'Social Change'.

CLARKE, F., *Education and Social Change* (Sheldon Press, 1940).

COLEMAN, J. S. (ed.), *Education and Political Development* (Princeton Univ. Press, 1965).

COSER, L., *The Functions of Social Conflict* (Free Press, Glencoe, 1956).

COTGROVE, S., *Technical Education and Social Change* (Routledge, 1958).

DUNCAN, O. D., (ed.), *William F. Ogburn on Culture and Social Change* (Univ. of Chicago Press, 1964).

EGGAN, F., 'Cultural Drift and Social Change' in *Current Anthropology*, No. 4, October 1963, pp. 347–360.

EISENSTADT, S. N., 'Institutionalization and Change' in *American Sociological Review*, Vol. 29, April 1964, pp. 49–59.

EISENSTADT, S. N., 'Social Change, Differentiation and Evolution' in *American Sociological Review*, Vol. 29, No. 3, June 1964, pp. 375–86.

ETZIONI, A. and E. (eds), *Social Change* (Basic Books, 1964).

FIRTH, R., *Social Change in Tikopia* (Allen and Unwin, 1959).

FOSTER, P. J., *Education and Social Change in Ghana* (Routledge, 1965).

FRASER, W. R., *Education and Society in Modern France* (Routledge, 1963).

GINSBERG, M., 'Social Change' in *British Journal of Sociology*, Vol. IX, No. 3, September 1958, pp. 205–29.

GREEN, B. S. R. and JONES, E. A., *An Introduction to Sociology* (Pergamon Press, 1966; reprinted 1968), pp. 112–19, 'Functionalism and Social Change'.

HAGEN, E., *On the Theory of Social Change* (The Dorsey Press, Homewood, Ill., 1962).

HANS, N., *Comparative Education: A Study of Educational Factors and Traditions* (Routledge, 1949; 3rd edition (revised) 1958).

HODGKINSON, H. L., *Education, Interaction and Social Change* (Prentice-Hall, 1967).

KELLER, A. G., *Societal Evolution* (Yale Univ. Press, New Haven, 1915).

KING, E. J., *Education and Social Change* (Pergamon Press, 1966).

LESTER SMITH, W. O., *The Impact of Education on Society* (Blackwell, 1949).

MACIVER, R. M., *Society: Its Structure and Changes* (Holt, Rinehart and Winston, 1937).

MACIVER, R. M., *Social Causation* (Ginn, Boston, 1942).

MACIVER, R. M. and PAGE, C. H., *Society: An Introductory Analysis* (Macmillan, 1950), Book III, 'Social Change'.

MALINOWSKI, B., *Dynamics of Culture Change* (Yale Univ. Press, 1945).

MANNHEIM, K., *Man and Society: In an Age of Reconstruction* (Routledge, 1940: reprinted 1960).

MEAD, MARGARET, 'Social Change and Cultural Surrogates' in Kluckhohn, C., and Murray, H. (eds.), *Personality in Nature, Society and Culture* (J. Cape, 1949).

MOORE, W. E., 'A Reconstruction of Theories of Social Change' in *American Sociological Review*, Vol. 25, December 1960, pp. 810–18.

MOORE, W. E., *Social Change* (Prentice-Hall, 1963).

MOORE, W. E. and COOK, R. M. (eds.), *Readings on Social Change* (Prentice-Hall, 1967).

MUSGRAVE, P. W., *Technical Change, the Labour Force and Education* (Pergamon Press, 1967).

NEWCOMB, T. M., *Personality and Social Change: Attitude Formation in a Student Community* (Dryden Press, N.Y., 1943).

OGBURN, W. F., *Social Change* (Viking Press, N.Y., 1932).

OGBURN, W. F., 'Cultural Lag as Theory' in *Sociology and Social Research*, 1957, pp. 167–74.

OGBURN, W. F. and NIMKOFF, M. E., *A Handbook of Sociology* (Routledge, 1947), Part VII.

PARSONS, T. (ed.), *Theories of Society* (Free Press, Glencoe, 1965), Part V, pp. 1,207–405, 'Social Change'.

SAMUEL, R. H., and THOMAS, R. H., *Education and Society in Modern Germany* (Routledge, 1949; 2nd impression 1963).

SCHOOLS COUNCIL, *The Educational Implications of Social and Economic Change* (*Working Paper No. 12*) (H.M.S.O., 1967; 2nd impression 1968).

SMELSER, N., *Social Change in the Industrial Revolution* (Univ. of Chicago Press, 1959).

SOROKIN, P. A., *Social and Cultural Dynamics* (Sargent, Boston, 1957).

TÖNNIES, F., *Fundamental Concepts of Society* (*Gemeinschaft und Gesellschaft*, translated by Loomis, C. P.) (American Book Co., N.Y., 1940).

TOYNBEE, A., *A Study of History* (abridged and edited by D. C. Somervell, O.U.P., 1946).

WEBER, ALFRED, *Fundamentals of Culture-Sociology* (Columbia Univ. Dept of Social Science, N.Y., 1939).

WEBER, MAX, *The Theory of Social and Economic Organization* (Free Press, Glencoe, 1947).

WILSON, G. and M., *The Analysis of Social Change* (C.U.P., 1945).

ZOLLSCHAN, G. K. and HIRSCH, W. (eds), *Explorations in Social Change* (Routledge, 1964).

Chapter 5

The State, Politics and Education

A. THE ROLE OF THE STATE IN EDUCATION

'Order is the first requirement of the diverse, specialized, interdependent activity of modern man, and this order the state alone can maintain' (1).

It is obvious that whether we are considering a primitive group or a complex, sophisticated society we are vitally concerned with the problem of order. In a simple society power may reside in the person of a tribal chief or in a group of headmen; in a highly developed society it may reside in what is referred to as 'the state'. In broad, general terms, a state is an association of people, a specific organization of society which is responsible for performing political functions, and which possesses the ultimate power of coercion and sanction. In their introductory work, *Society*, MacIver and Page go on to emphasize not merely the importance of order within the micro-society, but also the necessity of order within the macro-society of the world, that is, the necessity of some form of international order.

Without such 'state' order and regulation it is impossible for a society to make any concerted effort at progress. This applies equally within the realm of education, to which no state can be indifferent since, as Durkheim emphasizes, education is basically and essentially a social function (2). Yet, despite his insistence that everything which in any way pertains to education 'must in some degree be submitted to [the state's] influence' (3), Durkheim was very liberal in his views about the existence of schools other than those for which the state was directly responsible. The state must, in the interests of the public, allow other schools to be opened, but in so doing must not remain aloof from what is going on in them. 'On the contrary,' argues Durkheim, 'the education given in them must remain under its control' (4). The 1944 Education Act made it quite clear that the state regarded it as part of its function to keep a register of independent schools and to inspect such schools as it saw fit (5).

According to Durkheim the role of the state was largely one of outlining certain basic and essential principles in education, and of ensuring that these were mediated to children in all schools. Such principles involved respect for reason, for science, for ideas and for sentiments which are 'at the base of democratic morality' (6). But the prescription of basic and essential principles is by no means a facile task: they are not very easily isolated and defined. Moreover, it is clear that once the process of prescription is undertaken there must be established certain criteria (or underlying 'principles') whereby even such 'principles' as those mentioned by Durkheim are selected. This presents difficulties. Evidently concepts of both 'democratic morality' and 'democracy' vary from one state to another. There are always differing standards, criteria and emphases being applied which do not invariably result in the same 'basic and essential principles', and this applies also *within* any particular society. Whilst many may agree that it is vital to have some ultimate, common denominator, it is not easy – and, indeed, it sometimes proves perilous – to state precisely what that common denominator is.

Sophisticated attempts at a philosophical statement of 'aims and objectives', or at taxonomies of educational values, more often divide rather than unite the educationists. They certainly result in very different theoretical conclusions, if not in varied practical actions. James Mill must surely have considered such matters before he eventually decided to keep his son, John Stuart, at home and to provide him with a private tutor, 'lest the habit of work should be broken and a taste for idleness acquired' (7).

In a simple society it is the function of the 'state' to ensure that its members are educated in the ways of the fathers. The role of the state here is to provide for a certain homogeneity of mores, behaviour, activity and thought. In her study of the development of children in the New Guinea society of the Manus, Margaret Mead (8) has shown how their education is both a familial and socially collective responsibility. Schools may not exist, but the child is, nevertheless, 'schooled' in the knowledge, skills and proficiencies of the tribe. The society has its sanctions for any form of anti-social behaviour, and it is largely through these sanctions that the child is educated and initiated into the acceptable forms of behaviour of his society. Thus, the slightest infringement of social tabu is mercilessly punished. Margaret Mead provides one example where

'. . . a canoe from another village anchored near one of the small islands. Three little eight-year-old girls climbed on the deserted canoe and knocked a pot into the sea, where it struck a stone and broke. All night the village rang with drum-calls and angry speeches, accusing, deprecating, apologizing for the damage done, and denouncing the careless children. The fathers made speeches of angry shame and described how roundly they had beaten the young criminals. The children's companions, far from admiring a daring crime, drew away from them in haughty disapproval and mocked them in chorus' (9).

In a more developed society such as our own we sometimes feel that we do not leave matters quite so much to 'chance' in the realm of socialization. We naturally apply sanctions for various forms of misbehaviour, and we also make an attempt at socializing the individual so that he does not feel quite alien to his society when he becomes a full member of it. Of course, the so-called 'primitive' society does not really leave things to chance: its system of initiation is a very thorough-going affair. But it has not, to date, concerned itself with the more organized full-time schooling of the more developed society. In our own society the state has increasingly taken measures to ensure that children receive the somewhat artificial forms of socialization through schools. In 1876 Lord Sandon's Education Act attempted to put pressure on parents, through school attendance committees, in order to ensure that their children received efficient elementary instruction in writing, reading and arithmetic, with suitable sanctions where the parents failed to comply. The employment of children below the age of ten was forbidden, and children between the ages of ten and fourteen had to attain the education levels specified in the First Schedule of the Act before they could be employed.

But Sandon's Act did not, strictly, make provision for compulsory education, only for the production of children with certain minimum standards of attainment before they could be certified for employment. Mundella's Education Act of 1880 made it more difficult for both school boards and parents to evade responsibility; attendance at school was now compulsory between the ages of five and ten, and the upper limit was raised to eleven in 1893 and to twelve in 1899. The Fisher Education Act of 1918 enforced compulsory attendance at school up to the age of fourteen years, and the Butler Education Act of 1944 raised the school leaving age to fifteen years. The latter Act stated explicitly that: 'It shall be the duty of the parent of every child of compulsory school age to cause him to receive efficient full-time education suitable to his age, ability, and aptitude either by regular attendance at school or otherwise' (10).

In the 1944 Education Act the specific role of the state appears to be that of ensuring that every child shall receive the sort of *education* which is particularly suitable to him; but a superficial reading of Section 36, just quoted, seems to suggest that such education may be attained in some way other than by regular attendance at a school. A close examination and analysis of the Act reveals the fact that no definition of 'full-time education' is actually given. Moreover, when one examines what little case-law there is, the phrase 'or otherwise' does not, in fact, mean that a parent can educate his child as and where he pleases. Section 76 of the Act does, however, state that:

'In the exercise and performance of all powers and duties conferred and imposed on them by this Act the Minister and local education authorities shall have regard to the general principle that, so far as is compatible with the provision of efficient instruction and training and the avoidance of unreasonable public expenditure, pupils are to be educated in accordance with the wishes of their parents' (11).

E. G. West holds that one of the most conspicuous of the administrative failures of the 1944 Education Act has been 'the inability to fulfil Section 76' (12). He cites the case of Mrs Joy Baker, who was involved in litigation with local education authorities from 1952 to 1962, and who at the end of this long struggle heard an Appeal Court establish the fact that she had been providing *at her home* a form of education which was held to be suitable for them (13). This may seem a total victory for those parents who might wish to educate their children, in the terms of Section 36, 'otherwise'; but, as Tyrrell Burgess somewhat caustically remarks, the moral of the whole affair seems to be that 'you can keep your children at home all the time and refuse to send them to school provided you are prepared to fight it out with the authorities for eight years' (14). It is hardly surprising that the 'Table of Cases' reveals only one Mrs Joy Baker.

G. Taylor and J. B. Saunders, in *The New Law of Education*, contend that Section 76 does not say that children must in *all* cases be educated in accordance with their parents' wishes. It merely lays down a general principle to which local education authorities must 'have regard'; it is left open to the authority to have regard to other things as well, 'and also to make exceptions to the general principle if it thinks fit to do so' (15). This would seem to support West's contention that, when there is any contest on this subject between a local education authority and a parent, it is most unlikely that a local authority will admit that the services which it provides are less efficient than those which the parent is able to offer. Indeed, as West comments, 'The significant point is that in such situations the predominant authority is allowed to be judge in its own cause' (16).

Thus the state and its local representatives prescribe education by law, interpret the law, and both judge what is considered to be an infringement and provide enforcement. In a 'democratic' society, however, it should be important to emphasize not merely the 'duties' of parents in relation to their children's education, but also their right and freedom to select within limits the way in which their children shall be educated. The balances are, of course, weighted in favour of the authorities; the majority of parents will inevitably be content to send their children to the school or schools provided to serve their district – content through ignorance, if for no other reason. The 'Manual of Guidance Schools No. 1' (17), first issued on 23 August 1950, emphasizes that the exercise of any parent's choice is contingent upon its being 'compatible with the provision of efficient instruction and training', and also upon the 'avoidance of unreasonable public expenditure'.

This is not merely a statement of the practical problem which faces the parent: it is also an expression of the strength of the authority over and against the parent. What parents can really combat the experts who make educational provision? What parent is really in a position to estimate what represents 'reasonable public expenditure' in the field of the education of his child? It is not surprising that West comments, with some acidity, that 'Although the 1944 Education Act respects the parent by imposing on him the duty of seeing that his child is educated, in practice, and for most people, this means the "duty" of doing what the local authority tells him to do' (18). The unhappy parent must take what comfort he can from Administrative Memorandum No. 557, published on 15 July 1957 (19), where it is explicitly stated that a local education authority should not *ipso facto* conclude that a child is not receiving full-time education suitable to his age, ability and aptitude because he is attending an establishment which is not required to submit particulars to the Registrar of Independent Schools. Equally, the memorandum suggests that the attendance at a registered school of a child of compulsory school age will not, in itself, be evidence that the child is necessarily receiving 'efficient full-time education suitable to his age, ability and aptitude' (20).

The role of the state in the provision of compulsory education for all, and in relation to the duty of parents in this respect, may appear to have been laboured somewhat. It is important to note, however, that in times of social reform, social change, and social betterment for all, the concomitant erosion of certain individual liberties may take place, in the blessed name of 'equality', with perhaps a minimum of protest from those whose freedom is being abnegated. The attainment of the sort of equality, which some individuals seem to seek in the educational field, could well result in the complete abolition of parental choice. Some may well regard this as 'a good thing', but it is just possible that others may not be fully aware of what is happening. This is partly because there is too much confusion in the public mind between 'equality', or the cult of egalitarianism, and 'equality of opportunity' (21).

The state is, of course, concerned with other functions in the sphere of education besides the enforcement of compulsory attendance at state schools and other approved or registered establishments. One of its roles is to ensure the maintenance of certain standards of learning, and also to encourage a certain amount of experiment and innovation. It is the duty of the Secretary of State for Education

'to cause inspections to be made of every educational establishment at such intervals as appear to him to be appropriate, and to cause a special inspection of any such establishment to be made whenever he considers such an inspection to be desirable' (28).

To this end inspectors, called Her Majesty's inspectors, are appointed by

Her Majesty on the recommendation of the Secretary of State. Inspections may also be carried out at any time by local education authorities who employ their own officers for this purpose. But, increasingly, the role of both H.M. Inspectors and of the local inspectorate has become one of observing, collaborating, advising, researching, collating information, and organizing courses for teaching and lecturing staffs. The 'payment by results' hangover-image of the inspectorate is happily a thing of the past, although it must be admitted that it took some eradicating.

One of the functions deliberately taken on by the state, in the formulation of the 1944 Education Act, was that of guardian of the future society's religious and moral standards through the provision of religious and moral education. Section 7 of the Act provides, in general terms, for the three main stages of education – primary, secondary and further. It then proceeds to lay down the basic conditions of that system in the following terms:

> 'it shall be the duty of the local education authority for every area, so far as their powers extend, to contribute towards the spiritual, moral, mental and physical development of the community by securing that efficient education throughout those stages shall be available to meet the needs of the population of their area' (23).

This section undoubtedly implies the state's concern for the total education of its population: every side of human personality is catered for in this overall statement. And perhaps most parents and educators would have been satisfied with this particular expression of the duty of the L.E.A.s, especially in terms of the entire ethos of its schools rather than in terms of 'agreed syllabuses' and religious curricula. But it was the more precise delineation of these requirements that has caused so much heart-searching as well as disagreement at various levels of our society.

Sections 25 to 30 of the Act are concerned with general and special provisions as to religious education, including religious instruction and collective worship, in both county and voluntary schools. It is, finally, through the agreed syllabuses of the various county education authorities that 'spiritual' development receives its closer definition. There are clauses in Sections 25 and 30 which excuse both pupils and members of staff from participating in religious instruction and collective worship, if they so wish, on grounds of conscience (24). The weakness of collective provision of religion or morality 'on the rates' has been epitomized by E. G. West in his quotation from Vernon Harcourt in the 1870 debate on the conscience clause: 'It is like saying to the minority: "We have made you pay for a dinner consisting of materials which you cannot consume, but if you wish it we will be so gracious and liberal as to allow you not to eat it!"' (25).

It is felt, however, by many religious people that religious education has a specific contribution to make towards the *moral* development of the child. There are, on the other hand, humanists such as Margaret Knight who would argue that the deliberate association of religion with morality may be deleterious, and that when religious authority is finally given up any moral principles based upon such authority might conceivably be abandoned (26). This is clearly both a delicate and controversial area in the realm of education, and one which is receiving a considerable amount of attention and research at the present time. And whilst there are those who would argue that religious and moral education are not the direct concern of the state, there are others who would, as educationists, accept responsibility for these aspects of education but who would, at the same time, demand a new approach to the whole problem. The reader should refer to the extensive bibliographies in the works of John Wilson, William Kay and Professor M. V. C. Jeffreys (27).

B. POLITICS AND EDUCATION

We have seen that the role of the state through its legislature, and through the subsequent administration of the local education authorities, is to ensure that parents compel their children to go to school or, in the terms of the 1944 Act, 'to receive efficient full-time education' suitable to their age, ability and aptitude, either by regular attendance at school or otherwise. The state, however, has other interests in the realms of education besides the function of compulsion and the development of the necessary administration to enforce its education acts and to ensure efficient education.

In a discussion of consensus in relation to the political function of education, P. W. Musgrave draws a general conclusion that 'education may not be a sufficient condition for democracy, but it certainly is a necessary condition for its survival' (28). Musgrave has already argued in this section that the limited educational experience of many working-class children is being followed by 'low mental stimulation', and that in consequence there may develop a 'breeding ground for extremism'. But even if we accept that we know precisely what 'democracy' means in a society in which the choice of forms of education by parents for their children is strictly limited, the term 'education' may well require closer scrutiny. In his 'systematic disorganization of society' (29) Hitler employed a group strategy which, as a form of 'education', was a necessary condition for the survival of Nazism. As Mannheim points out, man is most easily influenced through his group ties, and he saw Hitler's group strategy as an attempt at breaking down the traditional groups of civilized society, and at rebuilding rapidly on the basis of a new group-pattern (30).

Mannheim believed very strongly that this group strategy, used by

Hitler for the destruction and disorganization of his society, could be utilized for constructive purposes. What Hitler did, according to Mannheim, was to misuse and distort the creative potentiality of group methods and experience. It is not our aim here to enter into Mannheim's social and political philosophy as applied to the practice of education, but his arguments underline the fact that, whatever political or social ideal we may adopt and seek to maintain, 'a necessary condition for its survival' is an educational system and pattern geared to that political aim. Consensus does not happen: it has to be planned; and this applies whether the society is a democratic or an ideological one. The survival of democracy depends no more, and no less, upon 'education' and the inculcation of certain qualities than does the survival of, for example, communism. But such an assertion does not, of course, solve the problem; it merely postulates it (31). It still remains to define democracy and precisely what those qualities are that the educational system must seek to instil, in contrast with anti-democracies and their characteristics.

There are, however, certain intrinsic difficulties about democratic planning, or planning for democracy, which do not apply in a fascist regime. If one accepts that there should be freedom for growth, change, criticism and reform, at once a policy of conditioning and intensive indoctrination would appear to be ruled out. Where, however, the end is the denial of all personal freedom, the means can be planned in almost nauseating detail. B. S. R. Green and E. A. Johns make the point when they say:

'Anti-democratic mass movements such as fascism or communism offer substitute loyalties to the alienated, unorganized masses in order to gain power. Once there they can maintain control through large-scale organization as well as through propaganda' (32).

Part, if not the most important part, of this large-scale organization and propaganda undoubtedly finds expression in and through the educational system.

We are obviously concerned here with political ideologies and also with doctrinaire approaches to education within political groups and parties. In a consideration of the manner in which a state, or government, through its political attitudes and policies, attempts to control or change the educational situation, we have perhaps no better example than the endeavour to establish the comprehensive system of schooling. We shall not here discuss the educational arguments for or against the system of comprehensive education: the literature on both sides is quite plentiful, and the reader may refer to it (33). What we are concerned with is the fact that the principle of 'equality of opportunity' has been identified by the Labour Party with the system of comprehensive schooling, whereby (it is averred) all pupils are provided with the same, or similar, social and educational environment.

The British Labour Party, at its conference in Margate in 1950, passed a resolution which called upon the Government to implement the party's policy on comprehensive schools, and to provide assistance to L.E.A.s prepared to plan such schools. The Labour Party's pamphlet, *A Policy for Secondary Education*, which was produced in 1951, was essentially a brief for the comprehensive school. It considered that the first two years of comprehensive schooling should be mainly diagnostic, and that the remainder of the children's school career should seek to provide them with courses adapted to their specific abilities and aptitudes. In 1953, *Challenge to Britain* further defined the political and social purposes behind this policy. The chief aim envisaged was to break down the existing class distinctions in our society, which they felt were being perpetuated by the existence of separate types of school under the tripartite, or virtually bipartite, system.

It was felt that there could never exist any parity of esteem between such schools so long as buildings and general amenities were different, and the qualifications and quality of staffs varied considerably. With the comprehensive system all courses and teachers in the same type of school would enjoy that parity of esteem to which so much lip-service had been given but which had, in fact, never effectively materialized. The Labour Party argued that such an organization was more democratic, would eliminate any real or imagined distinctions of status, and would contribute more than separate types of secondary school could to the development of common social understanding. In particular, class and intellectual distinction would be eliminated and there would be no elite of either fee-payers or the intelligent.

By the end of the year 1969, out of 163 L.E.A.s in England and Wales 129 had schemes for comprehensive systems either implemented or approved. Of these, 108 authorities had schemes implemented or approved covering the whole or greater part of their areas, and a further 21 authorities had schemes implemented or approved for part of their areas. In addition, 12 authorities had submitted schemes which were being considered by the Department of Education and Science, and 8 authorities had been asked by the Secretary of State to reconsider their submitted schemes. Of the remaining 14 authorities there were 6 which had not submitted any official scheme, and 8 had formally declined to do so (34). In January 1969, 17·6 per cent of the maintained secondary schools were comprehensive in character, and they were providing education for 26·1 per cent of the secondary school population.

However much pressure may have been brought to bear upon L.E.A.s to submit proposals and develop plans for the establishment of comprehensive schooling, it is clear from the foregoing figures that, under a Labour government, our society was rapidly becoming 'comprehensive'. With the advent of a Conservative government, however, in June 1970, some of this pressure was taken off. L.E.A.s were then told explicitly by the newly-appointed Secretary of State for Education that they might adopt the form of secondary education which they considered most suitable to their particular situation (35). This raises the very important question as to whether the schooling of children should be at the mercy of every change of government – whatever one may think of comprehensive education *per se*, or any other form of education. It is, of course, true, as T. S. Eliot has said, that 'one would indeed be surprised to find the educational system and the political system of any country in complete disaccord' (36).

But this does not imply that the educational system should be subordinated to the doctrinaire policies and vagaries of political parties. Government, however, in any country implies control, and in our own society the Department of Education and Science exercises a certain control over backward authorities through the powers afforded it by the 1944 Education Act (37). Few would deny that there must be *some* central control; that there must also be some participation in, or devolution and distribution of, authority and power in a complex society such as our own also appears to be generally agreed. The vital problem is to establish the limits of both control and freedom. Even freedom must, to some extent, be planned (38), but when planning finally infringes upon the personal liberties which it proposes to protect, it ceases to be planning for the public good. A state, which according to F. W. J. Schelling should be envisaged as 'the objective organism of freedom and a work of art in reality' (39), ceases to fulfil its true role when it destroys man's freedom.

Obviously, both the nature of the state and the function of education are viewed differently in different societies. Nigel Grant argues that in the U.S.S.R. the prime function of education is that of being a 'political tool for the construction of a communist society' (40). This view is amply supported by the statements of Soviet Education Ministers and leaders. For example, V. P. Yelyutin has written:

'The role of Soviet education is to assist in the building of a communist society, shaping the materialist world outlook of the students, equipping them with a good grounding in the different fields of knowledge and preparing them for socially useful work' (41).

Grant, in his section on 'Education and Ideology', goes on to show that everything in Soviet education is planned in great detail, whether it be matters of finance, questions of curriculum and teaching methods, or building programmes. Organization and policy are narrowly and closely controlled by the Communist Party (42).

In his book on *Education in the U.S.S.R.*, Professor Mikhail Prokofyev stated that, after Rabindranath Tagore's visit to the Soviet Union, Tagore wrote that he had felt there 'a profound movement of human thought'. According to Prokofyev, Tagore had nowhere else seen such widespread education, and he had noted that 'in the Soviet Union education of all was in the education of one', whilst in other countries the fruits of education were reaped only by those who received it. Prokofyev goes on:

> 'Insufficient education of one was felt by all. With the help of universal education Soviet people sought to succeed in the nation-wide building of a collective brain. They were acting on a global scale, so they needed a big brain and a real education, also on a large scale. . . . The Indian sage was right. By the time he is seventeen a Soviet boy has acquired a broad education which later opens before him all the roads leading to the career of his choice. It is no exaggeration to say that the entire Soviet Union is studying and working, thinking and remaking life in order to improve the material and intellectual level of everyone, no matter where he lives and works' (43).

These words were, of course, written by Professor Prokofyev for foreign consumption. But they reveal very much the political attitudes to education of both the writer and his society, if not of the Indian sage. The building of a 'collective brain' such as that conceived by the writer involves throughout a singleness of aim and purpose firmly based upon a political and social ideal. Whether one accepts, in principle, this ideal or not, the total picture of the Russian educational process is one of commitment to education as 'a matter of first-rate national importance' (44). Any state which has this view of education cannot fail to make a success of it in terms of its own educational objectives.

REFERENCES

1 MacIver, R. M. and Page, C. H., *Society: An Introductory Analysis* (Macmillan, 1957), p. 459.
2 Durkheim, E., *Education and Sociology* (Free Press, Glencoe, 1956), p. 80.
3 Ibid., p. 80.
4 Ibid., p. 80.
5 *Vide Education Act, 1944* (7 and 8 Geo. 6. Ch. 31, H.M.S.O., 3 August 1944), Sections 70 and 77.
6 Durkheim, E., op. cit., p. 81.
7 Mill J. S., *Autobiography* (Henry Holt, N.Y., 1873), p. 36.
8 Mead, Margaret, *Growing Up in New Guinea* (Penguin, 1942; reprinted 1963), Chapters 3, 13 and 14 in particular.

9 Ibid., p. 32.

10 *Vide Education Act, 1944*, Section 36.

11 Ibid., Section 76.

12 West, E. G., *Education and the State* (The Institute of Economic Affairs, 1965), p. 188.

13 *Vide* West, E. G., op. cit., pp. 191–5, and Baker, Joy, *Children in Chancery* (Hutchinson, 1964), pp. 53–4.

14 Burgess, T., *A Guide to English Schools* (Penguin, 1964), p. 130.

15 Taylor, G. and Saunders, J. B., *The New Law of Education* (Butterworth, 6th edition 1965), p. 194, note (c).

16 West, E. G., op. cit., p. 18.

17 *Vide* Taylor, G. and Saunders, J. B., op. cit., pp. 510–16, 'Manual of Guidance Schools No. 1'; first issued 23 August 1950, reprinted with minor amendments in September 1960, and again in 1967.

18 West, E. G., op. cit., p. 17.

19 *Vide* Taylor, G. and Saunders, J. B., op. cit., pp. 524–5, 'Administrative Memorandum 557', 15 July 1957.

20 Ibid., p. 525, para. 4.

21 *Vide* Maude, A., 'The Egalitarian Threat' in Cox, C. B. and Dyson, A. E. (eds), *Fight For Education: A Black Paper* (The Critical Quarterly Society, 1969), pp. 7–9; Cox, C. B. and Dyson, A. E. (eds), *The Crisis in Education: Black Paper Two* (The Critical Quarterly Society, 1969), p. 14; Vaizey, J., *Education for Tomorrow* (Penguin, revised edition 1966), Chapter 2, 'Equality and Ability', pp. 14–25.

22 *Education Act, 1944*, Section 77.

23 Ibid., Section 7.

24 Ibid., Section 25, sub-sections (4) and (5); and Section 30.

25 West, E. G., op. cit., p. 81.

26 *Vide* Knight, Margaret, *Morals Without Religion* (Dobson, 1955); Elvin, L., 'Moral Values in a Mixed Society' in *Aspects of Education: Morality and Education* (University of Hull Institute of Education Press, July 1964); Hemming, J., 'The Development of Children's Moral Values', *British Journal of Educational Psychology*, June 1957; Kay, W., *Moral Development* (Allen and Unwin, 1968), pp. 17, 34, 124–5, 248.

27 *Vide* Wilson, J., *Logic and Sexual Morality* (Penguin, 1965); Wilson, J., Williams, N. and Sugarman, B., *Introduction to Moral Education* (Penguin, 1967); Kay, W., *Moral Development* (Allen and Unwin, 1968), and *Moral Education* (Allen and Unwin, 1973); Jeffreys, M. V. C., *Education: Its Nature and Purpose* (Allen and Unwin, 1971).

28 Musgrave, P. W., *The Sociology of Education* (Methuen, 1965; reprinted 1968), p. 147.

29 Mannheim, K., *Diagnosis of Our Time* (Routledge, 1943), Chapter V1, 'Nazi Group Strategy', pp. 95–9.

30 Ibid., p. 95.

31 For an interesting discussion on 'Democracy and Education', *vide* Hans, N., *Comparative Education* (Routledge, 3rd revised edition 1958), pp. 235–53.

32 Green, B. S. R. and Johns, E. A., *An Introduction to Sociology* (Pergamon Press, 1966; reprinted 1968), p. 78.
33 *Vide* Chetwynd, H. R., *Comprehensive School, the Story of Woodberry Down* (Routledge, 1960); Cox, C. B. and Dyson, A. E. (eds), *Fight for Education: A Black Paper* (The Critical Quarterly Society, 1969), and *The Crisis in Education: Black Paper Two* (The Critical Quarterly Society, 1969); Gould, R. (ed.), *Inside the Comprehensive School* (Schoolmaster Publishing Co., 1958); L.C.C., *London Comprehensive Schools: a Survey of Sixteen Schools* (L.C.C., 1961); Miller, T. W. G., *Values in the Comprehensive School* (Oliver and Boyd, 1961); N.A.S., *The Comprehensive School – An Appraisal from Within* (N.A.S., 1964); Pedley, R., *The Comprehensive School* (Penguin, revised edition 1966).
34 D.E.S., *Education and Science in 1969* (H.M.S.O., 1970), pp. 34–5.
35 D.E.S., *Circular 10/70* (H.M.S.O., 30 June 1970).
36 Eliot, T. S., *The Idea of a Christian Society* (Faber, 1939), p. 36.
37 *Vide Education Act, 1944*, Section 99.
38 Cf. Mannheim, K., *Diagnosis of Our Time* (Routledge, 1943), pp. 8–11.
39 Quoted in Mannheim, K., *Essays on Sociology and Social Psychology* (Routledge, 1953; 3rd impression 1966), p. 173.
40 Grant, N., *Soviet Education* (Penguin, 1964), p. 23.
41 Yelyutin, V. P., *Higher Education in the U.S.S.R.* (Soviet Booklet No. 51, London, 1959), p. 41.
42 Grant, N., op. cit., pp. 23–31.
43 Prokofyev, M., *Education in the U.S.S.R.* (Novosti Press Agency Publishing House, Moscow, 1968), pp. 51–2.
44 Grant, N., op. cit., p. 162.

BIBLIOGRAPHY

BAKER, JOY, *Children in Chancery* (Hutchinson, 1964).
BANKS, OLIVE, *Parity and Prestige in English Secondary Education* (Routledge, 1955).
BANKS, OLIVE, *The Sociology of Education* (Batsford, 1968; 2nd impression 1969), Chapter 6, 'Who controls our schools?', pp. 111–28.
BANTOCK, G. H., *Freedom and Authority in Education* (Faber, 1952).
BEALES, A. C. F., *Education under Penalty: English Catholic Education from the Reformation to the Fall of James II* (Athlone Press, 1963).
BOTTOMORE, T. B., *Sociology: A Guide to Problems and Literature* (Allen and Unwin, 1962; 2nd edition 1971), Chapter 9, 'Political Institutions', pp. 147–61.
BURGESS, T., *A Guide to English Schools* (Penguin, 1964).
BUTLER, D., *The Study of Political Behaviour* (Hutchinson, 1958).
CRAIK, H., *The State in its Relation to Education* (Macmillan, 1896).
CRUICKSHANK, M., *Church and State in English Education: 1870 to the Present Day* (Macmillan, 1963).
DE MONTMORENCY, J. E. G., *State Intervention in English Education* (C.U.P., 1902).

DENT, H. C., *The Educational System of England and Wales* (Univ. of London Press, 4th edition 1969), Chapter 3, 'Control and Direction', pp. 65–90.

DURKHEIM, E., *Education and Sociology* (Free Press, Glencoe, 1956), pp. 78–81.

DURKHEIM, E., *Professional Ethics and Civil Morals* (Routledge, 1957).

EAGLESHAM, E. J. R., *From School Board to Local Authority* (Routledge, 1956).

EAGLESHAM, E. J. R., *The Foundations of Twentieth-Century Education in England* (Routledge, 1967).

EDMONDS, E. L., *The School Inspector* (Routledge, 1962).

GARFORTH, F. W., *Education and Social Purpose* (Oldbourne Press, 1962).

GREEN, B. S. R. and JOHNS, E. A., *An Introduction to Sociology* (Pergamon Press, 1966; reprinted 1968), pp. 76–8, 91–5.

HANS, N., *Comparative Education* (Routledge, 1949; 3rd edition 1958), Chapters X, XI, XII.

KAZAMIAS, A. M., *Politics, Society and Secondary Education in England* (Univ. of Pennsylvania Press, 1966).

KORNHAUSER, W., *The Politics of Mass Society* (Free Press, Glencoe, 1959).

LASSWELL, H., *Politics: Who Gets What, When, How* (McGraw-Hill, 1936).

LESTER SMITH, W. O., *To Whom do the Schools Belong?* (Blackwell, 1942; 2nd edition 1945).

LESTER SMITH, W. O., *Compulsory Education in England* (UNESCO, 1951).

LESTER SMITH, W. O., *Education* (Penguin, 1962).

LESTER SMITH, W. O., *Government of Education* (Penguin, 1965).

LIPSET, S. M., *Political Man* (Doubleday, 1960).

LOWNDES, G. A. N., *The Silent Social Revolution* (O.U.P., 1937; 2nd edition 1948).

MACIVER, R. M., *The Web of Government* (N.Y., 1947), Chapter XII.

MACIVER, R. M., and PAGE, C. H., *Society: An Introductory Analysis* (Macmillan, 1950; reprinted 1957), Chapter 18, 'The Great Associations: Political', pp. 453–67.

MANNHEIM, K., *Ideology and Utopia* (Routledge, 1936; reprinted 1966).

MANNHEIM, K., *Diagnosis of Our Time* (Routledge, 1943).

MANNHEIM, K., *Freedom, Power and Democratic Planning* (Routledge, 1951; 2nd impression 1965).

MANNHEIM, K., *Essays on Sociology and Social Psychology* (Routledge, 1953; 3rd impression 1966), Chapter III, 'The History of the Concept of the State as an Organism', pp. 165–82.

MANNHEIM, K., and STEWART, W. A. C., *An Introduction to the Sociology of Education* (Routledge, 1962).

MONTMORENCY, J. E. G., *State Intervention in English Education* (C.U.P., 1902).

MUSGRAVE, P. W., *The Sociology of Education* (Methuen, 1965; reprinted 1968), Chapter 10, 'The Political Function', pp. 143–54.

MUSGRAVE, P. W., *The School as an Organization* (Macmillan, 1968), Chapter 3, 'The Overall Structure of British Education', pp. 23–37.

MYERS, E. D., *Education in the Perspective of History* (Harper, 1960).

OTTAWAY, A. K. C., *Education and Society* (Routledge, 1953; 2nd edition 1962, reprinted 1968), pp. 53–6.

PARSONS, T. *et al.* (eds), *Theories of Society* (Free Press, Glencoe, 1965), Part II, Section D.

PEACOCK, A. T., and WISEMAN, J., *Education for Democrats* (Institute of Economic Affairs, 1964).

RELLER, T. L., and MORPHET, E. L., *Comparative Educational Administration* (Prentice-Hall, 1962).

RUSSELL, B., *Education and the Social Order* (Allen and Unwin, 1932).

RUSSELL, B., *Power* (Allen and Unwin, 1938).

TAYLOR, G. and SAUNDERS, J. B., *The New Law of Education* (Butterworth, 6th edition 1965).

VAIZEY, J., *The Control of Education* (Faber, 1963).

WEST, E. G., *Education and the State* (Institute of Economic Affairs, 1965).

WOOTTON, B., *Freedom under Planning* (Allen and Unwin, 1945).

Chapter 6

The Economy and Education

A. SOME PROBLEMS OF THE ECONOMICS OF EDUCATION

Education is a service provided by a society for its members; it is an industry like any other with certain inputs and outputs (1); and it is a product as well as one of the factors of production. It is because education has such a multifarious function and role in the social structure that the economics of education present problems of decision-making of a very special and peculiar kind. The Industrial Revolution, with its rapid introduction of mechanical inventions and new forms of power, gave rise to questions of training in certain skills at a variety of levels; and the more complex industrialization became, the more involved also became the learning processes attached to those skills.

In an age of biotechnic development and cybernetic invention we are involved in the education and training of individuals for a different sort of life and a different sort of world. In any definition of aims and objectives one must have, therefore, a clear vision not merely of the present but also of the probable and foreseeable future. This is vitally so in the realm of education where millions of pounds are being spent annually, not merely for 'the development of fully rounded personalities' and similar woolly (if sound) aims, but also as an investment in the future of society and for the initiation of each individual youth into adulthood, citizenship, social responsibility and a highly complex mobile society.

Professor Fritz Machlup has suggested that educational efforts may be regarded as 'consumption, investment, waste or drag' (2). When, however, he goes on to say: 'They are consumption to the extent that they give *immediate* satisfaction to the pupil or student (e.g., the joy of learning) or to others (e.g., mothers and neighbours enjoying some peaceful hours while the youngsters are at school)' (3), one must argue that it is precisely here that the productive contribution of education differs fundamentally from most other forms of economic contribution. Perhaps only an economist could refer to the immediate satisfaction to the pupil or student as 'the joy of learning'; certainly at the school level most children's joy derives from a blissful unconsciousness that they are learning, otherwise it would be quite pointless in disguising the fact by the subterfuges of 'play-way' and 'discovery' methods. The simple fact is, however, that much of learning is not joyous in the present, but only in retrospect – and not always then. And if educational efforts are consumption to the extent that mothers and neighbours are able to enjoy some peaceful hours while the youngsters are at school, then there is nothing specific about education; the children might just as profitably be locked up in some strongly built community hall.

But the educational efforts are, nevertheless, to be regarded as consumption and not simply investment. The only *immediate* satisfaction to the pupil will remain, in a large proportion of instances, simply at the level of the fulfilment of an external requirement imposed upon him; but in so far as education is an element of economic production, it is as much a matter of economic consumption as of educational consumption. The 'satisfaction' of wants in economic terms may not necessarily provide any pleasure and joy, whether immediate or remote, and this applies whether one is speaking of material or mental wants. There is simply a want, or a demand, whether recognized by the individual or not, which is met or satisfied by some form of supply.

In the educational process something is provided and consumed at the personality level which is not always (indeed rarely) measurable even in educational terms, to say nothing of economic terms. It may well be possible to say, for example, that three thousand pounds have been spent on John Smith's education; in personality terms one might equally be able to say that this was money well spent, but in economic terms there will certainly be somebody always prepared, and perhaps able, to prove that it was all 'a dead loss'. The real difficulty is to elicit a satisfactory set of economic criteria by which to measure educational production and consumption.

Nor is it always safe to speak of education as an 'investment', particularly when one is thinking of investment in terms of human potential. A youth's economic capabilities must relate very closely to the sort of society in which he is *going to live*, perhaps for many years, rather than simply the one in which he is living at the present moment. As educationists we may 'invest' in him all the wrong things for a computerized and cybernetic civilization. We may develop interesting, even 'full' or 'integrated', personalities who are quite unfitted to live productive lives, economically speaking, in the society into which they graduate. Indeed, one suspects that a lot of the so-called 'drop-outs' and 'hippies' in our midst are invested with considerable human potential which is quite unrelated to their existing society. In fact, they would not have it otherwise since they approve neither of the present society nor of the direction that society is taking.

But in thinking of education as an investment one must not, in any case, think simply in terms of economic returns. If we are educating for life we are educating also for those hours during which the individual is not engaged in working, but rather in leisure pursuits. Indeed, for many this will be the only time when they will begin to feel that life, for them, is really worthwhile, and when an opportunity will be presented to them to use their potential in an enjoyably creative way. Thus, future gains in economic productivity are not the sole – nor perhaps even the most important – criterion for educational effort. A really positive contribution to social or community living may, in the long run, counterbalance a certain poverty of economic potential.

In any consideration of further expenditure on education, however, the theme of 'education for leisure' is not likely to be a particularly popular one; nor are objections entirely from the political or economic quarters. Many parents are goaded into suggesting that their children are 'not at school to play, but to learn'; and they are often, of course, parents who are quite incapable of organizing their own leisure time. There are strong proponents of education for leisure today, who regard this as one of the most important themes for future education, and they may perhaps be forgiven for their failure to remember that it was as long ago as 1926 that the Hadow Report first explicitly said: 'Finally, we would urge the desirability of generating from the school studies interests which will continue through after-life and will enlarge the opportunities for a fuller enjoyment of leisure' (4). If the theme is an urgent one, as well as one particularly relevant to the immediate future, it is by no means a new one.

One must recognize, however, that whilst the cry of 'education for leisure' may still be the same as it was over forty years ago the situation has considerably changed. Thus, in 1938, the Spens Report considered it a serious educational heresy to believe that culture and practical utility were mutually exclusive; and it accepted with some reserve even the view that education should train for the right use of leisure, 'lest it should lead to a dichotomy between studies important for serious life and those pertinent only to hours of leisure' (5). The dichotomies of liberal and technical education, and of culture and utility, have been more than adequately dealt with in the past by such thinkers as A. N. Whitehead (6) and John Dewey (7). But it must be confessed that today their arguments sound strangely unrelated to the life situation. Times have changed, and 'serious life' has for many become more and more divorced from 'hours of leisure'. There is a dichotomy whether we like it or not, and there are some forms of labour which not even the ivory-towered philosopher would care to relate to leisure. Nor should the educational process pretend that they are related, unless one is prepared to stretch language in such a way that one cannot avoid equating 'useful' with everything that is pursued in education from the most academic or technical to the most trivial.

If, as in the words of Professor Machlup, educational efforts are 'investment to the extent that they create either future nonpecuniary satisfaction (e.g., the joy of reading and learned discourse) or future gains in productivity' (8), then almost anything pursued in education *can* be an investment, although Professor Machlup invariably selects his examples from the more intellectual pursuits. It may well be an 'investment' to teach a boy how to play chess, or bridge, or rugby, or the guitar. The Spens Report, however, would not go so far as this in its concept of educational investment or education for leisure. Activities were 'useful' for the Consultative Committee only in the sense that they tended 'to raise the level and quality of life in all its phases and moments' (9).

Machlup contends that any educational effort is a waste in so far as it does not contribute either to pleasure or to productivity (10). But here again we are dealing with incommensurables both in hedonistic and in economic terms. Presumably, to eliminate everything in education which did not contribute to present or future productivity would be to eliminate waste. But since, on the hedonistic side, pleasure is not something which can be measured anyway – one man's meat is another man's poison – and, since productivity in economic terms cannot be certainly known until a man has almost finished his course, it is virtually impossible on this criterion to predict what is, or is not, wasteful in education. And if we cannot predict waste we cannot eliminate it.

Lastly, Professor Machlup considers that educational efforts may be regarded as a handicap, or drag, to the extent that they make the preferences of the workers and the opportunities of employment incompatible (11). This is a much more serious possibility than anything stated so far; and it is one of the reasons why it is both difficult and dangerous to make simple statistical comparisons between the educational services of one country and those of another. It is, of course, equally dangerous to imagine that a highly successful system and method of education in one country is easily transferable to another. There are, for example, areas in India where the extent of higher education has outstripped the opportunities of employment, but where, at the same time, the popular levels of literacy are palpably low (12).

In our own society it is interesting to note the rapid increase in the figures for full-time students in universities between 1938 and 1969, and also the figures projected by the Robbins Report for the years 1974 to 1980. These latter figures are now considered a very conservative estimate, but at least they indicate a trend (13). There is an ever-increasing demand for further and higher education, which is being met by expanded and new universities, the Open University, the Council for National Academic Awards, polytechnics, colleges of further education, liberal arts colleges and reconstituted colleges of education.

There are at least two ways of looking at this expansion: one is an increasing awareness on the part of people generally that education is a life-long process, that it does not end when school is over; the other is

TABLE ONE

STUDENTS IN FULL-TIME UNIVERSITY EDUCATION
IN GREAT BRITAIN

Year	No. of Students	Year	No. of Students
1900/01	20,000	1955/56	85,194
		1956/57	89,866
1924/25	42,000	1957/58	95,442
		1958/59	100,204
1938/39	50,000	1959/60	104,009
		1960/61	107,699
1946/47	68,452	1961/62	113,143
1947/48	78,507	1962/63	118,404
1948/49	83,690		
1949/50	85,421	1967 (Oct.)	199,372
1950/51	85,314	1968 (Oct.)	212,000
1951/52	83,458	1969 (Oct.)	219,000
1952/53	81,474		
1953/54	80,602	1974/75 (projected)	228,000
1954/55	81,705	1975/76	240,000
		1980/81	346,000

that workers generally are becoming alert to the importance of paper qualifications, not merely at G.C.E. 'O' and 'A' level, but also at the diploma and degree level. But the ever louder demands for 'equality of opportunity' in the realm of higher education can, in fact, lead only to an increase in the competition for a scarce number of better occupations.

This is where, in Machlup's terms, educational efforts may well become a handicap or drag, in that the preferences of the qualified workers may well be incompatible with the opportunities of employment. All animals may well be equal at an ever-increasingly higher level: but some will inevitably, and as always, be more equal than others. We may eventually destroy an elite possessing one university degree by the production of a large number with such a qualification; but a new elite will arise with two, three or four degrees and of a higher level. No one would suggest, of course, that it is a bad thing, *per se*, for most people to acquire a degree or to be educated at a higher level. But will the graduate in the humanities, the sciences, the social sciences, or whatever, be content to be a cog in the technological machine when he finds that his qualification is, in fact, incompatible with the chances of employment?

Professor Papi may well be right in his contention that we can today observe the slow decline of the so-called civilization of the elites, and the dawning of a new era, the era of mass civilization, in some advanced countries. But, he warns,

'The slow decline of the elite civilization gradually giving way to mass civilization, must not be allowed to lead to the suppression of human values in society. In the very act of promoting social progress, education must rise to the defence of values which have the names of individuality, of liberty, of civic consciousness' (14).

All this may well be true, and one might in fact question any promotion of 'social progress' which resulted in the disappearance of such values. But it is also true to say that the decay of one set of elites seems invariably to make way for another sort. Someone has to run the 'mass civilization' in any particular country; it is largely the sort of expertise required for this purpose that has changed, and it is here that human potential is perhaps being assessed in somewhat different terms from a purely economic standpoint. We have to learn to distinguish between 'social progress' and 'social process'. And the values which Papi specifies – individuality, liberty and civic consciousness – may well be the sort of values considered at depth by the philosophers of education, but they do not always have a mention in the writings of economists who comment on the education system and the control of education.

In his article on the 'General Problems of the Economics of Education', however, Professor Papi considers some of the consequences of investment in human potential (15). He argues that among the factors of production there are two which are amenable to improvement by education, including training. These two factors are labour and entrepreneurial ability. Papi insists that in the absence of human potential or, as he puts it, of 'personnel of adequate quality', the contributions which are made by capital and the relatively artificial establishment of productive activities are insufficient (16). In his consideration of the investment of human potential it is interesting to note throughout that Professor Papi, a President of the International Economic Association, places emphasis upon the personality and character factors as well as upon the development of particular and specific skills. It is not merely the training of individuals in certain industrial and other abilities that must be evaluated when considering the economic criteria of educational efforts; it is also the changing and moulding of attitudes and the evolving of personality itself.

According to Papi, education of the right sort should make individuals more receptive to inventions and innovations and should ensure that

'those individuals who are responsible for making major technical, economic and political decisions possess the width of knowledge and the breadth of view, which, associated with a high moral sense, enable them to avoid potentially dangerous mistakes' (17).

In addition to these essential personality characteristics, education for

Professor Papi must promote the division of labour and the use of machinery; it must permit increasingly advantageous combinations of the factors of production; it must help to expedite the operating of any new technical discovery; and it must promote an extensive mobility of labour and of entrepreneurial ability. Here Professor Papi is stating in more precise economic terms the sort of 'aims of education' which frequently remain at the somewhat abstract and mental level when discussed by educationists *qua* educationists. When we speak of educating for 'flexibility of mind', or 'mobility of thought', or 'breadth of vision', the economist naturally wishes to see how this applies to a developing technological and inventive society.

Flexibility of mind is not necessarily a good quality *in vacuo*, for it might well result in something like a grasshopper attribute. It implies the ability, however, in specified and particular contexts to think in new terms, and with considerable application, concerning sometimes well-established social, economic, industrial concepts and processes. This is investment in human potential; this is capital in economic terms.

Again, according to Professor Papi, every effort made to promote economic and social development in any country or society must begin by improving the human factor. But as soon as we contemplate the improvement of the human factor we are faced with competing wants; and before the problem of these competing – and sometimes conflicting and scarce – wants can be resolved it is necessary to define pretty closely what sort of society we are aiming at. Granted that our society desires a basic minimum of education and literacy for all from the age of five to that of fifteen or sixteen, what does it require beyond that?

This is a question of establishing priorities; and this, in turn, cannot be finalized without a consideration of the social economy, its desirable direction of development, and such a banal consideration as costing. When all these matters have been entered into there are still other economic problems to be considered – such as the priority of education itself in relation to, say, defence, or public health, or unemployment benefits or family allowances. It is, therefore, not without significance that, particularly since the Second World War, the central education authority has seen the necessity of appointing economists and social administrators to the membership of committees and advisory councils investigating a variety of educational problems within all sectors. Any responsible body, making proposals for educational expansion or change, must consider and count the cost of its proposals and its order of priorities.

But competing areas of educational effort and want may have to find new ways of solving economic problems. Thus, for example, should our country spend more money at the moment on the expansion of higher education, in particular the number of university places, or should it invest in full-scale nursery education between the ages of three and five years, and day nurseries for children under three? The Plowden Report recommended that:

'There should be a large expansion of nursery education and a start should be made as soon as possible ... Nursery education should be available to children at any time after the beginning of the school year after they reach the age of three until they reach the age of compulsory schooling' (18).

One might argue that it would be a long time before one saw the results in society of this very early investment in education, whereas the return from higher education at university level would begin to accrue within three or four years. Again, one has to balance a better mass education against elitism; and one also has to consider comparative costs, and the principle, already mentioned, of complementarity. Any expansion and improvement of education at the initial levels must inevitably affect education at the higher levels.

In a consideration of the comparative cost situation here it may prove to be possible to have the best of both worlds. The need for nursery schools is very urgent and bound up with the increasing tendency for married women to engage in professional and industrial activities. No one could doubt the need for nursery schools, as well as day nurseries, to meet this situation. At the same time, any growing and competing society which seeks to keep its place in the world must develop every element of human potential that it possesses. Indeed, it is only at the upper end of the educational ladder that the real potential of the educands becomes more explicit. Assuming that the cost effectiveness of universities is not as great as that of other institutions of higher education, it would seem that there must be a limit to their expansion, in sheer economic terms. Despite this limit, beyond which one can speak only in terms of diminishing returns, whether one is thinking of human capital or eventual productivity, it is important to note the comment made by the Robbins Committee on Higher Education:

'Considered, therefore, as an investment, there seems a strong presumption in favour of a substantially increased expenditure on higher education. Even if we cannot produce detailed computations of comparative yield, there is a strong probability that the country would have to go a good deal beyond what is contemplated in our recommendations before the return in terms of social net product could be said to suggest general over-investment in this sector' (19).

There are, however, institutions whose cost effectiveness in the realms of higher education is such that, assuming the requisite teaching and tutoring expertise, they could make the necessary provision for an increasing number of students desirous of non-vocational degree courses. The polytechnics, colleges of technology, and colleges of commerce have already proved their competence in this direction, in connection with both the external degrees of London University and the degrees of the Council for National Academic Awards (C.N.A.A.). The colleges of education are also geared to degree work (B.Ed.) in a wide variety of main subjects as well as in the disciplines of education, and in many interdisciplinary areas of inquiry. These latter colleges need an alternative to teacher-education for a number of reasons, not the least being their own survival and the need for a more balanced education for their students with a greater variety of possibilities of occupation at the end of it all.

The Open University arranged for 25,000 students to begin, in January 1971, one or two of its first four foundation, or first level, courses in arts, science, mathematics and social science. Another 17,000 men and women had to be disappointed for the time being, but there can be little doubt that the degrees of the Open University will become increasingly popular and available, particularly with its system of credits which is already accepted by many universities in other countries. And there seems little doubt that a considerable area of higher education expansion will in time be absorbed by the Open University, and that this will be, in pecuniary terms, a cheaper method of production.

B. THE DEMAND, SUPPLY AND COST OF EDUCATION

We have, in our discussion, already entered into some of the problems of supply and demand, and of cost efficiency. In any attempt to cost education, or to express educational expenditure as a percentage of the gross national product (G.N.P.), or as a contribution to the growth of national income, we must carefully note the warning of Professor Machlup when he says:

> 'Fifty years ago statistical data of national income were virtually non-existent. Now we have them for most countries. It is sometimes forgotten, however, that the preparation of the data involves a good deal of artful juggling of ideas and figures that are, not the result of observation, but of invention, imaginative construction, and heroic guesswork. Hence, the use of these statistical series for "measuring" exactly how much each of a variety of things has contributed to the "observed" growth of national income may strike some of the more cautious economists as excessive boldness' (20).

Simon Kuznets also emphasizes the virtual impossibility of any economist escaping from his subjective preconceptions in making estimates of national income; his estimates are 'appraisals' rather than objective state-ments of fact. Kuznets maintains that these appraisals are predetermined by criteria which are 'at worst a matter of chance, at best a matter of deliberate choice' (21).

The subject of the costs of education becomes even more problematic when we are involved in a comparison of educational expenditures in a variety of countries, from the developing to the most technologically sophisticated societies. Professor John Vaizey has pointed out that such a problem as that of price comparisons makes international comparisons 'more or less invalid' (22). Vaizey, however, makes another point which is of considerable importance in the 'costing' of education, if not in the evaluation of its cultural content. He maintains – and perhaps only those inflicted with 'inconceivable prejudice' would deny it – that much of our educational outlay does not contribute to economic growth: on the contrary much of what is done in the educational system is 'deleterious to economic growth' (23).

With these warnings in mind one must obviously approach the questions of both the productivity and the cost of education with considerable caution. Moreover, when comparisons are made between one country and another, one must take into account the price levels and the price struc-tures of those countries, the salaries of teachers, the cost of materials and so forth. Percentages of the G.N.P. are the roughest of guides only, and what is required is a much more precise composite numerical index as a basis for comparison. But, although economists are undoubtedly coming closer to some such index, they are not yet agreed entirely on what elements should contribute towards it (24).

Perhaps more useful modes of comparison as between countries are what are referred to by Professor F. H. Harbison of Princeton University, U.S.A., as 'available human resource indicators', which he regards as only second-best measures but ones which, nevertheless, are more readily avail-able for a large number of countries. He uses seven of these resource indicators as follows:

1. The number of teachers at first and second levels of education (i.e. primary and secondary schools) per 10,000 population.
2. The number of engineers and scientists per 10,000 population.
3. The number of physicians and dentists per 10,000 population.
4. The number of pupils enrolled at first level education as a percentage of the estimated population aged five to fourteen years inclusive. This is an 'unadjusted' ratio because the duration of first level education varies from one country to another.
5. The 'adjusted' school enrolment ratios for first and second levels combined, which are designed to correct distortions arising from

varying lengths of time spent in primary and secondary schools in different countries.
6. The number of pupils enrolled at second level (secondary) education as a percentage of the estimated population, fifteen to nineteen years inclusive, adjusted for the length of schooling at this level.
7. The enrolment in third level, or higher, education as a percentage of the age group from twenty to twenty-four years (25).

That these indicators all have their own peculiar and in-built problems according to the particular country one is discussing, Professor Harbison has made adequately clear, and the reader must pursue such problems in the article itself, and in the discussion of his paper which followed (26). In the Statistical Annex to his article Harbison provides a Table which puts seventy-five countries in rank order according to a composite index based on human resource and economic development. The sixteen 'advanced countries' appear in the order given in Table Two (27).

Whatever else these figures may or may not show, they at least demonstrate the difficulties of making *absolute* comparisons between one country and another in terms of the economics of education. And if Harbison's 'composite index' is a sound basis for comparison, then clearly the expenditure on education as a percentage of national income is not, and *vice versa*. It is also true that one cannot make the same sort of judgements about a developing country as one can about an advanced country – hence Harbison's league table involving four different levels, namely, 'under-developed countries', 'partially-developed countries', 'semi-advanced countries' and 'advanced countries'. But even in plain economic terms there are similar difficulties in comparing the annual productivity of one country with that of another. The principles of the development of education in one society are not necessarily applicable to another. In our own society, for example, we firmly believe in the principle of 'equality of opportunity for all' at all levels of education; but Professor Machlup argues that

'Instead of aiming at social justice in providing schooling for all, a poor country does much better in having only one-fifth or even less of its children go to primary school, but providing secondary education for some of the more talented. To offer several years of schooling for fewer children seems to be the optimum educational plan for the poorest countries ... To aim for large enrolment ratios in the lower grades is especially wasteful if the drop-out rate is very high' (28).

Now the demand for education and educational services generally will tend to increase with any increase in population or in economic development. But, in economic terms, this does not necessarily mean that a larger number of people will be educated at the first level – certainly not to begin

TABLE TWO

EXPENDITURE ON EDUCATION IN SIXTEEN
ADVANCED COUNTRIES

Country	Composite Index	Expenditure on Education as a percentage of National Income
Denmark	77·1	2·9
Sweden	79·2	3·2
Argentina	82·0	2·5
Israel	84·9	3·0
West Germany	85·8	3·6
Finland	88·7	6·3
U.S.S.R.	92·9	7·1
Canada	101·6	4·5
France	107·8	3·0
Japan	111·4	5·7
U.K.	121·6	4·2
Belgium	123·6	5·6
Netherlands	133·7	5·2
Australia	137·7	2·2
New Zealand	147·3	3·7
U.S.A.	261·3	4·6
Mean	115	4·2

with. Nor, as Professor Machlup points out, does it of necessity mean a great increase in higher education initially. This mistake has already been made in such a country as Colombia, where a large percentage of the university graduates have discovered that it is impossible to find employment in which their education could be viably used (29). This is equally true of some parts of India where there has been an imbalance in university and college education compared with primary education (30).

That the supply of education is concerned with the total economic and social structure of a particular society, and not simply with the popular demand for it, is well demonstrated by the recommendations made by the Report to the Governor of Mauritius in 1961:

'106 A strong effort should be made through the medium of the education system to change the current attitude of young people that it is undignified to work with their hands . . .

109 The government should not at present press the idea of compulsory schooling . . .

112 The temptation to expand (rather than to improve) secondary education should be resisted' (31).

In its *Annual Report on Education for 1968* (32), the Government of Mauritius estimated that 89 per cent of the total population of children in the five to eleven age group were attending primary schools. And whilst it is true that there has also been a steady expansion of secondary education it has nowhere met the popular demand for it.

There is, of course, something cumulative about supply and demand. Supply in educational services creates a demand, because (like Everest) it is there. In an age in which the catchwords are 'equality' and 'equal opportunity for all', there is an increasing demand for opportunity at all levels of education. Any *pretence* of equal opportunity must ensure that there is a supply adequate to meet the demand. But this is precisely where economic considerations must enter in, and where economic concepts such as 'efficiency', 'productivity' and 'waste' must be allowed their rightful place.

It may well be that the 'equality of opportunity' increasingly demanded must inevitably affect both curriculum content and teaching method. The traditional 'subjects' and their apparently insuperable confines are gradually giving way, even at degree level, to areas of study in which equally rigorous disciplinary approaches are demanded, but in which a wider spread of individual interests is catered for. The Open University, as well as the C.N.A.A., has taken the point; and the 'credit' system of the former institution makes provision for both wide and changing interests. Dr P. H. Coombs (33) made the point when he stated:

'In discussing the effectiveness for which education resources were used, one became involved with questions of curriculum content and the technology of teaching, and it was unfortunately true that university teachers in particular, whilst ready to suggest changes in many fields, were extremely conservative in relation to their own technology of teaching. He himself doubted whether the pupil-teacher ratio was really a measure of quality but this ratio was another sacred cow of the educationalists' (34).

It is a 'sacred cow' which, at the higher education level, is quite certainly in the process of being desacralized and slaughtered. The group dynamics of large tutorial units have, out of sheer economic necessity, been developed in colleges of further and higher education ever since the Second World War; whilst the development of educational technology is making it increasingly possible for large numbers to pursue the same or similar educational interests at the same time, although scattered throughout a whole country. Machlup makes the same point at the end of his *Education and Economic Growth*. He foresees the time when alternative methods and techniques are developed in education which will be less personal, and more mechanical and automated, but 'reasonably effective and much less expensive' (35).

There were three clear principles laid down by Professor Papi in relation to the supply of educational services: time precedence, unity and complementarity (36). Briefly, time precedence means that supply must be available many years before it is actually needed; this involves the preparation of teachers, adequate equipment and accommodation, and everything else that goes to make up the education service. The concept of unity in supply implies that all levels of education must expand at the same time; there is little point in raising the school-leaving age to sixteen, and in developing the potential of all children at the secondary level, unless society is prepared at the same time to expand higher education in order to absorb and fructify the increasing investment of human resources (37). But Papi rightly warns that

> 'Too rapid an expansion at one level tends to provoke, on the one hand, a deterioration in the quality of the services offered at that level: less qualified teachers may have to be used, classrooms will be cramped and equipment scarce, and less gifted students may be admitted to courses . . .' (38).

Thirdly Papi suggests that there must be complementarity of the components of supply, such as teachers, premises, equipment and non-teaching staff, including research workers, technicians and clerical staff. Papi argues that if even only one element varies, the others must vary in due proportion, or the supply will remain inadequate. This may or may not seem obvious when stated in these terms, but it is not always apparent in the administration of ministries, departments of education and science, and local education authorities. It is a matter of planning, of costing and of clearly defining roles.

If, through raising the school leaving age, more teachers are required, then larger premises are required not simply for the schools to absorb another year of pupils, but also for the colleges of education and university departments of education, in order to absorb a larger number of student teachers. But students in training will require more tutors, most of whom must be recruited from the very schools which already require more teachers. In order to meet this situation very careful provision and planning have to be effected in the realm of 'complementarity'.

An increased number of tutors in, say, a college of education will demand not simply more premises but more equipment of every conceivable kind, as well as more technicians and secretarial staff. A careful defining of roles might ensure, for example, that a lecturer in a senior position, such as head of a large department, was not in fact performing additionally the duties of a filing clerk and a secretary.

In a very interesting article on 'Criteria for Public Expenditure on Education' (39), John Vaizey discusses some of the internal logistics of the education service. All of Vaizey's writings indicate the importance of educational policies, not merely in terms of education theory, but also in terms of economics and the principles of unity and complementarity, which he develops in the following passage:

'For instance it may be shown that the expansion of medical faculties in universities entails expansion of the arts faculties because, in order to get more medical students, there have to be more secondary school graduates, all of whom take a curriculum which requires more teachers who are arts graduates. In addition, many universities have a concept of the balance between faculties which, from one year to another, they try to maintain' (40).

Some of the difficulties both of estimating the costs of education and in the use of the grammar of economics are discussed by Professor Machlup, who argues that if we measure society's demand for education by what it spends on education, and if, in turn, these expenditures are represented as the cost of education, we arrive at a 'sterile tautology' in which cost and demand mean precisely the same thing (41). Machlup also points out the difficulties of defining precisely what we mean by 'demand' in education. If, for example, the number of pupils in the secondary stage of education increases because there are now more children in that particular age group, does the resulting increase in *cost* really represent an increase in the *demand* for education, or is it to be recognized as simply an increase in the 'required cost' of a 'given task'? And so one could go on to levels where the increased sophistication of the argument comes close, as Machlup indicates, to sophistry (42).

This is obviously a realm full of pitfalls, not merely for the educationist untutored in economics, but also for the economist untutored in such questions as the comparative quality of educational services, the assessment of the contributions of education to economic growth, 'unproductive' education, education and manpower needs, and so forth. The interested reader is recommended to read the works of Professor John Vaizey (43), Professor Fritz Machlup (44), and the excellent source book edited by Professors Robinson and Vaizey, which records the proceedings of a conference held by the International Economic Association (45). However precise and exact the science of economics attempts to become, one must recognize that, within the realm of 'human capital' and human investment in a rapidly changing society, it is at times impossible to give little more than an inspired guess in relation to the costing of education. It is gratifying, as well as salutary, to find someone of the stature of Professor F. Edding (46) using a term such as 'guestimate' when discussing the expenditure on education per head in relation to national income per head in the U.S.S.R. in 1960 (47). But quite apart from 'guestimates' where figures are not available, it is clear, as Professor F. Harbison has emphasized, that for analytical purposes such concepts as those of the costs of in-service training and of earnings forgone are certainly useful, but at the same time extremely difficult to quantify and 'if used in international statistics would introduce a large area of unreliability. For international comparisons, it would be better to reduce the content but to improve the quality of statistics' (48).

Sometimes educational expenditures, expressed as a percentage of the G.N.P., are used for purposes of international comparison. But such percentages need to be taken into consideration with other macro-economic data before any firm conclusions can be drawn from them; and, since there is no clear measure of purchasing power, such percentages of educational expenditure may be misleading even within the same society over a large number of years. Table Three, which has been compiled from a variety of sources, may be used by the student, not to draw comparisons between the educational system of one society and another, nor to make immediate inferences about the development of education in any one society, but rather as the raw-material for an exercise in investigating some of the basic problems involved in the economics of education (49).

TABLE THREE

TOTAL EDUCATIONAL EXPENDITURE EXPRESSED AS A
PERCENTAGE OF THE GNP AT CURRENT PRICES

Year	Germany	Japan	U.S.A.	Netherlands	England	India
1909			1·98			
1921					1·50	
1933			4·10			
1935			3·65			
1938					2·75	
1943			1·83			
1950	2·46	4·09		2·62		
1951			3·41			
1952					3·20	
1954		4·91				
1955		4·52			3·50	
1956				4·01		
1057			4·77		3·80	
1958	2·94	4·55		4·46		
1959	2·89	4·16	5·10	4·76		
1960	2·95	4·27				2·30
1961					4·50	2·40
1962					4·80	2·50
1963						2·40
1964					5·10	2·20

REFERENCES

1 *Vide* Vaizey, J., *The Control of Education* (Faber, 1963), pp. 21–2.
2 Machlup, F., *Education and Economic Growth* (University of Nebraska Press, 1970), p. 5.
3 Ibid., p. 5; my italics.
4 Board of Education, *The Education of the Adolescent* (Hadow Report) (H.M.S.O., December 1926; reprinted 1948), para. 116.
5 Board of Education, *Secondary Education* (Spens Report) (H.M.S.O., 1938; reprinted 1959), p. 161.
6 Whitehead, A. N., *The Aims of Education and Other Essays* (Williams and Norgate, 1929). *Vide* in particular p. 74: 'The antithesis between a technical and a liberal education is fallacious. There can be no adequate technical education which is not liberal, and no liberal education which does not impart both technique and intellectual vision.'
7 Dewey, J., *Democracy and Education* (Macmillan, 1916; reprinted 1955). *Vide* in particular p. 305: 'Of the segregations of educational values discussed in the last chapter, that between culture and utility is probably the most fundamental. . . . The problem of education in a democratic society is to do away with the dualism and to construct a course of studies which makes thought a guide of free practice for all and which makes leisure a reward of accepting responsibility for service, rather than a state of exemption from it.'
8 Machlup, F., op. cit., p. 5.
9 Op. cit., p. 161, para. 18.
10 Machlup, F., *The Production and Distribution of Knowledge in the United States* (Princeton Univ. Press, Princeton N.J., 1962), pp. 108–10, 115.
11 Machlup, F., *Education and Economic Growth*, p. 5.
12 *Vide* Morrish, I., *The Background of Immigrant Children* (Allen and Unwin, 1971), Chapter 9 on 'Education of the Indians'.
13 *Vide* Table One. This table is a composite effort compiled from the following documents: Committee of Higher Education, *Higher Education* (H.M.S.O., 1963), p. 161; U.G.C. *University Development: 1957–1962* (H.M.S.O., 1964), p. 67; D.E.S., *Education and Science in 1967* (H.M.S.O., 1968), p. 84; D.E.S., *Education and Science in 1968* (H.M.S.O., 1969), p. 87; D.E.S., *Education and Science in 1969* (H.M.S.O., 1970), p. 74.
14 Papi, G. U., 'General Problems of the Economics of Education' in Robinson, E. A. G. and Vaizey, J. E. (eds), *The Economics of Education* (Macmillan, 1966), Chapter 1, p. 23.
15 Ibid., pp. 3–6.
16 Ibid., p. 4.
17 Ibid., p. 3.
18 D.E.S., *Children and their Primary Schools* (Plowden Report) (H.M.S.O., 1967), p. 469.
19 Committee on Higher Education, *Higher Education* (Robbins Report) (H.M.S.O., 1963), p. 207, para. 630.

20 Machlup, F., *Education and Economic Growth*, pp. 9–10.
21 Kuznets, S., *National Income and Its Composition, 1919–1938* (National Bureau of Economic Research, N.Y., 1941), Vol. 1, p. 3; quoted in Machlup, F., *Education and Economic Growth*, pp. 9–10, footnote 2.
22 *Vide* Robinson, E. A. G., and Vaizey, J. E. (eds), *The Economics of Education* (Macmillan, 1966), p. 611. Compare also Professor Vaizey's comments on pp. 612, 629 *et passim*.
23 Ibid., pp. 637–8.
24 Cf. Kaser, M. C., 'Education and Economic Progress: Experience in Industrialized Market Economics' in Robinson, E. A. G., and Vaizey, J. E. (eds), op. cit., p. 89, where he states that 'Gross national product, as an annual rate of growth and *per capita*, is used as the best available measure of economic progress'. In his comment on a previous paper by Professor F. Edding, in the same book, Professor John Vaizey stated on p. 611 that 'On the question of the relationship between increased educational expenditures and rising G.N.P. he had to confess himself something of an agnostic.'
25 Harbison, F. H., 'Quantitative Indicators of Human Resource Development' in Robinson, E. A. G. and Vaizey, J. E. (eds), op. cit., pp. 352–7.
26 *Vide* ibid., pp. 352–7 and 652–69.
27 Ibid., adapted from Table 8, Level IV: Advanced. Sixteen Countries, pp. 378–9. Harbison's figures appear to be derived from a variety of sources up to the year 1961.
28 Machlup, F., *Education and Economic Growth*, pp. 24–5.
29 Schultz, T. P., *Returns to Education in Bogotá, Colombia* (Rand Corporation, Santa Monica, Calif., 1968), pp. 37–40; referred to by Machlup, F., op. cit., p. 17.
30 Blaug, M. *et al.*, *The Causes of Graduate Unemployment in India* (Allen Lane, Penguin Press, 1969). See note 12.
31 *Vide* Meade, J. E. *et al.*, *The Economic and Social Structure of Mauritius* (F. Cass and Co., 1961; new impression 1968), p. 239.
32 Government of Mauritius, *Annual Report on Education for 1968* (L. Carl Achille, Government Printer, Port Louis, Mauritius, October 1969), p. 3.
33 Dr Philip H. Coombs of the International Institute for Educational Planning, UNESCO, Paris.
34 *Vide* Robinson, E. A. G. and Vaizey, J. E. (eds), op. cit., p. 637.
35 Machlup, F., op. cit., p. 100.
36 *Vide* Robinson, E. A. G. and Vaizey, J. E. (eds), op. cit., pp. 9–13.
37 Ibid., pp. 461–2 on 'Internal Logistics'.
38 Ibid., p. 11.
39 Ibid., pp. 451–62.
40 Ibid., pp. 461–2.
41 Machlup, F., *Education and Economic Growth*, p. 83.
42 Ibid., pp. 85–6.
43 Vaizey, J., *The Costs of Education* (Allen and Unwin, 1958); *The Economics of Education* (Faber, 1962); *The Control of Education* (Faber, 1963); and

with Sheehan, J., *Resources for Education* (Allen and Unwin, 1968: 2nd impression 1969).
44 Machlup, F., *The Production and Distribution of Knowledge in the United States* (Princeton Univ. Press, 1962); *Education and Economic Growth* (Univ. of Nebraska Press, 1970).
45 Robinson, E. A. G. and Vaizey, J. (eds), op. cit.
46 Professor F. Edding, Hochschule für Internationale Pädagogische Forschung, Frankfurt am Main, Germany.
47 *Vide* Robinson, E. A. G. and Vaizey, J., op. cit., Table 3, p. 41.
48 Ibid., p. 615.
49 Table Three is compiled from the following sources: Robinson, E. A. G. and Vaizey, J., (eds), op. cit., Tables 1A, 1B, 1C, 1D, pp. 28–31; Vaizey, J., *The Control of Education*, p. 13; Research and Reference Division, Ministry of Information, *India – A Reference Annual, 1968* (Publications Division, Ministry of Information and Broadcasting, Govt. of India, 1968), pp. 61 and 156.

BIBLIOGRAPHY

ANDERSON, C. A. and BOWMAN, MARY J. (eds), *Education and Economic Development* (Aldine, Chicago, 1965).
BANKS, OLIVE, *The Sociology of Education* (Batsford, 1968; 2nd impression 1969), Chapter 2, 'Education and the Economy'.
BECKER, G. S., *Human Capital* (Columbia Univ. Press, 1964).
BLAUG, M., *Economics of Education: A Selected Annotated Bibliography* (Pergamon Press, 1966).
BLAUG, M. (ed.), *Economics of Education, I and II* (Penguin Books, 1968–9).
BLAUG, M., LAYARD, R. and WOODHALL, MAUREEN, *The Causes of Graduate Unemployment in India* (Allen Lane, Penguin Press, 1969).
BOTTOMORE, T. B., *Sociology: A Guide to Problems and Literature* (Unwin Univ. Books, No. 13, Allen and Unwin, 1962; 2nd edition 1971).
BOWMAN, MARY J. et al (eds), *Readings in the Economics of Education* (UNESCO, Paris, 1968).
CAPLOW, T., *The Sociology of Work* (Univ. of Minneapolis Press, 1954).
CARTER, M. P., *Home, School and Work* (Pergamon Press, 1962).
CARTER, M. P., *Education, Employment and Leisure* (Pergamon Press, 1963).
COMMITTEE ON HIGHER EDUCATION, *Higher Education* (Robbins Report) (H.M.S.O., 1963), Chapter XIV, pp. 199–216.
D.E.S., *Education and Science in 1969* (H.M.S.O., 1970), Section VII, 'Finance and General', pp. 111–46.
D.E.S., *Statistics of Education 1969 – Volume 5: Finance and Awards* (H.M.S.O., 1970).
EDDING, F., ELVIN, H. L. and SVENNILSON, I., *Targets for Education in Europe* (O.E.C.D., 1962).
FLOUD, J., HALSEY, A. H. and ANDERSON, C. A. (eds), *Education, Economy and Society* (Free Press, Glencoe, 1961).

GREEN, B. S. R. and JOHNS, E. A., *An Introduction to Sociology* (Pergamon Press, 1966; reprinted 1968), pp. 80–91.

HANS, N., *Comparative Education* (Routledge, 3rd revised edition 1958), Chapter IV, pp. 63–84.

HARBISON, F. and MYERS, C. A., *Education, Manpower and Economic Growth* (McGraw-Hill, 1964).

LAMBERT, R., *The State and Boarding Education* (Methuen, 1966).

LAUWERYS, J. A. (ed.), *Education and the Economy* (Evans Bros, 1969).

MACHLUP, F., *Education and Economic Growth* (Univ. of Nebraska Press, 1970).

MINISTRY OF EDUCATION, *15 to 18* (Crowther Report) (H.M.S.O., 1959), Chapter 5, pp. 45–53.

MISRA, A., *Educational Finance in India* (Asia Publishing House, 1962).

MOORE, W., *Industrial Relations and the Social Order* (Macmillan, N.Y., revised edition 1951).

MUSGRAVE, P. W., *Technical Change, the Labour Force and Education* (Pergamon Press, 1967).

MUSGRAVE, P. W., *The Sociology of Education* (Methuen, 1965; reprinted 1968), Chapters 6, 7 and 12.

PARSONS, T., *The Social System* (Free Press, Glencoe, 1952).

PARSONS, T. and SMELSER, N., *Economy and Society* (Free Press, Glencoe, 1956).

PARSONS, T. et al. (ed), *Theories of Society* (Free Press, Glencoe, 1965), 'Occupation and Economy', pp. 405–513.

ROBINSON, E. A. G. and VAIZEY, J. E. (eds), *The Economics of Education* (Macmillan, 1966).

SCHULTZ, T. W., *The Economic Value of Education* (Columbia Univ. Press, 1963).

SEXTON, P., *Education and Income* (Viking Press, 1961).

SMELSER, N., *The Sociology of Economic Life* (Prentice-Hall, 1963).

VAIZEY, J., *The Costs of Education* (Allen and Unwin, 1958).

VAIZEY, J., *The Economics of Education* (Faber, 1962).

VAIZEY, J., *Education for Tomorrow* (Penguin, 1962; 2nd impression 1966).

VAIZEY, J., *The Control of Education* (Faber, 1963).

VAIZEY, J. and SHEEHAN, J., *Resources for Education* (Allen and Unwin, 1968; 2nd impression 1969).

WEST, E. G., *Education and the State* (The Institute of Economic Affairs, 1965).

WISEMAN, J., *The Economics of Education* (British Association for the Advancement of Science, August 1958).

YOUNG, M., *The Rise of the Meritocracy* (Penguin, 1958).

Chapter 7

Social Stratification and Education

A. CASTES AND ESTATES

Wherever societies have existed in the past there has also existed some form of hierarchy or stratification among their members. Indeed, it may well be argued that even the so-called 'classless' societies of our present era have their hierarchical systems, implicit if not explicit. We may disguise the situation by the introduction of different terms, such as 'status' or 'prestige', but outside the realms of sophistry the result seems to be very much the same.

Even within the Israeli 'classless' *kibbutzim*, where there may indeed be no economic 'class' or class struggle, there are the leaders, the branch managers, and the important personalities generally who inevitably involve their society in some form of differential social status. The recognition of such a differential also involves stereotyped attitudes, the playing of distinct roles, and a variety of expression in terms of social philosophy (1).

As long as efficiency and control are valued in any society there are bound to be established managerial and administrative positions which represent power, and which are relatively permanent. A rapid turnover in such positions would inevitably result in a loss of both efficiency and production. Eva Rosenfeld has cogently argued that, when scarcity places a premium upon competent and trusted members of society who possess powers of initiative and leadership, prestige eventually becomes associated with the positions they hold, and these positions are then 'used as an index of high social status' (2).

Thus, even if inequalities were not intrinsic to the very genetic make-up of man, and even if environmental conditions were capable of eradicating the major inequalities of nurture, the very fact that men must play a variety of roles, vital or unimportant, in society would create its own social and status differential. This is intended, at this point in the discussion on social stratification, merely as a warning to the reader that there are dangers in looking at the caste system of Hinduism, on the one hand, as a prime example of a closed iron-clad class hierarchy, and at the *kibbutz*, or commune, system of Israel, on the other hand, as a perfect exemplification of the open, 'classless' society. Indeed, with regard to the latter, R. D. Schwartz has stated that many expressions of job dissatisfaction by members of *kibbutzim* appear to stem from the fact that 'they do not feel that their skills are being utilized, e.g. that their jobs are dull, that their manager is oppressive, or that they could be doing far more constructive work' (3). Classless, non-hierarchical societies are largely the mental constructs of philosophers, the dreams of museum-bound political prophets, and the visions of religious idealists or the promise of the demagogues. Detailed examinations of them, in practice, inevitably reveal that George Orwell's dictum that 'all animals are equal, but some are more equal than others', is one which applies to the most 'egalitarian' of societies.

The Hindu caste society is interesting to us for a variety of reasons and, today, the merely academic and comparative one is perhaps the least important. It represents, for a start, one of the oldest societies in the world, but it is also important because, for over three millennia, its fundamental structure has remained virtually unchanged. In addition, however, as a developing multi-cultural society Great Britain is likely to see more and more of the caste system at work in small, closely-knit communities within its larger society.

Caste, broadly speaking, represents a social class system in which membership is determined at, and by, birth, and from which there is little vertical mobility. But it is perhaps important, before we go farther, to make the distinction between the caste *system*, such as that in India, and the caste *principle* which might well apply anywhere. This point is made by R. M. MacIver and C. H. Page in their discussion of 'caste' in an open-class society:

'For the caste principle, assigning status strictly in terms of birth, enforcing endogamous marriage, vastly limiting social contacts between groups, and restricting certain occupations to the "right-born", is one that, in some degree, is manifested in all societies, including our own. Whenever status is predetermined by birth, whenever one's colour or ethnic origin or religion or "name" automatically assigns one special prestige or privilege, or special social handicaps, the *principle* of caste is at work' (4).

There are societies other than the Hindu caste society which are practising the caste principle mainly because of colour, and the existence of apartheid is a prime example of this.

About 1500 B.C. the Nordics, Aryans or Indo-Aryans left the northern plateau of Iran and made inroads into northern India. The Aryans (or *aryas*, i.e. 'the noble ones') were a light-skinned race of people who were very proud of their origin, their purity of race and their nobility. Gradually they conquered the indigenous peoples of India who were, for the most part, darker in colour; and they subdued and colonized them. They were somewhat contemptuous of their conquered victims and virtually enslaved them; and during the ensuing millennium the caste system became firmly established. According to Romila Thapar (5), the Aryans were already divided into three social classes when they arrived in India, namely, the aristocracy or warriors, the priests, and the commoners. This division of the Aryan society was largely an economic one. Generally speaking, however, the great division was not within Aryan society itself, but rather between the Aryans and the non-Aryans. Gradually the former assumed the status of the three upper castes, and the latter became the fourth caste.

There seems little doubt that the original Hindu caste system was a form of colour discrimination reinforced by the fact of conquest (6). The three upper castes, formed from the Aryans, were known as the 'twice-born' because they had gone through the process of natural, physical birth and that of spiritual initiation. They were the *brahmins*, or priestly caste, who at some point gained ascendancy in the caste system; the *kshatriyas* or warriors; and the *vaishyas* or agriculturalists. The conquered non-Aryans formed the lowest caste and were the labourers, the herdsmen, the serfs and the slaves, collectively termed *shudras*.

These four broad divisions do not by any means constitute the total complexity of the caste system. Taya Zinkin (7) states that there are over two thousand *jatis*, or sub-castes, among the brahmins alone, so that there are altogether literally thousands of sub-castes and kin-groups. According to orthodox Hinduism inter-caste marriage is not permitted; in fact, a caste has been defined as 'a group of families whose members can marry with each other and can eat in each other's company without believing themselves polluted' (8). One form of inter-caste marriage, however, seems to have been permitted, namely *anuloma* marriage in which the bridegroom was of a higher caste than that of the bride. Children born of such a marriage usually belonged to their father's caste. Marriage customs seem, today, to vary from caste to caste, or sub-caste, and the orthodox Hindu ideals of non-intermixture of caste are obsolescent.

Nevertheless, one group remains outside the caste system and is referred to as the 'outcastes': these number at least fifty million, or about 10 per cent of the Indian population. They were formerly known as untouchables or pariahs; and they are not only without caste, but have also always been regarded as social outcasts without opportunities of labour or contact with members of the caste system. Their chief occupation has been that of begging and making sure that they do not in any way pollute their benefactors by personal contact. During his lifetime Mahatma Gandhi worked very hard on behalf of the untouchables, and he refused to accept that any sort of contact with them incurred pollution. He was the first to refer to them as *harijans*, or 'children of God', and this name has remained with them.

Today there exist laws against the deliberate practice of avoidance or untouchability but one clearly cannot, by legislation, change overnight the habits and customs of at least three millennia. Discrimination against members of lower castes when being interviewed for work is also illegal; but there is a tendency for this sort of legislation to act in reverse, and it can very quickly lead to discrimination against the so-called privileged members of the *brahmin* and *kshatriya* castes.

Whilst Taya Zinkin maintains that caste is not class, not colour, not occupation, and not exclusively Hindu or Indian (9), there is a sense in which caste is involved in class, colour (or *varna*) and occupation; and although there are undoubtedly institutions analogous to caste elsewhere, and the *principle* of caste applies elsewhere, the Indian Hindu caste system would appear to be unique among the systems of social stratification (10). Professor T. B. Bottomore states that 'The only cases in which a caste system has been established outside Hindu India are those of non-Hindu groups in India (e.g. Muslims) or of Hindu settlement outside India, notably in Ceylon' (11). The ultimate sanction of the Hindu caste system is religion and the concept of *karma*. None can avoid *karma*, which is the debt we have to pay, and the work and deeds we have to do, in order to work out our own personal salvation. The fact that one is born into a particular caste, and that there is no possibility of advance up the caste scale in this life, pales into insignificance when one realizes that there is a certain inevitability about return after death.

Such return and its nature are contingent upon the sort of life one has lived here and now: this is the important thing in the philosophy of caste – not the fact that I am born a humble *shudra*, but the fact that if I want to return next time in a more favourable position in a higher caste, as a *vaishya*, for example, I must live as near a perfect life as possible in my present condition and caste. My ultimate release from the apparently ceaseless round of *samsara*, or rebirth, will occur only when my karmic debt is fully paid, and my personal purification has led to an acceptance of the *dharma*, or universal law of goodness, truth and righteousness. The final goal is one of 'no return', when the chains of desire and of the illusion (*maya*) of life are broken, and when *moksha*, or salvation, is attained.

Thus, the Hindu caste system is a closed one – it is a stratification fixed for all individuals by the nature of their birth. Originally it was most probably connected with colour through the lightness of the skins of the upper castes and the blackness of the skins of the lowest caste. Because, inevitably, the Aryan conquerors held certain positions and occupations, caste also became linked with occupation: the *brahmins* were priests, the *kshatriyas* were warriors, the *vaishyas* were agriculturalists, and the *shudras* were labourers. The large variety of sub-castes and *jatis* that grew up further defined the occupations of their members, so that some sub-caste groupings were responsible for particular occupations and none else. Over the centuries, in somewhat broader terms, the *vaishyas* have tended to become increasingly an educated class who have spent their wealth in providing their children with a better education. Hence merchants, doctors, teachers and lawyers tend increasingly to be associated with this caste. On the other hand, the 'drop-outs' of the *brahmin* caste, who have been unable or unwilling to pursue the strenuous and rigorous training of the priest, might well perform any menial task in society.

In a very interesting essay on 'The Social Structure of a Mysore Village' (12), M. N. Srinivas describes in some detail the village of Rampura which had at the time 1,523 inhabitants and seventeen sub-castes. These sub-castes relate closely to the occupations which are pursued by them, and Srinivas has described the Rampura economy in the following terms:

'A self-sufficient economy is possible only if each sub-caste adheres to its traditional occupations. The occupations are complementary. This is true to a great extent in Rampura even today, though every caste either has agriculture as its main occupation, or practises agriculture along with its main occupation. The members of the Peasant caste practise agriculture, the Barber shaves, the Washerman washes clothes, the Potter makes pots, the Banajigas are traders, the Ganiga works the oil-press and sells oil, the Besthas are fishermen, the Indigas sell toddy, though they no longer tap it, the Medas make baskets, and the Koramas are swine-herds. The Untouchables are labourers and servants. But most of the Kurubas are agriculturists though their traditional occupation is keeping sheep and making woollen blankets. There are a few Muslims in Rampura who are recent immigrants, and they are traders and contractors. A few Peasants and a Lingayat have opened grocery shops, and a Potter and a Fisherman sew clothes on a sewing machine. The priestly castes also cultivate land. But even today it is considered proper to follow one's traditional occupation' (13).

Thus, the manifold sub-castes of Indian society, particularly those living in village communities, are linked very closely with the economy, its division of labour, and its necessary production. There is, however, in this village system an internal vertical link through agriculture, and an external horizontal link through the sub-caste occupation. But the relative invariableness of the total situation has been established by tradition and the attitudes of the villagers towards caste itself.

It has been argued that castes are similar to the *estates* of medieval Europe. Estates were status groups, such as the nobility or lords temporal, the clergy or lords spiritual, and the commons, who all had legal rights, privileges and obligations. Each estate, in fact, was subject to a similar legal system, but justice was meted out somewhat differently to each estate via the manorial and ecclesiastical courts. There were different sanctions and modes of punishment even for the same offences; and whilst a duel might suffice for a noble, there might well be a hanging for a commoner, peasant or serf. Thus the status of each estate was known, and the role and function of all the members of the estates were clearly defined. An individual's status, or estate, was (as in caste) decided at birth, and was a legal matter; only the law could change the estate of any individual. Apart from recruitment from the laity into the Church, and the possibility of a villein becoming a small trader or artisan, there was very little social mobility within the estate system.

B. SOCIAL CLASS

Social mobility will be considered in greater detail in Chapter 8, but it is obvious that in any discussion of the development of social class in our society we are, *ipso facto*, concerned with the mobility and fluidity of the social structure. Social class in our own society developed from the more static and legal system of estates largely through the rise of the merchant class, and the ownership of wealth in terms of money as distinct from land or property. And just as there was the possibility, however remote, of the serf or villein becoming an artisan or trader, so the rich merchant, who was both useful and favoured, might well become elevated to the nobility. It was therefore the rise of capitalism, and its inevitable adjuncts, which really led to the expansion of what today is referred to as 'the middle class'. It also helped to establish a distinction between the peasants involved almost exclusively in agriculture, who lived on their own produce, and the ever-increasing numbers of industrial workers who were developing in the urban areas as wage-earners.

Whatever 'class' may signify today to different sociologists, and however much they may distinguish economic and social factors, it is fairly true to say that, initially, economic considerations were of prime importance in establishing these new classes. The acceleration in the expansion of the industrial revolution in this country during the nineteenth century led to the hardening of distinctions between the agricultural worker, the wage-earning industrial class, the 'middle' class merchants and industrialists, and the aristocracy. There was thus established a certain correlation between the social class and the occupation pursued. This, in turn, inevitably resulted in training and education for specific skills and areas of occupation, which meant that each class gradually developed its own peculiar interests and culture.

Individuals in any society seek an identity, and steadily they identify with the class structure. Whether we like it or not, life demonstrates a continuous struggle of individuals to improve their position, and equally it indicates that many fail to emerge from the social rut into which they were born. People are much more self-conscious of their social status according to the class structure of their society than were the individual members of the estate or caste systems which were legalistic and established by birth. There is nothing 'legal' about the vertical stratification or hierarchy within our society which we term class. The distinctions between classes, however, are certainly no longer economic: a docker may earn more than a schoolmaster but this does not necessarily put both of them in the same class – indeed, neither would claim to be in the same class.

Class has become associated with standards and modes of behaviour, as well as with patterns of expenditure and consumption. Leisure-time pursuits may often be a more accurate criterion of class status than even the possession of particular articles and amenities. Individuals in a lower class may copy those in a higher class, especially in the realm of possessions, in order to try and establish an identity that they would very much like to have. But the *nouveau riche*, for all his wealth, never quite acquires the manner of even the most destitute or impoverished of aristocrats. Class is certainly not just a question of economics, of wealth; it is a question of breeding, of mode of speech, of culture, of being able to say and do the right things at the right time – in whatever stratum one is. The former luxuries of the upper classes have rapidly become, in our own time, the basic necessities of all classes. It is no longer the possession of a car or a television which establishes class, it is the make and type of car, or even the number of cars, and whether one has the most expensive colour television set.

Any attempt, therefore, to group individuals within our society according to the income bracket within which they fall would be statistically unsound if one suggested at the same time that there was a complete correspondence between income and social class. There may, in fact, be a fairly high correlation but there are many other factors involved, relating more to the intangible and mental qualities of individuals, as well as their type of occupation, which help to establish their social status. And our concepts of social status are also largely subjective, which inevitably makes it difficult to provide criteria for statistical measurement. It could well be that our 'class' terminology is altogether outmoded, and no longer represents a satisfactory way of describing the social structure. R. J. Stalcup defines social class as: 'A level in society made up of people who consider themselves equals due to similarities in family background, level of education, occupation, race, and attitudes toward social issues' (14).

But attitudes towards specific social issues may well cut across all social class barriers, whilst the introduction of race immediately provides the possibility of a great variety of classes and sub-classes which may be regarded as inferior or superior for reasons of colour alone. It is interesting to note that in a contemporary book devoted entirely to an examination of the middle class, the author, John Raynor, states very clearly

'We prefer to use the term middle stratum rather than middle class, because its components are not a solid or homogeneous group. Rather it is a disparate grouping of people who may perceive themselves as middle class, from the variety of everyday experience which feeds their perceptions of social inequality, but who lack any kind of common ideology to bind themselves together. Members of this middle stratum do share a broad economic orientation that distinguishes them from the working class, and they do share different life-styles, levels of prestige and power that distinguish them further' (15).

Thus the middle class is not a monolithic stratum of society, but rather a stratum comprising a number of sub-groups which have arrived there and identified themselves, or have been identified by others, as middle class for a great variety of reasons.

J. Hall and D. Caradog Jones (16) attempted, in 1950, to classify occupations according to the social prestige attached to them, and they provided a standard classification of seven grades as follows:

1. Professional and High Administrative
2. Managerial and Executive
3. Inspectional, Supervisory and other Non-Manual (Higher Grade)
4. Inspectional, Supervisory and other Non-Manual (Lower Grade)
5. Skilled Manual and routine grades of Non-Manual
6. Semi-skilled Manual
7. Unskilled Manual

Whilst it may not be difficult to classify many people in specific occupations as upper class or working class, there are a variety of occupations in which the individuals who are engaged may classify themselves variously as working, or lower middle, or even middle class. And one can only agree with G. D. Mitchell when he says that the 'concept of "middle class" as popularly used is a vague and ill-defined one' (17).

Perhaps, whether in popular or sociological terms, the time has arrived when not only is it impossible to be precise about the criteria of class and the demarcation of classes, but it is also less useful statistically to talk in these terms. The occupational classification may prove to be more valuable both descriptively and analytically. Groups of people may best be described by means of their role and function in society – as, to a large extent, the individuals were in M. N. Srinivas' Mysore village. The great difference in our society is that a trader is a trader *de facto*; he has somehow worked himself into that position because that is what he wants (or at some time wanted) to be. In the Mysore village of Rampura a trader is such *de iure*, because he has been born into the sub-caste of the Banajigas, and therefore religious, social and legal sanctions support him in that occupation, as over against the Ganiga who works the oil-press and sells oil, or the Bestha who is a fisherman.

In his article on 'The Professions and Social Structure', Talcott Parsons discusses in some detail the specificity of function and role of individuals in particular professions (18). Parsons emphasizes the technical competence which is one of the principal defining characteristics of the professional role and status, and which is 'always limited to a particular "field" of knowledge and skill' (19). In so far as a professional man is an authority only in his own field, to that extent his economic worth can be measured in terms of scarce resources. If he is the only one of his kind he is clearly invaluable, and power, prestige and status, as well as economic reward, will accrue to him in an open society.

If one goes to the other extreme to unskilled labour where there is a minimum of specificity, and where knowledge and ability are easily transferable from one form of unskilled activity to another, then the occupation is certainly not prestigious nor possessing social status, and its economic rewards are likely to be low. Thus, functional specificity provides one form of criterion for establishing the position of professions and occupations within the social scale.

C. SOME THEORIES OF SOCIAL STRATIFICATION

In his discussion of the 'class struggle' (20), Karl Marx (1818–83) states that:

'The modern bourgeois society that has sprouted from the ruins of feudal society, has not done away with class antagonisms. It has but established new classes, new conditions of oppression, new forms of struggle in place of the old ones. Our epoch, the epoch of the bourgeoisie, possesses, however, this distinctive feature; it has simplified the class antagonisms. Society as a whole is more and more splitting up into two great hostile camps, into two great classes directly facing each other: Bourgeoisie and Proletariat' (21).

Marx goes on to explain that by *bourgeoisie* he means the class of modern capitalists or owners of the means of production and employers of wage-labour; the *proletariat* is the class of modern wage-labourers who have no means of production of their own, and are therefore reduced to selling their 'labour-power' in order to live.

Like Weber after him, Marx was fundamentally influenced by the historicist dynamic of German social thought (22). The Hegelian polarization of thesis and antithesis was interpreted by him in terms of a class struggle which had been going on throughout the history of man, whether one thought in terms of patricians and plebeians or nobles and commoners. The synthesis would result only at the end of a very bitter struggle between the bourgeoisie and the proletariat, during which the social distance would have developed so much that the proletariat would revolt and bring about a transformation of society through the violent overthrow of its capitalist masters.

It is just as easy to underplay Marx's historical thesis as it is to overplay it. Of course, Marx could not anticipate the great expansion in capitalist societies of the 'middle class', nor the somewhat peaceful transformation of his dichotomy of bourgeoisie and proletariat, and social distance, into a highly complex, manifold-graded society, in which the so-called proletariat are very often better off than the so-called bourgeoisie; and a society in which sub-classes are for ever knocking on each other's doors. Indeed, the terms themselves, as applied to our own society, are today archaic and virtually meaningless. But Marxism, like Christian theology, is quite capable of revision in terms of evolving and changing situations.

Depressed classes or groups have a habit of finding new enemies somewhere; new terms are employed, such as 'under-privileged' and 'over-privileged', and 'the means of production' may well be translated into terms of 'human capital' or education. The clamouring for 'equality of opportunity' is to some degree an extension of the class struggle depicted by Marx; and the demand for the eradication of public-school education and the expansion of 'comprehensive' schooling is a further attempt to eliminate social distance.

But, as was pointed out earlier (23), societies which have developed the 'classless' theme are not necessarily free from class distinctions, or at least some of the expressions of class distinction. And even if the 'ruling class' has been overthrown in Russia, there are still rulers who form an elite, and there are few signs of the 'withering away' of the state. With regard to the latter it was Nicolai Lenin who said:

> 'The state will be able to wither away completely when society has realized the formula: "From each according to his ability; to each according to his needs"; that is, when people have become accustomed to observe the fundamental principles of social life, and their labour is so productive, that they will voluntarily work *according to their abilities*' (24).

Lenin was the first to recognize that this was not to be achieved by the mere conversion of the means of production into public property, that is, by the mere expropriation of the capitalists. What was essential as the economic basis for the complete withering away of the state was the disappearance of the distinction between brain and manual work – a principal source of modern *social* inequality.

In his examination of class in the Soviet Union, A. Inkeles has argued that not only is there a social stratification, but that it is a stable one and it is such that it would in all probability require a new revolution, both political and social, in order to arouse the sort of dynamism required to create the classical Marxist 'classless' society (25). Although Inkeles wrote his paper in 1950, there seems to be little evidence to suggest that the social structure, as he delineated it, has changed very much. Inkeles identified the following differentiated groups or strata within the Soviet society:

1 Ruling elite
2 Superior intelligentsia
3 General intelligentsia
4 Working-class aristocracy
5.5 White collar
5.5 Well-to-do peasants
7 Average workers
8.5 Average peasants
8.5 Disadvantaged workers
10 Forced labour

The German sociologist, Max Weber (1864–1920), defined class in purely economic terms; that is, class covered the 'life chances' of the individual members of the class in terms of the economic opportunities and expectations they might reasonably have. In real terms this means that, statistically speaking, the chances of a young man in the upper-middle class are greater not only in economic terms than those of a young man of the same age in the working class, but also in terms of housing, health, medical care, food and education. Class is a question of the power or potential of the individual in relation to the production or acquisition of goods.

Weber distinguishes status groups from classes, in that status groups are concerned with, and aligned with, the modes or patterns of the consumption of wealth. People spend their money in a variety of ways, and even if an unskilled worker should earn as much as, say, a university lecturer, he is likely to spend his money in a different way, on different sorts of amenities and forms of recreation. He is, in fact, less likely to invest his money in order to improve the life chances of his children. His whole life-style will be totally different; in Weberian terms, his social status is different. Weber, however, does not see the class struggle in the same terms as Marx: conflict is not inevitable, although of course it is always a potential.

This section would be incomplete without some reference to the ideas of Ralf Dahrendorf, who has admirably summed up his views in his essay entitled 'Recent Changes in the Class Structure of European Societies' (26).

It is impossible to analyse fully here Dahrendorf's delineation of social stratification. Briefly, however, he relates the class structure of a society to the relationship of its members to the exercise of power. Society is divided up by him into four main groups:

1. *The Ruling Groups*: these are those in a given country who, by virtue of their position, are able to lay down the law for others in both the literal and the metaphorical sense.

2. *The Service Class*: this comprises those individuals who help the ruling groups in their legislative task by executing and adjudicating law, in addition to advising and generally assisting those in power. It is the emergence of this group which continues to be a disturbing fact to all those who believed that Marx's prediction of the polarization of classes was inevitable. Moreover, there has been an enormous expansion of this class at the expense of all the others.

3. *The Ruled or Subjected Groups*: these are those individuals who are subject to the power of both the ruling groups and the service class, even if their citizenship rights enable them from time to time to make their voice heard. In all society there is no boundary more cruelly felt than the one between those who are just above and those who are just below the line dividing power from impotence. 'Even today, it would be useless to deny that in terms of power there is this boundary, and that its existence testifies to the potential of class conflict all over Europe' (27).

4. *The Intellectuals*: this group stands outside the whole structure of leaders and led. They are the 'free-floating intellectuals', whom Bertrand Russell has characterized as those who withdraw and do not easily fit into the social structure, but who in various ways seek a refuge where they can enjoy a relatively solitary freedom (28).

Dahrendorf concludes his essay by suggesting that whilst the gross inequalities of life chances have given way to a common basis of citizenship, there is, nevertheless, a universal social necessity for inequality which is expressed in other terms and other areas of life. Status is more a matter of prestige than of rights and privileges; and prestige is more and more attached not merely to occupations but also to leisure activities and patterns of consumption. A new society is developing, variously termed managerial, leisure-time, consumer's, advanced industrial and mass. Dahrendorf adds another name in claiming that Europe is advancing towards a 'service class society'; and he argues that, although only a small percentage of the population can be reckoned among the service class proper, the values of the latter group have spread to all other groups. He considers that

'Paramount among these values is the replacement of cohesive feelings and groupings by individual competition. In the past, progress was a matter of immense public interest; in the present, progress has become a private affair or, rather, a matter of the abstract sum of innumerable advances in individual happiness' (29).

As we come to consider some of the relationships between social stratification and education we must bear in mind that, in all the variety of theories concerning class and group structure, certain vital facts emerge regarding such concepts as power, status, prestige, life chances, life-styles, patterns of consumption, leisure activities, and occupations. These are concrete facts amongst a considerable amount of abstract theorizing, and they are closely related to problems of culture, education and socialization. In all the ramifications of the literature on class and social groupings it is not easy for anyone, whether pundit or dilettante, to obtain any final and clear-cut view on social stratification. Human personality and development, whether considered in group or in individual terms, defies the strictly statistical analysis that so many seek in the sociology of the future.

At least Dahrendorf's analysis recognizes the problem of the increasing number of 'classless' individuals who, as 'floating intellectuals', wander through the many areas of society, doing everything from working in sewers, singing pop-songs, producing or otherwise participating in TV shows, to lecturing in colleges and universities. But, no doubt, B. S. R. Green and E. A. Johns are right in their conclusion on the question of class:

'While it may be agreed that socio-economic changes in our own society have largely invalidated the class conflict model, it must not be assumed that the concept of social class has been made irrelevant. The fact remains that people can be classified according to occupational prestige, income, education or other closely associated indicators of social status and that such classifications are not merely statistical categories but reflect differences in values, goals, attitudes and behaviours. For example, high social status is associated with greater political involvement, with more favourable attitudes towards further education and with a more rational mode of decision-making in such situations as occupational choice' (30).

D. SOCIAL CLASS AND EDUCATION

In this section we are mainly concerned with the effects of social class or stratification upon education. In Chapter 8 we shall be more directly concerned with the effects which education may have upon society and social mobility. The division is more one of literary convenience than of sociological differentiation. It is also clear that a great deal of reference must be made by the reader to the particular research material available in connection with the problems discussed: we can do little more here than indicate what the problems are.

Emile Durkheim (1858–1917) maintained that there were as many different kinds of education as there were social *milieux* in any given society (31). In ancient Rome the education of the plebeian was very different from that of the patrician; in India, certainly until recent years, the education of the *brahmin* was considerably different from that of a *shudra*; whilst in medieval England the education of a knight, or of his attendant squire, was far removed from that of a villein or peasant. No one questions the difference of education according to caste or estate in the past, or even in relation to class in our own society when a good grammar-school or public-school education had to be paid for. But is Durkheim's statement any longer true in a society in which provision is made for each child to be educated according to his 'age, ability and aptitude'?

The simple fact is that 'equality of opportunity' cannot be provided merely through Education Acts. Each child in our society has certain social positions by ascription: it is born into a particular family, in a particular place, as a male or female, and in a relative position with regard to brothers and sisters. The child may be the eldest or the youngest or at some point in between, but each different position in the family organization provides, in fact, a slightly different *milieu*. But its position even within the family may not be a static one: older siblings may leave home in order to get married, younger children may be born. The child is also born into a family which will belong to a particular part of the structure of society – it may be a working-class family, it may be a middle-class one, and so on.

Again, the family fortunes may change, and so the social *milieu* may well be a moving one. The family will live in a certain area which may be rural or urban; it may be an agricultural village, an industrial small town, a large city, a seaport, and so on. Inequalities in opportunity for educational development may arise out of any of these particular factors – familial, economic, class or regional. Studies such as those produced by Dr J. W. B. Douglas (32), J. E. Floud, A. H. Halsey and F. M. Martin (33), A. Davis (34) and J. Barron Mays (35), are all concerned to demonstrate some of the effects of environmental factors upon children.

Class differentials in life chances, to use Weberian terminology, are expressed initially in terms of birth and health. Both J. W. B. Douglas (36) and T. Arie (37) have pointed out that many of the differentials between classes in relation to these two factors are reflections of their disparities in terms of wealth and education. The chances of being born and of staying alive are relatively greater the higher up the social scale one goes, and Arie's conclusion is that in the crucial area of birth and infancy some of the gaps between the classes have hardly changed in current times. Douglas indicates, similarly, that infant care and management, as well as the use of medical services, improve considerably as one passes from the 'lower manual working-class' mother to the 'upper middle-class' mother.

Thus equality of educational opportunity is not something that can suddenly begin at the age of five when compulsory education begins. Both physical and mental damage may have been done to the child in his early infancy to such an extent that very little that the school can do will be really effective in equalizing his opportunity. If his total constitution is undermined, his general health bad, and his physique malformed through ignorance, carelessness or sheer uninterest, he may be backward in his general educational progress.

Equally important are the parental interests and aspirations for their child in terms of education. It is a truism among teachers that somehow they always seem to be interviewing the 'wrong' parents. This, of course, is not strictly true since it is the very interest that these parents show in visiting the school that, in many instances, helps to provide the motivation for the child to do well or better and, therefore, they are in a very real sense the 'right' parents. But the teachers are right in the sense that the children who desperately need such parental attention and encouragement very often do not get it. J. W. B. Douglas has attempted to show that the children whose parents are interested in their educational welfare tend to pull ahead of the rest whatever their initial starting ability. He says:

'The children who are encouraged in their work by their parents are, it seems, at an advantage both in the relatively high scores they make in the tests and in the way they improve their scores between eight and eleven years' (38).

Douglas rightly asks the question how far the children have improved simply because they have been stimulated by their parents, and how far because the interested parents are likely to be relatively successful, and so will provide a more cultural environment for their children in the home. However, after the overlapping effects of the size of family, the standard of home, and the academic record of the school on test performance had been removed, the advantage of children with 'interested' parents, although reduced somewhat, was still considerable (39). But the parents' interest in, and their educational aspirations for, their children cannot be divorced from their own personal educational and cultural levels and the home environment they provide for their children. There is no such thing as 'interest' *in vacuo* in this context: there are only interested parents, and their interest is not something that can be 'partialled out' from the totality of their social, cultural, educational and personal development and experience.

There is no doubt that parents' attitudes help to condition their children's attitudes. A parent who shows a complete disregard for education, literacy, the niceties of social behaviour, or any form of social advancement is bound to have some adverse effect upon his children's educational progress. Children need, in a very real sense, to be *educated* to appreciate education. It is the example of parents – not so much their precepts, but what they really are – which affects children most. Parents who have not only left their schooldays behind them, but who also lack any further desire to learn or to continue their education through life, must inevitably demonstrate to their children the paucity of their own education and their lack of interest in it. One of the possible long-term effects of the Open University is the acceptance in an ever-increasing number of homes of the continuing influence of an educational ethos. But it is clearly something the school itself must seek to perpetuate – the concept that the school is merely one medium of education, and that education itself is a lifelong process.

Because there is a positive correlation between the measured I.Q. of parents and child (about $+ 0.5$), children in the higher social strata will *tend* to have higher measured I.Q.s than children in the lower social strata. Much can be done to promote the innate potential of a child; equally, a good deal is done to frustrate and depress it. In recent years there has been some considerable discussion as to whether intelligence is something that is fixed at birth or whether it can be 'acquired'. When the Newsom Report was published in 1963, the then Minister of Education (40) provided a Foreword in which he referred to the potentialities of pupils of average or less than average ability, between the ages of thirteen and sixteen, as

> 'no less real, and of no less importance, because they do not readily lend themselves to measurement by the conventional criteria of academic achievement. The essential point is that all children should have an equal opportunity of *acquiring intelligence*, and of developing their talents and abilities to the full' (41).

The assumption here is that intelligence is not entirely fixed at birth, but there do appear to be limits to the possibilities of further acquirement. Professor A. R. Jensen (42) has concluded, after some intensive research into the problem, that the inheritable component, as judged from the best overall estimates obtained from intelligence-test scores, is about 80 per cent.

In so far as I.Q. tests are used to establish the innate intellectual endowment of children, they are obviously limited if Professor Jensen and other psychologists are right. At the same time, they are 80 per cent or more reliable even in this respect. But as indicators of future academic success, by allocation to particular types of school, according to the findings of the National Foundation for Educational Research (N.F.E.R.) and other bodies, such I.Q. tests have been highly accurate in their prediction, as judged by the educational performance of pupils two to five years later. Sir Cyril Burt, in his discussion of 'The Mental Differences Between Children', quotes from the findings of the Report of the N.F.E.R. which maintains that 'the number of errors involved in such allocations amounts to about 10 per cent of the candidates' (43).

According to Burt, the time to assess each child's innate intelligence is when he first enters school, and not at eleven-plus, and it should be the responsibility of the child's class teacher to make these assessments. Such assessments should not be merely of general ability, but also of special talents and disabilities as they appear; moreover, for successful academic achievement it is necessary to take into account a child's physical health and fitness as well as his temperament and character (44). All these things are elements in the life chances of the pupil, and they are clearly not a matter simply of education or of the provision of 'equal opportunity' within education, whatever that might mean. Apart from the production of a society of genetically identical clones, there is very little one can do about making temperament and character equal, to say nothing of general intelligence. J. W. B. Douglas has emphasized that there are still wide inequalities in educational opportunity in different parts of the country and in different types of family (45). The child of working-class parents who has high innate intelligence potential may certainly suffer in comparison with a child of equal potential whose parents and home environment are middle class.

The danger of the perpetuation of such inequalities is increased, says Douglas, by the very 'self-fertilizing nature' of education. Well-educated parents will wish their own children to benefit as they have done from their good education, and will provide the necessary ethos, as well as sometimes the necessary cash, in order that this may be accomplished. A particular class, or occupation groups within a class, will build up a tradition of valuing education as of functional importance in society. In the Crowther Report of 1959, it was indicated that the chances of the children of professional and managerial parents continuing their education to seventeen or beyond were twenty-five times as many as those of the children of unskilled workers (46). Similarly, in 1963, the Robbins Report registered that 15 per cent of boys from non-manual classes entered university degree courses as against 3 per cent from manual classes (47). These figures were based on a sample survey and were admittedly subject to sampling errors. The corrected figures of 16·8 per cent and 2·6 per cent showed an even greater gap between the life chances of the children of non-manual and manual workers (48).

If the Crowther Report indicates the close association between a father's level of occupation and his children's educational achievement at school, the Robbins Report confirms that

'the association with parental occupation is, if anything, still closer where higher education is concerned. For example, the proportion of young people who enter full-time higher education is 45 per cent for those whose fathers are in the "higher professional" group, compared with only 4 per cent for those whose fathers are in skilled manual occupations. The underlying reasons for this are complex, but differences of income and of the parents' educational level and attitudes are certainly among them. The link is even more marked for girls than for boys' (49).

Thus, not only is there inequality as between social classes, there is also, for a variety of reasons, an inequality according to sex.

The Newsom and Plowden Reports in particular have emphasized that potential, as distinct from realized, ability among the children of the lower classes has been 'masked by inadequate powers of speech' (50). Linguistic inadequacy is closely associated with the home and social background, and this in turn affects the eliciting of intellectual potential. Professor B. Bernstein has done a considerable amount of research into this problem, and his main written contributions to date are quoted in the bibliography at the end of this chapter. We obviously cannot go into this important problem in any considerable detail here, but because of the cardinal importance of Bernstein's work and his contentions it is necessary to comment upon it at this juncture.

We understand, or apprehend, our world through our perceptions, and through the organization of our perceptions by means of language. We frame our concepts according to our vocabulary, our understanding of the meanings of words, and our competence in syntactical expression. In this respect it becomes clear that the working-class child, generally speaking, is at a disadvantage compared with the middle-class child. In the process of learning, the spoken language has a central role to play, and it is therefore not surprising that children are handicapped or helped in this respect long before they reach the age of compulsory schooling.

Status groups are distinguishable today much more by the forms of language they use than by any particular accent. The working-class child tends to use a 'restricted code' of language, in which the individual selection and manipulation of words will be severely restricted as well as highly predictable. Whilst the middle-class child may also use this code of language, particularly in the company of working-class children, he will not be restricted to it in the same way, and will eventually develop away from it. Some of the characteristics of the 'restricted code' are listed below, but for a fuller examination of both the restricted and the elaborated codes the reader is referred to the work of Professor Bernstein and to the critical analysis by D. Lawton (51):

1. The use of short sentences, which are simple in grammatical structure and uncomplicated in syntax.
2. Conjunctions employed are simple and repetitive, e.g. and, so, then, because ('cos).
3. Very few subordinate clauses are employed.
4. Short comments, commands and questions are repeatedly used.
5. There is very little competence in developing a sustained theme with sequential speech.
6. Information is purveyed in a disjointed and dislocated way.
7. There is a limited use of adjectives and adverbs, indicating a lack of imaginative and creative power linguistically.
8. There is a general inability to impersonalize or to create conditional statements by the use of such impersonal pronouns as 'it' or 'one'.
9. The symbolism employed is of a very low order, and there is a general incapacity to verbalize abstractions, or to express in a formal way any sort of abstract thought.
10. Much of the restricted code is implicit; statements and comments are expressed in a partial and unfinished manner so that the hearer is expected, or compelled, to make his own inference.
11. Statements are broken up with such stabilizers as, 'You see?', 'You know?', in order to gain confidence and the hearer's sympathetic acquiescence.

The middle-class child is much more likely to be brought up in an ethos of formal language, or in what Bernstein terms an 'elaborated code'. We are concerned here with the children of parents whose occupations will be largely involved in the use of words and their precise connotations. Language will tend to be much more an individual matter, and to form the vehicle for the expression of individual personality with its opinions and qualifications. Whilst the language of the working-class child is highly predictive, that of the child of middle-class parents is not nearly so. One thing that is important is that the child brought up in the atmosphere of the 'elaborated code' will have available to him a language structure capable of articulating and structuring his perceptions of the world and society around him, as well as his rapidly accumulating knowledge of an increasing variety of areas of learning. Socialization involves the ability to live in society in an understanding way: the child brought up with an 'elaborated code' will be able more competently to express the meanings of his world. The characteristics of the 'elaborated code' are as follows:

1. The sentence construction is more complex, introducing a greater variety of stress and logical modification. The grammatical order employed and the regulating syntax are accurate.
2. A larger range of conjunctions is employed, many of them introducing a variety of subordinate clauses.
3. Prepositions are employed not merely to express spatial contiguity but also logical and temporal relationships.
4. There is an increasing ability to impersonalize ideas, statements and opinions, by the introduction of impersonal pronouns.
5. There is a richer employment of both adjectives and adverbs, indicating a greater creative linguistic ability.
6. There is a greater use of subordinate clauses.
7. There is a considerable use of symbolism of a higher order to discriminate and distinguish between meanings within speech sequences. There is a greater facility in the expression of abstract thought in concrete terms.
8. The elaborated code is explicit; statements and comments are completed, and ideas are mediated and modified through the actual structure of the sentences.
9. The child's conceptual hierarchy is gradually formulated in verbal terms in an increasingly accurate and meaningful way (52).

In his *Social Class, Language and Education*, D. Lawton applies the principle of restricted and elaborated codes to written work as well as to speech. The problem for education, as he sees it, is deliberately to intervene in the language habits of the working-class family in order that those individuals who have higher innate intellectual ability may be facilitated through the media of communication to realize that potential. There is also a suggestion, in this intervention or compensatory programme, of the employment of social workers who might be attached to schools in order to co-operate with working-class parents and ensure that their children are in no way disadvantaged because of their social class background.

But can education really compensate for society in this way? Can it, in fact, compensate for society at all? There are clearly limits to such compensation (53). The whole environment of the working-class child militates against any formal sort of education, for the school demands responses which, on the whole, are very different from those to which the child is accustomed in the home. The child finds himself faced by a teacher who belongs to a different class from himself, and to whose speech patterns and mental concepts he is not 'cued in'. The working-class child will react strongly against any attempts to improve his speech and expression, and because of this he will find the manipulation of abstractions difficult, if not impossible. The disjointed and naïve description of concrete events will come much more easily to him than abstract analysis of ideas and concepts. He is already disadvantaged. And, moreover, the different patterns of the school and the staff may well be viewed as a criticism of those of his own home and his peer group, a criticism which he will strongly resist and which may well create an attitude of antipathy towards the school's socializing influence (54).

In his discussion of 'A New Society?' Professor Robin Pedley states that our first need is a culturally rich environment of the neighbourhood, the home and the school within which children can both learn and grow (55). And this principle applies whatever name we may, in the end, give to the school. A non-purpose-built neighbourhood 'comprehensive' school in a socially deprived, slum area can be as culturally and education-ally damaging as a 'secondary modern' school might be in the same area. There may certainly be little cross-fertilization of social classes, for as Mr R. R. Pedley, Headmaster of St Dunstan's College, has pointed out the 'social mix' in such a school as Manchester Grammar School is far greater than in the normal neighbourhood comprehensive school (56). The home and social class influences are stronger than those of the school and are in fact taken into the school. A child's home environment will fundamentally affect his perceptions, his personality development and his inter-personal relationships, and the school may well fight a losing battle in the realm of the evocation of a child's potential because of a social barrier at the level of communication.

We have considered the question of language in some detail because of its sociological importance. There are many other important questions that we can do no more than mention in an introductory work of this sort. For example, the opportunities for leisure-time activities are increasing, but the nature of the activities pursued by individuals is largely a reflection of their social background and learning. If the sum-total of our happiness depends not only upon work, but also upon leisure – indeed, for many it may depend far more on the latter than on the former – then somehow the education of the school must provide for the successful fulfilment of this need.

Again, the welfare state has increased the life chances of many in terms of further and higher education, in particular of university education. Many have availed themselves, and many more will continue to avail themselves, of the opportunity of studying for three or more years at a university. Much of this opportunity is provided without a consideration of how far and in what way society can absorb an ever-increasing number of intellectuals, many of whom have no immediate vocational aims in mind, and who form an open stratum referred to by Karl Mannheim as the 'relatively uncommitted Intelligentsia' (*relativ freischwebende Intelligenz*), because they are least uniform in their social and political behaviour or allegiance (57). The creation and perpetuation of such an intelligentsia must inevitably involve also the production of many who cannot find any commitment or allegiance at all, nor indeed any real vocation in life. Short of detailed research it would be a matter of mere speculation as to whether the largest number of intellectual 'drop-outs' came from one particular class or another; but the question may well be related to the extent of social mobility and social acceptance experienced by the lower strata of society.

There is in our society an increasing attempt to provide conditions for equality of opportunity in education. It is at the same time being realized that such equality of opportunity as can be achieved in a democratic society is not simply a matter of educational legislation whereby all children are able, or are made, to attend precisely the same types of school. The existing social stratification inevitably presents a variety of conditions which, prior to the beginning of the period of compulsory schooling, to a large extent determine the child's perceptive ability, his character and personality, and his relationships. Whatever may be done by the educational system for the child from the age of five onwards, if he is largely socially determined before he reaches that age, and if he is still greatly influenced by forces outside the school throughout his period of education, we cannot really speak in terms of 'equality of opportunity'.

If we still have egalitarian ideals we must push the educational and socializing process farther and farther back, and take fuller control of it, through day nurseries and nursery schools. Or, perhaps we may be driven to agree with Durkheim when he says:

'In sum, education, far from having as its unique or principal object the individual and his interests, is above all the means by which society perpetually recreates the conditions of its very existence. Can society survive only if there exists among its members a sufficient homogeneity? Education perpetuates and reinforces this homogeneity by fixing in advance, in the mind of the child, the essential similarities that collective life presupposes. But, on the other hand, without a certain diversity, would all co-operation be impossible? Education assures the persistence of this necessary diversity by becoming itself diversified and by specializing. It consists, then, in one or another of its aspects, of a systematic socialization of the young generation' (58).

Homogeneity and diversity are both essential ingredients in any society, and any educational or socializing process must be concerned with the preservation of both.

REFERENCES

1 *Vide* Rosenfeld, Eva, 'Social Stratification in a "Classless" Society', *American Sociological Review*, Vol. 16, December 1951, pp. 766–74.
2 Ibid., p. 774.
3 Schwartz, R. D., 'Functional Alternatives to Inequality', *American Sociological Review*, Vol. 20, August 1955, p. 426.
4 MacIver, R. M., and Page, C. H., *Society: An Introductory Analysis* (Macmillan, 1950; reprinted 1957), p. 358.
5 Thapar, Romila, *A History of India: Vol. I* (Penguin Books, 1966), pp. 38–9.
6 The Sanskrit word for 'caste' is *varna*, meaning 'colour'.
7 *Vide* Zinkin, Taya, *Caste Today* (O.U.P., 1962).
8 Wint, G., *The British in India* (Faber, 1947), p. 41.
9 Zinkin, Taya, op. cit., pp. 1–2.
10 *Vide* Hutton, J. H., *Caste in India* (O.U.P., 4th edition 1963), pp. 133–48.
11 Bottomore, T. B., *Sociology: A Guide to Problems and Literature* (Allen and Unwin, 1962; 2nd edition 1971), p. 189.
12 Srinivas, M. N., 'The Social Structure of a Mysore Village', in Srinivas, M. N. (ed.), *India's Villages* (Asia Publishing House, N.Y., 2nd revised edition 1960), pp. 21–35.
13 Ibid., p. 29.
14 Stalcup, R. J., *Sociology and Education* (C. E. Merrill Pub. Co., Ohio, U.S.A., 1968), p. 78.
15 Raynor, J., *The Middle Class* (Longmans, 1969), p. 11.
16 Hall, J. and Caradog Jones, D., 'Social Grading of Occupations', *British Journal of Sociology*, Vol. 1, No. 1, 1950.
17 Mitchell, G. D., *Sociology: The Study of Social Systems* (University Tutorial Press, 1959; reprinted 1963).
18 Parsons, T., 'The Professions and Social Structure', *Social Forces*, Vol. 17, May 1939, pp. 457–67.
19 Ibid., p. 460.
20 *Vide* Marx, K., *Manifesto of the Communist Party* (C. H. Kerr, Chicago, 1888), Section 1, pp. 12–32.
21 Ibid., p. 12.
22 *Vide* Birnbaum, N., 'Conflicting Interpretations of the Rise of Capitalism: Marx and Weber', *British Journal of Sociology*, Vol. IV, June 1953, pp. 125–41.
23 *Vide* Rosenfeld, Eva, op. cit., in note 1.
24 Lenin, Nicolai, *State and Revolution* (International Publishers, N.Y., 1932), from Chapter V, pp. 84–105, reprinted in Parsons, T., *Theories of Society* (Free Press, Glencoe, 1965), p. 586.
25 Inkeles, A., 'Social Stratification and Mobility in the Soviet Union: 1940–1950', *American Sociological Review*, Vol. 15, August 1905, pp. 465–79.
26 Dahrendorf, R., 'Recent Changes in the Class Structure of European

Societies', *Daedalus*, Vol. 93, No. 1, Winter 1964, pp. 225–70. This important essay has been reprinted in the Bobbs-Merrill Reprint Series in the Social Sciences, S-564.

27 Ibid., p. 252.

28 *Vide* Russell, B., *Power: A New Social Analysis* (Allen and Unwin, 1938; 7th impression 1957). Cf. also Cole, G. D. H., *Studies in Class Structure* (Routledge, 1955; 3rd impression 1964).

29 Dahrendorf, R., op. cit., pp. 262–3.

30 Green, B. S. R. and Johns, E. A., *An Introduction to Sociology* (Pergamon Press, 1966; reprinted 1968), p. 88.

31 Durkheim, E., *Education and Sociology* (originally published by Alcan, Paris, 1922; Free Press, Glencoe, 1956), p. 67.

32 Douglas, J. W. B., *The Home and the School* (MacGibbon and Kee, 1964; Panther 1967).

33 Floud, J. E. *et al.*, *Social Class and Educational Opportunity* (Heinemann, 1956).

34 Davis, A., *Social Class Influences on Learning* (Harvard Univ. Press, 1948).

35 Mays, J. B., *Education and the Urban Child* (Liverpool Univ. Press, 1962).

36 Douglas, J. W. B., op. cit., p. 75; and 'Class Differences in Life Chances 2', in Butterworth, E. and Weir, D., *The Sociology of Modern Britain* (Fontana, Collins, 1970), pp. 218–19. This article is reprinted from Meade, J. E. and Parkes, A. S. (eds), *Biological Aspects of Social Problems* (Oliver and Boyd, 1965), p. 86.

37 Arie, T., 'Class and Disease', *New Society*, 27 January 1966.

38 Douglas, J. W. B., *The Home and the School*, p. 86.

39 Ibid., p. 86 and Table C, p. 170.

40 The Rt Hon. Sir Edward C. G. Boyle, Bart., M.P.

41 Ministry of Education, *Half Our Future* (Newsom Report) (H.M.S.O., 1963), Foreword, p. iv; my italics.

42 Jensen, A. R., 'How Far Can we Boost I.Q. and Scholastic Achievement?', *Harvard Educational Review*, Vol. 39, 1969, pp. 1–123.

43 *Vide* Burt, C., 'The Mental Differences Between Children', in Cox, C. B. and Dyson, A. E. (eds), *The Crisis in Education: Black Paper Two* (The Critical Quarterly Society, 2 Radcliffe Avenue, London, N.W. 10, 1969), pp. 16–25; especially pp. 19–20.

44 Ibid., p. 20, col. 2.

45 Douglas, J. W. B., 'Class Differences in Life Chances 2', in Butterworth, E. and Weir, D., op. cit., p. 219.

46 *Vide* Ministry of Education, *15 to 18*, Vol. II (Crowther Report) (H.M.S.O., 1959), Part One, 'The Social Survey', Chapter 1, 'Home Background and Some Factors affecting the Age of Leaving School', and Part Two, 'The National Service Survey', Chapter 1, 'The Distribution of Latent Ability School and Family, School Leaving'.

47 *Vide* Committee on Higher Education, *Higher Education* (Robbins Report) (H.M.S.O., 1963), Table 21, p. 50.

48 *Vide* Committee on Higher Education, *Higher Education: Appendix I*

(Robbins Report) (H.M.S.O., 1963), 'The Demand for Places in Higher Education'.

49 *Higher Education* (Robbins Report), pp. 50–1.
50 *Vide Half Our Future*, paras. 3, 50 and 86; and D.E.S., *Children and their Primary Schools* (Plowden Report) (H.M.S.O., 1967), paras 53–64, 97 and 302.
51 *Vide* Lawton, D., *Social Class, Language and Education* (Routledge, 1968).
52 *Vide* ibid.
53 *Vide* Bernstein, B., 'Education cannot compensate for Society', *New Society*, 26 February 1970.
54 *Vide* P. W. Musgrave's discussion of some of the problems of social class learning in his *The Sociology of Education* (Methuen, 1965; reprinted 1968), pp. 66–76.
55 Pedley, Robin, *The Comprehensive School* (Penguin Books, 1963; reprinted with revisions 1966), p. 31.
56 Pedley, R. R., 'Comprehensive Disaster' in Cox, C. B. and Dyson, A. E. (eds), *Fight for Education: A Black Paper* (The Critical Quarterly Society, 1969), p. 47.
57 Mannheim, K., *Essays on the Sociology of Culture* (Routledge, 1956; 2nd impression 1962), p. 106.
58 Durkheim, E., *Education and Sociology*, pp. 123–4.

BIBLIOGRAPHY

A. *Books*

BANKS, OLIVE, *The Sociology of Education* (Batsford, 1968; 2nd impression 1969), Chapters 3–5, pp. 39–110.
BARBER, B., *Social Stratification: A Comparative Analysis of Structure and Process* (Harcourt, Brace and Co., 1957).
BELL, C. R. *Middle Class Families* (Routledge, 1969).
BENDIX, R. and LIPSET, A. M. (eds), *Class, Status and Power* (Routledge, 1953; 3rd impression 1966).
BOTTOMORE, T. B., *Sociology* (Allen and Unwin, 1962; 2nd edition 1971), Chapter 11, pp. 185–214.
BOTTOMORE, T. B., *Elites and Society* (C. A. Watts, 1964; Penguin Books, 1966).
BOTTOMORE, T. B., *Classes in Modern Society* (Allen and Unwin, 1965; 4th impression 1969).
BRANDIS, W. and HENDERSON, D., *Social Class, Language and Communication* (Routledge, 1969).
BRIEFS, G., *The Proletariat* (McGraw-Hill, 1938).
BURNHAM, J., *The Managerial Revolution* (Putnam, 1943; Penguin Books).
BUTTERWORTH, E. and WEIR, D. (eds), *The Sociology of Modern Britain: An Introductory Reader* (Fontana Library, Collins, 1970).
CARR-SAUNDERS, A. M. and CARADOG JONES, D., *A Survey of the Social*

Structure of England and Wales as Illustrated by Statistics (O.U.P., 1927; revised edition 1958).

CARR-SAUNDERS, A. M. and WILSON, P. A., *The Professions* (Clarendon Press, 1933).

COLE, G. D. H., *Studies in Class Structure* (Routledge, 1955; 3rd impression 1964).

COTGROVE, S., *The Science of Society* (Allen and Unwin, 1967; 9th impression 1970).

DAHRENDORF, R., *Class and Class Conflict in Industrial Society* (Routledge, 1959; revised edition 1965).

DAVIS, A., *Social Class Influences on Learning* (Harvard Univ. Press, 1948).

DAVIS, K., *Human Society* (Macmillan, 1948).

DOLLARD, J., *Caste and Class in a Southern Town* (New Haven, U.S.A., 1937).

DOUGLAS, J. W. B., *The Home and the School* (MacGibbon and Kee, 1964; Panther 1967).

FLOUD, J. E. et al., *Social Class and Educational Opportunity* (Heinemann, 1956).

FORD, JULIENNE, *Social Class and the Comprehensive School* (Routledge, 1969).

GERTH, H. and MILLS, C. W. (eds), *From Max Weber: Essays in Sociology* (Routledge, 1948; 5th impression 1964).

GLASS, D. V. (ed.), *Social Mobility in Britain* (Routledge, 1954; 2nd impression 1963).

GOLDTHORPE, J. H. et al., *The Affluent Worker in the Class Structure* (C.U.P., 1969).

HALBWACHS, M., *The Psychology of Social Classes* (Heinemann, 1958).

HALSEY, A. H. et al., *Education, Economy and Society* (Free Press, Glencoe, 1961).

HARGREAVES, D. H., *Social Relations in a Secondary School* (Routledge, 1967).

HICKS, J. R., *The Social Framework* (O.U.P., 3rd edition 1960).

HUTTON, J. H., *Caste in India* (O.U.P., 4th edition 1963).

JACKSON, B., *Working Class Community* (Routledge, 1968).

JACKSON, B. and MARSDEN, D., *Education and the Working Class* (Routledge, 1962).

JACKSON, J. A. (ed.), *Social Stratification* (C.U.P., 1969).

KAHL, J. A., *The American Class Structure* (Holt, Rinehart and Winston, 1959).

LAWTON, D., *Social Class, Language and Education* (Routledge, 1968).

LEWIS, R. and MAUDE, A., *The English Middle Classes* (Penguin Books, 1953).

LOCKWOOD, D., *The Blackcoated Worker: A Study in Class Consciousness* (Allen and Unwin, 1958; 2nd edition 1966, 3rd impression 1969).

MACIVER, R. M. and PAGE, C. H., *Society: An Introductory Analysis* (Macmillan, 1950; reprinted 1957), Chapter 14, pp. 348–83.

MARSHALL, T. H., *Citizenship and Social Class* (C.U.P., 1950).

MARSHALL, T. H. (ed.), *Class, Conflict and Social Stratification* (Le Play House, 1938).

MAYER, K. B., *Class and Society* (Doubleday, N.Y., 1955).

MAYS, J. B., *Education and the Urban Child* (Liverpool Univ. Press, 1962).

MCKINLEY, D. G., *Social Class and Family Life* (Free Press, Glencoe, 1964).

MERTON, R. K., *Social Theory and Social Structure* (Free Press, Glencoe, 1949).

MILLS, C. W., *White Collar: The American Middle Classes* (O.U.P., 1951).

MILLS, C. W., *The Power Elite* (O.U.P., 1956).

MITCHELL, G. D., *Sociology* (University Tutorial Press, 1959; reprinted 1963), Chapters VII and VIII, pp. 109–39.

MUSGRAVE, P. W., *The Sociology of Education* (Methuen, 1956; reprinted 1968), Chapters 4 and 5, pp. 48–82.

MUSGROVE, F., *Youth and the Social Order* (Routledge, 1964).

NADEL, S. F., *The Theory of Social Structure* (Cohen and West, 1957; 2nd impression 1962).

OTTAWAY, A. K. C., *Education and Society* (Routledge, 2nd edition, revised 1962; reprinted 1968), Chapter VI, pp. 103–24.

PARSONS, T., *Theories of Society* (Free Press, Glencoe, 1965), Part Two, 'Differentiation and Variation in Social Structures', pp. 237–682.

PEAR, T. H., *English Social Differences* (Allen and Unwin, 1955).

RADCLIFFE-BROWN, A. R., *Structure and Function in Primitive Society* (Cohen and West, 1952; 5th impression 1963), 'On Social Structure', pp. 188–204.

RAYNOR, J., *The Middle Class* (Longmans, 1969).

ROSE, G., *The Working Class* (Longmans, 1968).

RUNCIMAN, W. G., *Relative Deprivation and Social Justice* (Routledge, 1966).

SCHUMPETER, J., *Imperialism and Social Classes* (Blackwell, 1951).

SPINLEY, B. M., *The Deprived and the Privileged* (Routledge, 1953).

SRINIVAS, M. N., *Caste in Modern India* (Asia Publishing House, 1962).

TAWNEY, R. H., *Equality* (Allen and Unwin; 5th edition 1965).

TUMIN, M. M., *Social Stratification: The Forms and Functions Of Inequality* (Prentice-Hall International, 1968).

VEBLEN, T., *The Theory of the Leisure Class* (Allen and Unwin, 1925; 3rd impression 1957).

WEBER, MAX, *The Theory of Social and Economic Organization* (tr. Henderson, A. M. and Parsons, T.; Free Press, Glencoe, 1947).

B. *Articles*

BERNSTEIN, B., 'Some Sociological Determinants of Perception', *British Journal of Sociology*, Vol. 9, June 1958, pp. 161–6.

BERNSTEIN, B., 'A Public Language: Some Sociological Implications of a Linguistic Form', *British Journal of Soiology*, Vol. 10, 1959, pp. 159–74.

BERNSTEIN, B., 'Language and Social Class', *British Journal of Sociology*, Vol. 11, September 1960, pp. 271–6.

BERNSTEIN, B., 'Social Class and Linguistic Development: A Theory of Social Learning', in Halsey, A. H. *et al.*, *Education, Economy and Society* (Free Press, Glencoe, 1961).

BERNSTEIN, B., 'Social Structure, Language and Learning', *Educational Research*, Vol. 3, No. 3, June 1961, pp. 163–76.

BERNSTEIN, B., 'Linguistic Codes, Hesitation Phenomena and Intelligence', *Language and Speech*, Vol. 5, 1962, pp. 31–46.

BERNSTEIN, B., 'Social Class, Linguistic Codes and Grammatical Elements', *Language and Speech*, Vol. 5, 1962, pp. 221–40.

BERNSTEIN, B., 'A Socio-Linguistic Approach to Social Learning', *Penguin Survey of the Social Sciences* (Penguin Books, 1965), pp. 144–66.

BERNSTEIN, B., 'A Socio-Linguistic Approach to Socialization', in Gumperz, J. and Holmes, D. (eds), *Directions in Socio-Linguistics* (Holt, Rinehart and Winston, 1969).

BERNSTEIN, B., 'Social Class, Language and Socialization', in Minnis, N. (ed.), *Language at Large* (Gollancz, 1970).

BERNSTEIN, B., 'Education cannot compensate for Society', *New Society*, 26 February 1970.

BERNSTEIN, B. and BRANDIS, W., 'Social Class Differences in Communication and Control', in Brandis, W. and Henderson, D. (eds), *Social Class, Language and Communication* (Routledge, 1969).

BERNSTEIN, B. and HENDERSON, D., 'Social Class Differences in the Relevance of Language to Socialization', *Sociology*, Vol. 3, No. 1, January 1969, pp. 1–20.

BERNSTEIN, B. and YOUNG, D., 'Some Aspects of the Relationship between Communication and Performance in Tests', in Meade, J. E. and Parkes, A. S. (eds), *Genetic and Environmental Factors in Human Ability* (Oliver and Boyd, 1966).

BIRNBAUM, N., 'Conflicting Interpretations of the Rise of Capitalism: Marx and Weber', *British Journal of Sociology*, Vol. 4, June 1953, pp. 125–41.

DAHRENDORF, R., 'Recent Changes in the Class Structure of European Societies', *Daedalus*, Vol. 93, No. 1, Winter 1964.

DAVIS, K. and MOORE, W. E., 'Some Principles of Stratification', *American Sociological Review*, Vol. 10, 1945, pp. 242–9.

DEUTSCH, M., 'The Role of Social Class in Language Development and Cognition', *American Journal of Orthopsychiatry*, Vol. 35, No. 1, 1965.

GOLDTHORPE, J. H., 'Social Stratification in Industrial Society', *Sociological Review*, Monograph 8, October 1964, pp. 97–122.

GOLDTHORPE, J. H. and LOCKWOOD, D., 'Affluence and the British Class Structure', *Sociological Review*, Vol. 11, No. 2, July 1963, pp. 133–63.

GOLDTHORPE, J. H., LOCKWOOD, D., BECHHOFER, F. and PLATT, J., 'The Affluent Worker and the Thesis of *Embourgeoisement*: Some Preliminary Research Findings', *Sociology*, Vol. 1, No. 1, January 1967, pp. 11–31.

HALL, J. and CARADOG JONES, D., 'Social Grading of Occupations', *British Journal of Sociology*, Vol. 1, No. 1, 1950.

HATT, P. K., 'Occupation and Social Stratification', *American Journal of Sociology*, Vol. 55, May 1950, pp. 533–43.

INKELES, A., 'Social Stratification and Mobility in the Soviet Union: 1940–1950', *American Sociological Review*, Vol. 15, August 1950, pp. 465–79.

LEE, D. J., 'Class Differentials in Educational Opportunity and Promotions from the Ranks', *Sociology*, Vol. 2, No. 3, September 1968, pp. 293–312.

MACRAE, D. G., 'Social Stratification', *Current Sociology*, Vol. 2, No. 1, 1953–4.

MARSHALL, T. H., 'Social Class – A Preliminary Analysis', *Sociological Review*, Vol. 26, 1934, pp. 55–76.

PARSONS, T., 'The Professions and Social Structure', *Social Forces*, Vol. 17, May 1939, pp. 457–67.

PARSONS, T., 'Analytical Approach to the Theory of Social Stratification', *American Journal of Sociology*, Vol. 45, 1940, pp. 841–62.

ROSENFELD, E., 'Social Stratification in a "Classless" Society', *American Sociological Review*, Vol. 16, December 1951, pp. 766–74.

RUNCIMAN, W. G., 'Embourgeoisement: Self-Rated Class and Party Preference', *Sociological Review*, July 1964.

SCHATZMAN, L. and STRAUSS, A., 'Social Class and Modes of Communication', *American Journal of Sociology*, Vol. 60, January 1955.

SCHWARTZ, R. D., 'Functional Alternatives to Inequality', *American Sociological Review*, Vol. 20, August 1955, pp. 424–30.

SWIFT, D. F., 'Social Class and Achievement Motivation', *Educational Research*, Vol. 8, No. 2, 1966, pp. 83–95.

TOOMEY, D. M., 'Home-Centred Working Class Parents' Attitudes towards their Sons' Education and Careers', *Sociology*, Vol. 3, No. 3, September 1969, pp. 299–320.

NOTE: Many of the articles referred to in the text and in the bibliographies have been reprinted in the Bobbs-Merrill Reprint Series in the Social Sciences, Bobbs-Merrill Company Inc.

Chapter 8
Social Mobility and Education

A. THE MEANING OF SOCIAL MOBILITY

Social mobility is basically the movement of individuals, or groups of individuals, from one social position to another; such a movement may be up or down between the classes in any social hierarchy or stratification (that is, vertical mobility), or it may occur within a particular social class (that is, horizontal mobility). In his discussion of this topic, J. A. Schumpeter (1) regarded the abilities of persons as the key to upward mobility, although he provided a variety of reasons why both individuals and families might rise or fall within a particular class, or might move from one class to another. Without considering all the details of his arguments, we may note his suggestion that the history of mobility has elicited the following causes, some of which are more important factors in mobility than others.

Thus, for example, a man whose status and wealth are really invested in his possession of land may find that his property has suddenly, or over a period of years, appreciated or depreciated. This will mean that, although he still has the status of a landowner, his style of living may be considerably improved or may suffer. Social mobility may also occur through the sort of power which accrues to certain families, not merely via nepotism but because of the fact that they are in a favourable position for self-advancement. Skill and success in war have also been the cause of advancement of certain notable individuals, including many others who have suddenly discovered that the services were, in fact, their particular *métier* and their ideal *milieu* for upward mobility. Some, more particularly women, have improved their social status through marriage; others have found the economic and social climate right – or wrong – for them through large-scale industrialization, automation, or investment.

The barriers of class are clearly not insurmountable, but the French philosopher Edmond Goblot, in his sociological study of the modern French bourgeoisie, has made the point that the latter attach considerable importance to keeping their distance from manual labour (2). It is not sufficient for the social climber to have the qualities, aptitudes, intelligence and knowledge requisite for his profession; both he and his family must be able to live in a social *milieu* consonant with that profession. The barriers, indeed, may not be insurmountable, but there is already implicit in the social stratification a certain 'social distance' that has to be negotiated. There are patterns and life-styles that have to be learned and inculcated for full acceptance, and very often the successful confidence-trickster is a person who knows how to 'cue in' to the levels of a particular social group.

There are, of course, many who believe that, so long as they have developed the patterns of consumption of a higher class, they have automatically moved into that class. Vance Packard makes the point that advertisers are continually inviting the factory operative to upgrade, not through his productive role in life, which is the cause of his 'social distance' but by adopting the consuming patterns of people in the higher classes (3). But social stratification is not just, or even, a question of patterns of consumption. Many factory workers and unskilled labourers have reached their maximum pecuniary reward at a relatively early age, whilst many a white-collar worker is still struggling on the lower rungs of a ladder which may eventually lead to high position, power and reward. However comparable or incomparable their levels of consumption may be at the moment, the consumption potential of the white-collar workers is greater than that of the factory wage-earners even though, as Packard suggests, the former are attempting to live like the 'semi-upper-class people, often on working-class incomes' (4).

B. THE THEORY OF 'EMBOURGEOISEMENT'

This leads us to a discussion of the thesis of *embourgeoisement* which has received considerable attention during the past decade, mainly due to the research of John H. Goldthorpe, David Lockwood and their associates. In their essay, 'Affluence and the British Class Structure' (5), Goldthorpe and Lockwood emphasized that, as a result of increasing educational opportunity, the extent of inter-generational mobility has tended to increase. In consequence, the *stability* of social strata has diminished, and although the system of social stratification has become increasingly fine in its gradations, it is at the same time less rigid and extreme (6).

In recent years a claim has been made that, through the increasing 'affluence' of the working class, a more prosperous section of the latter is in the process of losing its identity and is becoming merged into the higher, middle class. In other words,

'The contention is that today many manual wage-earning workers and their families are becoming socially indistinguishable from the members of other groups – those of blackcoated workers, minor professionals and technicians, for example – who were previously their social superiors' (7).

This contention implies, in turn, not merely economic advance but also changes in aspirations, attitudes, values, behavioural patterns and in social relationships.

This social trend is graced with the term *embourgeoisement*, or the turning of the working-class 'proletariat' into 'bourgeoisie'. And it has also been invested with political implications, particularly in regard to the third successive defeat of the Labour Party in 1959, where it is suggested there occurred an erosion of traditional working-class attitudes by the steady increase of affluence. Thus, 'People who would be objectively classified as working class in terms of occupation or family background have acquired a middle-class income and pattern of consumption, and sometimes a middle-class psychology' (8).

In passing, it is interesting to note that there is usually a greater emphasis upon mobility *upwards* than upon mobility *downwards* in discussions on social mobility. In terms of human aspirations this is only natural; in terms of sociological objectivity it may tend to conceal the true facts. In this respect it is also of some significance to note the definition of 'proletariat' in a contemporary dictionary of politics, which states that:

'Definitions of the limits of the proletarian class vary; at one time only manual workers were included, but a process of "proletarianization" of the middle class is discernible in some countries, particularly where (as in the U.K.) many manual workers can earn more than professional or white-collar workers' (9).

In the long run this might prove to be a fairer description of the social process under consideration, but obviously a lot depends upon whether the criteria one is using are of an economic or social status nature, or both.

Goldthorpe and Lockwood go on to analyse the chief sociological implications of the *embourgeoisement* of the more prosperous of our manual wage workers (10). These implications are three in number, namely, economic, normative and relational. The *economic* aspect of class suggests that these workers and their families are in the process of acquiring a standard of living which, in terms of both income and material possessions or consumption, puts them on a level with at least the lower strata of the middle class. The *normative* aspect of class suggests that these workers are also acquiring new norms of behaviour, and new attitudes and perspectives, which are more characteristic of the middle class. The *relational* aspect of class suggests that these workers are being accepted by the middle class on terms of equality in both formal and informal interaction, because they are essentially similar to many middle-class persons 'in their economic position and their normative orientation' (11).

The treatment of the *economic* aspect of class in the theory of *embourgeoisement* is considered both incomplete and unconvincing by

Goldthorpe and Lockwood. Economic parity is not just a question of income and consumption patterns, important though these may be. Terms of employment, for example, are very relevant in any sort of comparison between members of the working and middle classes. Few manual workers are employed on the basis of long-term wage contracts, and so, unlike the professional classes, are more likely to be dismissed at short notice. Some teachers may earn less than some factory workers, but they are far less likely to become redundant. Moreover, there is far more occupational upward mobility within the middle class generally than within the working class.

Thus, the prospects of advancement, coupled with such fringe benefits as pension schemes and sickness benefit, all add up to security for the middle-class person. Economic parity certainly does not of itself provide equal opportunities for parity of esteem in society; and in the division of labour the importance of the actual role played by the individual has status value which brings its own rewards. And although matters may have changed somewhat during the past twenty years, A. Inkeles reported that, even in Soviet Russia, where one might have expected 'proletarianization', if not *embourgeoisement*, on a large scale,

> 'Ordinary citizens, of course, have very slight chances of qualifying for awards in the arts and sciences, but even in the case of prizes granted for inventions and fundamental improvements in production methods there is almost no representation of the rank and file worker or even of the lower ranks of industrial management such as foremen' (12).

Equally, the *relational* aspect of class is almost entirely disregarded by proponents of the *embourgeoisement* thesis. Goldthorpe and Lockwood argue that research studies tend to emphasize a status segregation within the realms of housing, neighbourhood relations both formal and informal, friendship groups, and membership of local clubs, organizations, societies and so forth. Certainly there is a need to investigate this 'status gap' further and to analyse the reasons for it, including the extent to which differences in work status are carried over into the context of voluntary associations.

In the factory and the workshop there are clear lines of demarcation between the management and the manual worker, between the wages clerk and the factory assistant. There is the area of authority and the area of subordination involving different social amenities within the same institution for different groups – a variety of canteens and clubs, as well as conditions of work, from time-keeping to toilets. How far do these separate status groups meet outside the walls of their work institution, even if they live in the same area? There is no clear evidence at present that economic parity necessarily involves with it a closing of the status gap and an acceptance of the manual workers by the middle class on terms of equality in both formal and informal social interaction.

The *normative* aspect of class is discussed by Goldthorpe and Lockwood at some length, and they regard the arguments relating to the changing patterns of family and community life, as well as the attitude and opinion surveys of manual workers, as being generally unsatisfactory. Those who argue in favour of *embourgeoisement* as a fact point to the decline of gregariousness and of the communal forms of sociability which are held to be characteristic of the traditional type of urban working-class locality. They speak of the emergence of a home-centred and family-centred existence, and of a growing preoccupation with money and with the acquisition of material possessions. Coupled with this there is, it is argued, an increasing concern with personal status instead of class solidarity, with an emphasis on the welfare of the children and their future hopes and aspirations.

The authors conclude, however, that these normative factors cannot be viewed in isolation, but that they must be seen as

'closely linked to changes in the structure of social relationships in industrial, community and family life, which are in turn related not only to growing prosperity but also to advances in industrial organization and technology, to the process of urban development, to demographic trends, and to the solution of mass communications and "mass culture"' (13).

In consequence, they conclude that what we are experiencing in our society is not a general movement towards 'middle-classness' or the *embourgeoisement* of the working classes, but rather a far-reaching adaptation and development of the traditional working-class way of life under considerably changed physical and economic conditions. In a later essay on the same theme (14), the authors have reiterated and reinforced these conclusions with a considerable amount of research material, and emphasized that the *direction* of the changes involved is not towards 'middle-classness', but rather towards a more 'privatized' mode of living on the part of certain elements among the working classes.

C. EDUCATION AND SOCIAL MOBILITY

The important question now arises concerning the relationship between education and social mobility. Some writers have suggested that education acts as a sort of 'blocking' agent, reinforcing the present social situation; others seem to suggest that the only gospel of salvation for the 'have-nots' is through improved forms of education. Olive Banks has stated unequivocally that 'Opportunity to rise in the economic and social scale depends less and less upon the accumulation of small capital, more and more on the possession of degrees and diplomas' (15). P. W. Musgrave agrees that one can hardly be considered to be a member of the middle class unless the occupation one pursues requires 'a relatively high level of education' (16). Thus it would appear that social mobility is achieved through the passing of examinations rather than through any sort of *embourgeoisement* process. And in our society the examinations which have been of supreme importance at the school level have been the eleven-plus selection, and the 'O' and 'A' level examinations. Success in these examinations has, by and large, spelt success in upward social mobility; individual achievement in the realms of education has been the key to success in the realms of society.

But to state it thus is perhaps to oversimplify the situation somewhat, and studies of comparative social mobility are not always convincing or helpful since they present comparisons between essentially different situations. Different societies have very different sorts of social structure, and any comparison of mobility between the United States, Great Britain and Soviet Russia, for example, must bear in mind not simply differing classificatory systems but also questions of political and social ideology.

In a study of comparative social mobility, S. M. Miller researched the inter-generational mobility within a total of eighteen countries (17). He concluded that there was, in general, a far more widespread movement of the sons of manual workers into white-collar jobs than had been anticipated. The percentage of such mobility in nine of the countries was between 24 and 31; in one urban sample from industrial Poona the mobility rate was of the order of 27 per cent. Miller, however, indicated that *downward* mobility was equally common and, quoting Puerto Rico, Great Britain and the Netherlands as examples, he found that more than 40 per cent of the sons of men in white-collar jobs became manual, industrial workers (18).

Obviously one cannot take comparative statistics such as these at their face value since we are dealing with societies, not only with different forms of social structure, but also with different systems and ideas of education. In addition, there are greatly differing economic forces and roles in operation. Upward mobility in one society may well be due to increased educational opportunities; in another it may be largely a result of affluence or social change. Again, downward mobility in one society may be quite unrelated to educational causes.

For our purpose, the work of R. H. Turner on 'Modes of Social Ascent Through Education' is far more important and suggestive (19). R. H. Turner argues that the mobility which occurs in the United States is a *contest* mobility as distinct from that which occurs in England, which is a *sponsored* mobility. These are undoubtedly useful terms to express general tendencies provided they are not used to polarize trends completely. Such terms and the situations they describe are relative rather than absolute. Contest mobility is compared to a race in which everyone is a competitor on equal terms for a limited number of places. No one is prevented from entering the race. But, to be realistic, this is a little like saying that an 'Open Mile' race in an athletic contest is an invitation to anyone to run a mile in competition. There may be nothing in the rules to prevent the severely handicapped from running, or hobbling, around. But it would be a somewhat cynical comment to suggest that they were all competitors 'on equal terms'.

We cannot here go into any details concerning the whole American educational system; we can, however, say that although there may be no selection mechanisms, such as the eleven-plus, which 'sponsor' some children as against others for better or higher levels of education, there are all sorts of social and economic 'sponsorships' at work within the system of common or comprehensive schools, which make the educational road much easier for some than for others. And the social and educational deprivation which many experience in the United States (20) presents the concept of contest mobility as a somewhat frightening one, rather than as one of the finer expressions of an 'open' society.

Turner compares the *contest* mobility of the United States with the *sponsored* mobility of England. He says of the former that 'Since the "prize" of successful mobility is not in the hands of the established elite to give out, the latter are not in a position to determine who shall attain it and who shall not' (21). But under the English system there is throughout a sponsorship of upward mobility through the selection process. The established elite and their 'agents' choose elite recruits and give them elite status on the basis of some criterion of supposed merit. Elite status cannot, says Turner, be *taken* by any amount of effort or strategy; in fact,

> 'Upward mobility is like entry into a private club, where each candidate must be "sponsored" by one or more of the members. Ultimately, the members grant or deny upward mobility on the basis of whether they judge the candidate to have the qualities that they wish to see in fellow members' (22).

This is a somewhat exaggerated statement of the general selective procedures in our society. No one doubts that there is a great deal of wasted talent, but this is due not so much to selection procedures *per se* as to limited places, particularly in higher education. Our society sets high standards: professions are entered by means of qualifying examinations, and entry to these qualifying examinations requires the attainment of certain preliminary academic standards. These standards, again, are established by examinations and other forms of assessment.

If this is what constitutes 'sponsorship' then the English society is a relatively sponsored one. We are, however, gradually increasing the variety of roads to higher education, through more and larger universities, polytechnics and colleges of technology, colleges of further education and colleges of commerce, colleges of education, external degrees through correspondence courses, the C.N.A.A., and the Open University. We are also reducing the initial qualifications required to start a course. But selection procedures still go on – even for the Open University. If, in Turner's terms, the contest can be judged to be fair only if all the competitors are allowed to compete 'on an equal footing', and victory may be achieved solely by one's own efforts, equally in the words of Turner, 'The most satisfactory outcome is not necessarily a victory of the most *able*, but of the most *deserving*' (23).

One can only emphasize that the phrase, 'on an equal footing', requires a very close definition. Even education according to one's 'age, ability and aptitude' does not suggest that all are on an equal footing, even if it seeks to give some sort of equality of opportunity. Indeed, quite the contrary. Abilities and aptitudes have to be described, analysed and, if possible, measured by some specific criteria. In the *contest* mobility this process appears to come at the end of a long and what must be to many a very unequal and frustrating road. And it is at this point that 'sponsorship' takes up the process. In *sponsorship* mobility there is some recognition at an early stage of the differences between individuals; the great problem is to harmonize what is best for society and what is best for each individual in the selection or sponsoring of elites.

Finally, Turner's dichotomy of the 'most able' and the 'most deserving' is, if not completely meaningless, quite invalid in any society. We do not appoint doctors, professors, engineers, and so forth, primarily because they are 'most deserving', but because they are the 'most able'; they may, of course, be most deserving as well – because they are, amongst other qualities, the most able. No one but a fool, however, would entrust his health to a man because he was 'most deserving', irrespective of his ability as a doctor, or the building of an important bridge to another 'deserving' man, irrespective of his competence as an engineer.

We will leave the American and English societies for a moment and consider how the question of contest and sponsorship mobility applies in Soviet Russia, where one might expect everyone, perhaps, to be 'on an equal footing'. In discussing the history of education in the U.S.S.R., Professor Vyacheslav Yelyutin has said that

'As soon as it was organized, Soviet Government took vigorous steps to democratize the higher school and ensure its rapid growth. Education was to be made accessible *to the more gifted* regardless of property, social status, nationality, sex, religion or political convictions' (24).

At the time he wrote this Professor Yelyutin was Minister of Higher and Specialized Secondary Education of the U.S.S.R., and he was writing for Western consumption. According to his statement, it was clearly the more gifted and able to whom higher education was to be made available, not those who were 'deserving' on any other grounds.

A closer study of the Soviet system of education reveals one or two interesting features. There is a general rejection, in principle, of selection or streaming as a result of any sort of mental tests. Professor A. N. Leontiev, of Moscow University, has argued that, at best, the results of measurements undertaken with tests provide only 'a superficial orientation to the level of development' (25). What is the consequence of this principle of non-selection and non-streaming in the Russian experience? According to Khrushchev, before 1958 20 per cent of all children in seven-year schools repeated their school work so often, because they had not satisfactorily passed the year tests for promotion, that they never managed to finish the course (26). But the selection of a group of children to repeat work that they were not sufficiently able to master is merely another way of streaming, or of selecting for promotion the brighter children who have satisfactorily passed the tests set on the year's work.

In his *Public Education in the U.S.S.R.* (27), Professor Mikhail Prokofyev discusses the Five-Year Plan for 1966–70 in relation to educational developments. Compulsory eight-year schooling was introduced in 1963, which meant that a child began such schooling at the age of seven, and passed through a primary stage of four years until he reached the age of eleven. A secondary stage lasted for another four years until the age of fifteen or sixteen years. Prokofyev, writing in 1968, stated that 63 per cent of children who completed the eight-year course went on to study for another two years in a variety of secondary schools. Many more would enter schools which provided a general secondary education as well as vocational training, and among which were specialized secondary schools known as technicums, and some vocational training schools. Thus eventually, in fact by 1970, all Russian youth has been promised some form of secondary education up to the age of seventeen or eighteen years (28).

At the end of the eight-year school, the pupils all sit for examinations and they will receive certificates which entitle them to take a job, or to continue their studies in a general school, in evening secondary schools for young workers or farmers, or in a variety of vocational or specialized secondary schools (29). The Soviet School thus

'prepares pupils both to continue their education and to work. These two principles should be in organic unity since training for work and for continuing education complement each other and furnish conditions for the harmonious development of the personality' (30).

DIAGRAM OF SOVIET EDUCATIONAL INSTITUTIONS

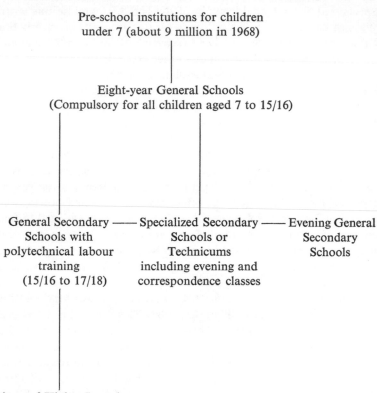

Pre-school institutions for children
under 7 (about 9 million in 1968)

Eight-year General Schools
(Compulsory for all children aged 7 to 15/16)

General Secondary —— Specialized Secondary —— Evening General
Schools with   Schools or   Secondary
polytechnical labour   Technicums   Schools
training   including evening and
(15/16 to 17/18)   correspondence classes

Institutions of Higher Learning:
Colleges and Universities
(including evening part-time and
correspondence departments)

Therefore Soviet education has in mind that the student will go on educating himself throughout life by the extension of education, in many instances, into his working life. The county college idea may be a dead duck in our own society, but it also had this concept in mind.

Entrance to higher education in the U.S.S.R. reveals a mixture of contest or open competition, age restriction, sponsorship and preferential discrimination, and privilege based upon merit. How one characterizes all this in Turner's 'contest' and 'sponsorship' terms it is difficult to say. Any citizen, provided he is under thirty-five, may be admitted to colleges once he or she has passed certain competitive examinations based upon the syllabuses of the secondary school. The stated aim of these examinations is to discern whether the candidate has absorbed sufficient at school in order to cope with the college curriculum and, in time, become a competent specialist. In the words of Yelyutin, 'The system of competitive examinations makes it possible to select the more capable, well-prepared applicants. The marks received at school are also taken into account' (31).

Professor Yelyutin goes on to explain that there are separate competitive examinations for school leavers and production workers, ensuring that there are equal conditions for both categories of applicants. This system is considered 'democratic' because it ensures 'equal opportunities for all' whether they go to college after a period spent in work or whether they go straight from school. But, to underline that some are more (or less) equal than others, Yelyutin adds that workers who are officially recommended by their enterprises also have to pass the examinations, just like the others, 'but in the event of equal marks *they are given preference*' (32). There are also privileges granted to gold and silver medallists from secondary schools in that they have to pass only one major examination.

Whether one is speaking of the U.S.A., England, or Russia, an elite is eventually elicited by one means or another. The size or proportion of the elite will vary according to the resources available; and the means adopted for the selection of such an elite will vary according to political and social ideologies as well as educational principles. In the end some sort of competitive examination based upon a common band of knowledge seems to be the chief method adopted in each case. Privilege, in all three countries, appears increasingly to depend upon prowess or achievement, at some point, rather than upon somewhat dubiously measured potential. And educational mobility, whether of the *contest* or *sponsored* variety, or some combination of both, appears to be at least one of the keys, if not the chief one, in unlocking doors which hinder social mobility.

The supporters of the comprehensive system in this country hoped for a number of things within the context of the present discussion. One, undoubtedly, was the lessening in the social distance between various classes, and the increase of social mobility, whether one speaks in terms of *embourgeoisement* or proletarianization. In a recent study of the comprehensive school, Julienne Ford throws some doubt on the assumption that the comprehensive reorganization of secondary education will achieve this aim (33). Her book suggests that, in fact, for a variety of reasons, including the streaming which goes on in many comprehensive schools almost along eleven-plus selection lines, social relations between members of different social levels are not being promoted; and that the former tripartite division is being reproduced upon a single campus. Moreover, of course, many comprehensive schools are neighbourhood schools in which there is no question or possibility of different social strata mixing.

Perhaps, after all, the grammar schools have greater possibilities of social mixing than the comprehensives. The real problem, however, is the conflict between home environment and school, which may be felt by pupils in any type of school. The problems, for example, of the restricted linguistic code are not solved by the few hours spent in the *milieu* of the school, whose standards may be rejected anyway because they contrast so strongly with those of the home. Perhaps, after all, the Russians have the right idea in encouraging parents to send their children to kindergartens between the ages of three and seven. Most kindergartens there operate for nine to twelve hours daily; and children attending them are divided into three groups: junior from three to five years of age, middle from five to six years, and senior from six to seven years. In 1968 about nine million children were in attendance at pre-school institutions (34). The nursery school stage, pin-pointed by the Plowden Report, may well be one of the most important agents in the promotion of social mobility (35). One must not ignore, however, the warning of Susan Isaacs when she says that

'the nursery school is not a substitute for a good home: its prime function . . . is to supplement the normal services which the home renders to its children and to make a link between the natural and indispensable fostering of the child in the home and social life of the world at large . . .' (36).

Further up the education scale in Russia, boarding schools have been widely introduced. In 1958 there were some 180,000 pupils at these schools, whilst in 1968 there were nearly four million pupils. Children remain at such schools during the whole of the week, but return home for the weekends and holidays (37). The U.S.S.R. plans to build sufficient boarding schools for all parents who wish to send their children there. In addition to boarding schools there are also prolonged-day schools at which pupils remain from 8 a.m. until 6 p.m., and all homework is done at the school. Thus, not only do parents get some sort of choice of the type of school for their children, but the children themselves have more continuous social contact with their school, their teachers and with one another.

N. Grant points out, however, that the boarding schools are in no sense special schools for an elite: there exists a system of priorities for entry, which affords preference to orphans, children of widows and unmarried or invalid mothers, and children from large and overcrowded families. But many teachers consider the boarding school as more successful than the ordinary day school in the realms of social and moral education (38). If there is a solution to social inequality in our own society along educational lines, it may well be that the Russian experiments in the above areas provide a possible answer. But, again, it would be wrong to assume that what works in the Soviet socialist regime would necessarily work in the same way in our own society.

At the higher levels of education, competition is becoming increasingly keener not merely to obtain a first degree, but to go on to further research.

There was a time in our society when a Ph.D. was something of a rare bird, but today in many areas of study, and levels of academic work, those with a doctorate, or at least some higher degree, are rapidly becoming the norm. For example, at the time of writing one polytechnic has something in the region of 60 per cent of its lecturers with a Ph.D. Another designated polytechnic has eighty-six members of staff with some sort of doctorate or other, representing about 20 per cent of its total lecturing staff. In almost every area of life, where any specialist knowledge or skill is required, the pressures for more, better and higher qualifications are being exerted, and competition becomes keener.

As Professor Prokofyev intimated, the school should not only prepare the pupil for work but also to continue his education. Education and academic achievement certainly do not end with school, college or university; if members of the middle classes desire upward social mobility, higher status, or just more money, they must continue to strive for further qualifications virtually throughout their lives. It is, therefore, one of the functions of the school to train the individual in the skills and techniques which will assist him to pursue his personal education and development throughout life.

REFERENCES

1 *Vide* Schumpeter, J. A., *Imperialism and Social Classes* (B. Blackwell, 1951).
2 *Vide* Goblot, E., *La Barrière et le Niveau* (Presses Universitaires de France, Paris, 1925), Chapter 3, pp. 38–59.
3 Packard, V., *The Status Seekers* (Penguin Books, 1961; reprinted 1963), p. 270.
4 Ibid., p. 270.
5 *Vide* Goldthorpe, J. H. and Lockwood, D., 'Affluence and the British Class Structure', *Sociological Review*, Vol. 11, No. 2, July 1963, pp. 133–63. A large part of this essay is reprinted in Butterworth, W. and Weir, D. (eds), *The Sociology of Modern Britain: An Introductory Reader* (Fontana Library, Collins, 1970), pp. 206–13.
6 Ibid., pp. 133–4.
7 Ibid., p. 134. The authors refer here to the semi-official document, *Social Changes in Britain* (Central Office of Information, H.M.S.O., December 1962).
8 Quoted by Goldthorpe, J. H. and Lockwood, D., ibid., p. 135, from Crosland, C. A. R., *Can Labour Win?* (Fabian Tract 324, 1960), pp. 4, 11–13.
9 Elliott, Florence, *A Dictionary of Politics* (Penguin Books, 1957; 6th edition, 1969).
10 Ibid., pp. 136–48.
11 Ibid., p. 136.

12 *Vide* Inkeles, A., 'Social Stratification and Mobility in the Soviet Union: 1940–1950', *American Sociological Review*, Vol. 15, August 1950, p. 470. Inkeles notes that of 121 awards made in 1948 for inventions and improvements in production methods, only four went to persons with the rank of foreman and below (p. 470, n. 22).

13 Goldthorpe, J. H. and Lockwood, D., op. cit., p. 155.

14 *Vide* Goldthorpe, J. H., Lockwood, D., Bechhofer, F. and Platt, J., 'The Affluent Worker and the Thesis of *Embourgeoisement*: Some Preliminary Research Findings', *Sociology*, Vol. 1, No. 1, January 1967, pp. 11–31.

15 Banks, Olive, *Parity and Prestige in British Education* (Routledge, 1955), p. 240.

16 Musgrave, P. W., *The Sociology of Education* (Methuen 1965; reprinted 1968), p. 51.

17 *Vide* Miller, S. M., 'Comparative Social Mobility', *Current Sociology*, Vol. 9, No. 1, 1960, pp. 1–89.

18 Ibid., p. 34.

19 *Vide* Turner, R. H., 'Modes of Social Ascent Through Education: Sponsored and Contest Mobility and the School System', *American Sociological Review*, Vol. 25, No. 5, 1960, pp. 855–67.

20 Cf. Berreman, G. D., 'Caste in India and the United States', *American Journal of Sociology*, Vol. 66, September 1960, pp. 120–7; Dollard, J., *Caste and Class in a Southern Town* (Doubleday and Co., N.Y., 1957); Gallagher, B. G., *American Caste and the Negro College* (Columbia Univ. Press, 1938).

21 Turner, R. H., op. cit.; quoted in Butterworth, E. and Weir, D. (eds), *The Sociology of Modern Britain: An Introductory Reader*, p. 221.

22 Ibid., p. 221.

23 Ibid., p. 221; my italics.

24 Yelyutin, V., *Higher Education in the U.S.S.R.* (Novosti Press Agency Publishing House, Moscow, 1968), pp. 9–10; my italics.

25 Leontiev, A. N., 'Principles of Mental Development and the Problem of Intellectual Backwardness', in Simon, B. and J. (eds), *Educational Psychology in the U.S.S.R.* (Routledge, 1963), p. 69.

26 Grant, N., *Soviet Education* (Penguin Books, 1964).

27 Prokofyev, M., *Public Education in the U.S.S.R.* (Novosti Press Agency Publishing House, Moscow, 1968).

28 Ibid., p. 8.

29 Ibid., p. 22. *Vide* 'Diagram of Soviet Educational Institutions'.

30 Ibid., pp. 33–4.

31 Yelyutin, V., op. cit., p. 35.

32 Ibid., p. 35; my italics.

33 Ford, Julienne, *Social Class and the Comprehensive School* (Routledge, 1969).

34 Prokofyev, M., op. cit., pp. 16–17. Note that 'the headmistress of a kindergarten must be a trained teacher, with at least five years' experience and special medical training. Teachers must have a secondary education and additional training as educators' (p. 16).

35 *Vide* D.E.S., *Children and their Primary Schools* (Plowden Report) (H.M.S.O., 1967), Chapter 9, pp. 116–34.
36 Isaacs, Susan, *Educational Value of the Nursery School* (Pamphlet No. 54, Nursery Schools Association, 1938). Quoted in the Plowden Report, para. 309 (a).
37 Prokofyev, M., op. cit., pp. 43–4.
38 Grant, N., op. cit., pp. 94–5.

BIBLIOGRAPHY

A. *Books*

BANKS, OLIVE, *The Sociology of Education* (Batsford, 1968; 2nd impression 1969), Chapter 3, 'Education and Social Mobility', pp. 39–65; also pp. 194–7.
BENDIX, R. and LIPSET, S. M. (eds), *Class, Status and Power* (Routledge, 1953; 3rd impression 1966).
BENDIX, R. and LIPSET, S. M., *Social Mobility in Industrial Society* (Heinemann, 1959).
BOTTOMORE, T. B., *Elites and Society* (Penguin Books, 1964; reprinted 1967), Chapter III, pp. 48–68.
BUTTERWORTH, E. and WEIR, D. (eds), *The Sociology of Modern Britain: An Introductory Reader* (Fontana Library, Collins, 1970), Chapters 3 and 5.
CARLSSON, G., *Social Mobility and the Class Structure* (Gleerup, Lund, Sweden, 1958).
COLE, G. D. H., *Studies in Class Structure* (Routledge, 1955; 3rd impression 1964).
DAHRENDORF, R., *Class and Class Conflict in Industrial Society* (Routledge, 1959; revised edition 1965).
FLOUD, J. E. *et al.*, *Social Class and Educational Opportunity* (Heinemann, 1956).
FORD, JULIENNE, *Social Class and the Comprehensive School* (Routledge, 1969).
GLASS, D. V. (ed.), *Social Mobility in Britain* (Routledge, 1954; 2nd impression 1963).
GOLDTHORPE, J. H., *et al.*, *The Affluent Worker in the Class Structure* (C.U.P., 1969).
GOLDTHORPE, J. H., *et al.*, *The Affluent Worker: Vol. I – Industrial Attitudes and Behaviour; Vol. II – Political Attitudes and Behaviour* (C.U.P., 1968/9).
HARRIS, AMELIA and CLAUSEN, ROSEMARY, *Labour Mobility in Great Britain* (H.M.S.O., 1966).
LAWTON, D., *Social Class, Language and Education* (Routledge, 1968).
MUSGRAVE, P. W., *The Sociology of Education* (Methuen, 1965; reprinted 1968), Chapters 4 and 5, pp. 48–82.
PACKARD, V., *The Status Seekers* (Penguin Books, 1961; reprinted 1963), Chapter 21, pp. 269–79.

160 / *The Sociology of Education*

PARETO, V., *Mind and Society* (Harcourt, Brace and Co., 1935), Vols. III and IV.

PARSONS, T. (ed.), *Theories of Society* (Free Press, Glencoe, 1965), pp. 517–73.

ROGOFF, NATALIE, *Recent Trends in Occupational Mobility* (Free Press, Glencoe, 1953).

SCHUMPETER, J. A., *Imperialism and Social Classes* (B. Blackwell, 1951).

SOROKIN, P. A., *Social and Cultural Mobility* (Free Press, Glencoe, 1959).

SWIFT, D. F., *The Sociology of Education* (Routledge, 1969), pp. 93–9.

TURNER, R., *The Social Context of Ambition* (Chandler, San Francisco, 1964).

YOUNG, M., *The Rise of the Meritocracy, 1870–2033* (Thames and Hudson, 1958; Penguin Books, 1961).

ZWEIG, F., *The Worker in the Affluent Society* (Heinemann, 1961).

B. *Articles*

ANDERSON, C. A., 'A Skeptical Note on the Relation of Vertical Mobility to Education', *American Journal of Sociology*, Vol. 66, 1960, pp. 560–70.

BANKS, OLIVE, 'Social Mobility and the English System of Education', *International Review of Education*, Vol. 4, 1958, pp. 196–202.

CENTERS, R., 'Occupational Mobility of Urban Occupational Strata', *American Sociological Review*, Vol. 13, 1948, pp. 197–203.

CENTERS, R., 'Education and Occupational Mobility', *American Sociological Review*, Vol. 14, February 1949, pp. 143–4.

CHINOY, E., 'Social Mobility Trends in the United States', *American Sociological Review*, Vol. 20, April 1955, pp. 180–6.

COHEN, E., 'Parental Factors in Educational Mobility', *Sociology of Education*, Vol. 38, 1965, pp. 404–25.

DUNCAN, O. D., 'The Trend of Occupational Mobility in the United States', *American Sociological Review*, Vol. 30, No. 4, August 1965, pp. 491–8.

FLOUD, JEAN, 'Education and Social Mobility', *Yearbook of Education 1950* (Evans Bros, 1950).

FOLGER, J. F. and NAM, C. B., 'Trends in Education in Relation to the Occupational Structure', *Sociology of Education*, Vol. 38, No. 1, 1964.

GERSTL, J. and PERRUCCI, R., 'Educational Channels and Elite Mobility', *Sociology of Education*, Vol. 38, No. 2, 1965, pp. 226–32.

GOLDTHORPE, J. H. and LOCKWOOD, D., 'Affluence and the British Class Structure', *Sociological Review*, Vol. 11, No. 2, July 1963, pp. 133–63.

GOLDTHORPE, J. H. *et al.*, 'The Affluent Worker and the Thesis of *Embourgeoisement*: Some Preliminary Research Findings', *Sociology*, Vol. 1, No. 1, January 1967, pp. 11–31.

GREENBLUM, J. and PEARLIN, L. I., 'Vertical Mobility and Prejudice: A Socio-Psychological Analysis', in Bendix, R. and Lipset, S. M. (eds), *Class, Status and Power* (Routledge, 1953; 3rd impression 1966), pp. 480–90.

HAVIGHURST, R. J., 'Education and Social Mobility in Four Societies', in Halsey, A. H. *et al.*, *Education, Economy and Society* (Free Press, Glencoe, 1961).

HAVIGHURST, R. J., 'Social Class in the United States: An Overview', in Kallenbach, W. W. and Hodges, H. M. (eds), *Education and Society* (C. E. Merrill Books, Inc., 1963), pp. 380–6.

INKELES, A., 'Social Stratification and Mobility in the Soviet Union: 1940–50', *American Sociological Review*, Vol. 15, August 1950, pp. 465–79.

LEE, D. J., 'Class Differentials in Educational Opportunity and Promotions from the Ranks', *Sociology*, Vol. 2, No. 3, September 1968, pp. 293–312.

LIPSET, A. M. and BENDIX, R., 'Social Mobility and Occupational Career Patterns', *American Journal of Sociology*, Vol. 57, January and March 1952, pp. 366–74, 494–504.

LIPSET, S. M. and ZETTERBERG, H. L., 'A Theory of Social Mobility', *Transactions of the Third World Congress of Sociology, Vol. II* (International Sociological Association, London, 1956), pp. 155–77.

LITTLE, A. and WESTERGAARD, J., 'The Trend of Class Differentials in England and Wales', *British Journal of Sociology*, Vol. 15, No. 3, 1964, pp. 311–14.

MATRAS, J., 'Social Mobility and Social Structure: Some Insights from the Linear Model', *American Sociological Review*, Vol. 32, No. 4, August 1967, pp. 608–13.

MILLER, S. M., 'Comparative Social Mobility', *Current Sociology*, Vol. 9, No. 1, 1960, pp. 1–89.

RUNCIMAN, W. G., '*Embourgeoisement*: Self-Rated Class and Party Preference', *Sociological Review*, July 1964.

SWIFT, D. F., 'Social Class, Mobility Ideology and 11+ Success', *British Journal of Sociology*, Vol. 17, 1967, pp. 165–86.

TURNER, R. H., 'Modes of Social Ascent Through Education: Sponsored and Contest Mobility and the School System', *American Sociological Review*, Vol. 25, No. 5, 1960, pp. 855–67.

L

Chapter 9

The Family and Education

A. FAMILY STRUCTURES

The family is one of the primary groups of society, concerned with face-to-face relationships. Throughout man's history, however, and throughout the world both the family and the institution of marriage display a considerable cultural variability. But whatever form such institutions take they have regard to the fact that the human child is for a long time dependent for its biological survival upon the adult members of those institutions. The precise functions of the family will be discussed in the next section, but in general terms it is sufficient to note here that marriage provides a certain secure framework for the process of reproduction, and the family affords a medium for primary socialization.

There are two main types of family, namely the *extended* family and the *nuclear* family. The extended family or kin-group is found in the West Indies and in such countries as India and Pakistan, and includes a span of three generations within the total household. On the other hand the *nuclear* family comprises basically the father, the mother and the children. Our own society is composed of a vast number of these small social 'cells' or nuclear families, which are gradually becoming smaller in size with the increase in the knowledge and practice of contraception. G. P. Murdock (1) makes the distinction between two sorts of nuclear family, which are not essentially different in their composition, but which involve rather a different point of view. Every normal adult belongs to a *family of orientation*, in which a man is born and reared, and which will include his father, mother, brothers and sisters. And he also belongs to a *family of procreation* which he establishes by his marriage, and which includes his wife and children.

Edward Westermarck (2) held that the family was not rooted in marriage, but that marriage was an institution arising out of the family. This institution is found in a variety of forms which fall into the two broad categories of *monogamy* and *polygamy*. Polygamy implies a marriage in which there is more than one partner. *Polygyny* occurs where one man is married to more than one woman; the Koran, for example, permits a Muslim male to have up to four wives at any one time. It should, however, be noted that even in this context there are certain admonitions about the capacity of a husband to look after them properly, and with a sense of fairness and the maintenance of equality among them (3). *Polyandry* occurs where one woman is married to more than one man, as for example in certain areas of Tibet where one woman may set up house with a man who may, in turn, be the eldest of seven sons; and his brothers will share his wife with him.

The fear of incest is strongly ingrained in man (4), and he has created a variety of tabus in order not to be guilty of this moral and social crime. Our own 'Table of Kindred and Affinity' clearly establishes those relationships which are not permitted within our society. Out of this incest fear there arises a variety of possibilities and tabus in relation to marriage. *Exogamy* implies that marriage may occur only outside the kinship group: in this way incest is avoided altogether. On the other hand, *endogamy* is an attempt to retain the purity of the group; at the same time there will be very precise rules to avoid any possibility of incestuous marriage.

In some societies there occur *levirate* and *sororate* marriages. The law of levirate among the ancient Israelites (5), for example, was a custom whereby, if a married man died without a male heir, his eldest brother was bound by law to marry the widow in order to ensure a posterity for the dead man. The first son born of this new union would take on the dead man's name and his inheritance. The principle of levirate marriage was based upon the view that a man lived on in his children, particularly in his sons. Sororate marriage (6) is one in which a widower is permitted to marry the sister of his dead wife, although the principle is similar to that of levirate marriage, namely, it is a method whereby a man ensures the continuance of his lineage.

The locations of the marriage households are defined by the terms *patrilocal, matrilocal* and *neolocal*. When the new home is set up near or within the groom's household, it is referred to as patrilocal residence; when it is set up near the bride's household it is termed matrilocal residence; and, when it is set up in some neutral area which is completely independent of either household, it is referred to as neolocal residence.

In some societies there has been a tendency for descent privileges, rights and obligations to be traced through the female line, and this is called *matrilineal* descent. In other societies descent has been traced through the male line, that is, *patrilineal* descent. *Bilateral* descent traces the descent of children through relatives on both the female and male lines.

Similarly, some societies are ruled by the female element in society, and a *matriarchate* is formed. There are still relics of such matriarchates throughout the world, including those areas where, in fact, there is basically a *patriarchate*, or male rule, in existence. Thus, for example, in Jamaica there exists the 'maternal family', so called because

'the grandmother or some female relative, perhaps a sister, usurps the function of the father and at times that of the mother. Such a family can originate through the girl becoming pregnant while still living at home. The household may consist of her mother, her mother's sister, and the girl's siblings. The girl may remain at home and look after her child, but in many cases she leaves and the child is brought up by its grandmother' (7).

There is, however, a third form of social control in simpler societies in which the family complex comprises a woman, her children and a number of uncles. This relationship between the uncles and the children is an 'authority' relationship called an *avunculate*, in which 'fatherhood' or its equivalent is shared out among a number of men. Family structures are, therefore, varied and in consequence the modes of socialization will also be varied.

B. THE FUNCTIONS OF THE FAMILY

Whilst it is true that there is a great variety in the familial structures throughout the world, and certainly throughout man's history, by and large their differences arise out of the nature of the environment and a number of cultural factors. G. P. Murdock (8), in his cross-cultural study of kinship, suggests that it is not merely the family that is universal but also the *nuclear* family. He further argues that the four functions of the family – sexual, economic, reproductive and educational – are universal. Melford E. Spiro has argued, however, in his essay entitled 'Is the Family Universal?' (9), that the Israeli *kibbutz*, or agricultural collective, does not conform to the criteria laid down by Murdock.

Spiro points out that, despite the emphasis upon children and children's houses (*bet yeladim*), it is not their own parents who provide directly for their physical care; it is the responsibility of the *kibbutz* as a whole to make this provision. Moreover, the education and socialization of the children are not the function of their parents, but rather of their nurses and teachers. The parents, however, are of considerable importance in the psychological development of their children within the collective; for they 'serve as the objects of his important identifications, and they provide him with a certain security and love that he obtains from no one else' (10). Later on, however, Spiro developed a non-enumerative definition of marriage which he felt would not only include all known cases termed 'marriage', but also the *kibbutz* form of marriage (11). But this is basically an attempt to formulate a definition which must inevitably ensure the universality of both marriage and the family. His definition is so broad and 'non-enumerative' as to provide no real or essential criterion. Marriage, he suggests, is 'any socially sanctioned relationship between non-sanguineally-related cohabiting adults of opposite sex which satisfied felt needs – mutual, symmetrical, or complementary' (12). We cannot, however, do full justice to Spiro's arguments here and the reader must pursue them in Spiro's articles.

We will confine ourselves here to a discussion of the actual functions of the family as enumerated by Murdock, namely, sexual, economic, reproductive and educational. Included in the educational function are certain social functions of both a psychological and sociological nature. Basic to man's needs are those of *sexual* expression and affection, and whilst it is obvious that these are attainable outside any such institution as marriage or the family, it is also clear that completely unrestrained fulfilment of sexual desires would lead to a breakdown in the organization of society, and in its relationships. According to 'The Form of Solemnization of Matrimony' of the Anglican Church (13) the institution of marriage was ordained 'for a remedy against sin, and to avoid fornication', in order that those individuals who 'have not the gift of continency might marry'. It is not necessary, however, to adopt a medieval or puritanical view of sex in order to see that, even if we no longer use such terms as 'sin', 'fornication' and 'continency', some form of marriage is inevitable if society is to be organized, orderly and lasting.

But, as P. W. Musgrave points out, the institution of marriage is not just a social contrivance to ensure its own security and futurity through the family. Indeed, 'the family has come to be used as a very specialized agency for providing the affection that helps to ensure the emotional stability needed if men and women are to manage their lives successfully under modern conditions' (14). This takes into account something beyond the crude and pressing biological urges of man. Emotional stability is, in the long run, far more vital for man than sheer physical excitement. Such stability in the male–female relationship is reached in and through an element of permanency and personal adjustment. In terms, however, of the growth and development of any children within the family institution, it is clear that what children require above all else in their early years is a feeling of security and stability.

The family also has a *reproductive* function as distinct from the mere exercise of the sexual function. The nuclear family, however small, is a social cell or social microcosm, through which society is perpetuated and recreated. The more stable the family the more secure the children will feel in the home. The child living in the shadow of the broken home is often bewildered by comings and goings, and by the mere fact that essential relationships are not promoted, or are broken off and disrupted at a very impressionable time. Both parents would appear to be essential elements in the growth and socialization of the child; the roles they have to play are different but, at the same time, complementary. In his study of the 'Principal Functions of the Nuclear Family' (15), Talcott Parsons emphasizes the fact that *human* personality is not 'born', but has to be 'made' through the socializing process. It is because of this that families are essential institutions in the first place; they are 'factories' which produce human personalities (16).

There is, therefore, a basic role-structure in the nuclear family which promotes such socialization. We shall consider socialization later as a part of the educational function of the family; we are more immediately concerned here with the roles that particular members of the family play. The family is in a very real sense a social network with role-relationships, and though Parsons himself rejects the term 'little society' as applied to the family (17), his term 'a differentiated subsystem of society' is not too far removed from the concept of a micro-society. The fact remains, however, that in the role-structure of the family Parsons sees the father as being superior in 'instrumental' power, and the mother as superior in 'expressive' power. He states that the area of the *instrumental* function of the father is concerned with the relations of the family system to its situation outside the system. It is concerned with meeting the adaptive conditions of its maintenance of equilibrium, and with establishing instrumentally the desired relations to *external* goal-objects. On the other hand, the area of the *expressive* function of the mother is more taken up with the internal affairs of the family system and with the integrative relations among its various members; it is concerned with the 'regulation of the patterns and tension levels of its component units' (18), that is, with the interplay, control and development of the emotions.

We shall take up some of these points again later on; at the present we are concerned to emphasize that mere reproduction does not require the institutions of marriage and the family for its occurrence. The continuance of a stable society, however, requires something more than just the production of children and their mass rearing in an institution of the order of a communal nursery. *Human* existence is something different from *animal* existence in that the development of the child physically and psychologically requires a role-structure such as that of the family. The 'stigma' of the child born out of wedlock should certainly not be that, throughout life, it is regarded as illegitimate and the product of socially and morally reprehensible behaviour. A stigma is a brand or a mark which is attached to something for as long as it exists and the real stigma, in this sense, as far as an illegitimate child is concerned, is the social and psychological deprivation that results from never experiencing the totality of the interaction process of the family. There is considerable cruelty involved in the social and legal sanctions attached to illegitimacy, but in the deepest sense these latter are not comparable with the psychological and emotional deprivation involved, although there is little doubt that the one element will aggravate the other.

Another important function of the family is the *economic* one. It would, of course, be quite wrong to single out the human family as the only animal group which is concerned with the 'economic' security of its young, or even of its developed members. Dr M. D. Sahlins has demonstrated that the social nature of the baboon, for example, is comparable with the human organization for economic and social survival, and that although in a sense its sex activity may be 'indiscriminate' within the baboon society, it is by no means 'promiscuous' (19). Competition with regard to partners may, in fact, be vicious and even fatal, but there is a certain group or social purpose, however unconscious or 'instinctive' it may be. Similarly, among human beings in their evolution there has been a gradual subordination of the sexual drive to the needs, social and economic, of the group. The progressive emancipation of sex from sheer hormonal and glandular control to cerebral and intellectual control means that man has seen the essential desirability of sexual order so as to fulfil social and collective ends. And the economic need of man is one of the most pressing.

It is in the area of its economic function that the family in a developed society such as our own has changed so much over the past thirty years. R. Fletcher argues quite strongly that it is untrue to suggest that the family in our present society

'has been "stripped of its functions" and has, as a consequence, become of diminished importance as a social institution. On the contrary, the modern family fulfils *more* functions, and in a far more detailed and sophisticated manner, than did the family before or during the nineteenth-century development of industrialization' (20).

This, of course, may be true, but there are at the same time certain elements which help to contribute to its earlier disintegration as a *stable* unit with more or less fixed role-relationships. Employment, for a start, is now almost completely separated from the family circle, since sons are no longer trained in the occupations of their fathers, and daughters do not stay at home to decorate the family living-room and entertain. For a large proportion of employed people life is one of commuting, and houses may be empty, or partially so, for a large part of the day. Someone has described the commuter in these terms:

> I am a commuter,
> And I spend my life
> Travelling to and
> From my wife.
> God! I will shave
> And take a train,
> And then go home
> And shave again.

Even if Fletcher is right and the family as a social institution has not become of diminished importance, there has been an ever-increasing mobility of labour which must result in some modification of the functions of the family, its role-relationships and its stability. Several factors are involved in this change in the familial structure and its resultant 'sophistication' of functions. Children begin their working career later than formerly, but in addition to becoming adult earlier – from a legal point of view at least – they also marry earlier and become self-supporting much more speedily. The instrumental and expressive functions evolve more rapidly, and the emotional and interpersonal relationships become much more complex and interstitial, mingling as they do with the cross-currents of the larger society; and although 'children' stay at school longer, they mature much more quickly and are concerned at an early age with the instrumental or external functions of the family.

Much of the pattern of family life has also been altered and modified by the participation of wives and mothers in the economic function. Married women are more and more taking up paid employment outside their homes, whilst many others are contributing to the family income by taking up part-time employment in the home in various forms of agency work. Some of it, such as typing and secretarial work, will keep them in the home almost all the time; other forms of agency will involve door-to-door calling or advertisement distribution. Where mothers who have young children are absent from home there always arises the problem of children left unattended, or left to their own devices in streets or playing-fields, or deposited in, perhaps, a third-rate private nursery. Certainly the increasing equality of men and women in the professions and in all forms of work, and the real need for married women to work in order to help balance the family budget, are facts which have made the economic function of the family a more intricate affair. And, additionally, in some families where older children are working the situation may arise in which some of the children will be earning more than their father, and between them may be making a greater contribution to the economic needs of their home.

C. THE FAMILY AND EDUCATION

Not only is the family an institution which permits some safeguarding of the child during its period of biological immaturity, it is also an institution which provides for the child's primary socialization and initial education. G. D. Mitchell has pointed out that parenthood 'is rapidly becoming a highly self-conscious vocation' (21); and it is in the realms of interpersonal relationships and social interaction that this self-consciousness operates. *Socialization* is simply the process whereby an individual is adapted to his social environment, and is eventually recognized as both a co-operating and efficient member of it.

The child has to learn how to live within the 'differentiated subsystem of society', that is, his family or home; but this is simply the playground, as it were, of socialization. His family life may in no way be typical of family life generally within his society. Certainly, in a society with a social stratification such as our own, it cannot epitomize every level of society. Nevertheless, as D. F. Swift points out, 'the child will learn some patterns of behaviour, perceptions of reality and habits of thinking which are features of the wider social environment and some of which are special to his family' (22). It is, however, the whole business of personality development with which we are here concerned. The eliciting of social attitudes, the promotion of self-awareness as well as other-awareness are all elements in the socialization of the individual.

At quite an early age a child begins to place himself in the position of others, that is, to take on the role of others, but it is done in a very imitative and uncomprehending way. For example, a boy may copy his father by 'reading' the newspaper even though the paper may be held upside-down. This is rather meaningless to him at first, except that he knows that he wants to do what others are doing within the family circle; but there is little self-awareness or self-observation.

In his *Mind, Self and Society* (23), George H. Mead has analysed the development of the self of the individual child, and has indicated in some detail that there is a strong relationship between this development of self or personality and socialization. Like Talcott Parsons, Mead rejects the idea that the infant is born as a personality. For him an infant has no idea of himself as a separate being: he is not yet a self, an Ego, or an 'I', for to become an 'I' in the fullest sense there must be social interaction. Professor Sprott refers to the infant as 'a bundle of needs' which arise out of 'inner tensions, and capacities to respond to stimulation' (24). The education which the family provides before the child enters an educational institution should assist him in fulfilling his needs and in relieving those inner tensions. The socializing and personalizing process of the home is the means whereby he gradually comes to regard himself as one individual among many, and at the same time as having relationships with other individuals.

Professor F. Musgrove has emphasized that the claims which schools make concerning their impact upon children's 'characters' are probably both extravagant and unfounded. He maintains that they are, in general, 'of negligible influence' (25). The real, prime and lasting influence is in the home, and if there is deprivation here – material, mental or spiritual – there will be some form of deprivation in the child's personality. In his work for the World Health Organization Dr John Bowlby concluded that observations of severely deprived children demonstrated that their consciences and their potentialities were not developed. He linked this with the fact that in the child's earliest years it was the mother who acted 'as his personality and his conscience' (26). Such deprivation was greatest in the case of children brought up in institutions, who displayed in consequence a serious and particular incapacity for abstract thought, which in turn resulted in lack of originality, value-judgement and decision-making.

Socialization in the family is much more than a mere question of house-training, learning a few rules and accepting or rejecting familial sanctions. It is the beginning of that internalization of the culture of the family's society which will go on throughout the individual's life, unless he suffers some partial or total alienation from that culture. It is true that his home and family may assist him in this internalization; it is equally true, however, that the very constellations of ideas, beliefs and practices of parents may militate against such internalization. Many children are unfitted for their society by the very teaching, or lack of it, provided by their parents. Moreover, the role-relationships which are required in society may be totally lacking in the home, not necessarily because it is a 'bad' home, in the generally accepted sense of the term, but because the beliefs of the parents are restricted and restricting. There may well be a conflict of loyalties developed in the child through this early socialization, which will result in an ambivalence of feelings and relationships. Such ambivalent feelings – love and hate, loyalty and rebelliousness, and so forth – are perhaps inevitable (27), but so long as they remain largely within the framework of the family they can be resolved by the individual members concerned. When they align the family over against society, however, there is a graver danger of complete disharmony and the dislocation of the individual in the development of his familial or social sentiments.

In the process of socialization within the home a large variety of instruments and techniques are employed, some consciously and some unconsciously. In an interesting paper on the part that ritual plays in family living, J. H. S. Bossard and Eleanor S. Boll (28) have argued fairly cogently that ritualizing has always, in fact, been a process of both culture transmission and family interaction, and that the role such ritual plays depends upon its content and the manner of its utilization. This is how they conclude:

> 'A ritual, appealing in content and manipulated wisely, becomes a powerful and constructive weapon in the integration of a family; and an ill-adapted ritual or a good ritual misused may become an agent in its disintegration' (29).

It is through the performance of a ritual that individuals find identity in a family group, a tribe, a race or a nation. The literature of anthropologists and writers in allied fields is replete with the amazing variety of ritual in simpler societies as well as the relics of ritual in more advanced societies (30).

The large proportion of the rituals of the simple societies are related to religion, fertility and social initiation. They are traditional, and they form one of the strongest elements in the stylization of the socializing process. The failure to perform such rituals would be quite unthinkable and would have disastrous consequences. No youth could possibly become an adult member of his tribe or social group without undergoing the initiation process, an almost invariably painful one. In our developed society at the present time it frequently seems, in anthropological terms at least, as if ritual were dead. Bossard and Boll, however, do not accept that this is so. According to them ritual is not dying, although it has, to a large extent, become secularized; on the contrary they believe it is on the increase and that it has been promoted by the mass media. It is important to see what the authors mean, in sociological terms, by ritual. To them it is a prescribed formal procedure which arises out of family interaction, and which involves a pattern of defined behaviour. This formal procedure is directed towards a specific purpose, and it acquires 'rigidity and a sense of rightness' as a consequence of its continuing history (31).

On the basis of this definition Bossard and Boll believe that ritual develops in family life in relation to such things as holidays, anniversaries, meals, religious worship, vacations and collective ways of using leisure time, gift giving, card sending and so on. At first sight this list does not seem either as impressive or as ritualistic as the various *rites de passage*, the scarification and cicatrization, subincision, flagellation, violent paroxysmal seizures, and fertility dances. But, firstly, one is dealing with different types of society; and, secondly, the principle of ritual does not depend upon the violence involved in it or even upon any element of the bizarre. Indeed, primitive traditional ceremonies and rituals do not appear in their own *milieux* as violent or strange; they belong to the very grass roots of those societies. In a more developed society such as the U.S.A. or Britain the rituals would inevitably be more sophisticated and related to the life of these two societies. But they are rituals notwithstanding.

Perhaps the most significant feature about the article by Bossard and Boll is their conclusion that the rituals for each class level of society are different, and have varying effects. In the lower class, children see very little that they desire to perpetuate, and the opportunities for emotional satisfactions in their homes are few. Hence, the rituals which arise from these situations are 'rituals of expediency' that is, their main purpose is to help the home to survive, and to 'facilitate escape from home into a more exciting or promising outside world' (32). Within the middle-class family there is more room to manœuvre, and the tone of the family has a general ethos of hope and optimism. Any habits which might tend towards a downward mobility are rejected, and there is developed in consequence a social and moral concern and carefulness. This is all reflected in the rituals which are developed and which reveal co-operativeness in a desire to reach the common goals, as well as genuine family 'togetherness'. The rituals of the upper class are more formalized than those in the other classes, and are perpetuated more easily from one generation to another 'because of the fortunate circumstances in their lives' (33).

When all is said, however, the rate of social change is so rapid in modern civilization that as a result a child is being reared in a *milieu* which is different from that of the parents. The resultant clashes that occur frequently result in a permanent situation of conflict. Kingsley Davis (34) makes the important point that in his attempt to socialize the child the parent tends to hark back to the old cultural content which was acquired at each stage of life, forgetting that, in the period of the birth-cycle, life has radically changed. Davis goes on to point out that these changes are found in the areas of physiological, psychosocial and sociological differences. In attempting to socialize the child into the established ways and institutions of society the parent tends to forget that what, for him, has become established is very much the object of youthful criticism and resentment, in that 'the old have in them a vested interest from which he [the young person] is excluded' (35). There is a conflict between the idealism of youth and the realism of the adult which remains unresolved.

Also, within the realm of parental authority, there is a confusion *within* the generations, and in consequence parents become confused themselves in relation to the conflicting norms presented to them by society. As a result, they become inconsistent in the rearing of their children, unable to decide what is 'best for them'. The variation between one family and another in this area of authority again leads to conflict because they are real arguing-points for the children. The sophistic teachers in the classroom, moreover, provide additional fodder for the children through periods of open discussion and social criticism. This is not written in any spirit of deprecation in relation to such discussions: it is merely an attempt to delineate the causes of increasing conflict and confusion, which may be but the growing pains towards social, and perhaps even global, maturity.

Kingsley Davis also points out that there is very little explicit institutionalization of the steps in parental authority (36). Some youths are completely emancipated from parental authority much earlier than others; some 'children' look adult at a very early age and resent any appellation which might suggest that they are, in fact, children or are still 'under authority'. Patterns of acceptance or rejection of authority vary from family to family, and there is no precise *rite de passage* which will decide conclusively that a child has now become an adult – except the present legal status acquired at the age of eighteen. But at eighteen a youth may be still at school, or possibly a student entering university and largely dependent upon his parents. Or he may, in any case, still share his parents' home. The rituals already referred to may no longer apply because new youth rituals and cultures may have been developed, and there results a rapid deceleration of the process of socialization as far as the parents are concerned.

In his conclusion in the article on 'The Sociology of Parent–Youth Conflict', Kingsley Davis emphasizes the important and complex variables which tend to disrupt the socializing process: (1) the rate of social change; (2) the extent of complexity in the social structure; (3) the degree of integration in the culture; and (4) the velocity of movement, that is, vertical mobility, within the structure and its relation to cultural values. Davis concludes that

'If ours were a simple rural-stable society, mainly familistic, the emancipation from parental authority being gradual and marked by definite institutionalized steps with no great postponement of marriage, sex taboo, or open competition for status, parents and youth would not be in conflict. Hence, the presence of parent–youth conflict in our civilization is one more specific manifestation of the incompatibility between an urban–industrial–mobile social system and the familial type of reproductive institutions' (37).

The frequent failure of socialization of individual youths in our society is not to be glibly attributed to what are popularly characterized 'bad homes' or poor home conditions; much of it is part and parcel of the total social change and the speed with which it is being effected, leaving a state in which norms themselves are variable and present differential possibilities.

It may well be that what the school can do to rectify the conflict in the home is minimal and that, as Professor F. Musgrove suggests (38), our examination of, and action relating to, the family must be far more courageous, ruthless and radical. We can no longer take familial role-prescriptions for granted, any more than we can assume that socialization and internalization of society will take place through the performance of a few social rituals. Even those groups in our society which have the strongest and most explicit familial rituals, particularly of a religious nature such as those of the orthodox Jews, have been the first to admit their concern that the ritualizing procedures may well be destroyed in the families of their children who have married gentiles. In socializing children the family must have some concept of the norms and values which it is attempting to inculcate; and there must at the same time be some deep understanding of the psychosocial effects of the cultural lag between one generation and another.

REFERENCES

1 Murdock, G. P., *Social Structure* (Macmillan, 1949), p. 11.
2 Westermarck, E., *The History of Human Marriage* (Macmillan, 1921).
3 *Vide The Koran*, sura 4.
4 *Vide* Freud, S., *Totem and Taboo* (Penguin Books, 1938; reprinted 1940) Chapter 1.
5 *Vide* Deuteronomy 25:6; cf. also Ruth 4:10. *Levir* is the Latin for 'brother-in-law'.
6 *Soror* is the Latin for 'sister'.
7 Henriques, F., *Family and Colour in Jamaica* (MacGibbon and Kee, 2nd edition 1968), p. 113.
8 Murdock, G. P., op. cit.
9 *Vide* Spiro, M. E., 'Is the Family Universal?', *American Anthropologist*, Vol. 56, October 1954, pp. 839–46.
10 Ibid., p. 844.
11 Spiro, M. E. in Bell, N. W. and Vogel, E. F. (eds), *A Modern Introduction to the Family* (Free Press, Glencoe, 1960), pp. 72–5.
12 Ibid., p. 74.
13 *Vide The Book of Common Prayer*.
14 Musgrave, P. W., *The Sociology of Education* (Methuen, 1965; reprinted 1968), p. 19.
15 *Vide* Parsons, T., 'Principal Functions of the Nuclear Family', in Parsons, T. and Bales, R. F. (eds), *Family: Socialization and Interaction Process* (Routledge, 1956; reprinted 1964), pp. 16–22.
16 Ibid., p. 16.
17 Ibid., p. 19.
18 Ibid., p. 47.
19 Sahlins, M. D., 'The Origin of Society'; reprinted from *Scientific American*, September 1960, as Offprint No. 602 (W. H. Freeman and Co.).
20 Fletcher, R., *The Family and Marriage in Britain: An Analysis and Moral Assessment* (Penguin Books, revised edition 1966), p. 76.
21 Mitchell, G. D., *Sociology* (University Tutorial Press, 1959; reprinted 1963), p. 157.
22 Swift, D. F., *The Sociology of Education* (Routledge, 1969), p. 68.
23 *Vide* Mead, G. H., *Mind, Self and Society* (University of Chicago Press, 1934; 13th impression 1965).
24 Sprott, W. J. H., *Human Groups* (Penguin Books, 1958), p. 23.
25 Musgrove, F., *The Family, Education and Society* (Routledge, 1966), p. 47.
26 *Vide* Bowlby, J., *Child Care and the Growth of Love* (Penguin Books, 2nd edition 1965), pp. 62–8.
27 *Vide* Fletcher, R., op. cit., p. 26; also Suttie, I. D., *The Origins of Love and Hate* (Penguin Books, Peregrine, 1963), *passim*.
28 Bossard, J. H. S. and Boll, Eleanor S., 'Ritual in Family Living', *American Sociological Review*, Vol. 14, August 1949, pp. 463–9.
29 Ibid., p. 469.

30 *Vide* the works of Margaret Mead, Ruth Benedict and Erik H. Erikson listed in the Bibliography.
31 Bossard, J. H. S. and Boll, Eleanor S., op. cit., p. 464.
32 Ibid., p. 467.
33 Ibid., p. 467.
34 Davis, K., 'The Sociology of Parent–Youth Conflict', *American Sociological Review*, Vol. 5, August 1940, pp. 523–35.
35 Ibid., p. 529.
36 Ibid., pp. 531–2.
37 Ibid., p. 535.
38 Musgrove, F., op. cit., p. 144.

BIBLIOGRAPHY

A. *Books*

BANKS, OLIVE, *The Sociology of Education* (Batsford, 1968; 2nd impression 1969), Chapters 4 and 5, pp. 66–110.
BELL, C., *Middle Class Families* (Routledge, 1968).
BELL, N. W. and VOGEL, E. F. (eds), *A Modern Introduction to the Family* (Routledge, 1961).
BENEDICT, RUTH, *Patterns of Culture* (Houghton, Mifflin Co., N.Y., 1934).
BOTT, ELIZABETH, *Family and Social Network* (Tavistock Publications, 1957).
BOTTOMORE, T. B., *Sociology: A Guide to Problems and Literature* (Allen and Unwin, 1962; 2nd edition 1971), Chapter 10, pp. 168–184.
BOWLBY, J., *Child Care and the Growth of Love* (Penguin, 2nd edition 1965).
BOWLEY, A. H., *The Problems of Family Life* (E. and S. Livingstone, 1946).
BURGESS, E. W., and LOCKE, H. J., *The Family* (American Book Co., N.Y., 1950).
BURLINGHAM, D. and FREUD, ANNA, *Infants Without Families* (Allen and Unwin, 2nd edition 1965).
BUTTERWORTH, E. and WEIR, D. (eds), *The Sociology of Modern Britain: An Introductory Reader* (Fontana Library, Collins, 1970), pp. 7–57.
CHAPMAN, D., *The Home and Social Status* (Routledge, 1955).
COOLEY, C. H., *Social Organization* (Free Press, Glencoe, 1956), Chapter III.
COTGROVE, S., *The Science of Society* (Allen and Unwin, 1967), Chapter 2, pp. 40–66.
CULLEN, K., *School and Family: Social Factors in Educational Attainment* (Gill and Macmillan, 1969).
DOUGLAS, J. W. B., *The Home and the School* (Panther, 1967).
ERIKSON, E. H., *Childhood and Society* (Penguin Books, 1957; reprinted 1965).
FARMER, MARY, *The Family* (Longmans, 1970).
FLETCHER, R., *The Family and Marriage in Britain* (Penguin Books, revised edition 1966).
FOLSOM, J. K., *Youth, Family and Education* (Washington, 1941).
FRAZER, ELIZABETH, *Home Environment and the School* (Univ. of London Press, 1959).

FRAZIER, E. F., *The Negro Family in the United States* (Univ. of Chicago Press, 1966).

GOODE, W. J., *World Revolution and Family Patterns* (Free Press, Glencoe, 1963).

GOODE, W. J., *The Family* (Prentice-Hall, 1964).

HALSEY, A. H. *et al., Education, Economy and Society* (Free Press, Glencoe, 1961).

HALSEY, A. H. (ed.), *Ability and Educational Opportunity* (O.E.C.D., 1961).

HARRIS, C. C., *The Family* (Allen and Unwin, 1969).

HASHMI, F., *The Pakistani Family in Britain* (Community Relations Commission, 1969).

HENRIQUES, F., *Family and Colour in Jamaica* (MacGibbon and Kee; 2nd edition 1968).

HIRO, D., *The Indian Family in Britain* (Community Relations Commission, 1969).

HOMANS, G. C., *The Human Group* (Routledge, 1951; 5th impression 1965).

JACKSON, B. and MARSDEN, D., *Education and the Working Class* (Routledge, 1962).

JAMES, E. O., *Marriage and Society* (Hutchinson, 1952).

LESLIE, G. R., *The Family in Social Context* (O.U.P., 1967).

LEWIS, M. M., *Language, Thought and Personality in Infancy and Early Childhood* (Harrap, 1963).

MACIVER, R. M. and PAGE, C. H., *Society: An Introductory Analysis* (Macmillan, 1950; reprinted 1957), Chapter 11, 'The Family', pp. 238–80.

MCKINLEY, D. G., *Social Class and Family Life* (Free Press, Glencoe, 1964).

MARRIS, P., *Widows and their Families* (Routledge, 1958).

MAYS, J. B., *Growing up in a City* (Liverpool Univ. Press, 1951).

MAYS, J. B., *Education and the Urban Child* (Liverpool Univ. Press, 1962).

MEAD, MARGARET, *Male and Female* (Penguin Books, 1962).

MEAD, MARGARET, *Growing Up in New Guinea* (Penguin Books, 1942; reprinted 1963).

MEAD, MARGARET, *Coming of Age in Samoa* (Penguin Books, 1943; reprinted 1963).

MEAD, MARGARET *et al., The Family* (Collier-Macmillan, 1965).

MERTON, R. K., *Social Theory and Social Structure* (Glencoe, Free Press, 1951).

MITCHELL, G. D., *Sociology: The Study of Social Systems* (University Tutorial Press, 1959; reprinted 1963), Chapter X, pp. 152–65.

MOGEY, J. M., *Family and Neighbourhood* (O.U.P., 1956).

MURDOCK, G. P., *Social Structure* (Macmillan, 1949).

MUSGRAVE, P. W., *The Sociology of Education* (Methuen, 1965; reprinted 1968), Chapters 2 and 3, pp. 17–47.

MUSGROVE, F., *Youth and the Social Order* (Routledge, 1964).

MUSGROVE, F., *The Family, Education and Society* (Routledge, 1966).

MYRDAL, G., *Nation and Family* (Routledge, 1945).

NEWSON, J. and E., *Infant Care in an Urban Community* (Allen and Unwin, 1963; 2nd impression 1964).

NEWSON, J. and E., *Patterns of Infant Care* (Penguin Books, 1965).
NEWSON, J. and E., *Four Years Old in an Urban Community* (Allen and Unwin, 1968).
NIMKOFF, M. F., *Marriage and the Family* (Boston, 1947).
OGBURN, W. F. and NIMKOFF, M. F., *Technology and the Changing Family* (Houghton, Mifflin and Co., 1955).
PAHL, R. E., *Patterns of Urban Life* (Longmans, 1970).
PARSONS, T. and BALES, R. F., *Family: Socialization and Interaction Process* (Routledge, 1956; reprinted 1964).
PHILP, A. F., *Family Failure* (Faber, 1963).
PRINGLE, W. L. KELLMER, *Deprivation and Education* (Longmans, 1965).
REISSMAN, F., *The Culturally Deprived Child* (Harper and Row, 1962).
ROSS, AILEEN D., *The Hindu Family in its Urban Setting* (Toronto Univ. Press/ O.U.P., 1967).
ROSSER, C. and HARRIS, C., *The Family and Social Change* (Routledge, 1965).
SCHLESINGER, B., *The One-Parent Family* (Toronto Univ. Press/O.U.P., 1969).
SEARS, R. R. *et al., Patterns of Child Rearing* (Row, Peterson, 1957).
STOTT, D. H., *Unsettled Children and their Families* (Univ. of London Press, 1956).
TURNER, C., *Family and Kinship in Modern Britain* (Routledge, 1969).
WESTERMARCK, E., *The History of Human Marriage* (Macmillan, 1921).
WILLMOTT, P., *Adolescent Boys in East London* (Penguin Books, 1969).
WILLMOTT, P. and YOUNG, M., *Family and Class in a London Suburb* (Routledge, 1960; 3rd impression 1965).
WINNICOTT, D. W., *The Child and the Family* (Tavistock Publications, 1957).
WINNICOTT, D. W., *The Family and Individual Development* (Tavistock Publications, 1965).
WISEMAN, S., *Education and Environment* (Manchester Univ. Press, 1964).
WORLD HEALTH ORGANIZATION, *Deprivation of Maternal Care: A Reassessment* (W.H.O., Geneva, 1962).
WYNN, M., *Fatherless Families* (Michael Joseph, 1964).
YOUNG, M. and WILLMOTT, P., *Family and Kinship in East London* (Routledge, 1957; Penguin Books, 1962).
YOUNGHUSBAND, E., *Social Work with Families* (Allen and Unwin, 1965; 2nd impression 1967).
YUDKIN, S. and HOLME, A., *Working Mothers and their Children* (Michael Joseph, 1963).

B. *Articles*

BALDWIN, A. L., 'Socialization and the Parent–Child Relationship', *Child Development*, Vol. 19, September 1948, pp. 127–36.
BOSSARD, J. H. S. and BOLL, E. S., 'Ritual in Family Living', *American Sociological Review*, Vol. 14, August 1949, pp. 463–9.
BURGESS, E. W., 'The Family in a Changing Society', *American Journal of Sociology*, Vol. 53, 1948, pp. 417–22.

178 | *The Sociology of Education*

DAVIS, K., 'The Sociology of Parent–Youth Conflict', *American Sociological Review*, Vol. 5, August 1940, pp. 523–35.

DEUTSCH, M., 'The Role of Social Class in Language Development and Cognition', *American Journal of Orthopsychiatry*, Vol. 35, No. 1, 1965.

ELDER, G. H., 'Family Structure and Educational Attainment: A Cross-National Analysis', *American Sociological Review*, Vol. 30, 1965, pp. 81–96.

FIRTH, R., 'Family and Kinship in Industrial Society', in *The Development of Industrial Society, Sociological Review*, Monograph No. 8, October 1964.

HOLLINGSHEAD, A. B., 'Class Differences in Family Stability', *Annals of the American Academy of Political and Social Science*, Vol. 272, November 1950, pp. 39–46.

KOHN, M. L., 'Social Class and Parent–Child Relationships: An Interpretation', *American Journal of Sociology*, Vol. 68, 1963, pp. 471–80.

LITWAK, E., 'Occupational Mobility and Extended Family Cohesion', *American Sociological Review*, Vol. 25, February 1960, pp. 9–21.

MUSGRAVE, P. W., 'Family, School, Friends and Work: A Sociological Perspective', *Educational Research*, Vol. 9, 1967, pp. 175–86.

ROBINSON, W. P. and RACKSTRAW, S. J., 'Variations in Mothers' Answers to Children's Questions', *Sociology*, Vol. 1, No. 3, September 1967, pp. 259–76.

SPIRO, M. E., 'Is the Family Universal?' *American Anthropologist*, Vol. 56, October 1954, pp. 839–46.

SWIFT, D. F., 'Family Environment and 11+ Success: Some Basic Predictors', *British Journal of Educational Psychology*, Vol. 37, 1967, pp. 10–21.

Chapter 10

The Self, Society and Education

A. THE DEVELOPMENT OF THE SELF

The problem of the origin, nature and development of the self is a perennial one which has been investigated and considered in a variety of universes of discourse. It is a central problem in psychology, philosophy and theology as well as in the fields of social psychology and sociology. Thinkers have presented a variety of 'models' of man's inner nature; some have assumed a supernatural element, called a 'spirit' or a 'soul'; others have accepted that nothing is 'given' beyond a biological and genetic heredity. But models of man's self, or personality, amount ultimately to no more than current descriptions of man's activity and function, the roles he plays and the modification of his attitudes and behaviour through socialization and education. And, as always, current descriptions are themselves modified by the data and evidence available in relation to man's behaviour.

We are not directly concerned here with the philosophical or neurological problems of body–mind relationships, since we do not begin with man in isolation, but rather with man as a social or political animal (1). As Durkheim puts it, 'Man is man, in fact, only because he lives in society' (2), and the individual self is discoverable only in the context of society. Even such a behaviourist as Professor B. F. Skinner, however, accepts that there is a complexity about the self which cannot be explicated in simply mechanistic or behavioural terms. He says that

> 'Whatever the self may be, it is apparently not identical with the physical organism. The organism behaves, while the self initiates or directs behaviour. Moreover, more than one self is needed to explain the behaviour of one organism. A mere inconsistency in conduct from one moment to the next is perhaps no problem, for a single self could dictate different kinds of behaviour from time to time. But there appear to be two selves acting simultaneously and in different ways when one self controls another or is aware of the activity of another' (3).

1. George Herbert Mead (1863–1931)
Man discovers himself as he discovers society. In sociological terms there is no assumption either that man is good or bad *ab initio*: he is simply a being with certain potentials which are evoked in a variety of directions in relationship with other people. One of the more interesting and fundamental

theories concerning the origin and development of personality at the naturalistic level is that of George Herbert Mead (4). Mead emphasizes that the self-conscious personality which is gradually being evolved by the child is a *social* product; behaviour in one individual causes behaviour in another, and the action of one acts as a cue to the action of another. Mead argues that animals act without conscious intention, whereas the peculiarity of human interaction is that it is purposeful. He gives the example of a dog which stands upon its hind legs and walks around only when we cue him in, as it were, by using a particular word. The dog, however, cannot give himself the stimulus which someone else gives to him – whilst he is able to respond to it he cannot himself actively condition his own reflexes. On the other hand, it is a characteristic of significant speech as used by human beings that precisely this process of self-conditioning is happening all the time (5).

Mead goes on to argue that human beings make gestures which are *calculated* to elicit a response, and that this comes about by the individual taking on the role of the other with whom he is in the process of interacting. The child, for example, gradually acquires the capacity to respond in a kind of *imaginative* way to his own projected conduct. Within himself he rehearses precisely what he is going to do, and inwardly he responds to himself. Should the response that he obtains prove to be unsatisfactory, he will then try again until an act is pictured in his mind which elicits within himself the reflection of the satisfactory response which, in turn, he hopes to evoke from the real Other outside him. He can then make a sign, a gesture or sound which is meaningful, in the sense that it is calculated to produce the desired effect.

Mead further argues that among the gestures which the human animal makes is speech, which is audible both to himself and to the person to whom he is talking. In speech the individual is able to respond to himself with the expected response of the Other more easily than is the case with other bodily gestures, for the vocal gesture has importance which no other gesture has (6). According to Mead the meaning of what we are saying is our tendency to respond to it: 'You are always replying to yourself, just as other people reply. You assume that in some degree there must be identity in the reply. It is action on a common basis' (7). An individual directs behaviour towards himself, converses with himself and passes judgement upon himself. Thus, the self, which is non-existent at birth, arises in social experience as a result of taking on the role of others.

For Mead, therefore, the self is not primarily the physiological organism (8), and although the physiological organism may be essential as a means of its outward expression, at least we can think of a self without it. The self is basically a social structure which arises in social experience. The conversation of gestures is simply the beginnings of communications and the individual starts to carry on a conversation of gestures with himself: he says something which calls out a certain reply in himself, and that in turn makes him change what he was about to say. This is what Mead terms 'significant speech'.

Thinking is thus preparatory to social action. It is interesting to note that Mead considers that Spearman's 'X factor' in intelligence is simply this ability of the individual to take the attitude of the other, or the attitudes of others generally, thus realizing the significance of the gestures and symbols in terms of which thinking proceeds, and so being enabled to carry on with himself the internal conversation by means of these gestures and symbols. Of all animals man appears to be alone, in his ability to have this sort of internalization of his social intentions by means of a species of self-dialogue. Professor Remy Chauvin, who has studied animal communication in considerable detail, states:

'As to mammals, we all know that they are far from dumb, but it cannot be said that sound is very important in their lives. The primates, our nearest cousins, are reasonably talkative, but do not have a true language. . . . Man alone has this distinction among the primates' (9).

In play a child takes on a succession of roles, such as his mother, his father, his brother or sister, with very little consistency in his behaviour, and so far no stable self has been formed. The game, however, introduces some definite unity into the organization of other selves; it is, in fact, an illustration of the situation out of which an organized personality arises, for in it the child becomes an organic member of society. 'The importance of the game is that it lies entirely inside the child's own experience' (10). There follows, in consequence, a development of unity and the building up of the self.

This process is exemplified by Mead in the playing of a ball game. Each one of the child's own acts in the game is determined by the assumption of the actions of others engaged in the game. What he does is controlled by his being everyone else in the team, at least in so far as the attitudes and actions of others affect his own particular response. We get, then, an 'Other' which is an organization of the attitudes of those involved in the same process. Mead points out that this organization is put in the form of the *rules* of the game. All children like and accept rules, and they take such an interest in them that if they are lacking in any particular game they will invent them in an *ad hoc* sort of way.

But, of course, as the child begins to understand the nature and the finer points of the game better, so he will take on the *role* of others not merely in an understanding of the rules of the game, important though these may be. If, for example, he is playing a game of cricket and he is bowling, he must so comprehend the functions of each of his fielders that he will be able to place them precisely where he knows, or thinks, that the batsman will send the ball: he must thus understand fully the role of the batsman. His wicket-keeper must also be completely aware of the type of bowling that he is about to send down so that, should the batsman miss the ball, he will be in a position to deal with the situation:

'In his game he has to have an organization of these roles; otherwise he cannot play the game. The game represents the passage in the life of the child from taking the role of others in play to the organized part that is essential to self-consciousness in the full sense of the term' (11).

The organized community or social group which gives to the individual his unity of self is termed, by Mead, 'the Generalized Other'; and the attitude of the Generalized Other is the attitude of the whole community. In any ball game, the team is the Generalized Other in so far as it enters, as an organized process or social activity, the experience of any one of the individual members of it. As a member of the team the individual antici-pates the behaviour of all the other members; he plays a number of roles simultaneously, a generalized role of a number of people. These roles, as we have said, are built around the rules, objects and techniques of the game, and as the individual appropriates these rules and techniques so he generalizes his behaviour – he plays the role of the Generalized Other.

Thus, the team with its rules is a prototype of the organized community; and eventually the whole community of which the child is a member becomes the Generalized Other with which he is identified. As this identi-fication takes place so the values of his society become incorporated into his neural system, or internalized. Thus the self, viewed in this way, consists in an organization of the roles taken over from the community as a Generalized Other.

The fullest possible development of the individual self depends upon the ability to get the broadest activities of any given organized society within the experimental field of the individuals included in that whole (12). The separate roles, of which we spoke earlier and which are now organized and internalized, become what we call 'social attitudes'. These attitudes imply that the social process, with its various implications, is in fact taken up into the experience of the individual and in consequence that which is going on in society takes place more effectively because the individual has rehearsed it (13). Not only does the individual fulfil his role better under these con-conditions, but he is able also to reach back upon the organization of which he is a fundamental part.

Once the self of the child begins to develop, a hard central core comes into being and grows harder as the years pass. According to Mead each child has its own innate range of potentialities, and he will receive the impact of society in his own peculiar way. Inevitably, therefore, the

Generalized Other will not be exactly the same for everyone, and the understanding of the roles of others will be conditioned by individual experience. Each individual also has his own biological needs for food, drink, sexual satisfaction and protection. These will certainly, from time to time, conflict with the demands of the Generalized Other.

If the socialized attitudes which go to make up the Other have been absorbed and internalized, then the individual may well come to terms with his own conflicting needs. But if these attitudes have not been absorbed, then the ensuing conflict may resolve into anti-social or deviant behaviour, and some form of reconditioning may have to take place in order that the individual may internalize the accepted norms of social behaviour.

When the organization of the self is fully launched it will then proceed under its own organizing and integrative principles. In the normal person this process of self-integration has due regard for the needs, the demands, the rules and the laws of society – but all selves are different, and in consequence the rules will be interpreted differently within the same society. There are, however, umpires within the society to ensure that deviation from the accepted interpretation is not too wide. Mead also maintains that when we reflect upon ourselves we become possessed of a cherished object, with prestige and merit; and so we have the power of reasoning, we acquire standards, and we have the ability to reflect upon them.

The self is not a substance but a process in which a conversation, as it were, between the 'I' and the 'Me' takes place. The 'Me' is the more or less integrated set of attitudes and ideas of other people which we have built together as our conscious experience, and from which we choose roles to represent our own ideas of ourselves. Many of these are roles which we know the community has come to expect us to perform. The 'I' is the self as actor or initiator, the agent of change, and without the 'I' there could not be the notion of novelty, unexpectedness or innovation in experience. While differing aspects of 'Me' depend upon my cultural and social training and upon the particular configurations of time and place, the 'I' represents the sense of self-identity in the one who possesses the experiences (14).

In a stable society the generalized image is relatively settled, and the varieties of interpretation are few because the main roles are appreciated and well understood. But in a heterogeneous society and a changing society we have a whole series of Generalized Others, as in large cities such as Chicago, Liverpool, etc. Only by taking the attitudes of the Generalized Others towards himself can man think at all; the self-conscious individual takes or assumes the organized social attitudes of the given social group or community of which he is a member, and towards the social problems of various kinds which confront that group or community at any given time.

For Mead there exists no human nature outside society, and what a personality internalizes is an object system, a role-expectation for the self and for the Other. This role-expectation is the basic unit of the social system, and two or more complementary role-expectations make up a role system. In *The Philosophy of the Act,* Mead maintains that it is the capacity of the human individual to assume the organized attitudes of the community towards himself, and towards others, that distinguishes the duties, rights, customs, laws and the various institutions and role systems in human society from the physiological relationships of an ant nest or a beehive. He certainly would not agree that man is an anthropoid ape trying to live like a termite (15). Mead goes on:

> 'The attainment of this attitude on the part of the individual is responsible for the appearance of a situation in which new values arise, especially within which society deals with the individual as embodying the values in himself. This situation is expressed in the appearance of institutions, e.g. the church, government, art, and education' (16).

Mead thus argues that social control is internalized, since the essence of all human experience is social; hence perception and communication are social. The internalization of the Other, 'the taking of the role of the Other', is an intrinsic aspect of human thinking, and leadership in any form in society becomes the prerogative of the individual most able to internalize the roles of others. The leader is a 'multiple participator'. As the individual becomes self-conscious so he becomes self-critical and, through self-criticism, social control over individual behaviour operates by virtue of the social origin and basis of such criticism. Self-criticism is essentially social criticism, and behaviour controlled by such self-criticism is essentially behaviour socially controlled.

2. Sigmund Freud (1856–1939)

We have spent some time on an outline of Mead's theory or description of the development of the self because his was one of the great original minds in the field of social psychology, and much of contemporary role theory has been an elaboration of his thinking. Freud's theory of the self was written from a somewhat different point of view, namely that of a psychoanalyst; it is, however, a description of the nature of the self which has clear social implications.

In the organization of the personality Freud recognized three major elements, or systems – the Id, the Ego, and the Super-Ego. In an individual who is mentally healthy these three systems work together harmoniously, but when the systems become disorganized, the individual becomes ill. Normally the three elements co-operate in order that the individual might cope with his environment and fulfil his basic needs and desires.

The Id (or the 'It') begins as a reflex apparatus which discharges the excitatory sensations that reach it; it does this by various motor activities, such as sneezing, eye-watering and so on. Stimuli may also come from within the body itself, such as pressure on the bladder and the emptying of its contents. New developments take place in the Id through the blocking, or frustration, of primary needs and tensions; thus an individual may be hungry without possessing any means of satisfying his hunger and this results in tension.

This new development in the Id is termed a primary process, and Freud believed that many of these tensions were released in wish fulfilment. Through our perceptual and memory systems we form a mental image of the object that will reduce tension – our dreams, said Freud, are often of this order: we dream about the things we want and so release our tensions. But it is clear that the Id does not always satisfactorily rid the individual of tension: it reduces through the pleasure-principle the amount of tension to a low and fairly constant level. Tension results in pain, relief in satisfaction – and so the aim of the pleasure-principle is to give satisfaction or pleasure and to reduce pain.

Whilst the Id is the sum-total of crude and unmodified instinctual needs, the Ego is 'the executive of the personality' (17). Its essential characteristic, according to Karen Horney, is its weakness (18). The sources of energy lie in the Id, and its preferences, goals, dislikes and decisions are determined by the interplay of the Id and the Super-Ego. The Ego is also very much concerned with the outside world, and it must ensure that the instinctual drives of the Id not only do not contravene the censorship of the Super-Ego, but also do not conflict too dangerously with the external world. Whilst it desires to submit to the pleasures of the Id, it also tends to submit to the prohibitions of the Super-Ego. When the Ego fulfils its executive functions with discrimination and wisdom, harmony and adjustment will prevail. Maladjustments in the personality occur when the Id, the Super-Ego or the external world exert too much power.

Just as the Id is controlled by the pleasure-principle, so the Ego is controlled by the reality-principle. The pleasure-principle moves us towards the gratification of drives: the reality-principle is established largely by the standards and mores of our society. It is through this latter principle, through the knowledge of reality, or that which exists, that the Ego learns to postpone action and to tolerate tensions until pleasure may be attained at the 'right' time, and in the 'right', or most fulfilling, way. This development in the Ego is termed a secondary process; it is developed after the primary process of the Id:

'The secondary process accomplishes what the primary process is unable to do, namely, to separate the subjective world of the mind from the objective world of physical reality. The secondary process does not make the mistake, as the primary process does, of regarding the image of an object as though it were the object itself' (19).

The Ego is the product of an interaction with the external world, or the environment, but Freud held that its general development was also controlled by heredity and the process of maturation. We all have innate powers of reasoning, which we more fully understand through the process of training, education and experience. Thus education itself is very much concerned with the development of the Ego in training it to think and to make increasingly more effective judgements, in order to arrive at truth or reality.

If the Id is concerned with pleasure, and the Ego with reality, then the Super-Ego, the moral element in the personality, is concerned with the ideal. The Super-Ego represents the individual's moral code, which is largely the internalization of parental authority, and then gradually of the other traditional and external values and ideals of his society. It is an inner agency of a forbidding character, detecting any trends of impulses that are not permitted, and punishing the individual if they are present.

The Super-Ego comprises the ego-ideal, which corresponds to what the individual considers, via his parents and society, to be morally good; and the conscience, which corresponds to what the individual has internalized as morally bad, and therefore requiring punishment. The Super-Ego rewards with feelings of pride and punishes with feelings of inferiority, shame and guilt. By such means it serves to regulate the impulses of aggression and sex, whose uncontrolled expression of the Id would endanger society. As B. F. Skinner says, these three selves or personalities in the Freudian scheme 'represent important characteristics of behaviour in a social milieu' (20). The internalization of the father figure, regarded as omniscient and omnipotent, gives to the resultant Super-Ego a dominant, authoritarian aspect in the socialization of the child; it is the inner representation of the moral demands of society (or some element of society), and in particular of its prohibitive aspects.

3. Some Other Views

Plato, in Book III of *The Republic*, discusses the art of imitation and suggests that the Guardians of the State

'should not depict or be skilful at imitating any kind of illiberality or baseness, lest from imitation they should come to be what they imitate. Did you never observe how imitations, beginning in early youth and continuing far into life, at length grow into habits and become a second nature, affecting body, voice, and mind?' (21).

Plato was clearly afraid that the mask (*persona*) which an actor perpetually wore might indeed become his face or 'personality'; for the roles in which we persistently participate will tend to become our identities. P. L. Berger has regarded the whole process of the development of the self in a dramatic or histrionic context. Thus the individual has a repertoire of roles, and the range and adaptability of his personality will be measured by the number of roles that he is capable of playing. The individual's biography appears as 'an uninterrupted sequence of stage performances', which will be played to different audiences, and may involve him in drastic changes of masks and costumes, but which will always demand that the actor *be* the part that he is playing (22).

In his study of 'Role Distance' (23), E. Goffman has outlined a pattern of role analysis involved in the development of the self. An individual becomes a *role incumbent* by the act of taking on a particular role. This role which he adopts consists of the sort of activity he would engage in if he were to act 'solely in terms of the normative demands upon someone in his position' (24). But his *actual* conduct while on duty in this position is referred to as *role performance*, or role enactment. In the fulfilment of the obligations of his role, however, the incumbent is involved or associated with a number of *role others*; and R. K. Merton has referred to these associated roles as a *role set* (25). Thus, in the example of the teacher in the school, his role-set will comprise other teachers on the staff, the headmaster, the pupils, the parents, the secretarial staff, the inspectorate, the L.E.A. and divisional executive, the school doctor, dentist and nurse, and not least the caretaker and cleaning staff.

Professor M. Banton has pointed out that the 'plethora of conflicting definitions' in role theory has caused some confusion where different sociologists and anthropologists have used different words for the same concepts. In consequence, Banton states that

'It is agreed: that behaviour can be related to a *position* in a social structure; that actual behaviour can be related to the individual's own ideas of what is appropriate (*role cognitions*), or to other people's ideas about what he *will* do (*expectations*), or to other people's ideas about what he *should* do (*norms*). In this light a role may be understood as a *set of norms and expectations applied to the incumbent of a particular position*' (26).

E. Goffman has added to these concepts that of *role distance*, which connotes for him the separateness between the individual and his positive role whereby he is, in effect, denying the self implied in the role (and not the role itself) for all accepting performers. Goffman's introduction of the term refers, he says, to those actions which convey effectively 'some disdainful detachment' of the performer from the role which he is performing

(27). Banton comments on this behaviour of those who are continually stepping out of role to indicate to others that they should not be identified with the part they are playing, and adds that 'superficial observation suggests that such behaviour is more common in the United States' (28). But to Goffman the concept of role distance provides a *sociological*, as distinct from an individual and psychological, means of dealing with the sort of divergent conduct that falls between role obligations and actual role performance. He regards role distance as a part of *typical* role, even though it is not part of the *normative* framework of role (29).

Any social system may be relatively maintained or relatively destroyed according to the fulfilment of the role system of that society. Thus the function of any specific role is delineated by the part it plays in perpetuating the social pattern. This fact will be of some consequence when we come to consider the roles of the school and the teacher in any particular social *milieu*. In so far as a particular role and role performance assist and support society, to that extent one may speak of its *eufunction*; in so far as the role and its enactment tend to disrupt or destroy society, one may refer to its *dysfunction*.

We have considered the development of the self as seen by G. H. Mead and Sigmund Freud, and the idea of the self in social relationships in the concept of role. In his *Stigma*, E. Goffman has considered what is meant by personal identity. A person's uniqueness involves, he suggests, the notion of a 'positive mark' or 'identity peg'; it is the idea of the photographic image which others have in their mind of the individual, or 'the knowledge of his special place in a particular kinship network' (30). It is perhaps not without significance that the word 'character' means a distinctive mark or stamp (31). In addition, according to Goffman,

> 'A second idea is that, whilst particular facts about an individual will be true of others too, the full set of facts known about an intimate is not found to hold, as a combination, for any other person in the world, this adding a means by which he can be positively distinguished from everyone else' (32).

And Goffman goes on to emphasize that, just because of its one-of-a-kind quality, personal identity is able to, and does, play a structured and standardized role in social organization.

Social structure is developed out of both differences in individuals as well as out of their similarities or sameness. In sociological science there is too often an attempt at a reduction of human qualities and culture to a lowest common denominator. It is, therefore, somewhat refreshing to note the value that W. I. Thomas placed upon personal life-records, which he regarded as the perfect type of sociological material; whereas the use of mass-phenomena or of events, without due regard to the life-histories of the individual participants, he regarded as a defect in sociological method (33). For Thomas the fundamental principles of personal evolution were to be sought both in the individual's own nature and in his social *milieu*. He saw this personal evolution as a perpetual struggle between the individual and society: it was a struggle for self-expression on the side of the individual, and for his subjection on the side of society. Out of this struggle the dynamic and evolving personality manifests and structures itself. There is change as well as stability which both derive from the relativity of the desire for new experiences and for continuity (34).

C. H. Cooley regarded the self as a reflection in a looking-glass: it was a mirror, as it were, of others. In his *Human Nature and the Social Order*, Cooley argues that we can know persons directly only as imaginative ideas in the mind; and the imaginations that individuals have of one another are the *solid facts* of society. The immediate social reality is 'the personal idea', the thing in which men exist for one another and in which they work directly upon one another's lives (35). Gradually through the consciousness and awareness of others, the individual develops a self which becomes capable of autonomous behaviour. Cooley further expands his theme in *Social Organization*, in which he concludes that there are at least three aspects of consciousness which are distinguishable: self-consciousness, which is what I think about myself; social consciousness, or what I think of others; and public consciousness, which is a collective view of self and social consciousness as organized in a communicative group. These are but three phases of a single unity (36), and their *locus* is found in the experience of the individuals; selves and others are, indeed, ideas in people's minds (37).

But, as G. H. Mead has indicated (38), although Cooley has demonstrated, within his own terms of reference, the total involvement of the self in society, and society in the self, his social psychology and psychological method inevitably resolve themselves into a complete solipsism. For Cooley society exists only in the individual's mind, and any social concept of the self is a product of the human imagination. But for Cooley, as for others, the social self must presuppose experience; and experience must presuppose the existence of other selves in interaction with whom the individual self or ego is evolved. There cannot be experience without an experiencer who is formed and developed by the *others*, who have already developed through their own experience.

B. THE SELF AND EDUCATION

In Freudian theory the Ego, or executive member of the personality, was slowly and often painfully reaching out towards freedom; that is, a freedom from the compulsions and authorities of the external world, as sometimes represented by the reality-principle in the Super-Ego; and also freedom from the instinctual urges and compulsions of the primitive levels of the Id, with its pleasure-principle. Once the Ego had been liberated from these 'alien' pressures, or had in some satisfactory way resolved and organized them, it could proceed to utilize the 'energized structures' and drives, generated in the Unconscious, for purposes which were consciously approved and creative.

For Freud freedom represented *consciously* motivated activity – activity that was self-directed and usefully channelled. Maturity occurred when the individual had organized and controlled the constellation of instinctual drives and the external forces: such a man was prepared to give love without seeking any return.

Many of the so-called 'free schools' that claimed to develop out of Freudian principles of no repression and free, unhindered development of the self, were likely to be as harmful as many of the more traditional schools, based upon a very strict and sometimes sadistic discipline. But Freud, in his analysis of the self, was not merely pointing the way of freedom from *external* compulsion; he was just as interested in man's, or the child's, freedom from *inner* compulsion, a compulsion which some of the 'free schools' exemplified. A truly psycho-analytical approach would emphasize the need for self-discipline and self-analysis (39), and also the need for the development of the integration or the wholeness of the individual, and of his capacity for health, happiness and love.

This is very relevant for education. Increasingly in a world of international and racial conflict, it is such values as love, happiness and wholeness that need to be emphasized – not just better academic qualifications. The works of Anna Freud, Melanie Klein and Susan Isaacs indicate the great importance of observing children, of understanding their problems, of seeking to help them to reorientate their ideas and values, and to develop the right sort of face-to-face relationships with them. And this, in turn, emphasizes the teacher's need to understand himself, as well as the children he teaches. In the words of Professor Ben Morris:

'. . . it seems to me that, far from reducing man to an automaton, a passive victim of instinct, a puppet controlled by unconscious desires, or a creature of conditioned response, Freud's work enables us to put the concepts of an integrated personality and an autonomous self at the centre of educational theory' (40).

A study of the sociology of education is as much concerned with the development of the individual self as psychology, for both disciplines must see the self, or personality, in the context of all the stimuli in society which eventually go to make the individual what he is.

We have seen already that for Mead the mind is a social emergent;

indeed, it is 'nothing but the importation of this external process into the conduct of the individual so as to meet the problems that arise' (41). Mead emphasizes the great importance of the social *milieu* in the development of the individual. In the discussion of the aims of education it is often, and somewhat loosely, claimed that the important goal to achieve is the fullest possible development of the personality, the eliciting of innate qualities, and so forth. But for Mead the self is not a seed in us, called 'personality', which must be carefully and tenderly nurtured, and allowed the maximum freedom for growth. Nothing could be farther from reality, for the type of environment in which the child is born and grows will determine the type of personality. A social environment which is permissive will shape and evolve one kind of personality; another environment which is authoritarian will elicit a different sort of personality. According to Mead, permission is not the *removal* of social influence so that the innate or 'natural' personality may have a chance to develop, *pace* Rousseau: permissiveness merely replaces one kind of social influence for another.

This would appear to imply that we can have ultimately in our society – indeed, *will* have – the sort of personalities we want to evolve according to the social context or environment that we provide for the growing child. This is a frankly behaviouristic approach to the nature of the self and to the meaning of personality. The self of the child emerges out of social experience. The conclusion drawn by Karl Mannheim is a very relevant one, namely, that:

> 'Responsibility is not a quality with which we are born but emerges out of the chances we have had to learn, according to our degree of maturity, how to act responsibly, so that as time has passed we have been able to develop a concept of what it means' (42).

It is obvious from the foregoing that it is vital to provide within the educational framework, which is an important part of the immediate social *milieu* to which the child belongs, the right sort of chances for the learning of responsibility and for its acceptance. This kind of experience can best be achieved in the relationship of individuals within community life. The infant's behaviour is diffuse and best considered in such terms as 'cycles of activity', but he has to learn what he can do, and how to do it, from the responses which others give to him and by the satisfaction which he experiences within himself. At this early stage he has no self-awareness or self-observation, and his behaviour flows out of him to others in an urgent desire for the immediate satisfaction of his rudimentary needs.

As the infant begins to demonstrate signs of becoming aware of others, he begins to include in his actions some anticipation of their response; and so he will direct and control his actions accordingly. He will utilize the whole apparatus of his face, hands and toes, and from time to time he will express signs of recognition by his smiles and gurgles. He is slowly learning both to control and to direct his behaviour in terms of what *others expect* of him, and this is one of the most vital elements in the educational process. The individual child must come to recognize and to develop the self-regulating and unifying function of this aspect of his experience.

Mead also emphasizes the importance in education of the initiation of activity. The awareness of identity emerges not out of action by the individual person, but out of *interaction* after one has perceived other people and established some sense of relationship with them and some idea of how actions or behaviour are called out. It is only when this sense of being able to *initiate* is present that we can say that there exists the beginnings of selfhood. Moreover, the kind of action which is initiated must arise out of a choice of possible actions, or else it would appear to be determined, and no question of initiation or selection would arise. Selfhood becomes possible, therefore, only when the child has had a sufficiently long experience, and an independent one at that. One of the chief tasks of education is to provide that sort of social context, possessing a wide variety of choice of experiences, which will help the child to initiate activity.

Obviously we can no longer treat young children as if they were little adults, somewhat deficient in morals and intellect, and needing to be disciplined in order to get them into the right attitude. This implies that there is a great need for the teacher to have a thorough understanding of both the intellectual and social development of the child, as expressed by such writers as Susan Isaacs and Jean Piaget. If, as Mead rightly argues, the child cannot possess the whole self-consciousness of the adult, then our development of modern educational practice rests to a large extent upon the 'possibility of the adult finding a common basis between himself and the child' (43).

The differences among people involve the recognition of varieties of experience. One has to accept that differing societies vary in their standards, their values and their evaluations, from the Hopi Indians, the Samoans and the Papuans to the sophisticated New Yorkers and Londoners. Different types of personality are formed by different types of society and it becomes, therefore, increasingly important to study the multiplicity of 'patterns of culture' (44) in order to see what sort of personality, what type of self, each is capable of producing. It is important, also, to see what changing effects culture contact may have upon a society and upon individuals within that society. The selves that we are, are to a very great extent the product of our social contacts; it is from society that we get the indispensable tool of language, our interests and our basic moral standards; selves change with the changes of society. In education we are helping individuals to prepare for and adapt to such social change. Mead has emphasized this educational importance of cultural and social *milieux* in the following terms:

'The getting of this social response into the individual constitutes the process of education which takes over the cultural media of the community in a more or less abstract way. Education is definitely the process of taking over a certain organized set of responses to one's own stimulation; and until one can respond to himself as the community responds to him, he does not genuinely belong to the community' (45).

Education is education for community and social living. Mead further insists in *The Philosophy of the Act* that the individual and the society are 'selectively and causally determinative of the environment', and that this, in turn, determines the individual or the society (46). Neither can be explained in terms of the other except as the other is determined by it. Thus Mead, in his social philosophy and psychology seeks to steer a middle course between what he regards as the Scylla of an impossible solipsism, such as that propounded (in his view) by C. H. Cooley, and the Charybdis of an equally impossible determinism.

Education must prepare for change – change within the culture-patterns, change within the basic moral standards, and change within the core values of society. In a developing multi-cultural society the necessity for such preparation, and the urgency of it, become increasingly apparent. Teachers are becoming ever more aware that the mediation of subject content is not, *per se*, enough – however necessary. We are educating for life, with its mobility, fluidity and change. One of the essential elements in education is the inculcation of the ability to absorb new situations, new experiences and novel ideas, as well as the capacity to initiate activity. All cultures suffer the hazards of internal dissension, human misery and mental disease: these social facts are, like all others, capable of being internalized by any individual member of society. A part of the essence of education is to develop the means of building the self in such a way that it is able not only to *adapt* itself to change, but also to *initiate* change, and can present within itself an opposing force to such hazards as those referred to above, which may well challenge its identity.

The kindergarten or nursery school has a large part to play in the social development of the small child (47). The small child readily plays out its experiences, and plays at a variety of roles including mother, father, teacher, the milkman, a burglar or a Red Indian. These roles are made the basis for training: they are very temporary roles, and a child will pass with considerable unconcern from that of a policeman to that of a crook. He will say something in one character and respond in another, and a certain organized structure arises in him, and in his 'other' which replies to it. It is true that such role-taking is purely for amusement and play, but gradually the process of role-taking becomes almost a conscious one for the better understanding of the 'other', or in anticipation of taking up that role later on. 'This outcome is just what the kindergarten works toward. It takes the characters of these various vague beings and gets them into such an organized social relationship to each other that they build up the character of the little child' (48).

The educational importance of role-taking becomes increasingly clear in our expanding and complex society. It is important that we understand other people, that we become 'members one of another', that we do not only see ourselves as others see us, but also see others as they see themselves. It becomes more and more important to be able to negotiate with others, to arbitrate fairly between others, and to find formulas acceptable to parties in disagreement. A social education implies the ability to identify with others, to get inside their skins, feel what they feel, know what they know, and experience what they experience – so that when they approach us in their particular role we have the fullest possible understading of what they seek from us and of how best we can come to terms with them. The face-to-face relationships which we every day encounter, the 'I-Thou' interaction in which complete identification is found with the 'other' (49) – these are the basic data of living together in harmony. Such harmonious living demands a deliberate educational policy: the multitudinous and intricate roles of society must go through a process of simplification so that our pupils may fully understand them. This raises the whole question of initiation for our society; and part of this process of simplification in roles is to be found in tradition, and in the transformation and re-interpretation of approved personality traits and accepted character types. In a simple society the whole process would be effected by its *rites de passage*.

All this points to a far deeper and wider understanding of our society than is at present the case; it points to courses in civics, neighbourhood and environmental studies, social studies and sociology at all levels of education. The Newsom Report (1963) was fully alive to the necessity of getting the child to understand more thoroughly the social *milieu* in which he lives, and to the need for realistic role-taking. Its recommendations (50) were all, in one way or another, involved in social interaction and role participation.

We noted earlier Mead's emphasis upon the importance of the organized game in developing a definite unity in the organization of the self. In passing from unorganized play to the more stringent role-taking and role-prescription in the game, the child is moving on 'to the organized part that is essential to self-consciousness in the full sense of the term' (51). What goes on in the game goes on in the life of the child all the time; he is continually taking on the attitudes of those about him, especially of those who in some sense control him and upon whom he depends. In fact, Mead suggests that the morale of the game takes hold of the child more than the larger morale of the whole community. The child takes part in a game and the game expresses a social situation into which he can completely and wholeheartedly enter; and its morale may exert, temporarily at least, a far greater hold on him than that of the family of which he is a part, or than that of the community in which he has been brought up and in which he now lives (52).

This complete identification with the roles of other members of the game is one of the strongest identifications which the child or the developing self makes. The team is the Generalized Other; it provides the rules and the limits of the individual's activity, and he has complete identity with them. This would indicate the educational value of the game as such: it is a means of internalizing the roles of other participants in the game itself, and by transference it is a means of finding identity with other human groups. The process of the Generalized Other is applied by the individual child in the family, the class, the school, the club, the church and so on. Eventually, if both internalization and transference are successful, the individual may find some identification with the macro-society – that is, the larger society of which he is a member.

There is a very real sense, if Mead's theories have validity, in which battles, projects, enterprises, and all organized efforts in which a number of people work together in a variety of roles, are 'won on the playing fields'. A team game becomes a serious, organized project in which each member must so fully understand the role of the other that he finds complete identity with it. A game, as we all know, frequently goes wrong because one or more of the members of the team may fail fully to appreciate the roles of the others, and therefore their *own* role. Just as the importance of the game is that it lies entirely within the child's own experience, so the importance of our modern type of education is that it is also brought as far as possible within this realm (53). This is life in miniature, and the organized teams and team games of the school have a function in preparing the pupil for the more serious organized group of the business firm, the factory, the research department and so on. Those who fail to make this internalization of the role of the Generalized Other become ill, maladjusted, deviant, delinquent or criminal. Perhaps it should be pointed out that one can, of course, know the rules and, in theory at least, understand the roles of others and yet not be a particularly good player – like the man who knows every stroke in cricket but can never somehow make contact with the ball.

Bound up with the question of taking on the roles of others is the great problem in our society of a communication – communication, that is, between different groups of people, with differing viewpoints, prejudices, standards and ideals. It is the problem of communication between the scientist and the non-scientist, between the technologist and the layman, between the employer and the employee, between the religious and the non-religious, between the old and the young, and between the 'with it' and the 'square'. This is, once more, a question of role-taking, of getting into the position of the other. Only a really enlightened education, able to range the great variety of social roles and *niveaux*, can help solve the difficulties of class barriers and struggles, colour bars and political doctrinaires.

For Mead, education implies the development of unity within the self, and the gradual building-up of the self through social interaction. The most effective form of learning and teaching can be found in community life, in which the child experiences the complex relationships of people. Neither social attributes nor personal qualities are acquired simply by taking thought or by understanding them intellectually. They are acquired in action, in role-taking or social interaction. It would seem to be the task of the educator to plan learning so that responsibility is being understood through action, and through the acceptance of the role which one knows others will expect one to play. We cannot, according to Mead, even be *ourselves* unless we are also members in whom there is a community of attitudes which control the attitudes of all. We cannot have rights unless we have common attitudes, and it is one of the functions of education to establish a sense of community through the internalization of common attitudes. Selves exist only in definite relationships to other selves. 'No hard-and-fast line can be drawn between our own selves and the selves of others, since our own selves exist and enter as such into our experience only in so far as the selves of others exist and enter as such into our experience also' (54).

The structure of the individual self reflects the general behaviour-pattern of the social group to which the individual belongs; there is a common structure of selves: we are members of a community. The self is a socio-logical phenomenon and one must be a member of a community in order to be a self. As a basis for the theory of education this implies a sociological approach to both learning and living.

In his consideration of a planned society and the problems of human personality, Karl Mannheim argues that society influences the human mind in four main ways: through the method of intelligent adjustment on the part of the individual; through learning; through conscious education, including re-education and post-education; and through psychoanalysis (55). For Mannheim conscious education was an arrangement of stimuli in such a way that an individual *responsible ego* is elicited which is competent to discriminate and discern good from bad, and healthy from unhealthy influences. Further, through its education the individual ego should be in a position to revise the values and standards of its environment, and gradually to transform its behaviour accordingly. It is this independence which the self eventually assumes that will inevitably bring it into conflict with other selves, and with groups and perhaps with society at large.

The works of both Carl Jung and Teilhard de Chardin have considered in some detail the genesis of the self and the development of personality. And both seem to have reached similar if not the same conclusions; the path to individuation is a movement towards some form of social or cosmic identity. Socialization is the beginning of personality: its end is some form of social identity. To be a 'person' is not to be isolated or divergent from others. Rather

'To be fully ourselves it is in the opposite direction, in the direction of convergence with all the rest, that we must advance – towards the "other". The peak of ourselves, the acme of our originality, is not our individuality but our person; and according to the evolutionary structure of the world, we can only find our person by uniting together. There is no mind without synthesis. The same law holds good from top to bottom. The true ego grows in inverse proportion to "egoism". Like the omega which attracts it, the element only becomes personal when it universalizes itself' (56).

REFERENCES

1 *Vide* Aristotle, *Politics*, Book 1.2: 'Clearly, then, the state is natural, and man is by nature an animal designed for living in states. The person who by nature, not accident, does not belong to a state is either a wild beast or a god.'

2 Durkheim, E., *Education and Sociology* (Free Press, Glencoe, 1956), p. 76.

3 Skinner, B. F., *Science and Human Behaviour* (Free Press, Collier-Macmillan, 1953), p. 284.

4 George Herbert Mead's theory is best expressed in his posthumous work, *Mind, Self and Society* (Univ. of Chicago Press, 1934; 13th impression 1965). *Vide* also Strauss, A. (ed.), *George Herbert Mead: On Social Psychology* (Univ. of Chicago Press, 1st Phoenix edition 1964).

5 Mead, G. H., *Mind, Self and Society*, p. 108.

6 Ibid., p. 65.

7 Ibid., p. 67.

8 Ibid., p. 139.

9 Chauvin, R., *Animal Societies* (Sphere Books Ltd, 1971).

10 Mead, G. H., op. cit., p. 159.

11 Ibid., p. 152.

12 Ibid., p. 155.

13 Ibid., p. 179.

14 Ibid., pp. 192–200.

15 *Vide* Linton, R., *The Tree of Culture* (A. A. Knopf, 1955), p. 11.

16 Mead, G. H., *The Philosophy of the Act* (Univ. of Chicago Press, 1938; 5th impression 1964), p. 625.

17 Hall, C. S., *A Primer of Freudian Psychology* (New English Library, Mentor Book, 15th printing 1954), p. 28.
18 Horney, Karen, *New Ways in Psychoanalysis* (Routledge, 4th impression 1961), pp. 184–5.
19 Hall, C. S., op. cit., p. 29.
20 Skinner, B. F., op. cit., pp. 284–5.
21 *Vide The Republic of Plato* (translated by B. Jowett) (O.U.P., 1927), Book III, 395 C-D.
22 *Vide* Berger, P. L., *Invitation to Sociology* (Penguin Books, 1966), pp. 123–4.
23 *Vide* Goffman, E., *Encounters* (Bobbs-Merrill Co., Inc., 1961), pp. 83–152.
24 Ibid., p. 85.
25 *Vide* Merton, R. K., 'The Role-Set: Problems in Sociological Theory', *British Journal of Sociology*, Vol. 8, June 1957, pp. 106–20.
26 Banton, M., *Roles* (Tavistock Publications, 1965), pp. 28–9.
27 Goffman, E., op. cit., pp. 105–10.
28 Banton, M., op. cit., p. 198.
29 Goffman, E., op. cit., p. 115.
30 Goffman, E., *Stigma* (Penguin Books, 1968), p. 73.
31 From the Greek χαρακτήρ (kharaktēr), meaning 'that which is cut in, marked or stamped; a likeness, image or exact representation'.
32 Goffman, E., ibid., p. 74.
33 *Vide* Thomas, W. I., *On Social Organization and Social Personality* (Univ. of Chicago Press, Phoenix Books, 1966), Chapter 2, 'Social Personality: Organization of Attitudes', pp. 11–36.
34 Ibid., pp. 32–6.
35 Cooley, C. H., *Human Nature and the Social Order* (Scribner's, 1902), pp. 120–3.
36 Cooley, C. H., *Social Organization* (Scribner's, 1909), p. 10.
37 *Vide* Mead, G. H., 'Cooley's Contribution to American Social Thought', *American Journal of Sociology*, Vol. 35, No. 5, 1929–30, pp. 693–706.
38 Mead, G. H., *Mind, Self and Society*, p. 224, note 26.
39 *Vide* Horney, Karen, *Self-Analysis* (Routledge, 1962; reprinted 1965), pp. 13–36.
40 Judges, A. V. (ed.), *The Function of Teaching* (Faber, 1959). Chapter 5 on 'Sigmund Freud' by Professor Ben Morris.
41 Mead, G. H., *Mind, Self and Society*, p. 188.
42 Mannheim, K. and Stewart, W. A. C., *An Introduction to the Sociology of Education* (Routledge, 1962), p. 94.
43 Mead, G. H., *Mind, Self and Society*, p. 317.
44 *Vide* Benedict, Ruth, *Patterns of Culture* (Routledge, 1935); Mead, Margaret, *Growing Up in New Guinea* (Penguin Books, 1942); Mead, Margaret, *Coming of Age in Samoa* (Penguin Books, 1943).
45 Mead, G. H., *Mind, Self and Society*, pp. 264–5.
46 Mead, G. H., *The Philosophy of the Act*, p. 153.
47 *Vide* Mead, G. H., *Mind, Self and Society*, pp. 152–3. Cf. also D.E.S.,

Children and their Primary Schools (Plowden Report) (H.M.S.O., 1967), Chapter 9, pp. 116–34.
48 Mead, G. H., ibid., p. 153.
49 *Vide* Buber, M., *Between Man and Man* (Fontana Library, Collins, 1961).
50 *Vide* Ministry of Education, *Half Our Future* (Newsom Report) (H.M.S.O., 1963), pp. 72–9.
51 Mead, G. H., *Mind, Self and Society*, p. 152.
52 Ibid., p. 160.
53 Ibid., p. 159.
54 Ibid., p. 164.
55 *Vide* Mannheim, K., *Essays on Sociology and Social Psychology* (Routledge, 1953; 3rd impression 1966), pp. 274–5.
56 de Chardin, Teilhard, *The Phenomenon of Man* (Fontana Library, Collins, 1965; 5th impression 1967), p. 289.

BIBLIOGRAPHY

A. *Books*

ADORNO, T. W. *et al., The Authoritarian Personality* (Harper, 1950).
ALLPORT, G. W., *Personality: A Psychological Interpretation* (H. Holt, N.Y., 1937).
ALLPORT, G. W., *Personality and Social Encounter* (Beacon, Boston, 1960).
ARGYLE, M., *The Psychology of Interpersonal Behaviour* (Penguin Books, 1967).
BANTON, M., *Roles* (Tavistock Publications, 1965).
BOSSARD, J. H. S., *The Sociology of Child Development* (Harper, 1948).
BRIM, O. G. and WHEELER, S., *Socialization after Childhood: Two Essays* (J. Wiley, 1966; 2nd printing 1967).
BUBER, M., *I and Thou* (Scribner's, 1958).
BUBER, M., *Between Man and Man* (Fontana Library, Collins, 1961).
COOLEY, C. H., *Human Nature and the Social Order* (Scribner's, 1902).
COOLEY, C. H., *Social Organization: A Study in the Larger Mind* (Scribner's, 1909).
EYSENCK, H. J., *The Scientific Study of Personality* (Routledge, 1952).
FREUD, ANNA, *The Ego and Mechanisms of Defence* (Hogarth, 1937).
FREUD, S., *The Ego and the Id* (Hogarth, 1947).
GERTH, H. H. and MILLS, C. W., *Character and Social Structure* (Harcourt, Brace and Co., 1953).
GOFFMAN, E., *The Presentation of Self in Everyday Life* (Anchor Books, N.Y., 1959; Allen Lane, Penguin Press, 1969).
GOFFMAN, E., *Encounters* (Bobbs-Merrill Co., Inc., 1961).
GOFFMAN, E., *Asylums* (Anchor Books, Doubleday, 1961).
GOFFMAN, E., *Stigma* (Penguin Books, 1968).
HARTSHORNE, H. and MAY, M. A., *Studies in the Nature of Character* (Macmillan, 1929–30).
HONIGMAN, J. J., *Personality in Culture* (Harper and Row, 1967).
HORNEY, KAREN, *New Ways in Psychoanalysis* (Routledge, 1939; 4th impression 1961).

ISAACS, SUSAN, *Social Development in Young Children* (Routledge, 1933; 9th impression 1964).

JUNG, C. G., *The Development of Personality* (Routledge, 1954).

KARDINER, A., *The Individual and his Society* (Columbia Univ. Press, 1939).

KARDINER, A., *The Psychological Frontiers of Society* (Columbia Univ. Press, 1945).

KLEIN, JOSEPHINE, *The Study of Groups* (Routledge, 1956; 3rd impression 1962).

KLUCKHOHN, C. and MURRAY, H. A. (eds), *Personality in Nature, Society and Culture* (A. A. Knopf, 2nd edition 1953).

KLUCKHOHN, FLORENCE, STRODTBECK, F. and ROBERTS, J., *A Study of Value Orientations* (Harper and Row, 1961).

LAING, R. D., *The Self and Others* (Tavistock Publications, 1960).

LAING, R. D., *The Divided Self* (Tavistock Publications, 1960).

LAZARUS, R. S. and OPTON, E. M., *Personality: Selected Readings* (Penguin Books, 1967).

LEWIN, K., *The Dynamic Theory of Personality* (McGraw Hill, 1935).

LEWIN, K., *Resolving Social Conflicts* (Harper, 1948).

LINTON, R., *The Cultural Background of Personality* (Routledge, 1947; 4th impression 1958).

LIPSET, S. M. and LOWENTHAL, L. (eds), *Cultural and Social Character* (Free Press, Glencoe, 1961).

MACIVER, R. M. and PAGE, C. H., *Society: An Introductory Analysis* (Macmillan, 1950; reprinted 1957), Chapter 3, 'Individual and Society', pp. 41–70.

MANNHEIM, K., *Essays on Sociology and Social Psychology* (Routledge, 1953; 3rd impression 1966), Part Four, pp. 253–310.

MANNHEIM, K. and STEWART, W. A. C., *An Introduction to the Sociology of Education* (Routledge, 1962), Part Three, 'Social Aspects of Personality', pp. 85–114.

MEAD, G. H., *Mind, Self and Society* (Univ. of Chicago Press, 1934).

MERTON, R. K., *Social Theory and Social Structure* (Free Press, Glencoe, 1957).

MILLS, C. W., *Character and Social Structure* (Harcourt, Brace and Co., 1953).

MORENO, J. L., *Who Shall Survive?* (Nervous Diseases Pub. Co., N.Y., 1934).

MORENO, J. L., *Psychodrama*, Vol. I (Beacon, N.Y., 1946).

MURPHY, G., *Personality: A Biosocial Approach* (Harper, 1947).

MURPHY, G., *Human Potentialities* (Allen and Unwin, 1960).

MURRAY, H. A., *Explorations in Personality* (O.U.P., 1938).

PARETO, V., *Mind and Society* (Harcourt, Brace and Co., 1935).

PARSONS, T., *Theories of Society* (Free Press, Glencoe, 1965), Part Three, 'Personality and the Social System', pp. 683–960.

PIAGET, J., *The Language and Thought of the Child* (Routledge, 1926).

RIESMAN, D., *The Lonely Crowd* (Yale Univ. Press, 1950).

ROLPH, C., *Personal Identity* (M. Joseph, 1957).

ROSENBERG, M., *Society and the Adolescent Self-Image* (Princeton Univ. Press, 1965).

RUITENBEEK, H. M. (ed.), *Varieties of Modern Social Theory* (E. P. Dutton, 1964), Chapters V, VII, VIII, and IX.

SHERIF, M. and CANTRIL, H., *The Psychology of Ego-Involvements* (Wiley, N.Y., 1947).

SKINNER, B. F., *Science and Human Behaviour* (Free Press, Collier-Macmillan, 1953), Chapter XVIII, 'The Self', pp. 283–94.

SPINLEY, B. M., *The Deprived and the Privileged: Personality Development in English Society* (Routledge, 1953).

SPROTT, W. J. H., *Human Groups* (Penguin Books, 1958; reprinted 1964), Chapter 2, pp. 23–38.

STORR, A., *The Integrity of Personality* (Penguin Books, 1963; reprinted 1964).

STRAUSS, A. L., *Mirrors and Masks* (Free Press, Glencoe, 1959).

THOMAS, W. I., *On Social Organization and Social Personality* (Univ. of Chicago Press, 1966), Chapters 2 and 8.

THORNDIKE, E. L., *Human Nature and Social Order* (Macmillan, 1940).

VOLKART, E. H. (ed.), *Social Behaviour and Personality* (Social Science Research Council, N.Y., 1951).

WHITING, J. W. M. and CHILD, I. L., *Child Training and Personality: A Cross-Cultural Study* (Yale Univ. Press, 1953).

YOUNG, K., *Social Attitudes* (H. Holt, 1931).

B. *Articles*

EISSLER, K. R., 'The Effect of the Structure of the Ego on Psychoanalytic Technique', *Journal of the American Psychoanalytic Association*, Vol. 1, No. 1, January 1953, pp. 104–43.

ERIKSON, E. H., 'The Problem of Ego Identity', *Journal of The American Psychoanalytic Association*, Vol. 4, 1956, pp. 56–121.

HALLOWELL, A. I., 'Behavioural Evolution and the Emergence of the Self', in *Evolution and Anthropology: A Centennial Appraisal* (Anthropological Soc. of Washington, Washington, D.C., 1959), pp. 36–60.

HILGARD, E. R., 'Human Motives and the Concept of the Self', *American Psychologist*, Vol. 4, September 1949, pp. 374–82.

KLUCKHOHN, C. and MOWRER, O. H., 'Culture and Personality: A Conceptual Scheme', *American Anthropologist*, Vol. 46, 1944, pp. 1–29.

LASSWELL, H. D., 'Person, Personality, Group, Culture', *Psychiatry*, Vol. 2, November 1939, pp. 533–61.

MERTON, R. K., 'The Role-Set: Problems in Sociological Theory', *British Journal of Sociology*, Vol. 8, June 1957, pp. 106–20.

RAPAPORT, D., 'The Autonomy of the Ego', *Bulletin of the Menninger Clinic*, Vol. 15, No. 4, July 1951, pp. 113–23.

RAPAPORT, D., 'The Theory of Ego Autonomy: a Generalization', *Bulletin of the Menninger Clinic*, Vol. 22, No. 1, January 1958, pp. 13–35.

SEWELL, W. H., 'Social Class and Childhood Personality', *Sociometry*, Vol. 24, pp. 340–56.

ZILLER, R. C., 'Individuation and Socialization', *Human Relations*, Vol. 17, 1964, pp. 341–60.

Chapter 11

The School and Society

A. THE SCHOOL AND ITS RELATIONSHIPS

Society is not composed of a number of institutions in complete isolation from one another, although it is true that some tend to be more isolated than others. Equally the school is not to be seen in isolation from the rest of society, although some schools and some types of school will be more involved with the total community than others. In so far as the school, in our own society, is an artificial institution set up for the purpose of socialization and culture transmission, it must have relations with political and quasi-political organizations which, either by central or local government, control the forms and the means of the education provided.

The current system of education in our society derives from the Butler Education Act of 1944, and from the subsequent acts making miscellaneous provisions and amendations (1). From 1 April 1964 the Ministry of Education became the Department of Education and Science. The D.E.S. is fully responsible for primary, secondary, and further levels of education in both England and Wales, whilst from that date the University Grants Committee (U.G.C.), which had previously been financed by and responsible to the Chancellor of the Exchequer, had to report to the Secretary of State. One must certainly not underestimate the powers of central authority in our society in the realm of education, which may at first sight seem to be virtually decentralized. Taylor and Saunders make this very clear when they say that if the Secretary of State

> 'cares to exercise his powers, he can assume almost complete control over the national educational system. Section 1 of the 1944 Act places upon him the duty to promote "the education of the people in England and Wales . . . and to secure the effective execution by local authorities, under his control and direction, of the national policy"; to underline the nature of his power, section 68 enables him to give directions to an authority which, in his opinion, is acting unreasonably or proposes so to act despite the fact that the issue lies within the discretion of the authority' (2).

Thus, the Secretary of State for Education and Science, as a Member of Parliament and Minister of the Crown, is the political head of the system of education in our society. Assisting the Secretary are Ministers of State who are responsible for such areas as school and other educational buildings, the supply of teachers and their training, further education, universities, educational broadcasting, the arts, civil science and sport. The Secretary of State and his Ministers may have as their assistants one or more Parliamentary Under-Secretaries of State, supported by a department of civil servants, including H.M. Inspectors.

Local Education Authorities (L.E.A.s) were created by the Education Act of 1902, which abolished the old School Boards; and the Education Act of 1944 established that the L.E.A. for a county was now the county council, whilst that for a county borough was the county borough council (3). Today there are 163 L.E.A.s in England and Wales (4). Some of the areas controlled by these authorities are very large, and in consequence provision has been made to partition them into divisions in order to ensure that the administration is both efficient and convenient. These divisions are controlled by bodies called Divisional Executives, whose duty it is to exercise on behalf of the authorities such functions relating to primary and secondary education as may be specified in a particular scheme (5).

Every L.E.A. has the duty to establish such education committees as they may consider expedient 'for the efficient discharge of their functions with respect to education' (6). The Education Act of 1944 also imposes upon the L.E.A.s the duty of appointing a Chief Education Officer, in full consultation with the Secretary of State for Education. The latter may, by law, prohibit the appointment of any candidate if, in his opinion, the latter is not a fit person for the post (7). The Chief Education Officer is assisted in his duties by a full staff of local government officers, who will include his deputy or assistant, county inspectors, advisers, and clerical members.

The relationships of a school depend very much, initially, on the nature of the school itself. The 1944 Education Act sought to establish a clear nomenclature and classification of the various types of school existing in the country. Under the Act a local education authority has the power and duty to establish primary and secondary schools, and to maintain them; these schools are known as *county schools*. By the Education Act of 1964 powers were also granted for the provision of new types of school (e.g. middle schools) for children between the ages of eight and thirteen (8).

The L.E.A. normally appoints and dismisses teachers in the county schools, unless some other provision is made by an article in the government of such schools. The local authority is responsible for the religious and secular instruction provided in these schools, although it must observe Sections 25 and 26 of the 1944 Act in regard to any religious instruction. In addition, the L.E.A. is responsible for the provision, improvement and development of the accommodation of its schools.

Primary and secondary schools maintained by L.E.A.s, but not established by them, are termed *voluntary schools*. Voluntary schools are, in turn, divided into three categories: controlled, aided and special agreement schools. After the publication of the 1944 Act, voluntary schools had to decide, within a fixed time limit, which category they wished to choose. The voluntary schools whose managers or governors were unable or unwilling to meet half the cost of alterations or necessary repairs to buildings became *controlled*, and the L.E.A.s were obliged to meet all costs. Two-thirds of the managers/governors were to be appointed by the L.E.A.s, and one-third were to be foundation managers/governors.

In such controlled schools the L.E.A.s were to be responsible for the appointment of all staff, but they had to consult the managers/governors when appointing head teachers or those teachers who were 'reserved' for religious instruction. All secular instruction was to be under the control of the local authority, whilst religious instruction was to be provided in accordance with any trust deed or particular practice in force before the school became a controlled school, and for not more than two periods per week, or else in accordance with an 'agreed syllabus', that is a syllabus which had been agreed upon by a conference representative of the various denominations, the authority and the teachers.

Managers/governors of any voluntary school which desired to become *aided* had to satisfy the then Ministry that they were both able and willing to defray whatever expenses were incurred in the day-to-day running of the school and in effecting those alterations to school buildings which the L.E.A. required in order to ensure that the school premises conformed to the prescribed standards of the Schools Buildings Regulations. By the 1944 Act the managers/governors agreed to contribute one-half of the costs, but this was later modified by the Education Act of 1959 to one-quarter; the Ministry was then made responsible for the maintenance grant of three-quarters of sums so expended (9).

The L.E.A.s were responsible for appointing one-third of the managers/ governors of the aided schools, whilst the remaining two-thirds were foundation appointments. The managers/governors were responsible for the appointment of staff, but in each case the local authority regulated the number of teachers actually employed. The secular instruction of the schools, if primary, was to be under the control of the L.E.A.; if they were secondary, it was to be under the control of the governors, unless alternative provisions were made in the rules of management or the articles of government. Religious instruction was normally to be given in accordance with the trust deed or former practice of the school but where parents so wished, provision had to be made for instruction to be given in accordance with an 'agreed syllabus'.

L.E.A.s had been empowered, by the Education Act of 1936, to assist financially towards the erection of what were termed 'non-provided' schools, that is, schools not provided by the state. By the same Act local authorities could pay grants ranging from 50 to 75 per cent of the cost of providing new senior schools of this type. Altogether 519 proposals for such developments were made, of which 289 were from Roman Catholic sources, but only a small number of these had actually been built before the outbreak of the Second World War. The Education Act of 1944 allowed these proposals to be revived, and in 1959 there were eighty-seven of these voluntary schools, now termed *special agreement schools*. In these latter the appointment of teachers was under L.E.A. control, and the authority had to consult foundation managers/governors in making the appointment of any reserved teacher. Of the managers/governors two-thirds were foundation members, and one-third were appointed by the L.E.A. Secular and religious instruction followed the same provisions as for aided schools.

Thus, both county and voluntary schools, as defined above, became maintained in various ways through the Education Act of 1944 and subsequent Education Acts making miscellaneous and specific provisions. There still remained outside these categories, however, a number of schools which had, under previous Education Acts, received grants from either local or central authority. In return for this assistance a certain proportion of pupil places were made either free or partially free. Schools receiving grants from L.E.A.s were usually required to keep a minimum of 25 per cent of their places for non-paying pupils, and those receiving grants from the central authority provided free places for 10 per cent of their admissions.

Those schools which did not wish to become voluntary aided could temporarily become *assisted* but had, eventually, to decide either to become *independent* or to apply for a *direct grant* from the Ministry. Any school accepted for direct grant by the Direct Grant Schools Regulations of 1959 (10) had to offer not less than 25 per cent free places to pupils who had been in attendance for two years at a maintained or grant-aided primary school. Up to another 25 per cent free places might be reserved for the L.E.A. if they found that the number of places already offered was insufficient. These reserved places were open to any pupils whether they had been educated in a grant-aided primary school or not. Any remaining places might be filled by the governors whose duty it was to ensure that preference for admission should be given to candidates who they considered were most likely to profit by such an education. Fees might be charged for these pupils, but parents could apply for remission of fees. The central authority would make a grant to the governors on a capitation basis, and would also encourage L.E.A.s to make special arrangements for nominated pupils to be admitted to independent boarding schools, if this form of education were thought to be desirable for them.

Finally, the Minister was declared responsible for seeing that no child was prevented through the poverty of his parents from pursuing the type of education suitable to his age, ability and aptitude, and this included education at a costly independent school – if that were really the best type of education for him. Any fees or expenses incurred would be paid by the central authority, which would also be responsible for inspections of independent schools and of the registers of pupils at such schools. Inspections by H.M. Inspectorate could take place at any time, and if any independent school were not up to the required standard it could be struck off the register, and there were heavy penalties to be imposed upon anyone running a school not so registered (11). The clause in the 1944 Act was not specifically aimed at public schools, but rather at the private schools which often outlived their educational value and efficiency. An *independent* school was defined by the Act as

> 'Any school at which full-time education is provided for five or more pupils of compulsory school age (whether or not such education is also provided for pupils over that age), not being a school maintained by a local education authority or a school in respect of which grants are made by the Minister to the proprietor of the school' (12).

It will be appreciated, from the foregoing brief analysis of the various types of school, that the relationship of any school with the controlling authority will depend upon its classification. Some schools will have little or no direct contact with the D.E.S.; others will have no contact with the L.E.A. There will in all cases, however, be some involvement with governors or managers who will in turn be concerned with the sort of staff appointed to their particular school, and although many of them may know little about education or the realm of the academic, *per se*, they may nevertheless possess sound business acumen and good judgement. It has become customary to make fun of the school governor who, without any noticeable education, 'governs' those who are responsible for educating; but the simple fact is that many of the governors are there simply because no one else is willing to do the job. Professor W. O. Lester Smith has emphasized the need for people such as parents and teachers to be represented on governing and managerial bodies; and he points out that the hopes expressed in this direction at the time of the passing of the 1944 Act have not been realized (13). F. W. Garforth has equally pointed out that the composition of many school governing bodies is merely a replica of the full education committee, 'faithfully reproducing the same political divisions and dominance of power. Thus educational considerations are subordinated to politics and the potential value of governing bodies lost' (14).

In his discussion on 'Administering Education' and on what the form of the authorities near the schools themselves should be, John Vaizey (15) suggests that the answer is to enlarge and change the jobs of the governors. Governors, he suggests, are too isolated and unaware of the problems of other schools in their district. In consequence, a group of governors should be responsible for more than one school, and Vaizey argues that parents and teachers should form a joint committee in a particular neighbourhood, which he terms the 'School Group'. The School Group would represent a unit of 5,000 to 10,000 children, and they would possess some of the 'major powers now exercised by the education authority, such as remodelling schools, re-equipping them, and re-allocating staff and pupils' (16), so that as a result its members' concept of the interdependence of their schools would become more realistic. The School Group would be provided with an annual budget, and panels of governors would be created, comprising members of each school or unit representatives and elected half by the teachers or their organizations in the School Group, and half by the parents.

It is true that very often both boards of governors and Parent-Teacher Associations (P.T.A.s) appear as ineffectual within the realm of school relationships, if only because they present themselves as separate bodies with vested interests – and sometimes almost in opposition to one another. But the school community today is a long way from that described by H. C. Dent, when the gates of the public elementary schools were locked, and permanent notices appeared, 'No parents allowed beyond this point' (17). Real participation by parents in the educational and socializing functions of the school, however, implies more than visits on 'Open Days', which often imply little more than a general agreement that some interesting work is somehow being done by someone somewhere. This is not, of course, to suggest that there is not considerable involvement in some schools; and certainly P.T.A.s are invariably drawn upon to provide for the schools those amenities which cannot be provided out of public funds. But there is something very parochial and disparate about many of these efforts in the promotion of *community*.

Perhaps something like John Vaizey's 'School Group' concept is required in order to overcome the narrower interests and introversion of schools in isolation, some of which will suffer seriously in their isolation because of the general deprivation of their environment; whilst others will benefit out of all proportion because of their parents' influence, interest and affluence. Vaizey argues that the School Group

'is a way of developing a wider loyalty among teachers and parents than that given to the school alone. In this way the problems of transfer of pupils and staff which are essential to the working of a genuine policy of "parity of esteem" can be discovered and overcome, and in this way the reluctance to be ordered about and experimented upon by "local politicians" can be avoided' (18).

The desire to develop the relationship of the school with the larger society and its other institutions led Mr Henry Morris, the Education

Secretary of the Cambridgeshire County Council at the time, to inspire in 1928 the building of the first village college at Sawston in Cambridgeshire. This was essentially the realization of a vision of a planned community. The village college aimed at bringing the whole life of the village, or group of villages, into one focal point. Here the children would attend day school; the adults would listen to evening lectures; youths would participate in dramatic productions, dances and sports; young women would learn the arts and skills of cookery and housewifery; the old would rest in the reading rooms with books borrowed from the lending library; and all would pursue their interests, hobbies and a variety of leisure activities together. The village college at Sawston was an undoubted success – it brought both old and young together in a communal life of learning and purposeful activity. Three more colleges were opened in Cambridgeshire before the Second World War curtailed this development, but by 1960 there were nine such colleges altogether in Cambridgeshire, Leicestershire and the Soke of Peterborough.

We shall consider later the school as a social system, in the somewhat narrower sense, but it is important to point out here that the school develops as a society to a very large extent through its relationships with other groups and institutions, as well as with individuals who visit the school in some official capacity. The School Health Service, for example, not only provides a necessary service with free medical and dental inspection and treatment, it also furnishes an induction for the child into the National Health Service. Similarly, the school-leaver is involved in the employment scene through the vocational guidance and placement provided by the Youth Employment Service.

Through H.M. Inspectorate the school is kept in touch with the standards of other schools and with the standards required by the D.E.S. H.M.I.s are appointed by the Crown and are, therefore, largely independent; their primary function is to make reports on schools and other educational institutions to the Secretary of State for Education. The ethos of the Inspectorate has changed somewhat over the years, and although their function is still to criticize, commend and advise, there is perhaps less emphasis today upon negative criticism and more upon constructive advice. The Parliamentary Select Committee on Education and Science investigated H.M. Inspectorate of Schools in 1968, and made the suggestion that the practice of formal inspection should cease and that the Inspectorate should concentrate more upon advising than upon inspection.

It is perhaps important that the school in its relationships should be able to accept both criticism and advice, but it is equally important that criticism and advice should be accepted as coming from within the framework of a normal relationship, and not as issuing from an elite body established specifically for the purpose of 'inspection'. Clearly the school cannot dispense with some criticism of its values and standards, or some evaluation of its educational methods and products. But whilst the precise functions of the Inspectorate seem to have been questioned from time to time, the basis of their appointment and establishment seems to have been left virtually unquestioned. Under their Senior Chief Inspector, H.M.I.s are responsible to the Permanent Secretary who is the chief administrative officer in the D.E.S.

In 1962 a curriculum study group was developed in order to supply information and advice to schools upon current curriculum developments. Two years later, in 1964, this group was established as the Schools Council, which exists as an independent body whose purpose it is to provide an entire service for the schools. Its stated aims are 'to promote and encourage curriculum study and development without diminishing any of the existing responsibilities of its members, and to sponsor research and inquiry where this is needed to help solve immediate and practical problems' (19). Such a body not only possesses the necessary expertise to produce valuable memoranda and working papers for the help of teachers and others work-ing in the field of education, it also acts as a valuable link between the staffs of the schools and the whole world of innovation, ideas and the possibilities of development under experimental and research conditions. The easy relationships which can be built up with the officers of the Schools Council will do much to offset the more 'official' relationship with H.M.I.s, which many find much more difficult to absorb.

The school is thus involved in a web of relationships with a variety and combination of bodies, councils, departments, committees and authorities which will change and permute according to the actual status of the school. There is obviously a great need to keep these relationships in some har-monized and coherent order; and there is also a need to define and appreciate sensitively the roles of every group, and to become associated with the roles of others in such a way as to maximize role performances. In the past, the relationships of the school have been viewed largely in terms of administration; today, they are seen more in terms of individual and group involvement and in terms of social dynamics.

B. THE SCHOOL AND ITS ORGANIZATION

In his *Theory of Social and Economic Organization*, Max Weber makes an analysis of authority in terms of rational–legal authority, traditional authority and charismatic authority (20). Rational–legal authority derives from an organized hierarchy and the relative position within it. Such an organization is a 'bureaucracy', and power exists in varying strengths at differing levels within the hierarchy. The legal element in this form of authority is the outward expression of the organization itself, its rules and

o

its regulations, whilst the rational element is the inner expression of the specialized knowledge and skill of those who hold office. Traditional authority is what it suggests – an inherited authority, generally through kinship, and bearing its own sanctions and sanctity. A third form of authority, namely charismatic authority, is expressed through individual and personal qualities of an unusual character. These traits indicate the power to command respect, awe and discipleship: it is an authority which depends neither upon tradition, nor upon any legal or rational situation. It exists in its own right, without dependence upon any hierarchical position or external investiture; it is something inexplicable or ineffable in normal socio-psychological terms.

Partly because of its origins, the word 'bureaucracy' is generally regarded in a pejorative way. It was a satirical invention which combined the Greek *kratein* (κρατεῖν) 'to rule', and the French word for 'a desk', namely *bureau*. Bureaucracy was conceived of as a form of rule from the desk, a rule by desk officials. Today it is used as a term for the rule of a caste of high officials, or 'bureaucrats'. But, although the word is still used by a large number of people derogatively, the simple fact is that no modern complex society can exist without some form of rule by officials. There can always, of course, be too many officials; there can be inefficient officials, and there can be oppressive ones. But society requires officials – the best that it can obtain – for planning and for putting its plans into execution.

The officials in charge of the educational process are concerned with planning and structuring the educational system within our society. Whether it be the members of Parliament who are appointed to the Department of Education and Science, or the Chief Education Officers in charge of the L.E.A.s, the divisional executives or the headmasters of schools – all are at the head of bureaucratic systems. Bureaucracy may seem to be a heavy term to use concerning the organization of the school, but in this respect the latter is no different from other institutions. They all have their hierarchical structures implying control, power, possibilities of promotion or of demotion. It may seem more pleasant, or idealistic, to regard the school as a large family, or as some sort of paternalistic or maternalistic institution, but the sheer force of modern social and political development has considerably changed the nature of the inner relationships and organization of the school.

The bureaucracy of the school may be a happy or an unhappy one, well organized or disorganized, efficient or inefficient, but it is still a bureaucracy. Once this is accepted one can go on to attempt some improvement of the bureaucracy. The school as an organizational unit has grown gradually larger over the years, and its structure has become more complex. Whilst some complain that the structure is becoming too large and unwieldy, others argue that the larger structure is more efficient and economical at a certain optimum level. Like any other bureaucracy the school may become a machine, dehumanized and thoroughly impersonal. This is one of the dangers of size, but it is not an inevitable consequence. It is, for example, often suggested that a child may get lost in the very large school unit; but this is not quite stating the reality of the situation. The child, even the intelligent one, is very rarely aware of the size of the school itself, once he is able to find his way to the relevant classrooms. It might possibly be truer to say that the teacher is more likely to get lost in the sense that he is inevitably in face-to-face relationships with a smaller total proportion of the school. This fact alone may strengthen the concept of a somewhat impersonal bureaucracy, in which some of the upper echelons of the hierarchy, including the headmaster, deputy head and heads of departments, have become more remote from both members of staff and pupils.

Another factor which will tend to increase this sense of impersonality about the structure of the school in modern society is the fact that increasingly the general mobility of society has invaded the realm of education. Teaching may or may not be a vocation, but it is today certainly *more* than that: teaching is a profession, and there are desirable positions of responsibility, and positions higher in the hierarchy or in general esteem, which attract ambitious teachers. There is also greater mobility for teachers from the school to the college of technology, to the polytechnic, to the college of education, or to the university. Since we are educating for fluidity of mind and mobility in action, it is inevitable that the teachers we produce should reflect this attitude of mind and behaviour. Those with an eye to the 'main chance' may, indeed, seek to obtain as varied an experience as possible in a large number of areas of teaching, where they can employ or improve their pedagogic expertise, in the hope that this will count in the promotion struggle. It is inevitable in this struggle that the rapid turnover of teachers should, in many schools, adversely affect the education of the pupils.

The source of authority in a school may be entirely a matter of the power of the hierarchy. Indeed, the 'discipline' of a school may depend very much upon a powerful prefect system, or upon the frequency with which the headmaster imposes a variety of sanctions, or upon the devolution of his authority throughout the staff. Rules will be laid down, as in any other society, and they will be enforced by some form of 'punishment'. But, as many schools have demonstrated, authority is not necessarily dependent upon punishment or the threat of sanctions. There are other and more pleasant forms of coercion than physical punishment, line-writing, standing in the corner or outside the classroom door, or a variety of types of detention – however effective some of these may at first sight appear to be.

The present writer recalls a very effective 'order-producing' punishment at a school in which the ultimate sanction was detention on Saturday mornings. In an area where most of the boys had a Saturday morning job this proved to be a real deterrent. But how far this could be regarded as really sound 'discipline' is another matter. Authority, however, may also be expressed by other forms of coercion in which the pupil may be persuaded in a variety of ways to conform, or rather to become a 'disciple' of the teacher, because of the latter's competence, expertise and understanding. This difference in the nature of authority is reflected in the way in which it is employed: it may be used to submerge and to override the wills of the pupils, or it may be employed to integrate their behaviour through a co-operative approach. Children are amenable to persuasion as well as to punishment.

Brian Jackson has referred to streaming as 'an education system in miniature' (21). In the past, streaming has been an essential element in the total organization of the school system; children have been selected for particular schools at the secondary level according to their general intelligence and ability, as well as attainment; and in most schools, both primary and secondary, there has also been some internal form of streaming and/or setting. With the advent of the comprehensive system the streaming of pupils *for* different types of school must necessarily be decreasing, but there may still, of course, be some form of streaming *within* all types of school. It is interesting to note that even within those schools which claim that their classes include children of all ranges of ability, there may still exist forms of grouping and setting which make the tacit admission that there are limits to the teaching together of children of widely varying abilities.

In his article on 'The Organization of Schools' (22), Sir Cyril Burt has argued that the teachers concerned usually know what system of streaming, or non-streaming, is best for their own particular schools. He concludes that

> 'what little evidence is available from recent research goes far to confirm the verdict of educational psychologists half a century ago: in general the mode of organization, whether of classes within schools or of schools within districts, matters far less than the personality, training, enthusiasm, and efficiency of the teachers themselves' (23).

Whatever ideological commitment teachers may have they are still largely in agreement that it is easier, if not also more efficient, to teach generally homogeneous groups. And even where classes are of mixed ability, if any real progress is to be made there must be some sort of grouping within the class. Indeed, as soon as remedial or compensatory facilities are made available within a school for dealing with backward or deprived children, there is an acceptance both in principle and in practice that not all animals are equal.

Increasingly the normal state school is concerned with problems of remedial and compensatory education in a large variety of areas of both mental and physical weakness or deficiency. But also, if a school is truly comprehensive, it must deal effectively with the really 'high-flyer'. If 'equality of opportunity' means anything at all in the context of the organization of the school, it signifies that each child has an equal opportunity with every other child of maximizing his own potential. A child with a very high level of intelligence could easily become frustrated and difficult in a mixed-ability situation in which there was little scope for his particular capacities, or for the fullest expression of his powers. Provided, however, one accepts these limitations of the unstreamed situation, one can go ahead and develop the means for dealing with the backward, the difficult and the brilliant; and in certain areas, with certain provisos, the technological aids, programmed texts and teaching machines have a great deal to offer. Team-teaching, and the employment of teachers' aids, may also do much to mitigate some of the problems and weaknesses of mixed-ability classes.

The questions of the size of classes and teacher-pupil ratios in any school have always been important and critical. It may be that in the open area situation of both the new first (infant) and middle schools (24), with team-teaching and the assistance of teachers' aides as well as ancillaries, the size of 'classes' becomes less critical. But this does assume that the school organization has regard to the importance of this sort of extra help just mentioned. As the Plowden Report emphasizes in relation to the staffing of schools:

'The continuous shortage of teachers and the increasing range of their duties have made the Department and the local education authorities anxious to use their services more efficiently. No longer are teachers expected to do everything that needs doing in school except clean it. School dinners have brought with them not only cooks but, in the end, "dinner helpers". Head teachers have some secretarial help. Other assistants are being appointed to relieve class teachers of some of the burden involved in looking after very young children. The process has gone a long way; but not, in our judgement, far enough. The ancillary services are not yet provided everywhere, and they are not comprehensive enough' (25).

It could well be, therefore, that the organization of the staffing situation, at least up to the secondary or comprehensive (third school) level is not so much a question of the maintenance of a specific teacher-pupil ratio, but more a question of the valuable ancillary help which teachers should get to relieve them of multitudinous time-consuming functions, including a lot of record-keeping, in order that they might get on with the prime work of educating.

Some educators would apply similar principles at the third school level. The Newsom Report, for example, quotes the opinion that buildings for secondary schools would need to be specifically designed for a more informal and less academic approach. There seemed to be little doubt that the prevalent subject curricula and traditional syllabuses and time-tables were not adequately meeting the needs of pupils of average and below average ability (26). That there are considerable functional deficiencies in many of our third schools no one would deny. Many of the buildings are quite unsuitable for the sort of work that the Newsom Report and the Schools Council have proposed (27). Necessity, nevertheless, is perpetually the mother of invention and many heads of third schools have so organized their leavers that they are involved in the construction of their own buildings, and with their decoration and maintenance. There is, in fact, an increasing awareness that a different sort of organization altogether is required for those pupils who are literally in a half-way house between the school pupil situation and social adulthood which is only two or three years away.

Built into the structure and organization of the school there must be a means of dialogue or communication. In sociological terms 'communication' is probably the better word since we are here concerned more with the actual channels which may be open in the organization for the passing of information, rather than any philosophical concept such as the word 'dialogue' might imply. Communication will occur through the hierarchy of the school from the head down to the pupil; it will also occur at peer level among staff, and among pupils. These means of communication are referred to as vertical and horizontal, and it is one of the aims of an institutional organization such as the school to maintain a balance or equilibrium in the communication systems. We all know from experience, however, that with the best will in the world (and often without it) there are often 'hang-ups' in the vertical channels of communication. Many such blocks, though accidental, are interpreted as deliberate by the lower echelons of the hierarchy.

Downward communication, however facile, is not enough. Any organization that hopes to work smoothly must ensure that there is some feed-back, and that there is some forum for the expression of opinion by all levels within the organization. The writer remembers a school in which no staff meeting had been held for years, and in which the prefects formed a sort of non-attached, free-floating cabal with more authority and a greater variety of sanctions to apply than even the staff had. Because there was no real feed-back, and no possibility of it except the sort of undercover rumblings that occur on most staffs, there was a considerable hiatus between higher levels of the bureaucracy and the rest. It was only when regular staff meetings were organized, and a school council was formed to provide a means of upward communication for the pupils, that many of the rumblings ceased – if only because the mere suggestion that a member should speak about his problem at the next staff meeting or the next school council was often enough to put the problem in its right perspective. And once the prefect system ceased to be an isolated, non-communicative, power group, exerting its own uncensored sanctions, a real form of total and structured communication began to develop.

The school as an organization may be almost as varied as the personalities who compose it. It is, however, a form of bureaucracy with authority vested in a hierarchy who may control by force, reward and punishment, persuasion, coercion, or by some enlightened or novel expression of self-discipline. The structure of the organization must allow for the maximum of communication in both vertical and horizontal directions, and for the possibilities of feed-back. It must also provide a sense of stability whilst not stifling the expression of dissent or of alternative opinion. Within its structure the school must also make room for experiment and development, since an organization which is too rigid tends to militate against any form of change. On the other hand, any organization which is too loosely structured may suffer nothing but change without the essential absorption and consolidation which turns change into an organized and evaluated development.

C. THE SCHOOL AS A SOCIETY

The school is an institution with its peculiar form of organization, but it is also a type of society. One of the most useful models in any discussion of social systems is that provided by Ferdinand Tönnies (1855–1936) in his *Gemeinschaft und Gesellschaft*, which was first published in 1887 (28). Tönnies distinguished between *Gemeinschaft*, or community, and *Gesellschaft*, society or association. In his 'Introductory Article', which represented some of Tönnies' latest thinking on the topic, he said:

'I call all kinds of association in which natural will predominates *Gemeinschaft*, all those which are formed and fundamentally conditioned by rational will, *Gesellschaft*. Thus these concepts signify the model qualities of the essence and the tendencies of being bound together. Thus both names are in the present context stripped of their connotation as designating social entities or groups, or even collective or artificial persons; the essence of both *Gemeinschaft* and *Gesellschaft* is found interwoven in all kinds of associations . . .' (29).

In his original discussion of this topic Tönnies made a somewhat stronger dichotomy between these two concepts. In *Gemeinschaft* there was an organic situation in which the individuals were members by virtue of their birth and general inheritance. There was a common bond between them all, and no man was an island; they all shared a common identity in the group or tribe to which they belonged. There was a coherence about the whole structure of their community that implied more than an external agreement or contract to behave towards one another in a certain way. There existed an inextricable linkage of all their mores, tabus, feelings, emotions, and attachments; they were all part and parcel of one another, their relationships were inclusive and individuals respected one another as ends and not only as means (30).

In *Gesellschaft* a society was developed by more artificial contracts and agreements. There was something anonymous about these associations; in fact, many of the transactions which occurred in this form of society might take place without any further contact ensuing. Whilst in *Gemeinschaft* the obligations of the members of the group ramified throughout the entire community, in *Gesellschaft* such obligations became more individual and specific; and since entry into these obligations was largely of a voluntary nature – that is, depending upon the rational will rather than the natural will – there was always the possibility of withdrawing (31).

As any society becomes larger and more complex there is a tendency for it to become increasingly the associational type of society rather than the communal type. And the larger the number of sub-groups, unions and so forth in the society, the more disparate and unconnected they become. The mass society, with its drop-outs and its general sense of lacking roots, aims or goals, also lacks that 'community' which is characteristic of the smaller unit in which people have grown and developed in a close sense of harmony and personal relation. It is, perhaps, only in times of considerable social danger and stress, in times of crisis or cataclysm, and when the society as a whole is in total conflict with another society that the sense of real community is revived.

The school is a society which may, theoretically at least follow either of Tönnies' two patterns, although it is more likely perhaps to follow his concept of the interweaving of both. Much will depend upon the views of the headmaster and staff concerning the aims of education and how those aims should be achieved. The size and nature of the school will also have something to do with the direction of its development. There is a general sense in which it is true to say that children have not voluntarily contracted to enter the school society; they are joining it, however, at an increasingly earlier age so that its norms and values will enter strongly into their consciousness. And, although the values of the home may have a stronger and more lasting effect upon them, there must inevitably be an awareness of the existence of other values in society at large and in the society of the school.

As the child grows older so he will desire more and more to participate in the government and control of the school. This does not mean that the school society necessarily requires pupil levels in its hierarchy such as the prefect system. What it does appear to require for a sense of shared responsibility and free communication is some sort of school council in which all age groups of the pupils are represented. If children are to develop a self-discipline within themselves, rather than a discipline imposed from outside, they must have some practice in the methods of discussion and dialogue that appertain to a democracy or free society. Rules, when imposed from above, always seem somewhat irksome; when, however, pupils are invited to make, and from time to time to revise, their own rules, the latter appear to them far more reasonable and acceptable – even though at times they may, in fact, be more rigorous and severe than those imposed by adults.

Pupils may also learn, within the forum of the school council, the many possibilities of the use and abuse of authority, the ease with which a facile talker may change the whole tenor and direction of a particular discussion, and the way in which ultimately even their seemingly most rational decisions may be frustrated and stultified by an unco-operative headmaster. The real lessons for life are not those just taught in the classroom: they are those which the pupils absorb through participation and action in the school society. And even the frustrations which many of them meet in decision-making within the school will certainly have their counterparts in the larger society when they enter it as full members.

It is this element of conscious, articulate and participatory conflict which is preferable to the unexpressed resentment which so many pupils feel in the face of an authoritarianism which will brook no discussion and no possibility of an alternative. It is important that the pupil should at least play the role of an active participant in the government of the school. In more recent times we have seen the extension of this participation in the various institutions of higher education where students may be represented at departmental meetings, academic boards, and governors' meetings. Whether pupils or students are competent to discuss the content and method of their courses is a matter for some dispute, but there are certainly a great many areas where they provide a view as members of a role-set, which it is both important and useful to know and to consider. It is equally important that, in recognizing their roles and functions, within the school or college, each individual should be cognizant of the limitations placed upon him as well as the freedom accorded to him. As Mannheim and Stewart have pointed out, 'The very concept of school and its function is a limit on the freedom of individual spontaneity and once we admit that we can begin to discuss realistically how to enable education to be as free and flexible as possible' (32).

In this sense, at least, the school reflects very much the general social condition. Initiation for the larger society must certainly take into account the *limits* which that society places upon the individual and his behaviour. A school in which there are no rules and no punishments, or forms of coercive sanction, is certainly not preparing the pupil for the sort of society in which he will participate, and to which he will in some way have to answer for his actions. Some deeper realization of this social relationship might help to take the sting out of the sort or polarity which, in Tönnies' terminology, appears to exist between *Gemeinschaft* and *Gesellschaft*. In the *Gemeinschaft*, human beings 'remain essentially united in spite of all separating factors'; on the other hand, in the *Gesellschaft* they 'are essentially separated in spite of all uniting factors' (33). It is, perhaps, one of the prime aims of the school to seek to eradicate this duality of will and purpose, and to attempt to develop some sense of identity with others not simply within the framework of the school, but also with others in the larger society who appear, at first sight, to be 'essentially separated'.

This cannot be achieved by lengthy dissertations about society and its complex associations; it is achieved by rejecting the notion that people in a variety of roles are 'essentially separated', and by accepting that we are members one of another. The Newsom concept of 'going out into the world' is sound provided that the institution of the school is not regarded as something at present separated and remote from society itself. The school is already an important dimension of society, and the educational process is, in part at least, an attempt to ease the child's passage in and through society, not *into* society. Increasingly, therefore, the work of the school may be seen as a real attempt to make each child socially aware throughout his school career, in such a way that the school is not viewed as an isolated phenomenon but as 'essentially united' with the macro-society.

It is the early recognition of this *essential* unity which helps to set the social limits and which, at the same time, prepares the way for neither uncritical acceptance nor unthinking rejection of the social *milieu*. A real identity implies a relationship which is capable of self-criticism as well as social criticism, without developing that sense of alienation which so often occurs during the period of adolescence. To this end it is quite inadequate to prepare children during their last year or two years to enter a quasi-alien society: for many it is too late, and for many others it may be too much in too short a time. Throughout his school career the child has to be made aware that society is here and now and not something in the future, or out there; that the school itself is not an element separate from the total society, but an integral part of it; and that freedom is not a quality granted at the end of a period of socialization, but something gained in free, but limited, social participation. If self-discipline is gained only through the assumption of responsibility, any real sense of social identity can be acquired only through its continuous practice. The school is not simply a training ground for life and the larger society: it is life itself, and social living.

REFERENCES

1 The 1944 Act was later amended by the Education Act, 1946; the Education (Miscellaneous Provisions) Act, 1948; the Education (Miscellaneous Provisions) Act 1953; the Education Act, 1959; the Education Act, 1962; the Remuneration of Teachers Act, 1963; the Education Act, 1964; the Remuneration of Teachers Act, 1965; the Education Act, 1967; the Education Act, 1968; and the Education (No. 2) Act, 1968. *Vide* Taylor, G. and Saunders, J. B., *The New Law of Education* (Butterworth, 6th edition 1965), and *Supplement* (1969).
2 Taylor, G. and Saunders, J. B., op. cit., p. 4.
3 *Vide* Education Act, 1944, Section 6 (1).
4 *Vide* D.E.S., *Education and Science in 1969* (H.M.S.O., 1970), p. 34.
5 *Vide* Education Act, 1944, Section 6 (2) and 1st Schedule, Part III, amended by Education Act, 1946, Section 13 (2).
6 Education Act, 1944, 1st Schedule, Part II, 'Education Committees', para. 1.
7 *Vide* Education Act, 1944, Section 88.
8 *Vide* Education Act, 1964, Section 1, and Circular 12/64 (12 August 1964).
9 Education Act, 1959 (7 and 8 Eliz. 2, Ch. 60) (H.M.S.O., 1959), p. 1, para. 1 (1).
10 *Vide* 'Direct Grant Schools Regulations', 1959 (H.M.S.O., 29 October 1959).
11 *Vide* Education Act, 1944, Section 73.
12 Education Act, 1944, Section 114.
13 *Vide* Lester Smith, W. O., *Government of Education* (Penguin Books, 1965), p. 21.
14 Garforth, F. W., *Education and Social Purpose* (Oldbourne, 1962), p. 136. Quoted in Lester Smith, W. O., op. cit., p. 22.
15 *Vide* Vaizey, J., *Education for Tomorrow* (Penguin Books, 1966), Chapter 8, 'Administering Education', pp. 104–13.
16 Ibid., p. 108.
17 Dent, H. C., *The Educational System of England and Wales* (Univ. of London Press, 4th edition 1969), p. 223.
18 Vaizey, J., op. cit., p. 109.
19 Dent, H. C., op. cit., p. 74.
20 *Vide* Weber, Max, *The Theory of Social and Economic Organization* (tr. Henderson, A. M. and Parsons, T.; O.U.P., 1947).
21 *Vide* Jackson, B., *Streaming: an Education System in Miniature* (Routledge, 1964).
22 Burt, Cyril, 'The Organization of Schools' in Cox, C. B. and Dyson, A. E.

(eds.), *Black Paper Three: Goodbye Mr Short* (Critical Quarterly Society, 1970), pp. 14–25.

23 Ibid., p. 25.

24 *Vide* D.E.S., *Children and their Primary Schools* (Plowden Report) (H.M.S.O., 1967), pp. 394–5, paras 1,092–5.

25 Ibid., pp. 317–18, para. 890. Note also pp. 330–2, paras 922–8, for 'Teachers' Aides'.

26 Ministry of Education, *Half Our Future* (Newsom Report) (H.M.S.O., 1963), p. 87, para. 264.

27 *Vide* The Schools Council, *Society and the Young School Leaver* (Working Paper No. 11) (H.M.S.O., 1967).

28 Tönnies, F., *Gemeinschaft und Gesellschaft* (1887; translated by Loomis, C. P. and published as *Community and Association*, Routledge, 1955). *Vide* also Parsons, T. *et al.* (eds), *Theories of Society* (Free Press, Glencoe, 1965), Section C, 'The Modes of Institutionalization of Action', pp. 181–236.

29 Tönnies, F., *Community and Association*, pp. 17–18. This 'Introductory Article' appeared in *Handwörterbuch der Soziologie*, Stuttgart, 1931, under the title 'Gemeinschaft und Gesellschaft'.

30 *Vide* ibid., pp. 42–73, 'Theory of Gemeinschaft'.

31 *Vide* ibid., pp. 74–116, 'Theory of Gesellschaft'.

32 Mannheim, K. and Stewart, W. A. C., *An Introduction to the Sociology of Education* (Routledge, 1962), p. 138.

33 Tönnies, F., op. cit., p. 74.

BIBLIOGRAPHY

ATKINSON, M., *Junior School Community* (Longmans, 1962).

AYERST, D., *Understanding Schools* (Penguin Books, 1967).

BANKS, OLIVE, *Parity and Prestige in English Secondary Education* (Routledge, 1955).

BANKS, OLIVE, *The Sociology of Education* (Batsford, 1968; 2nd impression 1969), Chapters 6, 8 and 9.

BARKER, R. G. and GUMP, P. V., *Big School, Small School* (Stanford Univ. Press, California, 1964).

BIDWELL, C. E., 'The School as a Formal Organization' in March, J. G. (ed.), *Handbook of Social Organization* (Rand McNally, 1965).

BLYTH, W. A. L., *English Primary Education*, Vols. I and II (Routledge, 1965).

BRIM, O. and WHEELER, S., *Socialization after Childhood* (J. Wiley, 1966).

BURGESS, T., *A Guide to English Schools* (Penguin Books, 1964).

CASTLE, E. B., *A Parents' Guide to Education* (Penguin Books, 1968).

CHESHIRE EDUCATION COMMITTEE, *The Secondary Modern School* (Univ. of London Press, 1958).

CHETWYND, H. R., *Comprehensive School, the Story of Woodberry Down* (Routledge, 1960).

CHILD, H. A. T. (ed.), *The Independent Progressive School* (Hutchinson, 1962).

COLEMAN, J. S., *The Adolescent Society* (Free Press, Glencoe, 1961).

CONANT, J. B., *The American High School Today* (McGraw-Hill, 1959).

DAHLKE, O. H., *Values in Culture and Classroom* (Harper, 1958).

DANCY, J. C., *The Public Schools and the Future* (Faber, 1963).

DAVIS, R., *The Grammar School* (Penguin Books, 1967).

DENT, H. C., *The Educational System of England and Wales* (Univ. of London Press, 4th edition, 1969).

D.E.S., *Children and their Primary Schools* (Plowden Report) (H.M.S.O., 1967).

DEWEY, J., *The School and Society* (Chicago Univ. Press, revised edition 1916).

EDMONDS, E. L., *The School Inspector* (Routledge, 1962).

EGGLESTON, S. J., *The Social Context of the School* (Routledge, 1967).

ETZIONI, A., *A Comparative Analysis of Complex Organizations* (Free Press, Glencoe, 1961).

ETZIONI, A., *Complex Organizations – A Sociological Reader* (Holt, Rinehart and Winston, 1962).

ETZIONI, A., *Modern Organizations* (Prentice-Hall, 1964).

FARLEY, R., *Secondary Modern Discipline* (A. and C. Black, 1960).

GRAMBS, J. D., *Schools, Scholars and Society* (Prentice-Hall, 1965).

GROSS, N., *Who Runs Our Schools?* (J. Wiley, 1958).

HARGREAVES, D. H., *Social Relations in a Secondary School* (Routledge, 1967).

HERRIOTT, R. E. and ST JOHN, N. H., *Social Class and the Urban School* (J. Wiley, 1966).

HIGHFIELD, M. E. and PINSENT, A., *A Survey of Rewards and Punishments in Schools* (G. Newnes, 1952).

HUGHES, A. G., *Education and the Democratic Ideal* (Longmans, 1951).

HUTCHINSON, M. and YOUNG, C., *Educating the Intelligent* (Penguin Books, 1962; reprinted 1964).

JACKSON, B., *Streaming: an Education System in Miniature* (Routledge, 1964).

JONES, J. R., *Your Child at School* (Pan Books Ltd, 1965).

KALTON, G., *The Public Schools: A Factual Survey* (Longmans, 1966).

KAZAMIAS, A. M., *Politics, Society and Secondary Education in England* (Univ. of Pennsylvania Press, 1966).

LESTER SMITH, W. O., *Education: An Introductory Survey* (Penguin Books, 1957; reprinted 1965).

LESTER SMITH, W. O., *Government of Education* (Penguin Books, 1965).

MANNHEIM, K. and STEWART, W. A. C., *An Introduction to the Sociology of Education* (Routledge, 1962).

MAYER, M., *The Schools* (Bodley Head, 1961).

MAYS, J. B., *Education and the Urban Child* (Liverpool Univ. Press, 1962).

MEAD, MARGARET, *The School in American Culture* (Harvard Univ. Press, 1951).

MILLER, T. W. G., *Values in the Comprehensive School* (Oliver and Boyd, 1961).

MINISTRY OF EDUCATION, *15 to 18* (Crowther Report) (H.M.S.O., 1959; reprinted 1962).

MINISTRY OF EDUCATION, *Half Our Future* (Newsom Report) (H.M.S.O., 1963).

MUSGRAVE, P. W., *The Sociology of Education* (Methuen, 1965; reprinted 1968).

MUSGRAVE, P. W., *The School as an Organization* (Macmillan, 1968).

MUSGROVE, F., *The Family, Education and Society* (Routledge, 1966).

OESER, O. A., *Teacher, Pupil and Task* (Tavistock Publications, 1955).

OTTAWAY, A. K. C., *Education and Society* (Routledge, 2nd edition 1962; reprinted 1968), Chapter IX, pp. 167–89.

PARSONS, T. (ed.), *Theories of Society* (Free Press, Glencoe, 1965), 'The Modes of the Institutionalization of Action', pp. 181–236.

PARTRIDGE, J., *Life in a Secondary Modern School* (Penguin Books, 1968).

PEDLEY, R., *The Comprehensive School* (Penguin Books, 1963; revised edition 1966).

PETERSON, A. D. C., *Educating Our Rulers* (Duckworth, 1957).

RÉE, H., *The Essential Grammar School* (Harrap, 1956).

REESE EDWARDS, K. H. R., *The Secondary Technical School* (Univ. of London Press, 1960).

RELLER, T. L. and MORPHET, E. L., *Comparative Educational Administration* (Prentice-Hall, 1962).

SHIPMAN, M. D., *Sociology of the School* (Longmans, 1968).

STALCUP, R. G., *Sociology and Education* (C. E. Merrill Pub. Co., 1968).

STENHOUSE, L., *Discipline in Schools* (Pergamon Press, 1967).

SWIFT, D. F., *The Sociology of Education* (Routledge, 1969), Chapter 3, pp. 29–58.

TABA, H., *School Culture* (American Council on Education, Washington, D.C., 1955).

TAYLOR, W., *The Secondary Modern School* (Faber, 1963).

TÖNNIES, F., *Community and Associations (Gemeinschaft und Gesellschaft)* (tr. C. P. Loomis; Routledge, 1955).

TURNER, R., *The Social Context of Ambition* (Chandler, N.Y., 1964).

WALLER, W., *The Sociology of Teaching* (J. Wiley, 1965).

WEBER, MAX, *The Theory of Social and Economic Organization* (tr. A. M. Henderson and T. Parsons; O.U.P., 1947).

WEINBERG, I., *The English Public School* (Atherton Press, 1967).

WILSON, J., *Public Schools and Private Practice* (Allen and Unwin, 1962).

Chapter 12

The Teacher and His Role

A. THE TEACHER AND HIS TRAINING

It is a somewhat commonplace view that the teacher exists in a world of his own between the world of children and the world of adults; he is, it is said, 'a man amongst children, and a child amongst men'. Like most facile gibes and aphorisms this is an exaggeration, but it does contain enough truth to highlight one of the problems of the teaching profession. There are large numbers of both men and women teachers who have gone straight from school to the college of education or university and back to school again to teach.

This traditional approach to teacher recruitment and training was broken as a result of the Second World War, when there threatened to be a serious shortage of teachers. In consequence, in 1943, the (then) Board of Education devised a scheme for the provision of emergency teachers' training colleges. The object of the exercise was to provide the additional number of teachers which would be required during the immediate post-war years, and the chief sources of recruitment were the Forces and other areas of National Service. By the end of 1947 a total of fifty-five such colleges, with 13,500 places, had been opened; eventually 35,728 students completed their training successfully, 23,808 men and 11,920 women. Two of the points emphasized by the Ministry of Education in its general appraisal of this scheme were that these students possessed a larger and deeper experience of life than the normal run of students, and that their greater maturity of personality and attitude provided them with a certain motivation which many younger students appeared to lack (1).

The importance of such an experiment, however, lay not simply in the highly motivated attitudes of these mature students towards their own learning, but also in the fact that they were in many ways more qualified to become involved in the socialization of the young than more youthful students who seemed to be barely socialized themselves. But anyone who has been involved in the training of teachers will know that it is possible to have some students who are *too* mature: in fact, they may be so experienced and fossilized in their ways that they are virtually incapable of learning anything. The younger student's mind is still fluid and malleable; and if he or she is still in the process of being socialized this is not necessarily a disadvantage. It may, indeed, give the student a keener insight into some of the more immediate problems of his older pupils.

Between the extremes of the naïve schoolgirl and the mature, worldly-wise but sometimes inflexible serviceman, there is a variety of possibilities. It has, for example, been suggested that all candidates for the teaching profession should have spent at least one year as an unqualified, or pupil, teacher before entering college. There is a lot to be said for this, since one year is enough to cure many of their original interest in teaching; it may also be sufficient to cause many others to realize that there is nothing they would prefer to do. It has also been suggested that it would be an excellent thing if all prospective teachers were to spend some time – a year or so – in some occupation other than teaching. All such suggestions are interesting and possess a certain validity, but there are other ways of providing experience for the inexperienced and of involving youth in the larger society.

In his *The Role of the Teacher*, E. Hoyle remarks that the teacher is 'intermediate between the "real" world and the "ideal" world' (2), and tutors are frequently accused by their students of providing pictures of very unreal or idealistic situations, of being remote from life as it is. Certainly in the past the training college has often looked upon itself as an institution divorced from society, and one in which students have been able to live a somewhat secluded, monastic or conventual life for two or three years, in order to concentrate upon their academic study and professional preparation. The teaching role was something *given*, and there were assigned or prescribed duties which were clearly accepted and defined. Today, however, as Bernstein has indicated, the teaching role is one which has to be *achieved*; it has to be made. We shall consider in more detail the precise nature of the role of the teacher presently; here we are more concerned with the nature of the teacher's training and the way in which he may become involved in life and society as a whole, although he is in fact preparing in an institution for a specific profession.

If the student is to move from the 'ideal' or perhaps 'unreal' world to the 'real' world, from the college community to the wider social environment or community, then the institution in which he lives for from one to four years must be an active element in that real community. In fact, the student's years of training, or education, must not simply make the transition more easy, they must rather make such a transition unnecessary.

There is more than a suggestion in current literature on this subject that the view of the college of education as a cosy, segregated, but cohesive unit standing apart from society is fast disappearing. In an article on 'Intergroup Studies and "Techniques of Manipulative Socialization" in Teacher Education' (3), Gerda Hanko underlines the increasing pluralism of our contemporary society, and the greater variety of groups with widely differing values. The writer also emphasizes the need for studying society in some detail in order to comprehend the many roles and role conflicts involved. The techniques of such socialization are not aimed at the mere promotion of the cohesion of the institution of the college of education, or of any outdated conceptions of group process or group loyalty. Gerda Hanko is suggesting that the social cohesion of the college is not something that we seek to promote in the pious hope that there might later be some sort of transfer of this cohesion to society as a whole. Today, there is the attempt, in a much broader way, to regard the college of education, and other similar institutions, as an active dimension of society itself – a dimension, it is true, in which students are being trained formally for participation in society, but also one in which they are becoming involved immediately in society, and not simply in three years' time.

This changing nature of teacher training has been emphasized by Miss M. S. Valentine in her article entitled 'Teacher Training – Retrospect and Prospect' (4). The new form of government of colleges, the new patterns of residence, with eighteen as the age of majority, the rejection by students of paternalism or maternalism, and of close tutorial contacts – all these signs indicate a changing view of the college of education and of the college community. One of the aspects in which there has been considerable change is that of the size of such colleges. The small and somewhat introverted college of two hundred students or less is very much a thing of the past, and G. Price (5) has drawn the contrast between the monocentric college, in which the principal was the king-pin in maintaining the unifying ethos, and the polycentric college. He argues that, when a college has between 400 and 500 students, it has become polycentric and communication from the top begins to break down. Information has now to be transmitted via academic boards and departmental meetings, or via a mass of xeroxed material, and the real, vital, human links begin to be broken.

Price also provides figures to show that the optimum size of a college from the point of view of cost-effectiveness is in the region of 700 students. If his figures are correct there is clearly a lack of coincidence between the optimum size for communication and the optimum size for cost-effectiveness. Somewhat wistfully Price goes on to suggest that

'our business is not only about the profitability of cost-effectiveness nor about "break-even" economics in which that which a nation puts into education in monetary terms is equalled by what comes out at the other end. Our business is also about the education of teachers as professional people' (6).

In this connection John Konrad has made an interesting survey of the role of the students' union as part of the wider education which colleges of education provide (7). He also regrets the breakdown of lines of social and academic communication, and the fact that the failure of the provision of social facilities to keep pace with the growth of student numbers has lessened the ability of the colleges to compete with the external pressures of society, with a proportionate weakening of their ability to transmit the professional values of teacher education.

In the college of education the immediate cohesion of the college *per se*, and the concept of group loyalty are perhaps no longer the vital matters that immediately concern us. Are these qualities not more likely to be by-products of larger social aims? Will not the unity in the college ultimately derive more from social diversification than from the creation of a closed and introverted students' union? Now if the college of education is an essential factor in social action and dynamic, what sort of criteria or conditions should determine the type of social involvement of most value to both students and society?

Clearly any formal or organized training within colleges must have in mind both the present and future roles and role-sets of the students. It would seem likely that the more the college community is involved in *realistic* terms, and not simply in the playing at roles within the limits of the college institution, the less will be the frictions within the college itself. By social involvement in realistic terms it is certainly not implied that teachers in training should become increasingly engaged in organized or disorganized political or pseudo-political demonstrations, which are more often examples of non-involvement than involvement. There is a Zen story of two monks who were returning home when they came to a river bank, where a pretty girl was waiting, fearful of making her clothes wet. One monk picked her up in his arms, forded the river and, having put her down, walked on. The other monk was horrified and kept spluttering his indignation, mile upon mile. Eventually the first monk became aware of the other's words and said, 'That girl? *I* put her down at the ford. Are *you* still carrying her?' Much of the so-called social participation is of this latter type. There is a great deal of discussion of social problems as well as indignation shown at what others do; but those who are really involved get on with it and do it.

How does the college of education set about achieving this sort of involvement? An ever-increasing number of colleges are running different types of courses concerned with community and social studies, and the background and integration of immigrants. There seems to be a general movement in higher education not merely to socialize the student, or make him more aware of the environment in which he will operate, but also to assist him to achieve the role that he will perform in society. The role-set of the teacher may be nominally the same as it was about fifty years ago; but whilst the complement of role relationships may be much the same, an examination of any one group in the role-set quickly reveals how much more complex these role relationships have become.

More will be said about the teacher's role later in this chapter, but in so far as it relates to his training and preparation within a college or department of education something must be said about it here. Pupils in our modern society are more varied in their background, culture and beliefs, and this fact alone implies a different sort of training of the teacher. Pupils mature more quickly and will be remaining at school for a longer period; this implies not only a different curriculum but also a different type of approach.

Teachers are beginning to function differently: there is far more team-teaching and interaction between one academic subject and another, and this is bound to affect personal relationships in the process. The teacher finds it increasingly difficult to hide behind a specialism and to pursue a segregated life in a subject-room. This, in turn, implies some change in method in the colleges themselves with an increasing emphasis on team-teaching and working in groups. All this may be observed in Humanities Projects, in topics involving interdisciplinary inquiry, and in similar experiments developing at the present time. There is also more emphasis upon personal initiative and responsibility, which is further underlined by a somewhat new relationship with other members of the role-set in the school situation, such as H.M.I.s and county advisers. The teacher must, therefore, be prepared to achieve the role of one who is himself an initiator and innovator of sound educational development. The teacher in training has to be educated not just to go along with change, but to be bold enough to analyse and criticize both method and content, as well as to experiment with them.

In broad terms, this all means the development of teachers who are responsible, critical, co-operative and courageous. These are all essential qualities in developing communication with their wider social environment. The role of the teacher in training does not, of necessity, involve any temporary withdrawal from society; and an increasing number of students are realizing this and are impatient with any concept that they are parasites or a drain upon society. They are not simply potential or future citizens, they *are* citizens, voting citizens, in present time.

It is interesting to note the students' developing sense of social responsibility in terms of voluntary community service. Colleges will obviously vary in the amount of 'extra-curricular' social work in which they are, or can be, involved. Some students organize and run play groups in deprived areas; some work with young people in youth clubs, probation hostels, approved schools and in homes for ex-prisoners; some assist the handicapped and old people; some work with spastics, visit hospitals for the mentally handicapped, provide soup kitchens for drop-outs and meths drinkers, or help to teach illiterates and backward children. All this is done in what is euphemistically called their 'spare time'. This work is motivated in some instances by religious ideals, in others by sheer humanitarian considerations. But in any case the community service rendered is a result of an awareness of communal responsibility.

Role-performance, however, is limited both by personality factors and by social structure. Some geographical areas are obviously more useful in this respect than others, and more productive for social service. Not all students wish to be involved during their college course, nor yet afterwards; the important thing is that such service should not be regarded as something alien or abnormal in the college *milieu*. In his *Encounters*, Erving Goffman speaks of playing *at* roles as well as playing them (8). Our students are, to begin with, playing *at* roles; but the mask the actor wears tends eventually to become his face, and our students finally *achieve* the roles at which they play.

B. THE TEACHER AND HIS PROFESSION

The professional and social status of the teacher has for a long time been in some doubt, particularly at a time when school teachers recognized a class difference among themselves. The graduate who taught in the grammar school, whether he was trained or not, was always considered – and certainly considered himself – as a somewhat more elevated being than the teacher in the primary school with perhaps two years' training. There was, in fact, a difference between a 'school-master' and a 'school-teacher'. It is true that teachers themselves contributed very much towards the concept of a hierarchy amongst themselves, particularly with their creation of a variety of unions and professional organizations which related to their elitism or non-elitism in connection with both graduation and appointment. This has certainly been one of the factors which militate against a unified profession of teaching, or indeed the recognition of teaching itself as a profession.

It has become increasingly clear since the Second World War that two things need looking at very closely in teaching in order to establish it as a profession of some standing, as compared with medicine and law, for example. One is the minimum requirement for entry, and the other is the final academic qualification before the student is accepted into the profession. In 1968 the entrance qualifications of students admitted to courses of initial training, excluding entrants to postgraduate and to one-year specialist courses, were as shown in table opposite (9).

This means that about 36 per cent of these students have two or more A Levels, and there is an apparent weakness in the academic attainment as well as intellectual stamina of the majority of the entrants to the teaching profession. A further detailed examination of these A levels would also reveal that the majority are not of a very high grade.

	Men	Women
G.C.E. and C.S.E. (*Grade* 1) *passes:*		
5 O's or C.S.E.s, no A's	966	2,165
6 O's or C.S.E.s no A's	881	2,103
7 or more O's or C.S.E.s, no A's	899	3,214
1 A and 3 or more O's or C.S.E.s	2,532	6,797
2 A's and 2 or more O's	2,398	6,468
3 or more A's	1,444	3,475
School Certificate	500	1,967
Equivalent Qualifications	236	490
Admitted Exceptionally	580	1,170
	10,436	27,849

It is sometimes suggested, in mitigation of these low standards, that a large percentage of the teachers trained, particularly those who teach at the infant stage, are little more than 'child-minders' who are concerned with early socialization and with mediating the three Rs, and who therefore do not require high academic standards. But this sort of argument is almost the equivalent of suggesting that a paediatrician does not require a rigorous general training in medicine since, after all, he will deal only with children. It is gradually being realized, however slowly, that the teacher in training is not being trained simply to go through the motions of teaching or class organization: he is going through a process of personal maturation as well as being educated in some academic depth.

It is only when this principle of good, sound, academic standards for the acceptance of entrants to the profession is recognized that teaching will be regarded on a par with other professions. This may well have happened already if the growth rate of the teaching profession had been steady and gradual. But its expansion had to meet the problems of population explosions and 'bulges', reduced pupil to teacher ratio, and the raising of the school-leaving age to fifteen. In a period of rapid and almost perpetual change, it is difficult to find a breathing space when standards can be established and maintained. But the sickness obviously does not remain there. A realistic look at the rewards of the teaching profession reveals a general situation in which the remuneration is incommensurate with the length of training required and the social status ultimately demanded. Such rewards are inadequate to attract some of the better qualified men into the profession when they are able to obtain more satisfactory conditions of employment in industry or commerce. If teaching is a profession one must take a professional attitude towards it in all its aspects.

But if demands for better entrance qualifications should be made, and greater rewards provided, it is equally clear that there should be more rigorous academic requirements in the educational process of the teacher, with a qualification at the end more substantial than a certificate. Unless the profession can tolerate an initial elite – which it cannot really afford to do any longer – nothing short of a full degree will be adequate for all qualified teachers. It is suggested here that the B.Ed. degree should be thrown open to many more students than it is at present, or than the 25 per cent in 1977 as predicted by the D.E.S., whose figure also includes students taking the four-year degree-cum-professional training course (10).

The demand by the teachers' unions for an all-graduate profession is soundly based on a desire for the recognition of parity with other professions, not merely at the level of remuneration but also at the level of initial training. In the first section of this chapter we have confined ourselves to some social aspects of the teacher's education, and it is no part of our purpose to outline an academic course for teachers here. But if the status of the teacher is to be regarded as a professional one in the way that a doctor or a lawyer is a member of a profession, it would seem that there ought to be some sort of rationalization of the professional courses being pursued in over 160 colleges of education. The 'interesting', 'exciting' and 'fascinating' courses going on in a variety of venues may often have greater appeal and attraction to adventurous tutors than to students in training. No one would deny the need for experiment and innovations – whether in education or in medicine – but these things must not be introduced at the expense of a basic and essential professional training which will fit every student for the job he has to do. At the same time there must be real evidence in the course of academic depth.

There are specific problems at present peculiar to the profession of teaching. There can be no question but that young women at the end of their present three-year college of education course are better prepared for the responsibilities of life and motherhood, as well as for teaching itself. They have extended their education and their knowledge of life, of people and of children. But there is a considerable and increasing wastage of young women teachers, which the Plowden Report expresses in these terms: 'We can expect that of every 100 women who enter the training colleges, only 47 will be in the schools after three years' service and after six years only 30' (11).

That this wastage is serious no one would deny, but the remedy proposed in 'A Suggestion on the Supply and Training of Teachers' by six members of the Central Advisory Council for Education (England) would create a lower level or second echelon of teachers who received two years of initial training and then returned after about five years of teaching for a final year (12). The implementation of this suggestion could do little but aggravate the already heterogeneous nature of the teaching profession; but the problem of wastage remains, nevertheless, a real one. An alternative solution to making the course and the career easier for young women is simply to make it more difficult. In this way those who would, in future, pursue the course to the new high academic and professional level would be those who had already reached a high standard of achievement, and who had more deliberately and thoughtfully chosen a profession rather than a further course in education. Such women would not only be more anxious to get back into teaching once their period of child-rearing was over: they would also be more competent and more mentally equipped to deal with new situations and problems.

Some of the present imbalance in numbers between male and female teachers (13) might possibly disappear if teaching were to become more attractive as a career for men, particularly at the primary or middle school level – although here again the D.E.S. has prescribed that 'the proportion of men in each type of intake will remain constant at its present level; this implies that men will be about 28 per cent of all new entrants' (14). But there is no reason why this should be inevitably so; and although women may now have equal pay with men, and claim equality with men, there can be little doubt that in the past much of the sense of a second-rate profession attached to teaching has been the fact that it was predominantly female in membership. A large number of well qualified and professionally minded men in teaching might not only give men a greater equality with women, but also improve the social status of teaching.

There is, finally, another social problem associated with the teaching profession as a whole. Social status is not difficult to establish in relation to the medical and legal professions, but what is the social status of the teacher? Where does he fit in the social structure of our society? In their interesting discussion of 'Problems of Status and Role', Professors F. Musgrove and P. H. Taylor refer to the acute condition of 'status incongruence', which occurs when any individual exhibits two or more discrepant status factors, for example, when a university professor does not possess a university degree, or when an H.M.I. speaks with a cockney accent (15). It is very difficult to say what is congruent or incongruent in the status of 'the teacher'. It may depend very much upon the type of school he teaches in, the sort of children he teaches, and the environment in which the school is situated. It may be quite incongruent for one teacher to speak in a particular way in a certain situation, but not for another. So much in teaching depends upon the individual teacher's personality, and, as Martin Buber would put it, 'the relation in education' (16).

The dialogue of education may, indeed, permit of that very 'status incongruence' previously referred to; but its incongruence will no longer be apparent since the teacher *qua* teacher may have to forget his professional status and dignity and get literally 'on all fours' with his children. This is what makes it so difficult to give professional advice and direction to students in training: at best one is often attempting little more than simulation exercises; at worst one is mouthing little more than hopeful exhortations. One can learn how to teach, or rather be a teacher, only by teaching in real situations.

To return, however, to the point made specifically by Professors Musgrove and Taylor, it is a fact that the teaching profession is one in which the path of upward mobility is far from clearly delineated. Moreover, it is one in which many individuals find themselves by force of circumstances in positions which are not justified by their qualifications. We have, indeed, 'the rather odd situation that people are trying to obtain university degrees not in order to get jobs, but because they have got jobs' (17). Equally, of course, there are teachers in jobs which in no way match up to their qualifications, and yet again, through a multiplicity of circumstances, they may be unable to make the necessary move to give them adequate 'status congruence'. There are, undoubtedly, certain personality and social factors which often count over and above academic qualifications.

In his valuable sociological analysis of the teacher's role, B. R. Wilson (18) makes one of the most telling points about the teaching profession, and one that probably carries more weight as a general as well as an economic criterion of judgement. Doctors and lawyers are dealing, in their social functions, with the abnormal and the anomic, with those critical issues in people's lives when they are desperately in need of the help of the experts. The teacher is concerned with a compulsory social service to all members of the public, which is taken for granted as a normal process in the lives of all children between the ages of five and fifteen. We quickly accept the normal with barely a comment: it is the abnormal and the dysnomic that attract our interest, and those who are involved in dealing with them may possibly attract a disproportionate respect and recompense. The positive establishment of teaching as a worthy and comparable profession demands higher standards of entry and qualification; in addition, it demands an adequate remuneration which will compare favourably with that of other professions, and which will help the teaching profession to compete on equal terms and not to exist as a second-choice profession.

C. THE TEACHER AND HIS ROLE

In the last two sections we have inevitably spoken of the teacher's role in general terms since this is involved in a consideration of his profession or job and, therefore, of his training. It is, however, virtually impossible to speak of '*the* role of the teacher', as if there were something clearly defined which one could state concerning all teachers in all schools and in all situations. In their analysis of 'Shaping the Contemporary Teacher's Role', Professors Musgrove and Taylor (19) examine some of the changes in the concept of the teacher's role according to the changing concepts of teaching method. As a result of some of these latter the teacher may become a 'stage-manager', or a 'chief clerk', or possibly some sort of social worker. But the 'prime requisite of the new teacher is that he shall not teach' (20), if he follows too closely his supervisors' censures on teaching practice during his initial training.

We are all only too painfully aware of the justice of some of these comments, and also of the high order of confusion in the theory and practice of the trainers of teachers to which Musgrove and Taylor refer; but in strict fairness to the latter they accept that lecturers in colleges and departments of education, whatever their conflicts and doubts may be, 'appear to be unanimous in the importance they attach to sympathetic understanding of children and to establishing a happy and harmonious relationship with pupils inside (and if possible outside) the classroom' (21).

In any examination and delineation of aims and methods in education, in fact its philosophy and methodology, we must inevitably become more and more conscious of the role of the teacher in the classroom. As we become more aware of the relation between the child's behaviour and his home environment, and between the school and society at large, in fact the sociology of education, so we become more involved in the social aspects of teaching and learning. As the psychologist makes us increasingly cognizant of the mental development of the child, so we become more involved in the individual problems of particular children in the classroom.

There may have been a time when a teacher could happily say that it was his sole function to mediate a particular body of knowledge to a particular group of children, and to inform them with certain skills and perhaps even attitudes and opinions. But, thanks to the changing social climate, as well as the closer examination of the process of education through its various disciplines, it is impossible any longer to epitomize the role of the teacher so narrowly. There may, of course, be teachers who still interpret their role in this way, but one can hardly accept that they have taken a serious look at their role *vis-à-vis* the role-set, its changing nature, and role expectations.

Moreover, as P. W. Musgrave has pointed out (22), the teacher stands in a peculiar relation to the rest of society. Like the priest or the psychiatrist, he plays a mediating role between two worlds, and so tends to belong to neither. As a role-incumbent he finds that many of his personal problems and conflicts arise from this very situation. He may not like, or may even be strongly opposed to, the form of society that his role expects, or demands that he shall mediate. This must inevitably give rise to a conflict in his mind. But other conflicts will arise from the fact that as an individual he plays many roles in life; he may be a father, a deacon in a parish church, a lay-preacher, or involved in local politics. His role-demands in these various areas may result in inter-role conflict at times, and may provide difficult and embarrassing situations for resolution. Conflict of a different order may arise between the various members of the role-set when their expectations and norms of behaviour are dissimilar. This intra-role conflict is not something which the individual can resolve by himself, and indeed he may never fully resolve it; whereas his inter-role conflict is something which requires the adjustment of his own inner personality and the integration of the self.

Any analysis of the role of the teacher, therefore, cannot afford to ignore the individuality of the teacher; yet in terms of that role this individuality can be spoken of only in generalizations. This has been well expressed by Karl Mannheim and W. A. C. Stewart in the following words:

'The teacher brings into the classroom his views of his job, his prejudices, his personal fears and inadequacies, his ambitions, his humanity and affection. The thirty-five twelve-year-olds whom he has to teach differ in physique, appearance, intelligence, sociability, temperament and social and personal background' (23).

This one statement embodies some of the philosophical, sociological and psychological implications of the teacher's role. Whether he is aware of it, and whether he has analysed it or not, every teacher embodies within himself, within his personality, a philosophy of life and of his role – 'his views of his job'. In so far as his teaching is child-centred he is concerned with the social blocks which prevent the child's adequate and expressive use of language, and with the personal problems of the individual pupil which may militate against his progress.

In less general terms, the teacher's role must be viewed in relation to the headmaster and staff, the pupils, the parents, the caretaker and cleaners, and any visitors who come into the school, including H.M.I.s, county inspectors and advisers, students and supervisors. In relation to the headmaster and staff a particular teacher may be a young probationer anxiously learning his role; or an experienced but new teacher gradually feeling his way and finding his place; or a well-established member of the staff hierarchy whose function, from an intra-role point of view, is to help newcomers and to try and keep a harmonious balance in staff relationships. The head himself may withdraw completely, or nearly so, from the academic side of his role, and may concentrate upon the intricacies of organization and administration.

Within the classroom itself the teacher may find, after his probationary period, that he has almost complete autonomy, and it is this very autonomy which so many teachers find difficult and some even bewildering. There can be little doubt that the role of the teacher in the classroom demands a considerable maturity and sense of responsibility by virtue of the very freedom that the teacher has. If he abuses this freedom, in whatever way, he is jeopardizing the future as well as the present development of his pupils. It is, therefore, vital that the role incumbent should understand his responsibilities and work out his role in relation to them. As a mediator of culture, information and values the teacher is involved as an academic expert as well as something of a character trainer. He is concerned to help in the socialization of each child that comes under his tuition and care, in the building up of his personality and character, and in the development of values and attitudes.

In any consideration of the role of the teacher we are concerned very much with what other people, from the pupils to the parents and the local education authorities, expect of him. These role expectations, or role norms (24), may place heavy burdens upon the teacher which he may, in some instances, be unwilling or unprepared to accept. Certainly parents and pupils alike expect him to teach, in the conventional sense of the term, but this may, in fact, be considered by him to be the least of his many roles, or he might possibly view this as his chief one. This latter is perhaps some-what unlikely in the present development of the educational situation, but it is just possible. A teacher may, however, see his role in a different light from the other members of the role-set. He may consider himself to be an adviser or counsellor to his pupils, ever ready and willing to listen to their problems and to give counsel where and when required. He may see himself as their friend and helper, as a sort of social worker, as well as their leader and judge.

As a member of society the teacher may accept that his role is primarily that of initiating his pupils into society; that is, he may feel that it is his chief duty to socialize them. In this socializing process he may discover that his role is concerned with a variety of rituals. In Chapter 9 we considered some of the rituals in family living, and it is clear that rituals similarly exist within the framework of the school and its processes of initiation. We commented there that ritual, in some form or other, was not dying (25); rituals change their nature and perhaps the timing of their impact, but they do not cease to exist in a more developed or sophisticated society. The same thing applies to the classroom, the nature of which is rapidly changing.

In his *A Study in the Psychology of Ritualism,* F. G. Henke (26) noted that the institution of rituals often occurred quite spontaneously without any deliberate design or thought. But, in fact, most of our rituals arose by giving voluntary attention to a particular problem, and they existed as a means of manipulating the world around us, and in consequence of making it more facile to understand and absorb. The rituals of the school and the classroom are designed to make living together simpler and easier, and to assist in the fulfilment of the teacher's role. This is why one school may differ very much from another, or why one classroom possesses an entirely different ethos from another. The rituals reflect to some extent the nature and personality of the role incumbent, and these are clearly things about which one cannot generalize. One of the elements that inevitably make the training of teachers so problematic is the factor of personality variables. The rituals in the classroom that suit the personality of one teacher will not necessarily suit another, whether they be concerned with seating and other classroom arrangements, or with the methods of coercion and the sanctions applied in order that the teacher may fulfil his role with minimum of conflict, and so that the strongest motivation may be supplied for maximum production. It is inevitable, also, that new concepts of team teaching, group activity, projects, interdisciplinary inquiry, open-plan classrooms, and so forth, should have a fundamental effect upon the delineation of role norms and role expectations as well as upon the nature of rituals.

At some point in his career the teacher has to give conscious thought to his aims and objectives in teaching, and the means whereby he may achieve them. His role becomes a serious business for analysis and validation within the context of pupil activity and fulfilment, and in relation to the expectations of parents and society as a whole. His job is made difficult simply because his traffic is with human personalities and human relationships, and he is caught up in an intricate web of relations of pupils, parents, heads, advisers, inspectors and many others. But he is also concerned with the mediation of knowledge and culture, as well as with the development of a number of skills. This is why his role may be interpreted in a variety of ways, and why he himself may see his job in a very different light from that of his colleagues.

REFERENCES

1 The full story of this 'experiment' may be read in the Ministry of Education Pamphlet No. 17, *Challenge and Response* (H.M.S.O., 1950).
2 Hoyle, E., *The Role of the Teacher* (Routledge, 1969), p. 74.
3 Hanko, Gerda, 'Intergroup Studies and "Techniques of Manipulative Socialization" in Teacher Education', *Education for Teaching*, No. 81, Spring 1970, pp. 48–50.
4 *Vide* Valentine, M. S., 'Teacher Training – Retrospect and Prospect', *Education for Teaching*, No. 81, Spring 1970, pp. 2–11.
5 *Vide* Price, G., 'Economics and the Size of Colleges', *Education for Teaching*, No. 79, Summer 1969, pp. 60–2.
6 Price, G., ibid., pp. 61–2.
7 Konrad, J., 'The Role of the Students' Union as Part of the Wider Education Provided by Colleges of Education', (John L. Konrad, Garnett College of Education (Technical), April 1968).

8   *Vide* Goffman, E., *Encounters* (Bobbs-Merrill Co. Inc., N.Y., 1961), and
    The Presentation of Self in Everyday Life (Doubleday, N.Y., 1959).
9   D.E.S., *Statistics of Education: 1968 – Volume 4, Teachers* (H.M.S.O.,
    1970), p.3.
10 Ibid., p. 86.
11 D.E.S., *Children and their Primary Schools* (Plowden Report) (H.M.S.O.,
    1967), p. 493.
12 Ibid., pp. 493–5.
13 *Vide* D.E.S., *Statistics of Education: 1968 – Volume 4, Teachers*, Table
    13[13], p. 17. In February 1970 there were a total of 393,672 full-time
    teachers in maintained schools and establishments of whom 186,907 were
    men and 206,765 were women.
14 Ibid., p. 86.
15 Musgrove, F. and Taylor, P. H., *Society and the Teacher's Role*, Chapter
    6, pp. 68–78.
16 Buber, M., *Between Man and Man* (Collins, Fontana Library, 1961), pp.
    125–31.
17 Musgrove, F. and Taylor P. H., op. cit., pp. 69–70.
18 Wilson, B. R., 'The Teacher's Role: a Sociological Analysis', *British
    Journal of Sociology*, Vol. 13, No. 1, 1962, pp. 15–32.
19 *Vide* Musgrove, F. and Taylor, P. H., op. cit., pp. 8–16.
20 Ibid., p. 13.
21 Ibid., p. 13.
22 *Vide* Musgrave, P. W., *The Sociology of Education* (Methuen, 1965), p.
    258.
23 Mannheim, K. and Stewart, W. A. C., *An Introduction to the Sociology of
    Education* (Routledge, 1962), p. 141.
24 *Vide* Banton, M., *Roles: An Introduction to the Study of Social Relations*
    (Tavistock Publications, 1965), pp. 28–9.
25 *Vide* Bossard, J. H. S. and Boll, Eleanor S., 'Ritual in Family Living',
    American Sociological Review, Vol. 14, August 1949.
26 *Vide* Henke, F. G., *A Study in the Psychology of Ritualism* (Univ. of
    Chicago Press, 1910).

BIBLIOGRAPHY

A. *Books*

A.T.C.D.E., *Handbook of Colleges and Departments of Education* (Lund
    Humphries, 1971).
BANKS, OLIVE, *The Sociology of Education* (Batsford, 1968), Chapter 7, 'The
    Teaching Profession'.
BEREDAY, C. Z. F. *et al., The Education and Training of Teachers* (Year Book of
    Education 1963) (Evans, 1963).
BIDDLE, B. J., *Role Theory: Concepts and Research* (Wiley, 1966).
BIDDLE, B. J. *et al., Studies in the Role of the Public School Teacher* (Univ. of
    Missouri Press, Vols. 1–5, 1961).
BYRNE, H. J., *Primary Teacher Training* (O.U.P., 1960).

CARR-SANDERS, A. M. and WILSON, P. A., *The Professions* (Clarendon Press, 1933).

CONANT, J. B., *The Education of American Teachers* (McGraw-Hill, 1963).

DENT, H. C., *To Be a Teacher* (Univ. of London Press, 1947).

GURNEY, P., *Education and Training of Teachers* (Longmans, 1963).

HOYLE, E., *The Role of the Teacher* (Routledge, 1969).

JEFFREYS, M. V. C., *Revolution in Teacher Training* (Pitman, 1961).

JUDGES, A. V. (ed.), *The Function of Teaching* (Faber, 1969).

KAYE, B. *et al., Group Work in Secondary Schools and the Training of Teachers in its Method* (O.U.P., 1968).

LIEBERMAN, M., *Education as a Profession* (Prentice-Hall, 1956).

MORRISON, A. and MCINTYRE, D., *Teachers and Teaching* (Penguin, 1969).

MUSGRAVE, P. W., *The Sociology of Education* (Methuen, 1965), Part III, 'The Sociology of Teaching', pp. 205–70.

MUSGRAVE, P. W., *The School as an Organization* (Macmillan, 1968), Chapters 4 and 5.

MUSGROVE, F. and TAYLOR, P. H., *Society and the Teacher's Role* (Routledge, 1969).

OESER, O. A. (ed.), *Teacher, Pupil and Task* (Tavistock Publications, 1955).

OTTAWAY, A. K. C., *Education and Society* (Routledge, 2nd edition 1962), 'The Role of the Teacher', pp. 185–9.

RICH, R. W., *The Training of Teachers in England and Wales During the Nineteenth Century* (C.U.P., 1933).

RICH, R. W., *The Teacher in a Planned Society* (Univ. of London Press, 1950).

RICHARDSON, C. A. *et al., The Education of Teachers in England, France and the U.S.A.* (UNESCO, Paris, 1953).

RICHARDSON, ELIZABETH, *Group Study for Teachers* (Routledge, 1967).

RYANS, D. G., *Characteristics of Teachers, Their Description, Comparison and Appraisal* (American Council on Education, Washington, D.C., 1960).

SARASON, S. B. *et al., The Preparation of Teachers: An Unstudied Problem in Education* (Wiley, 1962).

STENHOUSE, L., *Culture and Education* (Nelson, 1967), Chapter 12, 'Training of Teachers'.

STILES, L. J. *et al., Teacher Education in the United States* (Ronald Press, 1960).

TAYLOR, W., *The Secondary Modern School* (Faber, 1963), Chapter VII, 'The Modern School Teacher and Educational Change'; see also Appendix IV, 'The Modern School Teacher'.

TAYLOR, W., *Society and the Education of Teachers* (Faber, 1969).

TROPP, A., *The School Teachers* (Heinemann, 1957).

WALLER, W., *The Sociology of Teaching* (Wiley, 1932; reprinted 1965).

Official Reports, etc.

Board of Education, *Teachers and Youth Leaders* (McNair Report) (H.M.S.O., 1944).

Central Advisory Council, *15 to 18* (Crowther Report) (H.M.S.O., 1959), Chapter 37, 'Teachers'.

Central Advisory Council, *Half Our Future* (Newsom Report) (H.M.S.O., 1959), Chapter 12, 'Teachers Needed'.

Central Advisory Council, *Children and their Primary Schools* (Plowden Report) (H.M.S.O., 1967), Part Six, 'The Adults in the Schools'.

Committee on Higher Education, *Higher Education* (Robbins Report) (H.M.S.O., 1963).

Ministry of Education, *Challenge and Response* (Pamphlet 17) (H.M.S.O.,1950).

Ministry of Education, *Training of Teachers: Suggestions for a Three-Year Training College Course* (Pamphlet 34) (H.M.S.O., 1957).

Ministry of Education, *Supply and Training of Teachers for Technical Colleges* (Jackson Report) (H.M.S.O., 1957).

Ministry of Education, *Teachers for Further Education* (H.M.S.O., 1961).

Ministry of Education, *Women and Teaching* (Kelsall Report) (H.M.S.O., 1963).

N.A.C., *Three-Year Training for Teachers* (5th Report) (H.M.S.O., 1956).

N.A.C., *Scope and Content of the Three-Year Course* (6th Report) (H.M.S.O., 1957).

N.A.C., *The Future Pattern of the Education and Training of Teachers* (8th Report) (H.M.S.O., 1962).

C. Articles

BARON, G. and TROPP, A., 'Teachers in England and America', in Halsey, A. H. *et al., Education, Economy and Society* (Free Press, Glencoe, 1961).

BOGEN, I., 'Pupil-teacher Rapport and the Teacher's Awareness of Status Structures Within the Group', *Journal of Educational Studies*, Vol. 28, 1954, pp. 105–14.

CANNON, C., 'Some Variations on the Teacher's Role', *Education for Teaching*, No. 64, May 1964, pp. 29–36.

COHEN, L., 'The Teacher's Role as Liaison between School and Neighbourhood' in Croft, M. *et al., Linking Home and School* (Longmans, 1967).

CRAIG, H., 'The Teacher's Function: some observations on an aspect of the teacher's job in Scotland', *Journal of Educational Studies*, Vol. 34, 1960, pp. 7–16.

EVANS, K. M., 'A Study of Attitudes towards Teaching as a Career', *British Journal of Educational Psychology*, Vol. 32, 1952, pp. 63–9.

EVANS, K. M., 'Teacher Training Courses and Students' Personal Qualities', *Educational Research*, Vol. 10, No. 1, 1967, pp. 72–7.

FINLAYSON, D. S. and COHEN, L., 'The Teacher's Role: A Comparative Study of the Conceptions of College of Education Students and Head Teachers', *British Journal of Educational Psychology*, Vol. 37, No. 1, 1967, pp. 22–31.

FLOUD, J., 'Teaching in the Affluent Society', *British Journal of Sociology*, Vol. 13, 1962.

FLOUD, J. *et al.*, 'Recruitment in Teaching in England and Wales', in Halsey, A. H. *et al., Education, Economy and Society* (Free Press, Glencoe, 1961).

GEER, B., 'Occupational Commitment and the Teaching Profession', *School Review*, No. 74, 1966.

GETZELS, J. W. *et al.,* 'The Structure of Roles and Role Conflict in the Teaching Situation', *Journal of Educational Sociology,* Vol. 29, 1955.

JARRETT, J. L., 'American Teacher Education: Caricature and Promise', *Education for Teaching,* No. 77, Autumn 1968, pp. 49–54.

KOB, J., 'The Teacher in Industrial Society', in *Yearbook of Education 1963* (Evans, 1963).

KOB, J., 'Definition of the Teacher's Role', in Halsey, A. H. *et al., Education, Economy and Society* (Free Press, Glencoe, 1961).

MUSGROVE, F. and TAYLOR, P. H., 'Teachers' and Parents' Conceptions of the Teacher's Role', *British Journal of Educational Psychology,* Vol. 35, No. 2, June 1965, pp. 171–8.

OLIVER, R. A. C. *et al.,* 'Teachers' Attitudes to Education', *British Journal of Educational Psychology,* Vol. 38, 1968, pp. 38–44.

PAFFARD, M., 'Training the Graduate Teacher: An Unorthodox View', *Education for Teaching,* No. 79, 1969, pp. 48–54.

PECK, B. T., 'Tradition and Change in Scottish Teacher Education', *Education for Teaching,* No. 77, 1968, pp. 40–8.

PERRY, L. R., 'Training', *Education for Teaching,* No. 79, 1969.

PETERS, R. S., 'Theory and Practice in Teacher Training', *Trends in Education,* No. 9 (H.M.S.O., 1968).

PORTER, J. F. (ed.), 'Teachers for Tomorrow', *Education for Teaching,* No. 77, 1968, pp. 55–64.

RYAN, D. G., 'Teacher Behaviour Theory and Research: Implications for Teacher Education', *Journal of Teacher Education,* No. 14, 1963, pp. 274–93.

SHIPMAN, M. D., 'Theory and Practice in the Education of Teachers', *Educational Research,* Vol. 9, 1967, pp. 208–12.

SKINNER, J. E., 'College and Community', *Education for Teaching,* No. 75, 1968.

SOLES, S., 'Teacher Role Expectations and the Organization of the School', *Journal of Educational Research,* Vol. 57, 1964.

STONES, E., 'The Role of the Headteacher in English Education', *Forum,* No. 6, 1963.

TANSEY, P. J., 'Teacher Training in England', *Educational Sciences,* Vol. 3, No. 2 (Pergamon Press, 1969).

TAYLOR, P. H., 'Teachers' Role Conflicts in Infant and Junior Schools', *International Journal of Educational Sciences,* 1968.

WASHBURNE, C. *et al.,* 'What Characteristics of Teachers Affect Children's Growth?', *School Review,* No. 68, 1960, pp. 420–8.

WAYNE, G. C., 'The Role of the Teacher in the Social Structure of the High School', *Journal of Educational Studies,* 1955.

WESTWOOD, L. J., 'The Role of the Teacher – I and II', *Educational Research,* Vol. 9, No. 2 and Vol. 10, No. 1, 1967–8.

WILLIAMS, R. H., 'Professional Studies in Teacher Training', *Education for Teaching,* No. 61, 1963.

WILSON, B. R., 'The Teacher's Role – a Sociological Analysis', *British Journal of Sociology,* Vol. 13, No. 1, 1962, pp. 15–32.

Chapter 13

The Pupil in the Classroom

A. PEER GROUPS AND GROUP DYNAMICS

A peer is an equal, and a peer group is a group composed of individuals who are equals. In terms of a school the children in the classroom are members of a peer group, usually age peers, and their interaction is that of equals. This sense and awareness of identity with the group is one of the essential features of the socialization of the pupils and their feelings of stability and solidarity. The peer group provides the norms or standards of thought and behaviour to be pursued by its members, and establishes the attitudes, opinions and cultural ideas which they are expected to adopt. It is through such peer groups that sub-cultures are established which may provide variations in standards of social behaviour or dress and fashion.

It is this general sense of identity and solidarity which can be used and manipulated in a variety of ways in the classroom as well as in the school as a whole. The individual child is motivated not simply by his own basic needs and drives, but also by the stimulation provided by his peers. In 'A Theory of Motivation', A. H. Maslow elicits five sets of goals which he considers are basic needs (1). These basic goals are physiological, safety, love, esteem and self-actualization, and they are related to one another in a hierarchy of prepotency. The interaction of these basic needs, involving as they do the need for personal growth and deeper relationships, is something which to some extent the teacher can direct and control. On the other hand, it is also the sense of oneness with the group and its goals that can lead to a variety of mass behaviour in relation to the teacher, to the head, or to other peer groups within the school. In the classroom the teacher is separated, temporarily at least, from his own peer group; and he is faced with a very different, younger peer group which may represent for him the 'enemy' to be conquered, or youthful 'animals' to be tamed and restrained, or the educands to be won over and taught.

Different attitudes towards the peer group of the pupils will inevitably lead to a variety of ways of teaching, learning and class organization. A school such as Dotheboys Hall was obviously based upon the view that all children were undesirable little beasts who had to be kept strictly in their place, and the restrictive measures employed to keep them there were an unavoidable result of this philosophy. At A. S. Neill's school, Summerhill, the attitude held is apparently one of equality between staff and pupils, and in the dynamics of the group the teacher is regarded as simply another member of the peer group. Thus Neill says:

> 'Summerhill is a self-governing school, democratic in form. Everything connected with social, or group, life, including punishment for social offences, is settled by vote at the Saturday night general School Meeting. Each member of the teaching staff and each child, regardless of his age, has one vote. My vote carries the same weight as that of a seven-year-old' (2).

In a consideration of teacher-pupil relationships there is a tendency to think only in terms of extremes, of authoritarian and democratic styles of teaching; or of dominating and being dominated, and alternatively of fully integrating. Perhaps there is something almost inevitable about this type of polarization; man tends to think in terms of opposites, of black or white, good or evil, freedom or determinism, heredity or environment, and so forth. It is noticeable, for example, that when students go on teaching practice initially they think in terms either of a strict, authoritarian discipline or of a too free, democratic one. The actual class situation in a state school, however, does not demand that the teacher should count for one and only one, in Neill's terms, nor does it demand the repressive Squeers' approach of Dotheboys Hall. Between these extremes there exists a considerable variety of possibilities dependent upon such variables as the teacher's personality, the nature of the pupil peer group, the type of school, its environment and so on.

The classroom is in many senses an artificial reproduction of the conflict and stresses of the larger society, and the child has to be educated in attitude development as well as trained in the skills of social interaction, discussion, compromise and mediation. All these require the acceptance not merely of conflict and social distance between pupil groups and the teacher, but also of the possibilities of resolution of conflict, of the maintenance of respect even in the midst of disagreement and 'trouble shooting', and of the continuance of social interaction even in the presence of the threat of social sanction. It is, of course, never as simple as all that since it is a very rare thing to find a class composed of a completely balanced, integrated and cohesive peer group. There are invariably factions and cliques within the class, which will sometimes defy all attempts at unification. Sometimes an outstanding athlete or games player may dominate the peer group, and the attainment of academic standards may be regarded as quite unimportant. Sometimes the group leader may be a clever wit who is capable at any time of baiting the teacher; whilst occasionally prestige is acquired through an easy academic brilliance which is apparently independent of 'swotting'. In the areas of leadership children are as unpredictable as their elders, and the successful deviant or delinquent may well find favour with a smaller coterie within the class, until he loses face, perhaps, by being found out.

One essential feature in the motivation of the dynamics of the peer group is the desire to *belong*. All children basically want to belong; they want, as Maslow pointed out (3), a sense of security and esteem. But the ambivalence of the human being is such that he also needs fulfilment in the process of self-actualization (4). Man is more than a gregarious animal, and he consciously seeks, therefore, to become something, someone, which others do not become. His identity with the group is, in consequence, a limited identity. In fact, the class peer group may become for any particular pupil a reference group from which he may virtually contract out. His membership group, that is, the group to which he really belongs, may be one in which he feels himself actualized and fulfilled. It is because it does not represent the norm that he feels that he can belong to it, and within and through it acquire the esteem that he seeks. For him the behaviour of his membership group is 'better' than that of the reference group with its more orthodox, traditional or acceptable norms of behaviour. 'Better' here may imply some high moral tone and, with that priggishness which is perhaps specific to youth, the individual pupil may judge the norms of the reference group as low and unacceptable. It may, however, be 'better' than the peer group because it is more daring or even deviant. Most children seem to go through a phase when slightly deviant behaviour, at least, becomes acceptable as a challenge to authority; and if the individual child is lucky he may pass through this stage without advancing to a state of delinquency.

But if all children want to belong, to experience esteem from their peers, and to have a sense of security within the group, how does one account for the *isolate*? The immediate answer is, of course, that one does not – at least not in a section of this length. The 'isolate' is as much an abstraction as the 'delinquent' or the 'criminal'. Pupils are individuals, and a child's isolation within the context of the peer group may arise from a wide variety of causes. He may be naturally very introvert; he may be self-sufficient; he may be individualistic; he may be bordering on the autistic; he may be one coloured child among many white; or he may be deliberately ostracized by the group for his oddness, his priggishness, or simply because he has an unpleasant odour. The writer can well remember one isolate who, because of his lack of identity with his peers, was attacked by a master in the following terms:

'Smith, you're too old for the class.'
'But, sir, I'm just about the average age of the class.'
'I mean in disposition, boy, in disposition.'

Some children seem to be born 'old' in outlook and disposition, and they never quite identify with the mass or their age peer group. The isolate, however, is not necessarily a problem psychologically or sociologically: his relative isolation may result from a deep desire for self-actualization in a way that does not particularly involve his peer group. Clearly one has to be aware of the isolate in the class and the reasons for his isolation, but in his socializing role it is certainly not the function of the teacher to try and make every pupil a lusty extrovert.

The class has virtually two leaders (or more): there is the leader of the peer group, and the institutional leader, the teacher. In the dynamics of the classroom and interpersonal behaviour, these two leaders will inevitably have to come to terms at some stage. It may be done quite amicably and quietly, or it may come to something like a staged 'show-down' at some point – but it will be done. There are, of course, changes in class organization and method which have, at certain levels in some schools, altered the nature of the conflict as well as of the leadership and the peer group. An open-plan middle school situation in which there are three teachers and seventy children, divided into ten or twelve groups, has provided an entirely different problem, or set of problems, of group dynamics. In such a situation there is both an immediate reduction of social distance between teacher and pupil, and a strengthening of the teacher's leadership role through the backing of other representatives of his own peer group. But the leadership at the same time has a closer identity with the pupil peer group(s). In the give-and-take of group activity there is no possibility of the *noli me tangere* attitude which in the past often resulted in an exclamation such as, 'Stand off, boy; don't breathe down my neck!' Pupils and teachers are increasingly breathing down one another's necks, and many of the older concepts of role and of group behaviour are being modified in practice, if not in theory.

In such team-teaching and group-learning situations there are new and different problems of arousing motivation for much more co-operative work in small groups, as well as of maintaining a workable form of discipline where children are in a more fluid and mobile situation and may be immediately under the eye of a teacher for only a small proportion of the learning day. It is facile, of course, to talk in terms of self-discipline and of developing a sense of personal responsibility, but these qualities are not acquired simply by presenting the possibility of their attainment in a particular learning situation. If children have to learn how to learn, they equally have to learn how to become self-disciplined and responsible individuals. In the contemporary classroom scene, the teacher is more on top of the 'logic of dynamics', and its variety of overlapping situations. Certainly the 'field theory' of Kurt Lewin (5), with its attempt to deal with human behaviour in terms of topology and vectors within a space, would appear to have increasing application to the developing classroom situations.

Professor W. J. H. Sprott refers to the life-space as that which 'consists of the individual person at a particular moment of time in a setting partly determined by the physical objects present, partly by his interpretation of them, how he perceives them, their significance for him at that moment' (6). And the behaviour setting of the classroom, including the other pupils in his group or immediate surroundings, the amenities in the way of books of reference, useful materials, gadgets and so forth, the availability of the right instruments to fulfil his requirements – all these things may decide the success or otherwise of any particular project or piece of work for a specific pupil or group.

Thus, life-space and group interaction are vitally important for the full implementation of the new methodology and classroom organization in education. It is important to the teacher, therefore, to understand as fully as possible what is happening in the classroom in terms of group interaction; and in this context educational technology is of considerable assistance. The various techniques and hardware for analysing the learning situations are of importance not simply in the development of new methodology, but also as a means of understanding group processes. The recording and playing back of group and class discussions may reveal some of the problems involved in group situations and communication levels.

The work also of J. L. Moreno (7) has revealed something of the way in which groups are formed in a class when children are left to make their own selection of group mates. There are *starred* pupils, who agglomerate a constellation of adherents, as well as isolates who, being rejected by the starred pupils, may be forced to form an ineffectual group of their own. But it is part of the role of the teacher, in the freer society of the democratic classroom, to manœuvre children into new and more productive situations. The presence of an increasing number of sub-cultures in our society, as represented by immigrant groups, is reflected in the voluntary grouping in some classrooms. This grouping derives not so much from a sense of hostility towards others as from a feeling of solidarity and security in a *given* identity. Pakistanis will tend to group together, as also will Sikhs and West Indians. The resultant in the classroom is often an ethos of discrete and disparate groups, with a number of wandering isolates who may be Chinese or whites. It is a form of self-discrimination by group identity.

Much of this grouping in the classroom is based, initially, not simply on colour or country of origin, but upon facility of communication. Once they have identified one another and grouped together, immigrant children tend to converse in their native language within their sub-group. This, in turn, tends to seal off other groups speaking English or any other alien language. The writer has noticed the particular difficulties and consequent sense of isolation experienced by West Indian children who have come over speaking a creole or pidgin, plus perhaps some Standard Jamaican English. These pupils feel cut off not only from the other coloured immigrant groups but also from the English children who speak what to them is virtually a foreign language. The dynamics of such a mixed group are odd, to say the least, and they present unusual problems to a teacher who has any idea of welding them all into an integrated group.

Thus, within the peer group of the class there may be today not simply sub-groups representing constellations around starred pupils, and the deviant or 'delinquescent' sub-groups (8) who seek to oppose all forms of authority; there is also the increasing variety of coloured sub-cultural groups who cover a vast area of historical, religious and social development in Pakistan, India and the West Indies, and who present an additional variable within the group dynamics of the class. The integration of these various sub-groups involves not merely a knowledge of their socio-religious and cultural background, but also an understanding of their psychology at both the individual and social levels. It is the failure to appreciate the sheer anthropological differences of other peoples and races which results in sterile attempts at manipulating mixed groups in the dynamics of the classroom.

Much of this is the problem of establishing a new consensus out of a deeper comprehension of both the differences and the common ground which exists between the various groups. Karl Mannheim understood this problem as well as anyone when he suggested that 'Consensus is far more than theoretical agreement on certain issues – consensus is common life. To prepare the ground for consensus eventually means to prepare the ground for common life' (9). But common life derives from something deeper than agreed articles of political or social behaviour, or artifically created rituals. The symbols which are the heritage of the East are different from those of the West (10); an understanding of them is not only essential to any real comprehension of the patterns of thought and behaviour of Eastern children, but may also reveal the key to some possibility of their transformation in Western terms. Some of the work of Carl Jung is of particular significance here (11). Similarly, the mental symbols of Africans and West Indians are different from ours, and therefore if we are to have dialogue with them we need to understand the psychic forces which motivate their thinking (12). The dialogical relation in education, mentioned by Martin Buber, does not happen in some altogether miraculous way: it is finally elicited through a thorough understanding of the Other (13).

All societies and groups, whether simple or complex, undergo those 'paradigmatic experiences' to which Mannheim refers (14). These are basic and decisive experiences which in some way reveal the meaning of life in its entirety, and according to Mannheim their pattern is deeply engraved in our minds in such a way that a mould is provided into which other experiences might flow. The integration of any society depends very much upon the increasing identification of archetypes, paradigmata, symbols, myths and rituals. The psychological importance of these factors at the unconscious level has for a long time been recognized: we must now accept their sociological significance at the conscious level.

B. SOCIETY IN THE CLASSROOM

In Chapter 11 we discussed some aspects of the school in its relation to society as well as the school as a society, or micro-society, in its own right; we are here briefly concerned with the way in which the macro-society intrudes upon and is reflected in the classroom itself. Much, of course, will depend upon the nature of the school, its environment and so forth, but with the increasing development of the comprehensive type of school it is clear that our generalizations about society in the classroom may be coming closer to reality. It is, however, equally true that some neighbourhood comprehensive schools represent only one particular stratum of society, while many grammar schools have exemplified a fair cross-section of society drawn from a wide catchment area.

But whether in one particular school or in schools in general, it is true to say that the multiplicity of social variations and problems are all introduced in one form or another into the context of the classroom. Professor B. Bernstein has reminded us steadily and consistently of the linguistic problems which children bring to school with them (15). There are those children who suffer from a sort of language undernourishment at home which results in their bringing to school with them a very restricted code, and therefore limited powers of communication. This may not create too much of a limitation for them *vis-à-vis* the other pupils in their class or peer group, whatever their social background. Even those children whose home environment involves an elaborated code will adapt themselves to the restricted code of other children. But it is more *vis-à-vis* the teacher that the child is likely to experience problems. Unless the teacher himself can adapt to the child's code, he may find, particularly if he has a middle-class background, that he has considerable difficulty in making himself understood.

Social deprivation covers a wide area of disabilities, including those which are personal handicaps resulting in social difficulties. It is not merely that different social levels are replicated in the classroom: all life's physical deformities, moral and social deviances and personality disturbances are congregated there. This becomes increasingly so as the concept of separate education for the handicapped, the dull, the backward and so forth is considered less and less 'a good thing'. The severely handicapped, the autistic and the criminal may still be educated separately, but a 'normal' unstreamed class in a comprehensive school might include a complete cross-section from the E.S.N. – if one may still use the term – to the high-flyer.

It is inevitable that the general ethos of society should be reflected in its schools, particularly those which are state schools. It is inevitable because in a very real sense this is one of the main functions of the school, namely to mediate to the children the nature of the society in which they live. And as society and its general aims change so also does the school and its aims. Durkheim was in no doubt as to the main functions of education and of the school when he claimed that

> 'it is society as a whole and each particular social *milieu* that determine the ideal that education realizes. Society can survive only if there exists among its members a sufficient degree of homogeneity: education perpetuates and reinforces this homogeneity by fixing in the child, from the beginning, the essential similarities that collective life demands. But on the other hand, without a certain diversity all co-operation would be impossible; education assures the persistence of this necessary diversity by being itself diversified and specialized' (16).

The classroom reflects this homogeneity and diversity. Even the most unrepentant of egalitarians cannot prevent the development of individual personalities, abilities and skills; equally the most enthusiastic of individualists must accept that there are social norms which are essential if society is to cohere and survive. The school and the classroom provide a social base from which children can diversify, but to which they can, in addition, return for security and stability. It is also an artifically devised *milieu* in which the violent and sudden changes of the outside world may be softened and introduced in doses small enough for the class group and the individual child to absorb in a sort of homoeopathic way.

Something of the conflict that is experienced in the outside world is also reflected in the life and activities of the class. Its fears, its terrors, its sorrows and its aggression are all found in the literature read in the class, as well as in the pupils' interpersonal relations. The classroom sets the social scene in miniature so that the full impact of its conflicts may not be felt by the child too soon. But it also preserves a balance by reproducing something of the co-operation, the participation and the interest of the total society. It does this both in the interaction of the peer group and through the pupil-teacher relationship. The variety of teacher personalities will provide for the pupils a cross-section of a peer group at a different level in the social and age hierarchies. As M. D. Shipman remarks, 'Each pupil will not only respond to the teacher as a symbol, but will see him as a person, feel attracted, repelled or unmoved' (17). In his reaction to his teacher, and in the teacher's response, he will find something of the security, the love, the fear, the authority, the impatience or the friendship of the larger society.

It is in the give-and-take of classroom experience that the child's personality evolves and becomes gradually integrated both in terms of society and in terms of the child himself. In other children he is able to see the reflection of himself, even though he may not fully recognize it. He will see something of the development and arousal of enthusiasm in a variety of projects and inquiries, and its gradual decay and dissolution; he will experience both failure and success, encouragement and indifference, reward and punishment. He will also begin to understand what it is to have limited freedom and responsibility; and in many schools the pupil may find that he is actively participating in their organization and administration.

In some schools the pupil will certainly experience something of the selective procedures of a society in which there still exist intellectual elites and something in the nature of an evolving meritocracy. Some children will suffer from a sense of under-achievement and become problem children: others will rejoice in the realization of academic fulfilment. But all pupils need to feel not only some awareness of achievement in the present, but also that what they are doing is related to their role in society in the future. In the human struggle for individual survival it is not enough to tell children blithely that above all they should feel happy, and everything else will be added unto them. Indeed, a little 'misery' experienced at their books now may forestall a lot of unhappiness later on when jobs are scarce and will inevitably go to the best qualified in terms of paper qualifications. But examinations in themselves are not necessarily calculated to make children unhappy, and their wholesale condemnation derives from a misconception of the needs of an efficient and progressive society. Nor does it help very much to point to the exceptionally great ones who have led their countries without having passed a single examination. Only the very few really achieve such greatness, and their position regarding examinations is quite irrelevant. If a child wishes to enter a profession, his competence even to begin a course of study for it must be tested. And if he is really interested in pursuing such a profession as his life work, he will in all probability overcome any aversion to the examination as such. Even A. S. Neill, with all his emphasis upon freedom, happiness and so forth, has said:

'My staff and I have a hearty hatred of all examinations. To us, the university exams are anathema. But we cannot refuse to teach children the required subjects. Obviously, as long as the exams are in existence, they are our master. Hence, the Summerhill staff is always qualified to teach to the set standard' (18).

Few of us perhaps, even in our moments of greatest achievement, stop to consider what we are doing in terms of being happy in our work. Indeed, happiness or contentment is largely derivative and, if the behaviourists are in any sense right, reinforcement and immediate knowledge of results

(IKR) are more productive of efficient and satisfying results than anything else. Most healthy-minded children like to have their knowledge, understanding and skills put to the test, particularly if the accompanying teacher responses are encouraging rather than condemnatory. The child likes to compete with himself if with no one else, and in his advance in society he will certainly find that his own mobility within his social group or work group depends very much upon setting his own standards and goals, and seeking to improve upon his own levels of attainment. Education is not only education for life itself; it is also education for more education extending into each individual's future.

Earlier it was mentioned that life was something of a struggle for individual survival and, whilst many would deprecate the replication of such a struggle in the classroom, the fact is that the children who constitute the class are already the subjects, whether in a positive or a negative way, of such a struggle through their home environments. They bring their homes and their parents into the classroom with them. If children are to survive as individuals they must, above all, learn to become *themselves*; and the process of weaning themselves from their parents even in the context of the classroom may indeed be a painful one.

As the role of the teacher becomes less rigid and tradition-bound, he may well find himself participating in some sort of social therapy in which the teacher's former social distance has virtually disappeared. This is not something to be taken on, or participated in, lightly; the well-meaning teacher turned psycho-analyst or psycho-therapist can do a lot of harm. At the same time, once the teacher accepts a role which involves him more directly in the group dynamics of the class, he can no longer sit back as an observer in order to see what happens. However unattached he may be, he is nevertheless involved as an active member of the group, and his very personality and attitudes must affect his pupils. In his main writings, J. L. Moreno (19) has considered both the group situation and its conflicts, and the possibilities of therapy along certain lines. Of his work Karl Mannheim has said,

> 'Indeed Moreno has developed a technique of socio-drama and psycho-drama as a means of diagnosis and as a possible means of therapy in his whole theory of psychology. I am not suggesting that his techniques may be directly transferred for use with children in school as a part of the curriculum, but I have in mind that the principles on which his methods have been worked out could be adapted with profit to use in school – indeed it has already been used for this kind of purpose' (20).

Much of the conversation in school staff-rooms is inevitably about the pupils who present problems of one sort or another in the classroom. At one time such conversation referred largely to undirectional behaviour, that is, the attitude and behaviour of children towards the class teacher and towards authority in general. Increasingly such discussion today revolves around group behaviour in open-plan or team-teaching situations. It is more a question of social attitudes in relation to other pupils or to their participation in some project under way. It is in the dynamics of situations of this sort that the social identity of the child is revealed, and the nature of the stigmas of spoiled identity becomes more clearly delineated (21). Teachers have always been particularly prone to the use of stigma terms (such as 'moron', 'cretin', 'blithering idiot') in a colourful, metaphorical, and sometimes gently jocose sort of way. But it is clear from the work of sociologists such as Erving Goffman that, once a stigma has been established, an individual may use it for 'secondary gains' or as a perpetual crutch in order to explain why he is incapable of normal behaviour (22). Children – and adults – are very quick to latch on to real or implied stigmas and to behave in a predictable manner accordingly. A child, who has been repeatedly told that she is 'just stupid', will grasp the stigma and make it literally her own and often, in some strangely perverted way, she may feel that there is something special about her which does not demand the conformity required of other children.

The classroom, as also the school in its entirety, is very much a mirror of society with its social hierarchy and strata, its peer groups, its abnormalities, its deviances, its stigmas, and its interpersonal problems. The child, under direction and guidance from older peer groups, is learning to live with others and to establish as healthy and normal a social and personal identity as possible. In this process of socialization the teacher has an active part to play not simply at the level of providing information but also in the realm of personal interaction with the children in their learning processes. In all this the teacher obviously has a great responsibility to know what he is doing in his own particular situation; and there are no easy catch-phrases involving such words as 'love', 'happiness', freedom', 'self-realization' and so on, which solve all his own problems or those of his pupils. The educationist's panacea, like the alchemist's elixir of life, is just non-existent; what may work well for one teacher may be a dismal failure for another.

In his valuable discussion on 'Understanding Human Behaviour', A. K. C. Ottaway argues that we need to employ a sound knowledge of all our disciplines (23), and he concludes with a passsage on leadership which borders on the lyrical:

'The democratic leader, like the good teacher, does not restrict others unnecessarily, nor impose his own will in a dictatorial fashion, nor resist change. He invites co-operation and is unafraid and tolerant of disagreement, aiming to transmute differences into a new form of agreement. He leads by persuasion and reason rather than by arbitrary command. He is not a power-seeker for its own sake, and uses what authority he has for the general welfare. Above all he preserves the ideals of those he leads, and is linked with them, and with their purposes, by the bonds of an affection unmixed with fear' (24).

For the present writer, at least, this passage is virtually unrivalled in sociological literature concerning leadership and the use of power in the classroom. No doubt many would object to it on the grounds that it uses poetic and apparently prescriptive terms rather than objectively scientific and sociological ones. But one might well argue that what Ottaway has here described comes not so much within the scope of social philosophy as social observation. Where there is democratic leadership, where there is a 'good' teacher, this is what may be observed to occur. But whether this is factual observation or value-judgement, we cannot eventually, in any study of the sociology of education, avoid some selection of functions or delineation of roles in specific terms which will inevitably involve a consideration of values.

REFERENCES

1 *Vide* Maslow, A. H., 'A Theory of Human Motivation', *Psychological Review*, Vol. 50, July 1943, pp. 370–96.
2 Neill, A. S., *Summerhill* (Penguin Books, 1968), p. 53.
3 Maslow, A. H., op. cit., pp. 376–82.
4 Ibid., pp. 382–3.
5 *Vide* Lewin, K., *Field Theory in Social Science* (Harper, 1951). In his 'topological psychology', *life-space* is the term used for the totality of facts which determine the individual's behaviour at any given moment. It comprises everything in the individual and his environment which exercises any effect upon his present behaviour or the possibilities of future behaviour: that is, it includes physical, personal and social relationships. In his *Principles of Topological Psychology* (New York, 1935), Lewin refers to this space as *hodological* space.
6 Sprott, W. J. H., *Human Groups* (Penguin Books, 1958, reprinted 1964), p. 47.
7 *Vide* Moreno, J. L., *Who Shall Survive?* (Beacon Ho. Inc., 1953).
8 *Vide*, Hargreaves, D. H., *Social Relations in a Secondary School* (Routledge, 1967).
9 Mannheim, K., *Diagnosis of Our Time* (Routledge, 1943), p. 27.
10 *Vide* Jung, C. G., *Symbols of Transformation* (Routledge, 1956); *Psychology and Religion: West and East* (Routledge, 1958); and Eliade, M., *Patterns in Comparative Religion* (Sheed and Ward, 1958).
11 Jung., C. G., *Symbols of Transformation, passim*; and *Psychology and Religion: West and East,* Chapters VII, CVIII and IX, pp. 475–608.

12 *Vide* Morrish, I., *The Background of Immigrant Children* (Allen and Unwin, 1971), Chapter 2, 'Religion in the West Indies', pp. 31–51.
13 *Vide* Buber, M., *Between Mand and Man* (Collins, Fontana Library, 1961).
14 Mannheim, K., op. cit., pp. 131–43.
15 *Vide* Bibliography, *Articles*, Chapter 7.
16 Durkheim, E., *Education and Sociology* (Free Press, Glencoe, 1956), pp. 70–1.
17 Shipman, M. D., *Sociology of the School* (Harper, 1962), p. 137.
18 Neill, A. S., *Summerhill*, p. 23.
19 *Vide* Moreno, J. L., *Who Shall Survive?* (Beacon Ho. Inc., 1953), and *Psychodrama Vol. I* (Beacon Ho. Inc., 1946 and 1964).
20 Mannheim, K. and Stewart, W. A. C., *An Introduction to the Sociology of Education* (Routledge, 1962), p. 105.
21 *Vide* in particular Goffman, E., *Stigma* (Penguin Books, 1968), Chapter I, pp. 11–55.
22 Ibid., pp. 21–4.
23 Ottaway, A. K. C., *Education and Society* (Routledge, 2nd edition (revised) 1962; reprinted 1968), pp. 190–207.
24 Ibid., p. 207.

BIBLIOGRAPHY

A. *Books*

ARGYLE, M., *The Psychology of Interpersonal Behaviour* (Penguin Books, 1967).
ASCH, S. E., *Social Psychology* (Prentice-Hall, 1952).
ATKINSON, J. W., *An Introduction to Motivation* (Van Nostrand, 1964).
ATKINSON, M., *Junior School Community* (Longmans, 1962).
BALES, R. F., *Interaction Process Analysis: A Method for the Study of Small Groups* (Addison-Wesley Press, Mass., 1950).
BANDURA, A. and WALTERS, R. H., *Social Learning and Personality Development* (Holt, Rinehart and Winston, 1963).
BANKS, OLIVE, *The Sociology of Education* (Batsford, 1968; 2nd impression 1969), Chapter 9, 'The School as a Social System', pp. 180–200.
BLOS, P., *On Adolescence: A Psychoanalytic Interpretation* (Free Press, Glencoe, 1962).
BLYTH, W. A. L., *English Primary Education: A Sociological Description* (Routledge, 1965).
BUBER, M., *Between Man and Man* (Collins, Fontana Lib., 1961).
BUSH, R. N., *The Teacher-Pupil Relationship* (Prentice-Hall, 1954).
CARTWRIGHT, D. (ed.), *Group Dynamics* (Tavistock Publications, 1955).
CHARTERS, W. W. and GAGE, N. L. (eds), *Readings in the Social Psychology of Education* (Allyn and Bacon, Boston, 1963).
COHEN, A. R., *Attitude Change and Social Influence* (Basic Books Inc., 1964).
COLEMAN, J. S., *The Adolescent Society* (Free Press, Glencoe, 1962).
COLLIER, K. G., *The Social Purposes of Education* (Routledge, 1959; 2nd impression 1962).

COOK, L. A., *Community Backgrounds in Education* (McGraw-Hill, 1938).

CUTTS, N. E. and MOSELEY, N., *Teaching the Disorderly Pupil* (Longmans, 1957).

DAHLKE, O. H., *Values in Culture and Classroom* (Harper, 1958).

DEUTSCH, M. and KRAUSS, R. M., *Theories in Social Psychology* (Basic Books Inc., N.Y., 1965).

ERIKSON, E. H., *Childhood and Society* (Penguin Books, 1965).

EVANS, K. M., *Sociometry and Education* (Routledge, 1962).

FARLEY, R., *Secondary Modern Discipline* (A. and C. Black, 1960).

FESTINGER, L., *Conflict, Decision and Dissonance* (Stanford Univ. Press, 1964).

FLEMING, C. M., *The Social Psychology of Education* (Routledge, 1944).

HARGREAVES, D. H., *Social Relations in a Secondary School* (Routledge, 1967).

HEIDER, F., *The Psychology of Interpersonal Relations* (J. Wiley, 1958).

HIGHFIELD, M. E. and PINSENT, A., *A Survey of Rewards and Punishments* (Newnes, 1952).

HOMANS, G. C., *The Human Group* (Harcourt, Brace, 1950).

HORNEY, KAREN, *The Neurotic Personality of Our Time* (Routledge, 1937).

HOWLAND, C. I. and ROSENBERG, M. J. (eds), *Attitude Organization and Change* (Yale Univ. Press, 1960).

JACKSON, B., *Streaming: An Education System in Miniature* (Routledge, 1964).

JACKSON, B. and MARSDEN, D., *Education and the Working Class* (Routledge, 1962).

KLEIN, J., *The Study of Groups* (Routledge, 1956; 4th impression 1965).

KLEIN, J., *Working with Groups* (Hutchinson, 1961).

LEWIN, K., *A Dynamic Theory of Personality* (McGraw-Hill, 1935).

LEWIN, K., *Resolving Social Conflict* (Harper, 1948).

LEWIN, K., *Field Theory in Social Science* (Harper, 1951).

MANNHEIM, K., *Diagnosis of Our Time* (Routledge, 1943).

MANNHEIM, K. and STEWART, W. A. C., *An Introduction to the Sociology of Education* (Routledge, 1962), Chapters XII and XIII.

MASLOW, A. H., *Motivation and Personality* (Harper, 1953).

MAYS, J. B., *Education and the Urban Child* (Liverpool Univ. Press, 1962).

MEAD, G. H., *Mind, Self and Society* (Univ. of Chicago Press, 1934).

MILLER, N. E. and DOLLARD, J., *Social Learning and Imitation* (Yale Univ. Press, 1941).

MILLER, T. W. G., *Values in the Comprehensive School* (Oliver and Boyd, 1961).

MORENO, J. L., *Who Shall Survive?* (Beacon Ho. Inc., 1953).

MORENO, J. L., *Psychodrama, Vol. I.* (Beacon Ho. Inc., 1964).

MOWRER, O. H., *Learning Theory and Behaviour* (J. Wiley, 1960).

MUSGRAVE, P. W., *The Sociology of Education* (Methuen, 1965; reprinted 1968), Chapter 15, 'The Teacher in the Classroom', pp. 241–54.

MUSGRAVE, P. W., *The School as an Organization* (Macmillan, 1968), Chapter 7, 'The School Class', pp. 85–96.

NEWCOMB, T. M., *Personality and Social Change: Attitude Formation in a Student Community* (Dryden Press, N.Y., 1943).

OESER, O. (ed.), *Teacher, Pupil and Task* (Tavistock Publications, 1955).

OTTAWAY, A. K. C., *Education and Society* (Routledge, 2nd edition 1962; reprinted 1968), Chapter X, 'Understanding Human Behaviour', pp. 190–207.

PETERS, R. S., *The Concept of Motivation* (Routledge, 1958).

RIESSMAN, F., *The Culturally Deprived Child* (Harper, 1962).

SHIPMAN, M. D., *Sociology of the School* (Harper, 1962).

SKINNER, B. F., *Science and Human Behaviour* (Macmillan, 1953).

SPROTT, W. J. H., *Human Groups* (Penguin Books, 1958; reprinted 1964).

STRANG, R., *Group Work in Education* (Harper, 1958).

SWIFT, D. F., *The Sociology of Education* (Routledge, 1969), Chapter 5, 'The Social Functions of Education', pp. 83–111.

TAYLOR, W., *The Secondary Modern School* (Faber, 1963).

THIBAUT, J. W. and KELLEY, H. H., *The Social Psychology of Groups* (J. Wiley, 1959).

THOMAS, R. M., *Social Differences in the Classroom* (D. McKay Co. Inc., N.Y., 1965).

THOULESS, R. H., *General and Social Psychology* (Univ. Tutorial Press, 4th edition 1958; reprinted 1963).

WALLER, W., *The Sociology of Teaching* (J. Wiley, 1932; reprinted 1961).

YATES, A., *Grouping in Education* (J. Wiley, 1966).

B. Reports

D.E.S., *Children and Their Primary Schools* (Plowden Report) (H.M.S.O., 1967).

Ministry of Education, *15 to 18* (Crowther Report), (H.M.S.O., 1959).

Ministry of Education, *Half Our Future* (Newsom Report) (H.M.S.O., 1963).

C. Articles

BALES, R. F., 'A Set of Categories for the Analysis of Small Group Interaction', *American Sociological Review*, Vol. 15, April 1950, pp. 257–63.

BALES, R. F. *et al.,* 'Channels of Communication in Small Groups', *American Sociological Review*, Vol. 16, June 1951, pp. 461–8.

BRONFENBRENNER, U., 'Soviet Methods of Character Education: Some Implications for Research', *American Psychologist*, Vol. 17, No. 8, August 1962, pp. 550–64.

KOCH, S., 'The Logical Character of the Motivation Concept', *Psychological Review*, Vol. 48, January 1941, pp. 15–38.

MASLOW, A. H., 'A Theory of Human Motivation', *Psychological Review*, Vol. 50, July 1943, pp. 370–96.

PARSONS, T., 'The School Class as a Social System', in Halsey, A. H. *et al.,* *Education, Economy and Society* (Free Press, Glencoe, 1962).

RICHARDSON, J. E., 'Group Dynamics and the School', *British Journal of Education Studies*, Vol. 4, No. 2, 1956.

SKINNER, B. F., 'The Technology of Teaching', *Proceedings of the Royal Society*, B., Vol. 162, 1965, pp. 427–43.

SUGARMAN, B., 'Involvement in Youth Culture, Academic Achievement, and Conformity in School', *British Journal of Sociology*, Vol. 18, 1967.

WHITE, R. W., 'Motivation Reconsidered: The Concept of Competence', *Psychological Review*, Vol. 66, September 1959, pp. 297–333.

Chapter 14

The Sociology of the Curriculum

A. THE DEVELOPMENT OF THE CURRICULUM

In Chapter 4 we considered, in general terms, some of the effects of social change upon education; here we are concerned more particularly with the social effects upon the curriculum itself, and the relation between the curriculum and the needs and demands of society. This is not the place to describe in any great detail the history of the curriculum, but a brief outline of its development should help us to see perhaps a little more clearly how the pressures of society impinge upon the schools and what they seek to teach.

The traditional subjects curriculum has its origin in what were termed, during the Middle Ages, the 'seven liberal arts'. St Augustine of Hippo (A.D. 354–430), in his *Retractions*, wrote a short account of each of the seven *disciplinae*, or disciplines, as he termed them. It is interesting to note that throughout the Middle Ages the terms 'arts' and 'sciences' were virtually interchangeable for these disciplines. It was believed that a thorough and detailed study of such disciplines would be an excellent preparation for the deeper and arduous study involved in theology, law and medicine. Thus, the seven liberal arts were not merely a scholastic exercise but were, in fact, closely related to the roles and functions of individuals in at least three very important professions. The first three disciplines, or the *trivium*, were in essence language studies, namely, grammar, rhetoric and logic (or dialectic) and these were, in turn, preparatory to the next four disciplines, or the *quadrivium*, which comprised arithmetic, geometry, astronomy, and music.

During the sixteenth and seventeenth centuries grammar schools were endowed and instituted primarily to prepare their pupils to proceed to the university, and eventually to enter one of the four main professions, the church, law, medicine or teaching. Thus, in a very real sense, the *liberal* education which was being provided by the grammar schools and the universities was also a *vocational* one. In addition, many of the endowed grammar schools provided for a large number of their pupils, during the seventeenth century and later, a basis for apprenticeship to a trade, and so they were also offering something of a *technical* education (1). That there was no great divorce at this time between science and arts is revealed both by the actual content of the *trivium* and *quadrivium*, and by the fact that the

Arts degree of the older universities, Oxford and Cambridge, covered then (and now) the whole range of subjects from classics to the natural sciences.

Such terms as 'useful', 'practical', 'utilitarian' and 'pragmatic' are obviously relative to the social conditions of any particular age. And whilst there was a time when it could be claimed that such subjects as Latin were utilitarian the time inevitably came when some traditional subjects were being studied simply because they were traditional. Certainly by the end of the seventeenth century there was reflected in John Locke's *Some Thoughts Concerning Education* (2) something of the utility controversy between the 'ancient' and the 'modern'. There seems always to have existed some protest against what has been regarded as 'useless' study, and a demand for change. Locke certainly demanded a less traditional curriculum with a much more general mental, moral and physical education.

The story of the development of the curriculum from the eighteenth century on is one of the expansion of subject methods. The traditional curricula had, in turn, led to the establishment of traditional methods, in particular of repetition and rote learning, memorization of data and imitation. There was, naturally enough, a great emphasis upon bookwork, and upon learning from books. After the passing of the Reform Act in 1832 there was an increasing demand for the type of commercial school which made provision for subjects such as arithmetic, history, geography, English, physical science, book-keeping and land surveying. These schools provided what was considered to be a really *utilitarian* education for a business career; and the Spens Report mentions in particular that in Devonshire

> 'a scheme was started about 1855 to provide middle-class county schools for the sons of farmers and others concerned in agriculture. It was proposed to teach in these schools, in addition to the three R's, English, History and Religious Instruction, Mathematics including Arithmetic, Algebra, Euclid and Trigonometry, Book-keeping, Mensuration and the elements of Political Economy. Latin, Chemistry, Mechanics, European History and Music were suggested as extra subjects' (3).

This represented a broadening of the curriculum itself not only in terms of the number and variety of subjects, but also in terms of their social utility.

The Schools Inquiry Commission (1864–8), in its report on the choice of subjects for the curricula of various types of school, favoured general education rather than an education calculated to prepare children for specific occupations. For them the three chief subjects for all secondary schools alike were language, mathematics and physical science. They insisted that the study of language was of paramount importance since any clarity of thought was bound up with clearness of language, and one was impossible without the other. After about 1850 the curriculum of most secondary schools became increasingly determined by external examinations; this was further affected by the establishment in 1873 of the joint examining body of the Oxford and Cambridge Schools Examination Board which provided Higher and Lower Certificate Examinations for pupils of eighteen years and sixteen years respectively. These examinations were designed specifically for children in secondary schools, unlike the London Matriculation examination which was originally an examination for entrance into London University.

The *Report of the Royal Commission on Secondary Education* (1895) made it clear that the Commissioners considered that the curricula for secondary schools should contain three specific elements, namely, the literary, the scientific and the technical. With regard to the technical element the Commissioners felt that

'The sense of its practical utility in days when industrial and commercial competition grows constantly more severe is enough, perhaps more than enough, to secure its rightful place. . . . Technical instruction must be considered not as the rival of a liberal education but as a specialization of it, which, whether it comes earlier or later in the scholar's life, ought to be, as far as possible, made a means of mental stimulus and cultivation, and will be most successfully used by those whose intellectual capacity has been already disciplined by the methods of literary or scientific training' (4).

It is interesting that as far back as 1895 a Royal Commission on secondary education could speak about the curriculum in these terms. It is often thought that there is something very conservative and restrictive about officialdom in the realm of education. Nothing could be further from the truth, and whilst the officials in our educational system may not always be the innovators in curriculum reform, any examination of official reports and working papers will reveal that there has always been an acceptance of the need for reform and change which has usually been well ahead of *general* practice.

In discussing the curriculum in the newly conceived post-primary schools, the Hadow Report on *The Education of the Adolescent* urged the need for proffering 'realistic' and 'practical' studies as an instrument of general education rather than for purposes of technical or vocational education (5). In its consideration of the lines of advance of the curriculum the Report emphasized the interests and capacities of individual children as well as the local conditions, the opportunities for practical work, and the importance of education for leisure. It urged, in the strongest terms, 'the desirability of generating from the school studies interests which will continue through after-life and will enlarge the opportunities for a fuller enjoyment of leisure' (6). Thus, almost half a century ago the Hadow Report was very much concerned that the curriculum should provide for the child something more than academic competence or the ability to pass examinations. There is nothing new in the cry of 'education for leisure'; it is merely that its urgency becomes greater as leisure time itself becomes greater, and for many individuals in society their real time for living since their daily work provides for them neither satisfaction nor self-fulfilment.

In its consideration of the curriculum of the primary school the Hadow Report of 1931 recognized the uselessness as well as the danger of trying to inculcate what Professor A. N. Whitehead referred to as 'inert ideas'. Such ideas were those which 'at the time when they are imparted have no bearing upon a child's natural activities of body or mind and do nothing to illuminate or guide his experience' (7). The theme of the Hadow Primary Report is, not surprisingly, similar to that of the Secondary Report published five years earlier. It was vitally concerned with the growing experience of the pupil, and with the enrichment and enlargement of their 'instinctive hold on the conditions of life'. The Consultative Committee saw the problem of the curriculum as one to be visualized in terms of 'activity and experience rather than of knowledge to be acquired and facts to be stored' (8). The emphasis was upon 'the highest examples of excellence in life and conduct' rather than upon the outstanding genius in academic affairs.

The committee also saw the implications of this view of the curriculum in terms of methodology. They briefly discussed the project method and the possibilities of using this in teaching within the more traditional subject divisions. They also saw the method as one in which some centre of interest might be selected, and the studies of the children might for a while converge upon it or radiate from it. The great importance of these methods as seen by the committee consisted in that they provided a considerable variety of openings for independent inquiries by pupils who might bring special gifts to any problem, but who, in any case, would develop forms of co-operation with their fellows which would have social significance (9). The Report, however, was cautious with regard to the use of these methods: they could be abused and forced beyond their proper limits; and whilst it was important to integrate subjects in a natural way, it was equally important at some point to disentangle them.

The Spens Report of 1938 largely reaffirmed the Hadow Committee's convictions, and reiterated the importance of 'activity and experience' (10). It felt that one of the unfortunate effects of the current system of public examinations was that they emphasized that aspect of school studies which was least important. Since the activities of any community were both conservative and creative, both elements should have a place in the curriculum. Those activities which were richest in the creative element had, in fact, the strongest claim for a place in the curriculum since they sprang from man's deepest needs and represented his highest achievement (11). Careful planning of syllabuses would provide at suitable times that education for citizenship which was also of high priority in the school curriculum. The Spens Report completely disavowed any belief that culture and practical utility were in any way mutually exclusive. Education should train for the right use of leisure; and the committee was quite unprepared to accept that 'any of the activities of the secondary school, assuming them to be pursued in the spirit we have indicated, are not "useful" in the sense that they tend to raise the level and quality of life in all its phases and moments' (12). And the quality of many people's lives reaches its highest point most often in the moments when they are thrown back upon their own developed abilities and resources. The Spens committee agreed that the studies of the secondary school should be brought into closer contact with the practical affairs of life, and should also relate to man's needs during his non-working hours.

The Norwood Report, which was published in 1943 (13), had considerable sympathy with some of the current notions about education as a preparation for life and a livelihood, and education for the right use of leisure, but it had certain reservations concerning the way in which such preparation should be put into practice. The Report envisaged the possibility of an ever-extending curriculum to meet the many claims for which the school week would be certainly too short. In general it did not believe that life in its many phases could be anticipated, to the extent which had often been suggested, by school children 'through specific training to meet contingencies and situations' (14). The pupil had to *grow* into an enlarged experience, and any premature attempt at dealing with aspects of life beyond his experience could lead only to a self-defeating unreality. The school could make its best contribution to an understanding of life's problems if it were

(i) to foster the qualities of a sympathetic and understanding mind and a sense of responsibility;
(ii) to promote an attitude of free inquiry and to develop the power of intellectual alertness as well as independent judgement;
(iii) to give some knowledge and understanding of the facts and events which have determined the world in which its pupils will live; and
(iv) to make pupils, in response to their naturally widening interests, aware of the problems which will later on engage their attention (15).

The first three of these contributions could, the Report felt, be most effectively achieved through the ordinary life and work of the school, consciously directed with the end in view; but the fourth contribution should be the subject of a more direct attack in the classes containing older pupils. Here there should be a deliberate attempt to education for citizenship.

The Newsom Report, published in 1963, is very much a document on the content and nature of the curriculum as well as methods to be employed in giving life to some of the dry bones of the past (16). The current explosion of knowledge emphasizes increasingly the need for new curricula and new approaches. The aims of such new curricula would be:

(i) to develop basic skills of communication in speech, writing, reading with understanding, and in number and measurement;

(ii) to develop capacities for thought, judgement, discrimination, enjoyment and curiosity;

(iii) to elicit a code of moral and social behaviour which would be self-imposed;

(iv) to inculcate an understanding of the physical world and of the human society;

(v) to develop a sense of responsibility for their own work and towards other pupils;

(vi) to incorporate 'extra-curricular' activities into the total school programme;

(vii) to 'go out into the world' in order to explore the possibilities of society in relation to work, places of cultural interest, community service, recreation, and the continuation of their education (17).

In its chapter on 'The Aims of Primary Education' the Plowden Report began with what it considered to be an obvious purpose of the primary school, namely, 'to fit children for the society into which they will grow up' (18). For this it would be necessary to train children to be adaptable and sufficiently flexible to adjust to an ever-changing environment. It was, indeed, difficult to predict precisely what sort of society these children would grow up into; but it could safely be said that whatever else it might be like it would be a rapidly changing and developing one. The Report considered that the all-round development of the individual child was of vital importance, and it laid emphasis upon the acquisition of the basic skills considered necessary in contemporary society. The religious and moral development of the child was considered important, although it was clear that there were difficulties in relation to religious education which were reflected in the Notes of Reservation appended to Part Nine, 'Conclusions and Recommendations' (19).

Important in the priorities of the aims of primary education was the co-operation of school and home, and with this aim was 'that of making good to children, as far as possible, the deficiencies of their backgrounds' (20). The Report went on to emphasize the community aspects of the school, with its own intrinsic values: 'A school is not merely a teaching shop, it must transmit values and attitudes. It is a community in which children learn to live first and foremost as children and not as future adults' (21). It was partly the purpose of the school to attempt to equalize opportunities and to make what compensation it could for any handicaps the children might have. Children must discover things for themselves by means of first-hand experience and creative work. In seeking to attain these aims the curriculum must itself be flexible and should make a maximum use of the environment. The Report discussed the theme of 'discovery', which it considered to be both loosely interpreted and misunderstood. Heuristic methods could obviously lead to the discovery of trivial ideas, and could also be inefficient, but most methods could be abused and heurism was no exception to this (22). In the main the Report supported projects, topics, centres of interest, learning by acquaintance, and an integrated curriculum.

In 1967 the Schools Council produced a very significant Working Paper entitled *Society and the Young School Leaver* (23). This Working Paper proposed the development of certain areas of inquiry in interdisciplinary work in the realm of the humanities. The objectives of such areas of inquiry were quite specifically stated; they were:

(i) to encourage tolerance, the ability to think humbly, and the development of value-judgements based on something other than prejudice;

(ii) to assist the future members of society to achieve personal maturity;

(iii) to assist the pupil to fulfil his personal needs within the school community;

(iv) to help him to realize social needs, and to understand his own society;

(v) to extend the pupil's intellect in order to comprehend the complexity and totality of man's environment and civilization;

(vi) to inculcate values, attitudes and abilities to learn rather than to provide a body of knowledge (24).

B. SOME SOCIAL IMPLICATIONS

As society has expanded its knowledge, as well as its control, of its environment so it has become necessary for the school to mediate knowledge to children over a wider front, if not in greater depth. Some of the initial objections to this extension, as we have seen, were based on the fear that the school time-table would be overloaded or that the more basic and traditional 'subjects' would be crowded out. Schools have dealt with these objections in a variety of ways, whilst experimenting at the same time with new curricula. Some schools have extended their 'week' from five days to anything from six to fourteen days. In this way some of the new subjects of study may appear on the time-table once in six days, or perhaps once in a fortnight. Other schools have introduced into the time-table integrated days in which much of the new material is dealt with in some form of interdisciplinary inquiry.

But the question 'what *should* be taught?' has both sociological and philosophical implications. Changes in society and social needs imply changes in education and in school curricula for the maintenance and development of that society. We are not here concerned with any ideally conceived society, but rather with society as it is likely to be. In Durkheimian terms, 'The man whom education should realize in us is not the man such as nature has made him, but as the society wishes him to be; and it wishes him such as its internal economy calls for' (25). The pressures, demands and changes (political, social and economic) of society are reflected, almost willy-nilly, in the school curricula. The pressures are to make what is taught more 'relevant', 'useful' and 'outgoing', whilst philosophical arguments are adduced to support the view that there is no real antithesis between technical and liberal, and that the dualism of culture and utility is equally fallacious.

Something of the pressures of society is reflected in the examination system which was devised largely as a selective procedure and as a mode of entry into the universities and the professions. Because society demands certain levels of attainment for specific occupations, as well as a ready means of selection, there is certainly no likelihood of eradicating the examination system. The general acceptance of this fact is reflected in the increase in the number and variety of examinations. Indeed, the solution of the problem appears to have resulted in a movement in the opposite direction: there must now be qualifications for all, so that pupils who cannot make the G.C.E. 'A' or 'O' level grades may, nevertheless, be able to manage one of the modes of C.S.E. or some other certificate examination. In a very competitive society an increasing number of people are seeking ever higher levels of education, and more and more qualifications. Thus, although school curricula may be changing and developing new patterns, the social requirements in the realm of examinations have certainly not eased. And the social demands for increased higher education are being met by extensions of the universities, the new polytechnics, the colleges of technology, and other institutes of further and higher education including the Open University.

Examinations, and further education leading on to examinations, are clearly concerned with the individual's life-career, profession or vocation. But curricular demands today are concerned with more than the child's future career in society; they are, as the various Reports have underlined, involved with his patterns of behaviour, his beliefs, his attitudes, and his life-style. Education, from this point of view, is concerned with the child's language patterns and linguistic competence, his intellectual alertness, his capacity for making value-judgements, his creativity and his general and leisure interests.

As far as his language problems are concerned the pupil will find increasingly that the school curriculum will seek to compensate for his linguistic deficiencies and deprivations. In the realm of creativity, schools are today involved in eliciting the child's potential in and through a wide variety of musical, artistic and literary media. The school may not specifically say, in so many words, that it is educating for leisure but, in developing the interests of children in a way that might formerly have been known as 'extra-curricular activities', it is clear that the school has in mind the perpetuation of those interests in skills outside the school buildings and beyond the school life of the child.

In general, it is one of the aims of the curricula of schools today to initiate the child both into society itself and into new realms and possibilities of knowledge. Education is certainly for citizenship; it is also for family life, for parenthood, for work, for understanding life's problems. Perhaps one of the mistakes we make in what we are pleased to call 'sex education' is that we isolate one human function as if it were unrelated to social living and total personal integration. To educate for living in society, in a family, in marriage, in citizenship, will inevitably involve an understanding of a great variety of relationships which will demand more than the knowledge of a few biological or economic facts. Education for social living demands a realization of social needs, a sense of personal and social responsibility, the qualities of a sympathetic and understanding mind, and the development of a self-imposed code of moral and social behaviour.

Whatever form the curriculum may eventually take in any particular school, there would appear to be certain social aims which need to be fulfilled within that curriculum. It will be important to maximize the individual's powers of communication; his abilities and skills for pursuing the social and economic life of our society must be elicited and expanded; his critical powers must be so organized and developed that he will find himself able to make personal judgements and to assess a wide variety of individual and social situations; he must be trained to take on responsibility relative to his abilities, his intelligence and his chosen role in life as well as his role as a citizen, or husband, or father; he must learn to accept social authority as well as, at times, to question it; he must be trained to co-operate with others and to share the load of work when placed within a group situation; he must be encouraged to develop values which belong in a very real sense to himself because he has analysed, questioned and finally absorbed them. These values may be of a religious, moral or aesthetic nature, but the individual pupil will understand before he leaves school that he is in the position of someone growing and evolving within the *milieu* of a total social culture as well as within his own peer-group culture. He must discover, on the way, that he has not finally concluded his education at fifteen or sixteen, but rather he has merely begun to learn how to learn, that he has been educated for a life-time of education, for growth, for living.

The social relevance of what is being taught is obviously important, and it is essential in the discussion and framing of any curriculum to consider this relevance. There is always a tendency to lag behind the requirements of society, as D. K. Wheeler remarks: 'Educational services may be catering for needs that no longer exist, or there may be new needs which are not being met. In either case, the old objectives are no longer valid' (26). We live in an age of technology, scientific invention, space travel, cybernetics and computerization; children are aware of these developments in a very real way through the mass media of Press, radio and television; it should, therefore, be the most natural thing in the world to encounter these topics in the commerce of the classroom. With the raising of the school-leaving to sixteen the importance of the last two years for the initiation of children into the thought-forms and life-styles of society becomes paramount.

In the development of the curriculum there must be some balance between the needs of the individual and those of society. There is nothing inevitable about social equilibrium: it is a question of planning and design; and as soon as one engages upon a programme of planning one is involved to some extent in the manipulation of the social equilibrium – whether it be a decision to try and adjust the supply of scientists and mathematicians to meet the demand, or whether it be some doctrinaire attempt to equalize opportunities and forms of education for all.

There are two passages from very different sources, which between them sum up something of the dilemma of curriculum building for society and for the individual. The Hadow Report of 1926 argued:

'If, on the one hand, the education of older pupils be kept too general in the supposed interests of individual development, the pupil is apt to find himself ill-equipped on leaving school to cope with the demands of modern life. If, on the other hand, undue stress be laid in the school course on the needs of later life, and the training of the pupil be made too specific, the individual man or woman may be sacrificed to the workman or citizen. A well-balanced educational system must combine these ideals in the single conception of social individuality' (27).

In his *Education and the Social Order* Bertrand Russell was equally sensitive to the dichotomy between the educational needs of the individual and those of society, although his resolution of the problem was stated in somewhat different terms. He said:

'Considered *sub specie aeternitatis* the education of the individual is to my mind a finer thing than the education of the citizen, but considered politically, in relation to the needs of the time, the education of the citizen must, I fear, take the first place' (28).

But Russell makes the mistake of imagining, however briefly, that an 'individual' can ever be anything other than a 'citizen'. For Aristotle man was always the social or political animal; his very individuality could be exposed only in and through the social *milieu*. There is no such thing as the education of the individual in complete isolation – even Rousseau's Émile was finally destined to become a citizen. Whether *sub specie aeternitatis*, or in relative terms of here and now, man exists only in relation with others, or with the Other. Anthony Storr has put the point both succinctly and well when he says that 'to be completely related to another person is to be most oneself, to affirm one's personality in its totality. And so we have the paradox that man is at his most individual when most in contact with his fellows, and is least of all a separate individual when detached from them' (29). Whatever catch-phrases may be used about the nature of the curriculum, if ultimately the latter does not achieve this double purpose of social identity and the integrity of the individual personality, it will have failed.

REFERENCES

1 *Vide* Board of Education, *Secondary Education* (Spens Report) (H.M.S.O., 1938), pp. 7–8.
2 Locke, J., *Some Thoughts Concerning Education* (1693), in Adamson, J. W. (ed.), *The Educational Writings of John Locke* (Longmans, 1922).
3 Spens Report, op. cit., pp. 26–7.
4 *Report of the Royal Commission on Secondary Education* (1895), pp. 284–5.
5 Board of Education, *The Education of the Adolescent* (Hadow Report) (H.M.S.O., 1926; reprinted 1948), p. 85.
6 Ibid., p. 110.
7 Board of Education, *The Primary School* (Hadow Report) (H.M.S.O., 1931; reprinted 1946), p. 92.
8 Ibid., p. 93.
9 Ibid., pp. 102–3.
10 Op. cit., p. 152.
11 Ibid., p. 155.
12 Ibid., p. 161.
13 Board of Education, *Curriculum and Examinations in Secondary Schools* (Norwood Report) (H.M.S.O., 1943; reprinted 1944).
14 Ibid., p. 56.
15 *Vide* ibid., p. 58.
16 Ministry of Education, *Half Our Future* (Newsom Report) (H.M.S.O., 1963), especially Chapters 4, 14, and 23.

17 Ibid., paras 76–87, 208–39.
18 D.E.S., *Children and their Primary Schools* (Plowden Report) (H.M.S.O., 1967), para. 494.
19 Ibid., paras 489–93.
20 Ibid., para. 500.
21 Ibid., para. 505.
22 Ibid., paras 549–50. For an interesting discussion of heurism *vide* Bantock, G. H., 'Discovery Methods' in *Crisis in Education: Black Paper Two* (The Critical Quarterly Society, 1969), pp. 110–18.
23 The Schools Council, *Society and the Young School Leaver: Humanities Programme* (Working Paper No. 11) (H.M.S.O., 1967).
24 Ibid., p. 39.
25 Durkheim, E., *Education and Sociology* (Free Press, Glencoe, 1956), p. 122.
26 Wheeler, D. K., *Curriculum Process* (Univ. of London Press, 1967), p. 88.
27 Board of Education, *The Education of the Adolescent* (Hadow Report), p. 101.
28 Russell, B., *Education and the Social Order* (Allen and Unwin, 1932; 6th Impression 1961), pp. 27–8.
29 Storr, A., *The Integrity of the Personality* (Penguin Books, 1963; reprinted 1964), p. 36.

BIBLIOGRAPHY

A. *Books*

CARTER, M. P., *Home School and Work* (Pergamon Press, 1962).
CARTER, M. P., *Education, Employment and Leisure* (Pergamon Press, 1963).
DEMPSTER, J. J. B., *Education in the Secondary Modern School* (Pilot Press, 1947).
DEMPSTER, J. J. B., *Purpose in the Secondary Modern School* (Methuen, 1956).
DEWEY, J., *The School and Society* (Univ. of Chicago Press, 1900).
DEWEY, J., *The School and the Child* (Blackie and Son, 1906).
ELVIN, H. L., *Education and Contemporary Society* (Watts, 1965).
GILLETT, A. N. and SADLER, J. E., *Training for Teaching* (Allen and Unwin, 1961; 2nd impression 1962), Part V, 'The Curriculum', pp. 201–37.
GLOVER, A. H., *New Teaching for a New Age* (Nelson, 1946).
MACLURE, J. S., *Educational Documents – England and Wales: 1816–1967* (Methuen, 1968).
MUSGRAVE, P. W., *The School as an Organization* (Macmillan, 1968).
NEILL, A. S., *Summerhill* (Penguin Books, 1968).
NISBET, S., *Purpose in the Curriculum* (Univ. of London Press, 1957).
OLSON, W. C., *Psychological Foundations of the Curriculum* (Publication No. 26) (UNESCO, Paris, 1957).
OTTAWAY, A. K. C., *Education and Society* (Routledge, 2nd edition (revised), 1962; reprinted 1968).
PRITZKAN, P., *Dynamics of Curriculum Improvement* (Prentice Hall, 1959).

ROWE, A. W., *Education of the Average Child* (Harrap, 1959).
SHARP, G., *Curriculum Development as Re-education of the Teacher* (Columbia Univ. Press, 1951).
SHIPMAN, M. D., *The Sociology of the School* (Longmans, 1968), pp. 16–19.
TAYLOR, L. C., *Resources for Learning* (Penguin Books, 1971).
WALLER, W., *The Sociology of Teaching* (J. Wiley, 1932; reprinted 1961).
WHEELER, D. K., *Curriculum Process* (Univ. of London Press, 1967).
WILSON, J. et al., *Introduction to Moral Education* (Penguin Books, 1967).
YOUNG, M., *Innovation and Research in Education* (Routledge, 1965).

B. *Reports*

Board of Education, *The Education of the Adolescent* (Hadow Report) (H.M.S.O., 1926; reprinted 1948), paras 93, 106–16.
Board of Education, *The Primary School* (Hadow Report) (H.M.S.O., 1931; reprinted 1946), paras 73–86.
Board of Education, *Secondary Education* (Spens Report) (H.M.S.O., 1938), pp. 146–89.
Board of Education, *Curriculum and Examinations in Secondary Schools* (Norwood Report) (H.M.S.O., 1943), pp. 55–79.
D.E.S., *Primary Education – Suggestions* (H.M.S.O., 4th impression 1965).
D.E.S., *Children and their Primary Schools* (Plowden Report) (H.M.S.O., 1967), paras 508–57.
Ministry of Education, *Half Our Future* (Newsom Report) (H.M.S.O., 1963), paras 349–517.
N.U.T. Report, *Curriculum of the Junior School* (Schoolmaster Publications, 1958).

SCHOOLS COUNCIL PUBLICATIONS

A. *Working Papers*

No. 10 *Curriculum Development: Teachers' Groups and Centres* (H.M.S.O., 1967).
No. 11 *Society and the Young School Leaver: Humanities Programme* (H.M.S.O., 1967).
No. 12 *The Educational Implications of Social and Economic Change* (H.M.S.O., 1967).
No. 17 *Community Service and the Curriculum* (H.M.S.O., 1968).
No. 21 *The 1966 C.S.E. Monitoring Experiment* (H.M.S.O., 1969).
No. 22 *The Middle Years of Schooling from 8 to 13* (H.M.S.O., 1969).

B. *Other Schools Council Publications*

The New Curriculum (H.M.S.O., 1967).
Humanities for the Young School Leaver: An Approach Through English (H.M.S.O., 1968).

Chapter 15

School, Pupil and Social Pathology

A. DEVIANT AND DELINQUENT BEHAVIOUR

As soon as we begin to use words such as 'deviant', 'delinquent', 'delin-quescent' (1), or 'criminal', we encounter not only differences of definition but also a variation of degree within those differences. The term 'deviancy', for example, implies a norm from which individuals depart or deviate. Alex Inkeles, however, finds the designation 'deviant' very ambiguous in relation to certain forms of behaviour, and he considers that it poses the problem whether, whilst exceeding the speed limit on the highway may be against the law, it is still deviance if almost everyone is guilty of it (2). Thus, deviancy is relative not merely to established social laws but also to general practice and consensus. But one must distinguish here between a norm which is established by statistical averages and one which is estab-lished by social concepts of 'right' or 'moral' behaviour. The fact that most, if not all, people tell lies on occasion does not make it any less 'deviant' behaviour. And if all people were to steal in a society one might say that it was 'normal' behaviour in that society, but it would still be deviant in terms of the security and stability of the community.

There are norms of behaviour to which we expect individuals to conform in the larger society, and equally there are established norms in the society of the school. Sometimes a child who is perfectly law-abiding in society generally and in the home, may be deviant in his behaviour in the institu-tion of the school; and some parents will undoubtedly be puzzled by the reports concerning their children's activities in the classroom. On the other hand, a youth who is well-behaved in the school may be deviant or delinquent in some area of his behaviour in society. The concept of 'devi-ancy' is, therefore, a relative and contextual one, and it is perhaps easier, as well as more accurate, to speak of deviant forms of behaviour than to stigmatize individuals as deviant.

There is a tendency to restrict the term 'criminal' to adults and the term 'delinquent' to juveniles. The fact that 'juvenile' and 'delinquency' are so frequently used in juxtaposition, whereas 'adult' and 'delinquency' hardly ever appear together, emphasizes that there is a rather different attitude towards juvenile delinquency and adult criminality.

In his paper on 'Delinquency as the Failure of Personal and Social Controls', A. J. Reiss defines delinquency as 'the behaviour consequent to

the failure of personal and social controls to produce behaviour in conformity with the norms of the social system to which legal penalties are
attached' (3). The rules and norms of society have not been adequately
internalized by the delinquent individuals who, in consequence, find themselves in conflict with the forms and sanctions of social control. Reiss goes
on to argue that juvenile delinquency is largely the result of the failure of
primary groups to offer the child 'appropriate non-delinquent social
roles', or to provide that form of social control which will ensure acceptance of those social roles which are proffered in accordance with his
needs (4).

In this present chapter we shall use the term 'deviancy' to imply actions
and forms of behaviour, particularly that of a variety of sub-cultures,
which have not yet come within the orbit of *legal* social sanctions, but
which, nevertheless, are opposed to generally accepted norms. It is
behaviour which is on the road, very often, to becoming more explicitly
delinquent; and when this behaviour is applicable to a group of individuals
forming a sub-culture Hargreaves' term 'delinquescent' seems to be a
useful one. There are delinquescent sub-cultures which threaten the
stability of any minor social group or any major society (5). The motivation behind such behaviour is not always clear, either to those who are
performing it or to those who are seeking to analyse it. It is true, as
Robert Burns put it, that

> 'What's done ye partly may compute,
> But know not what's resisted.'

And it is true both that we do not fully know what is resisted in each
individual mind, and also that we cannot even properly compute what is
in fact being done.

A business director, for example, may for a number of years mulct his
company of fairly substantial sums of money on what is sometimes face-
tiously referred to as an 'expense account' – and, to be perfectly fair, the
firm may not object; indeed, it may be regarded as quite legitimate business. Another person may regularly take home small quantities of materials
from his workshop or office, and regard this simply as the 'perks' of his
trade. His employers might agree, or on the other hand – if they knew
about it – they might prosecute him. In December 1965 an old-age
pensioner, aged sixty-eight, picked up a roll of tape worth 1s 9d, and
walked out of a store without paying for it. She was arrested and charged
with petty larceny, and after three appearances before the magistrates,
and a wait of over forty days, she was 'given the benefit of the doubt'.
Every year colleges and universities lose hundreds of books from their
libraries which are 'borrowed', to use a euphemism, but never returned.
Thus even what society, by its very sanctions and legal terms of reference,

calls delinquent or criminal behaviour is (like deviant behaviour) a contextual matter. It all depends very much upon who does it, where it is done, and who discovers it as to whether it is termed petty larceny, fraud, 'perks', borrowing or expenses.

The motivation behind these various activities ranges from, perhaps, laziness, carelessness or forgetfulness, to sheer acquisitiveness or greed. Forgetfulness, kleptomania or a temporary mental aberration may be punished as larceny, whilst greed might conceivably be regarded as sound business economics. The computation of 'what is done' requires a great deal of understanding and knowledge of the individual, youth or adult, with some reference to the possible motivation behind the act as well as the controls, both social and individual, which are operating for each person involved. T. S. Eliot has said that

> 'Between the conception
> And the creation,
> Between the emotion
> And the response,
> Falls the shadow.'

It is this 'shadow' element, a sort of surd or irrational factor in human activity, which may ultimately determine whether our actions will be acceptable or not, whether they will be normal, deviant or delinquent. And if we 'chase a crooked shadow' we are liable to become 'crooked' or delinquent.

In general, then, deviant behaviour is any behaviour which deviates from the accepted norms of our society, or from the norms of some sub-group or micro-society within the larger society. But it is suggested here that deviant behaviour is not necessarily delinquent or criminal behaviour, although it may, of course, be the first step to some antisocial behaviour which may come within the sanction of the law and therefore irrevocably delinquent. Delinquent behaviour is some form of activity which has so far departed from the norms of our society that it is felt, in consequence, that some action must be taken of a disciplinary nature, and some sanction applied. A deviant act may be simply a question of 'bad manners', but a delinquent act interferes directly with the general welfare, security and survival of society. The distinction is perhaps best summed up by R. A. Cloward and L. E. Ohlin when they state that delinquent acts are those which are

> 'distinguished from this larger class of deviant acts by the fact that officials engaged in the administration of criminal justice select them, from among many deviant acts, as forms of behaviour proscribed by the approved norms of the society. These acts acquire their deviant

character by being violations of social rules; they acquire their specifically delinquent character by being typically treated as violations of
official norms by representatives of the official system' (6).

B. ANOMIE

Man, as a rational being, is always looking for the causes of things. In the
realm of wrong-doing, man has blamed everyone and everything for his
evil, from God to the Devil, either in singular or conjoint form, from
his stars to his genes, from his home and parents to his teachers and his
schools, and from Original Sin to society. It is virtually a psychopathic
reaction of us all to attempt to transfer our sense of guilt to someone,
something or some institution outside ourselves and our control. The
admission of *mea culpa* is one we would avoid at all costs; and it is perhaps
a sign of unusual maturity when someone volunteers the statement, 'Yes,
I did it; it was entirely my fault'. In her classic work, *Social Science and
Social Pathology*, Barbara Wootton discusses twelve criminological hypo-
theses (7) in the course of which she carefully reviews and examines
twenty-one studies of delinquency. She concludes that, although the results
of her review have been 'strikingly negative', the whole exercise has not
been altogether unprofitable:

> 'For on the one hand, it induces a wholesome scepticism; and on the
> other hand it shows up many of the major technical weaknesses in the
> work so far undertaken in this field; and since such work is still hardly
> out of the pioneering stage, concentrated attention on technical improve-
> ment can be a most constructive operation' (8).

This book was first published in 1959, but it remains a *locus classicus* on
methodology in this particular field, although no doubt most would argue
that there has been some technical improvement in the investigations into
criminal causation.

Barbara Wootton (9) goes on to state that, on the whole, offenders
appear to come from the relatively larger families, and that not infrequently
other members of the delinquents' families have also been in trouble with
the law. There is evidence that the offenders are unlikely to be regular
churchgoers, but there seems to be no solid evidence to support the view
that club membership discourages delinquency. The employment record
of delinquents indicates that those who have been employed at all are
likely to be 'poor' rather than 'good' workers. The majority of (appre-
hended) offenders come from the lower classes, and although the evidence
suggesting that they are from the exceptionally poor is apparently not
convincing, the urgent desire for social position or status would seem to
be a causative factor. Barbara Wootton also holds that there is no clear

indication that the juveniles' delinquency is associated with the employment of their mothers outside the home. During their schooldays many of
the delinquents were likely to have been truants, and it is also probable
that 'an unusually large proportion of them' have come from broken
homes of one sort or another. Generally speaking, their health is no
worse than that of non-delinquents, whilst their educational attainment at
school will probably be low; although, as Barbara Wootton puts it,
'many of them have earned poor reputations at school, though these may
well be prejudiced by their teachers' knowledge of their delinquencies'
(10).

The factors which contribute towards delinquency are, therefore, complex rather than simple; and if the fault for our offences does not lie
entirely within our genes, or our environment, there is a combination of
factors, or predisposing causes, which produces the right occasion and
opportunity for delinquency or crime. This is where the more general
concept of *anomie* comes in, which has already been referred to in Chapter
3. In a 'normal', or relatively stable and eunomic society, there is some
regulation of men's goals and aspirations, and a brake is placed upon those
egoistic trends which may lead to disunity, disaggregation and dysnomia
within the society. The very structure of society, with its varying class
levels, provides a pattern for work, behaviour and life-style. People within
such a structured society live their lives at these various levels according
to their social class, their environment, their work and their general
upbringing.

When, however, these social structures and levels begin to be ironed out,
the social norms which formerly controlled and delimited men's actions
begin to become blurred and to fade. In the name of 'equality' social
hopes and aspirations are frequently placed before less intelligent youths
of the lower classes which are not, in many instances, within their capabilities – nor indeed within their wildest dreams. Men may, as Durkheim
suggests, seek the fulfilment of their desires for power, or wealth, or
prestige, but there is an element of insatiability about it all. If there is no
external force to regulate man's aspirations, he will seek to fulfil them by
any means whatever. Since 'our capacity for feeling is in itself an insatiable
and bottomless abyss', unless this capacity is restrained we become a prey
to pathological morbidity and torment (11). This leads to an attempt at
fulfilment by illegal or delinquent means – an attitude and state of *anomie*
which is further fostered by rapid change and development within society
at commercial, industrial, scientific and technological levels. Social change
is reflected in both group and individual instability.

Our society appears to promise something for everyone. Even if we
cannot very happily defend the proposition that 'we are all equal', there
is still held out the promise of 'equality of opportunity', which is almost

as hollow-sounding as the former statement of total equality. The Incorporated Association of Head Masters seems to have summed up the situation very well when they suggested that the equality of opportunity granted by our educational system to every child was in order 'to display (their) inequality of capacity' (12). Even if we do not put children through organized and structured processes of selection, they will inevitably select themselves. But a form of self-selection which leaves a large group at the bottom is not necessarily more acceptable to the unfortunates who find themselves there than some form of external selection. If we suggest that success-goals are open to all, and that social status is of no consequence, there will invariably be those who immediately regard social advancement as their natural right; and they are not a little aggrieved when they discover that the old social blockages have now been replaced by those of 'merit'. The old elite, with the public-school tie, may have gone, but it is being firmly replaced by a new elite whose prescription is merit – it is the 'rise of the meritocracy' (13).

This sense of frustration, which results from the closing of what appeared to be open doors for all, leads to a general feeling-tone and attitude of rebellion and *anomie*; this, in turn, results in the development of sub-cultures and a retreat from the larger society. Some of these sub-cultures are relatively harmless, some are clearly and deliberately deviant and others are purposely delinquent. Their total sense of failure in a society that appears to offer so much, particularly through education, is compensated for by a sense of success in deviant behaviour. A. K. Cohen, for example, argues that within the delinquent sub-culture, behaviour is regarded as meritorious and worthy of reward because it represents a direct attack upon the respectable status system; the sub-culture is itself a logical response to the built-in frustration of the middle-class way of life (14). W. B. Miller has attempted to analyse the 'focal concerns' of the lower class adolescent street corner groups, and he argues that the dominant component of the motivation of delinquent behaviour among these groups involves a positive attempt to achieve 'status, conditions, or qualities valued within the actor's most significant cultural milieu' (15).

There is a hardening, as it were, of these focal concerns which results ultimately in the development of a sub-cultural group and identity which appears to be in opposition to the main culture. Miller's 'value conflict' or 'culture conflict' thesis has been criticized by R. A. Cloward and L. E. Ohlin (16). We cannot reproduce their arguments here, but their conclusion is that

'Nothing in Miller's account of lower-class life helps to explain the differentiation of delinquent sub-cultures. Even if his definition of lower-class values were accepted, it is not at all clear why this conflict would result alternatively in criminal conflict, or retreatist adaptations' (17).

In his study of adolescent boys in East London (18), Peter Willmott discusses the suggestion that their sense of failure and frustration was, in fact, the mainspring of delinquency, in particular of acts of theft, violence and hooliganism. These acts appear to be motivated by 'a desire to strike at society rather than acquire wealth', but Willmott considers that this applies only to some boys, not to most. Whilst many boys are deviant or delinquent in the sense that sometimes they break the law through such acts as petty theft, most boys do not feel that they are frustrated or rejected. Willmott, therefore, turns to a psychological explanation of what he views as the 'relatively trivial delinquency of the majority'. He regards such delinquency as part of the process of working out the adolescent resentments and tensions against their parents, teachers and adults in society. Their delinquency is further encouraged and fostered by the peer group, in the bosom of which they find refuge from the malign influences of social disapproval. Their weaning from delinquency occurs when they eventually wean themselves from the peer group and set up home with the woman of their choice (19).

If Willmott is right, then juvenile delinquency, and its expression in and through peer group sub-cultures, is a passing phase for a fairly large number of adolescents who seek release from the stresses which result from interpersonal relationships with the older generation.

C. DELINQUENCY AND CRIME TODAY

The crime for which the highest percentage of persons are found guilty today is larceny. This is an acquisitive, affluent society in which man is encouraged perpetually to acquire, to buy, to have. Those who lack the ability, or the enthusiasm, to work honestly to acquire, are led to a different form of acquisition – to theft, to embezzlement and to borderline activity.

The official figures for 1968 show that offences against property make up about 90 per cent of the indictable crimes. The remainder, that is crimes against the person, include not only murder and manslaughter but also such offences as bigamy and concealment of birth. Broadly, therefore, we can say that most crime today consists of offences against property.

As the following table shows, nearly half of the total of indictable offences in 1968 were committed by children and youths under the age of twenty-one, and increasingly delinquency appears to be coming within the school age limits (20).

PERSONS FOUND GUILTY OF INDICTABLE OFFENCES
1968

	Male	Female	Total	Percentage
Under 14	22,031	2,504	24,535	9·5
14 and under 17	35,136	4,700	39,836	15·5
17 and under 21	51,106	5,484	56,590	22·0
21 and over	114,334	22,032	136,366	53·0
	222,607	34,720	257,327	100·0

It is sometimes suggested that raising the school-leaving age would reduce the amount of juvenile crime, but this seems to be highly questionable. Already a high percentage of the crimes committed are offences by children and youths still attending schools. Much of their delinquency is motivated by frustration, stress, *anomie* and boredom. There is no certain guarantee that another year in school for fifteen-year-olds will relieve their boredom and frustration. A Crime Liaison Officer of a large London borough recently claimed that, in his division at least, there appeared to be more juvenile crime committed during term time than during school holidays; and that a fair proportion of the crime committed occurred during school time not only by truants but also by pupils who had actually been registered as present at their schools when they committed their crimes – mostly petty larceny and housebreaking. The Chief Liaison Officer was inclined to blame the size of the large comprehensive schools for much of this, since (in his view) there was far less close supervision of children after registration than in the smaller schools. No staff could keep track of the movement of children from one classroom to another, and it seemed inevitable to this officer that children – particularly the non-academic, the bored and the deviant or delinquescent – should make their way out of the school into the areas of temptation. At present, at any rate, the peak year of delinquency is the final year of compulsory education; another year of compulsory schooling could increase considerably the amount of delinquency within the school itself.

Crime appears to be basically an urban problem. The increasing number of large, self-service stores with open counters must inevitably be accompanied by a rise in the number of cases of shop-lifting and petty larceny. Similarly, motor vehicles have become more and more the preserve of the criminal – including the petty juvenile thief as well as the highly organized criminal coterie. The following table (p. 278) lists the crimes favoured by juveniles (21).

Thus, with a growing population and a rising standard of living, the presence of more and more material property available for pilfering and stealing will inevitably mean more crime. It does not seem to be really

	Males under 14 %	Males 14–16 %	Males 17–20 %	Males all ages %
1. Larceny	53·2	52·2	52·4	53·2
2. Breaking and Entering	37·0	33·1	25·6	22·8
3. Violence v. the Person	1·0	4·3	9·6	7·8
4. Receiving	5·6	5·4	5·0	6·5
5. Fraud and False Pretences	0·3	0·6	1·8	3·4
6. Sexual Offences	0·7	2·2	2·0	2·8
7. Robbery	0·6	0·8	1·4	0·9
8. Other Offences	1·6	1·4	2·2	2·6
	100·0	100·0	100·0	100·0

poverty that is the cause of most crime today, but rather an ever-increasing spirit of acquisitiveness, of rebellion against society, of *anomie*, of lawlessness as a consequence of the presentation of unlimited aims with a limited capacity for fulfilment, and of boredom with a somewhat uncreative existence in the midst of incredible creativity. The deprivation in our present society is not so much a deprivation in terms of material goods as of personal fulfilment through the expression of specific innate capacities and abilities. The mass media present a vast spectrum of possibilities which arouse and excite the imagination of the least able; and one of the inevitable results is the sense of inadequacy by the underachievers who seek by all means to succeed.

D. DEVIANCE, DELINQUENCY AND EDUCATION

There are at least two ways of looking at the question of the prevention of juvenile deviancy and delinquency: one is in general and the other is in particular terms. One is to look at society as a whole, and the other is to look at the deviant or delinquent individual in particular. If young people feel the need to develop sub-cultures, to deviate from the norm, and to become alienated from their society in and through anti-social behaviour, it may well be that something *is* wrong with society. In their lack of mutual understanding of one another, age and youth develop a peer-group solidarity which frequently resolves itself into positive antipathy and hatred. Dr F. Musgrove has commented that:

'The hatred with which the mature Western society regard the young is a testimony to the latter's importance, to their power potential and actual. The adolescent has not enjoyed such economic and social power as is his and hers in mid-twentieth-century Britain, Europe and America, since the early days of the classical Industrial Revolution, when rapidly declining rates of mortality among the young made them worth taking seriously, and technological change and the reorganization of industry gave them a strategic position in the nation's economic life' (22).

Youth finds that the older generation is somewhat hypocritical in that it pretends to inculcate one set of standards, but vigorously pursues another. Our Education Act of 1944 insists upon the mediation of the Christian religion in state schools as a way of underpinning social and moral behaviour as well as inculcating a religion. But however permeated our society may be with Christian concepts and ideals, it is clear that the practice of big business, the exploitation of the immature and the ignorant, the production of nuclear weapons, nerve gases and bacteria for biological warfare are all contrary to the principles of peace, love and goodwill to all men. Youth is increasingly sensible of these discrepancies, for any culture which is merely 'on the books', or on tablets of stone, but not really pursued by a society, is already in decay. Some of the sub-cultures which are developing in this decaying soil may seem pathetic and immature, but they represent a deep yearning for something that is real and can be followed with zest and without hypocrisy.

In the meantime, however, there is an alienation from a society that is rejected as meaningless and unfulfilling. It is clearly one of the functions of educators to try and explain to their pupils what is happening in society and to society. In general terms, it is one of the aims of education to prevent alienation occurring from the very beginning. This clearly does not mean the acceptance of all that is evil or wrong in our society, but it does imply a thorough understanding of our society before we reject or accept it and its culture, or before there occurs a retreat into some sub-culture of our own. It may well be necessary to try and demonstrate to pupils that acquisitiveness does not inevitably make for happiness; that happiness is ultimately both derivative and an inner attitude of mind and being; that 'things' merely minister to this, and then only when they are in some way related to our being. We cannot change the nature of our society, or its direction, except through the nature of the people who comprise it. But we can help our pupils to live more fully through a deeper awareness of their own nature, and of the nature of society.

Our society is becoming increasingly mechanized and automated; the computerized and cybernetic age is with us: these are facts which we have to face and come to terms with. But the consequences of the new technological age must also be faced; it seems inevitable that the time will come when people will spend more hours in leisure than in work. Now, if the spirit of alienation and *anomie* were to grow correspondingly, society would be unbearable. This is where education must not only be *about* society, and about facts; it must also be *for* society, and for the development of values. We cannot afford simply to seek to develop the individual for his own sake, for the individual can never exist alone. We become fully ourselves, we become persons, in and through the group, the society. If we do not understand this society, and if we are in no way prepared for the new society that is developing, we shall of course remain alienated. As educators we may fill our pupils' heads with all sorts of information and data, but unless it is all related in some way to the society in which they are going to live, they will reject it all and create a culture of their own. They may become deviant, delinquent or criminal.

As we educate we must clearly think more in terms of what our pupils *will* and *can* do during their leisure time. They have to be trained to create a really worthwhile culture: and they have to be assisted to fulfil themselves creatively and in a satisfying way. Every form of literary, artistic, aesthetic and physical activity in which the self can be expressed in creation should be an essential part of our curriculum for living. This is not education for play, but education for a full life, education for living, and education for being. Much deviant and delinquent behaviour derives from the inability of individuals to fill their leisure time creatively; and when individuals become frustrated in the dimension of their creative potential they frequently become destructive.

The great importance of leisure, and the sociology of leisure, was emphasized by Joffre Dumazedier in his article entitled, 'La Sociologie du Loisir' (23). In sum, Dumazedier stated that

'Leisure represents a liberation from other forms of time utilization. It is an end in itself, characterized by the fact that the individual's needs take precedence over those of the collectivity. It is a time for relaxation, entertainment and for fuller development of the individual and his personality ... In the future there will be a need for more surveys to measure the time, distance and monetary factors which limit free time from being transformed into leisure time in the cases of many classes and categories of workers; to evaluate leisure resources in the cultural development of collectivities; to determine the value of leisure in relation to other values held by a society. In the last analysis, the responses to these questions relate directly to the future of man in industrial and post-industrial society' (24).

This total approach to leisure is certainly one that is desperately needed in both educational and sociological terms. The 'free time' of many individuals in our society is transformed into further work time or, maybe, just wasted time. People do not 'naturally' know how to manage, organize and maximize their free time for leisure: it is something that has to be developed as part of the totality of their personality.

It has become one of the functions of the school to help to elicit and develop the innate capabilities and skills of children – other than those involving merely imitation and memory. Much can be done to prevision the possibilities of individual activity in terms of leisure time, and equally to forestall the possibilities of deviant behaviour, both individual and collective. The role of the school is thus partly a social one in that it seeks to make pupils more able to use their leisure creatively. The problem is one of self-fulfilment in a social context – and this seems to be true at all levels in education. Those youths, who might formerly have sought to express their masculinity by stealing or 'bashing' the defenceless, could conceivably be trained to use their free time in a constructive and creative way. In Book VIII of *The Politics*, Aristotle emphasized that there was one vital criterion of a good education, namely, the proper use of one's leisure time:

'Leisure of itself gives pleasure and happiness and enjoyment of life, which are experienced, not by the busy man, but by those who have leisure. For he who is occupied has in view some end which he has not attained; but happiness is an end which all men deem to be accompanied with pleasure and not with pain . . . It is clear then that there are branches of learning and education which we must study with a view to enjoyment of leisure and these are to be valued for their own sake; whereas those kinds of knowledge which are useful in business are to be deemed necessary, and exist for the sake of other things' (25).

But it is not sufficient to think simply in terms of making proper provision for the fullest extension of the leisure time of each individual. A. J. Reiss has emphasized the failure of primary groups to offer adequate social roles or to provide proper social control (26). Our society has already recognized the need for pre-school play groups and nursery schools; it is through such developments that some of the early social deprivations of children might be ameliorated. The failures of homes and families to provide a rich linguistic background or possibilities of helpful interpersonal relationships might be compensated for in the environment of such educational institutions (27). At the upper end of the secondary or comprehensive school it is quite clear that, in the words of the Newsom Report, there is 'no automatic transfer of values' (28). But the attempt must still be made to lead adolescents into the realm of values in such a way that stress, resentment and *anomie* are minimized. This has never been an easy task: in a world of changing and uncertain, if not conflicting, values it is easier to write about it than to do it.

REFERENCES

1 *Vide* Hargreaves, D. H., *Social Relations in a Secondary School* (Routledge, 1967), where the author uses the term 'delinquescent' to describe a sub-culture among pupils which is in opposition to the 'academic' climate, and which encourages behaviour that is contrary to the values and standards promulgated by the school.

2 *Vide* Inkeles, A., *What is Sociology?* (Prentice-Hall, 1966), p. 80.

3 Reiss, A. J., 'Delinquency as the Failure of Personal and Social Controls', in *American Sociological Review*, Vol. 16, April 1951, p. 196.

4 Ibid., p. 198.

5 *Vide* Hargreaves, D. H., op. cit.

6 Cloward, R. A. and Ohlin, L. E., *Delinquency and Opportunity* (Routledge, 1961), pp. 2–3.

7 Wootton, Barbara, *Social Science and Social Pathology* (Allen and Unwin, 1959; 3rd impression 1963), pp. 81–135.

8 Ibid., p. 83.

9 Ibid., pp. 134–5.

10 Ibid., p. 135.

11 Durkheim, E., *Suicide* (Routledge, 1952; reprinted 1963), p. 247.

12 Incorporated Association of Head Masters, *The Grammar School: A New Survey of the Purpose and Method of the Main School* (Second Brasenose, 1960) (Gordon House, 29 Gordon Square, London, W.C.1, December 1960), p. 6.

13 *Vide* Young, M., *The Rise of the Meritocracy* (Penguin Books, 1961).

14 *Vide* Cohen, A. K., *Delinquent Boys* (Free Press, Glencoe, 1955).

15 *Vide* Miller, W. B., 'Lower Class Culture as a Generating Milieu of Gang Delinquency', *Journal of Social Issues*, Vol. 14, 1958, pp. 5–19; and Kvaraceus, W. C. and Miller, W. B., *Delinquent Behaviour: Culture and the Individual* (National Education Association, Washington D.C., 1959).

16 *Vide* Cloward, R. A. and Ohlin, L. E., op. cit., pp. 65–76.

17 Ibid., p. 74.

18 *Vide* Willmott, P., *Adolescent Boys of East London* (Penguin Books, 1969).

19 Ibid., pp. 166–7.

20 Home Office, *Criminal Statistics: England and Wales – 1968* (Cmnd 4098) (H.M.S.O., 1969), p. xii.

21 Ibid., p. xiii (adapted).

22 Musgrove, F., *Youth and the Social Order* (Routledge, 1964), p. 10.

23 *Vide* Dumazedier, J., 'La Sociologie du Loisir', *La Sociologie Contemporaine*, Vol. 16, No. 1, 1968 (Mouton and Co., Paris), pp. 5–31.

24 Ibid., pp. 35–7.

25 Aristotle, *The Politics*, in Cahn, S. M. (ed.), *The Philosophical Foundations of Education* (Harper and Row, 1970), p. 127.

26 *Vide* references 3 and 4.

27 *Vide* D.E.S., *Children and their Primary Schools* (Plowden Report)

(H.M.S.O., 1967), Chapter 9, 'Providing for Children before Compulsory Education', pp. 116–34.

28 *Vide* Ministry of Education, *Half Our Future* (Newsom Report) (H.M.S.O., 1963), para, 161, p. 53.

BIBLIOGRAPHY

A. *Books*

AICHHORN, A., *Wayward Youth* (Imago, 1951).
ANDRY, R. G., *Delinquency and Parental Pathology* (Methuen, 1960).
BAGOT, J. H., *Juvenile Delinquency* (J. Cape, 1941).
BANDURA, A. *et al.*, *Adolescent Aggression* (Ronald Press, N.Y., 1959).
BARRON, M. L., *The Juvenile in Delinquent Society* (A. A. Knopf, 1956).
BOSS, P., *Social Policy and the Young Delinquent* (Routledge, 1967).
BOWLBY, J., *Forty-four Juvenile Thieves* (Baillière, Tindall and Cox, 1946).
BURN, M., *Mr Lyward's Answer* (Hamilton 1956).
BURT, C., *The Young Delinquent* (C.U.P., 1942).
CARR-SAUNDERS, A. M. *et al.*, *Young Offenders* (C.U.P., 1942).
CLINARD, M. B., *Sociology of Deviant Behaviour* (Holt, Rinehart, 1965).
CLOWARD, R. and OHLIN, L. E., *Delinquency and Opportunity* (Routledge, 1961).
COHEN, A. K., *Delinquent Boys: The Culture of the Gang* (Free Press, Glencoe, 1955).
COLEMAN, J. S., *The Adolescent Society* (Free Press, Glencoe, 1961).
DOWNES, D. M., *The Delinquent Solution* (Routledge, 1966).
DUNLOP, A. B. *et al.*, *Young Men in Detention Centres* (Routledge, 1965).
EAST, W. NORWOOD, *et al.*, *The Adolescent Criminal* (Churchill, 1942).
FERGUSON, T., *The Young Delinquent in his Social Setting: a Glasgow Study* (O.U.P., 1952).
FORD, D., *The Delinquent Child* (Constable, 1957).
FRIEDLÄNDER, KATE, *The Psycho-Analytical Approach to Juvenile Delinquency* (Routledge, 1947; 5th impression 1961).
FRY, M. *et al.*, *Lawless Youth* (Allen and Unwin, 1947).
FYVEL, T. R., *The Insecure Offenders* (Penguin Books, 1963).
GILES, F. T., *The Juvenile Courts* (Allen and Unwin, 1946).
GILES, F. T., *Children and the Law* (Penguin, 1959).
GITTINS, J., *Approved School Boys* (H.M.S.O., 1952).
GLOVER, E. R., *Probation and Re-education* (Routledge, 1949; revised edition 1956).
GLOVER, E., *The Roots of Crime* (Allen and Unwin, 1960).
GLUECK, S. and E., *1,000 Juvenile Delinquents* (Harvard Univ. Press, 1934).
GLUECK, S. and E., *Juvenile Delinquents Grown Up* (Commonwealth Fund, 1940).
GLUECK, S. and E., *Unravelling Juvenile Delinquency* (Harvard Univ. Press, 1955).

GLUECK, S. and E., *Predicting Delinquency and Crime* (Harvard Univ. Press, 1959).

GLUECK, S. and E., *Family Environment and Delinquency* (Routledge, 1962).

GOETSCHIUS, G. W. *et al.*, *Working with Unattached Youth* (Routledge, 1967).

HARGREAVES, D. H., *Social Relations in a Secondary School* (Routledge, 1967).

HEALY, W. and BRONNER, A. F., *New Light on Delinquency and its Treatment* (Yale Univ. Press, 1946).

HEMMING, J., *Problems of Adolescent Girls* (Heinemann, 1960).

HERBERT, W. L. *et al.*, *Dealing with Delinquents* (Methuen, 1961).

HOYLES, J. A., *The Treatment of the Young Delinquent* (Epworth Press, 1952).

JEPHCOTT, P., *Some Young People* (Allen and Unwin, 1954).

JONES, H., *Reluctant Rebels* (Tavistock Publications, 1961).

JONES, H., *Crime in a Changing Society* (Penguin Books, 1965).

KING, JOAN F. S. (ed.), *The Probation Service* (Butterworth, 1958).

KVARACEUS, W. C. *et al.*, *Delinquent Behaviour* (National Education Association, 1959).

LENNHOFF, F. G., *Exceptional Children* (Allen and Unwin, 1960).

MACINNES, C., *Absolute Beginners* (Penguin Books, 1964).

MATZA, D., *Delinquency and Drift* (J. Wiley, 1964).

MAYER, R., *Young People in Trouble* (V. Gollancz, 1946).

MAYS, J. B., *Growing Up in the City* (Liverpool Univ. Press, 1954).

MAYS, J. B., *On the Threshold of Delinquency* (Liverpool Univ. Press, 1959; 2nd edition 1964).

MAYS, J. B., *Education and the Urban Child* (Liverpool Univ. Press, 1962).

MAYS, J. B., *Crime and the Social Structure* (Faber, 1963).

MAYS, J. B., *The Young Pretenders* (Michael Joseph, 1965).

MERTON, R. K., *Contemporary Social Problems* (Hart-Davis, 1965).

MORRIS, T., *The Criminal Area* (Routledge, 1957).

MORSE, MARY, *The Unattached* (Penguin Books, 1965).

PAGE, L., *The Young Lag* (Faber, 1950).

QUAY, H. C., *Juvenile Delinquency* (Van Nostrand, 1965).

REAKES, G. L., *The Juvenile Offender* (C. Johnson, 1953).

REDL, F. *et al.*, *Children Who Hate* (Collier-Macmillan, 1962).

ROBISON, S. M., *Juvenile Delinquency* (Holt, Rinehart, 1965).

ROGERS, C. R., *Clinical Treatment of the Problem Child* (Houghton Mifflin, 1939).

SCHOFIELD, M., *The Sexual Behaviour of Young People* (Penguin Books, 1968).

SELLIN, T. (ed.), *Juvenile Delinquency* (Philadelphia Press, 1949).

SHAW, C. R., *The Jack-Roller: A Delinquent Boy's Own Story* (Univ. of Chicago Press, 1966).

SHAW, C. R. *et al.*, *Juvenile Delinquency and Urban Areas* (Univ. of Chicago Press, 1942).

SHAW, O. L., *Maladjusted Boys* (Allen and Unwin, 1965).

SHAW, O. L., *Prisons of the Mind* (Allen and Unwin, 1969).

SHELDON, W. H., *Varieties of Delinquent Youth* (Harper, 1949).

SHIELDS, R. W., *A Cure of Delinquents* (Heinemann, 1962).

SPINLEY, BETTY M., *The Deprived and the Privileged* (Routledge, 1953).

ST JOHN, H., *Probation – The Second Chance* (Vista, 1961).

STOKES, S., *Our Dear Delinquents* (Heinemann, 1965).

STOTT, D. H., *Delinquency and Human Nature* (Carnegie U.K. Trust, 1950).

STOTT, D. H., *Unsettled Children and their Families* (Univ. of London Press, 1956).

STOTT, D. H., *Saving Children from Delinquency* (Univ. of London Press, 1957).

STOTT, D. H., *33 Troublesome Children* (Nat. Ch. Home, 1964).

TAPPAN, P. W., *Juvenile Girls in Court* (Columbia Univ. Press, 1947).

TAPPAN, P. W., *Juvenile Delinquency* (McGraw-Hill, 1949).

THRASHER, F. M., *The Gang* (Univ. of Chicago Press, abridged edition 1963; 2nd impression 1966).

TRASLER, G., *The Explanation of Criminality* (Routledge, 1962).

VALENTINE, C. W., *The Difficult Child and the Problem of Discipline* (Methuen, 1950).

VENESS, THELMA, *School Leavers* (Methuen, 1962).

WARD, R. F., *The Hidden Boy* (Cassell, 1962).

WATSON, J. A. F., *The Child and the Magistrate* (J. Cape, 1942).

WATTENBURG, W. W., *Social Deviancy Among Youth* (Univ. of Chicago Press, 1966).

WEAVER, A., *They Steal for Love* (M. Parrish, 1959).

WEST, D. J., *The Young Offender* (Penguin Books, 1967).

WHYTE, W. F., *Street Corner Society* (Univ. of Chicago Press, 1943; 2nd edition, 1955).

WILLCOCK, H. D., *Report on Juvenile Delinquency* (Falcon Press, 1949).

WILLMOTT, P., *Adolescent Boys of East London* (Penguin Books, 1969).

WILLS, D., *The Hawkspur Experiment* (Allen and Unwin, 1941; 2nd edition 1967).

WILLS, D., *The Barns Experiment* (Allen and Unwin, 1947).

WILLS, D., *A Place Like Home* (Allen and Unwin, 1971).

WILSON, HARRIETT, *Delinquency and Child Neglect* (Allen and Unwin, 1962; 2nd impression 1964).

WOOTTON, BARBARA, *Social Science and Social Pathology* (Allen and Unwin, 1959; 4th impression 1967).

YABLONSKY, L., *The Violent Gang* (Penguin Books, 1967).

YOUNG, M. and WILMOTT, P., *Family and Kinship in East London* (Routledge, 1957).

B. *Home Office Pamphlets*

The Child, the Family and Young Offender (Cmnd 2742) (H.M.S.O.).

Approved Schools and Remand Homes (Cmnd 8429) (H.M.S.O., 1964).

Types of Delinquency and Home Background (H.M.S.O., 1967).

Children in Trouble (Cmnd 3601) (H.M.S.O., 1968).

Criminal Statistics: England and Wales – 1968 (Cmnd 4098) (H.M.S.O., 1969).

Chapter 16

Education and Social Philosophy

Facts are stubborn things, but sociologists (like politicians) know only too well that facts are open to a variety of interpretations, and that the evaluation of the same data will differ from one researcher to another. This is not just a question of levels of expertise; it is simply that, at the level of human activity, although techniques have considerably improved, there is no exact science of measurement. Indeed, some of the attempts at quantifying dimensions of human action and personality are both artificial and pretentious. There are areas and depths of both being and interpersonal relationship which defy measurement; man persistently refuses any form of reduction to 'the average' or to some statistical skew.

There is an element of unpredictability about humankind which challenges all forms of prognosis, whether medical, psychological or sociological. And whether the behaviourists like it or not, the uncertainty principle applies not only to particles of matter but also to human consciousness. Indeed B. F. Skinner believes that the Principle of Indeterminacy, particularly applicable to physics at the sub-atomic level, is also of significance in relation to people. He says that

'since human behaviour is enormously complex and the human organism is of limited dimensions, many acts may involve processes to which the Principle of Indeterminacy applies. It does not follow that human behaviour is free, but only that it may be beyond the range of predictive or controlling science' (1).

We may be creatures of habit, and we may display *trends* in our activities and in our behavioural choices and patterns; but there are times when we not only act 'out of character', but also drop the mask, or *persona*, which we normally wear, and for once really become ourselves. This unpredictability of individuals at the time of real, personal choice inevitably raises questions of an evaluative nature. We pass value-judgements as well as factual-judgements about human behaviour, and it is at this point that ethics and social philosophy, if not religion, enter.

It is one thing to analyse society as it is and to mediate this factual material to our pupils. But however essential this may be it is clearly not enough. A society without ideals is a society without motivation: and if it is important to know where we have been in our social development, it is equally (if not more) important to know the direction in which we are going, and to provide some leadership for those who are today becoming very quickly full members of our society. Writing in 1964 Dr Frank Musgrove said that

'There is a general need for lowering the age of admission into English social and cultural institutions, for taking in sixteen-year-olds and according them the rights, and imposing the responsibilities, which apply to their seniors. Political and legal maturity should be recognized at seventeen; the trend to more youthful marriage accepted and aided instead of deplored ... The sexual powers and needs of adolescents need frank recognition; heterosexual experience in adolescence must be accepted, instruction in birth-control given ... The contemporary social order and adult social attitudes are based, if not upon hypocrisy, on gigantic myths concerning the needs and nature of the young' (2).

This is a very realistic approach to the problems of the young, and, although many might quarrel with some of the detail of Dr Musgrove's suggestions, there can be little doubt that the main principle expressed is right. The sooner the 'tween-period' of the teenager is erased the better; the twilight period of youth between school-leaving and so-called adulthood is an anachronism in our modern society, and increasingly the last year or two years of school life must be regarded as the final period of initiation into society and into the responsibilities of earning and adulthood.

In pursuing this theme the reader can do no better than peruse the whole chapter in Dr Musgrove's book from which the above quotation comes (3). It is worth noting in passing that one of the recommendations of the Newsom Report was that more demands should be made upon pupils between the ages of thirteen and sixteen, both in the nature and the amount of the work required (4). In this respect Dr Musgrove has emphasized elsewhere the importance for the adolescent of 'an occupational identity' (5). Once the school-leaving age becomes sixteen, the choices of a career for adolescents are pushed farther into the future, and youth begins to 'lack the kind of focus for their image of themselves which our society approves' (6). Musgrove sees the possibility of a resultant increase in role conflict among adolescents in the future through the deferring of vocational choices. It is, no doubt, for this reason that much of the Newsom Report is taken up with a discussion of the possibilities of vocational choices and guidance (7). An education which makes sense, according to the Central Advisory Council, is one which is realistic, practical and vocational, and which leaves the way open to youths to make some choice. But this is not all. If it is to make complete sense it must also provide the opportunity for 'personal fulfilment – for the good life as well as for good living'.

The 'good life' suggests at once that there *are* standards and values of behaviour which are, at least, relatively ideal norms for mankind in any particular society; and that, difficult as it may be at times to define these norms precisely to the satisfaction of all the pundits, when it really comes to the crunch there are certainly some forms of behaviour which we can say with some confidence are deleterious to the health, welfare and happiness of both the individual and society. The wisdom and the accumulated store of knowledge of the ages must surely count for something in the field of human behaviour. There are also lessons we could learn from more recent human involvement in crime, social deviance, aggression and war. It is not all that difficult to delineate what is harmful if we really put our minds to it, without long disquisitions on the meaning of meaning, semantics and linguistic analysis. Some of the simplest of interpersonal relationships we have complicated by forms of casuistry which would in the long run make almost every action both isolated and autonomous. If one questions the necessity of a social order at all, it may well be that values and standards of morality are irrelevant. But so long as there remains the concept of a human society there must exist norms of behaviour, mores, customs, habits or morals – whatever one chooses to call them. Even at the purely pragmatic level, for example, it is essential in any society to have certain standards of truth, for without these no people could any longer communicate. Indeed, the success of a lie depends entirely upon the relative stability of truth. One has, also, to have respect for life, since without such respect there would be no guarantee of our own personal survival.

In his *The Integrity of the Personality*, Anthony Storr argues that it is only in the 'fruitful soil of satisfactory interpersonal relationships' that the full flowering of the human personality can take place (8). The child's fulfilment and happiness depend upon how far he is capable of having the fullest possible relationships with others: and this in turn depends upon how far he can identify with others and make their interests also his own. We may, indeed, as individuals have a limited vision of the truth, and of the ideals which move others to love, hope, faith and action; but that limited vision will inevitably restrict our own personal development and fulfilment. As Anthony Storr remarks:

'Truth has many aspects; and the limitations imposed by inheritance preclude each one of us from seeing more than a small part of it. The most that anyone can do is to be faithful to that aspect which he is able to see. Each of us has his own interpretation of the truth; but our very differences may link us more closely when we recognize that the man who is capable of the deepest human relationship is the man who is most surely himself' (9).

We return now once more to the functional approach of D. F. Aberle *et al.* discussed in Chapter 3, where certain prerequisites of society were delineated (10). Those prerequisites were considered in some detail there, but they inevitably represent a social philosophy in relation to education. The writers of the article obviously took the view that a society functioned only in so far as it fulfilled certain conditions: to that extent it really was a society. A functional view of education would take up the same standpoint. The general demands of the society in philosophical and ethical terms are also, ideally, those of the school, in so far as they are valid at all. The educational system must make the proper provision for adequate relationship to the environment; it must provide adequate role-differentiation and assignment for its pupils; it must develop the means of communication both in speech and writing; it must afford shared cognitive experiences; it must establish a shared and adequately articulated set of aims and objectives; it must prescribe the normative regulation of means; it must regulate children's affective as well as cognitive expression; and it must socialize its pupils (11). To develop these themes as functions of education would require another book, but they should leave the student with sufficient material to consider the possibilities of a philosophy of education derived from the sociological analysis of D. F. Aberle and his associates. It would be unfair to suggest that the latter regarded their list of functional prerequisites as definitive; nor is it argued here that they are any more definitive in the context of education. But they are suggestive and positive and provide a foundation for further expansion for anyone interested in social philosophy as a point of departure for a philosophy of education.

Society is composed of individuals, of people; but society is more than the individuals whom it comprises. It is true that men can and do change society, but it is also true that other things – inventions, events, revolutions – all help to change society. But as M. B. Katz suggests, there is an essential passivity about the school as a social institution; it cannot act apart from society or in complete divorce from society's aims; 'it must rationalize the outcome of institutional evolution while altering existing institutions as little as possible' (12). But it is certainly not the purpose of the school merely to reflect uncritically the values of society and its stratification. The teacher may be a servant of the state but he is not its slave: certainly he must live in society, some society of his choice, but he does not of necessity subscribe to all its values and aims. He should make sure, however, that his own values and aims are really better than those of his society before he seeks to improve upon them, or to propagandize his pupils with his own. He must seek to open the door to reality and to truth, beauty and goodness rather than to indoctrinate his children with his own limited and often visionless values, reality and truth. Indeed, as the Prophet said,

T

'No man can reveal to you aught but that which already lies half asleep in the dawning of your knowledge.

The teacher who walks in the shadow of the temple, among his followers, gives not of his wisdom but rather of his faith and his lovingness.

If he is indeed wise he does not bid you enter the house of his wisdom, but rather leads you to the threshold of your own mind' (13).

REFERENCES

1 Skinner, B. F., *Science and Human Behaviour* (Collier-Macmillan, 1953; Free Press paperback, 1965), p. 17.
2 Musgrove, F., *Youth and the Social Order* (Routledge, 1964), p. 157.
3 Ibid., Chapter 8, 'Youth and the Future', pp. 150–63.
4 *Vide* Ministry of Education, *Half Our Future* (Newsom Report) (H.M.S.O., 1963), paras 77–82 and p. 31, 'Recommendations' (b).
5 *Vide* Musgrove, F., 'Role Conflict in Adolescence', *British Journal of Educational Psychology*, Vol. 34, 1964; and 'Childhood and Adolescence' in The Schools Council, *The Educational Implications of Social and Economic Change* (*Working Paper No. 12*) (H.M.S.O., 1967), pp. 48–58.
6 The Schools Council, *Working Paper No. 12*, p. 58.
7 *Vide* op. cit., Chapter 14, 'An Education that Makes Sense', pp. 114–18.
8 *Vide* Storr, A., *The Integrity of the Personality* (Penguin Books, 1963), p. 134.
9 Ibid., p. 177.
10 *Vide* Aberle, D. F. *et al.*, 'The Functional Prerequisites of a Society', *Ethics*, Vol. 60, January 1950, pp. 100–11 (Bobbs-Merrill Reprint Series in the Social Sciences, S-1).
11 *Vide* Chapter 3 *passim*.
12 *Vide* Katz, M. B., 'Education', in Butterworth, E. and Weir, D., *The Sociology of Modern Britain: An Introductory Reader* (Collins, Fontana Library, 1970), pp. 296–300.
13 Gibran, Kahlil, *The Prophet* (Heinemann, 1926; 27th reprint 1969).

BIBLIOGRAPHY

BANTOCK, G. H., *Freedom and Authority in Education* (Faber, 1952).
BANTOCK, G. H., *Education in an Industrial Society* (Faber, 1963).
BANTOCK, G. H., *Education and Values* (Faber, 1965).
BENN, S. I. and PETERS, R. S., *Social Principles and the State* (Allen and Unwin, 1959, 6th impression 1968).
BOTTOMORE, T. B., *Sociology: A Guide to Problems and Literature* (Allen and Unwin, 1962; 2nd edition 1971), Part VI, 'Applied Sociology', pp. 313–42.
BOULDING, K., *The Meaning of the Twentieth Century* (Allen and Unwin, 1965).

BUTTERWORTH, E. and WEIR, D., *The Sociology of Modern Britain* (Collins, Fontana Library, 1970), Chapter 7, 'Values', pp. 285–335.

CLARKE, F., *Education and Social Change* (Sheldon Press, 1940).

CLARKE, F., *Freedom in the Educative Society* (Univ. of London Press, 1948).

COLLIER, K. G., *The Social Purposes of Education* (Routledge, 1959).

DEWEY, J., *Democracy and Education* (Macmillan, 1955).

DOBINSON, C. H. (ed.), *Education in a Changing World* (O.U.P., 1951).

DURKHEIM, E., *Education and Sociology* (Free Press, Glencoe, 1956).

DURKHEIM, E., *Moral Education: A Study in the Theory and Application of the Sociology of Education* (Free Press, Glencoe, 1961).

DURKHEIM, E., *Sociology and Philosophy* (Cohen and West, revised edition 1965).

ELVIN, H. L., *Education and Contemporary Society* (Watts, 1965).

FLUGEL, J. C., *Men, Morals and Society* (Penguin Books, 1955).

GINSBERG, M., *On the Diversity of Morals* (Heinemann, 1956).

HOBHOUSE, L. T., *Elements of Social Justice* (Allen and Unwin, 1922; 5th impression 1965).

HOLLINS, T. H. B., (ed.), *Aims of Education* (Manchester Univ. Press, 1964).

JEFFREYS, M. V. C., *Glaucon* (Pitman, 1950).

JEFFREYS, M. V. C. *Personal Values in the Modern World* (Penguin Books, 1962; revised edition 1966).

MANNHEIM, K., *Man and Society in an Age of Reconstruction* (Routledge, 1940; reprinted 1960).

MANNHEIM, K., *Diagnosis of Our Time* (Routledge, 1943).

MANNHEIM, K., *Ideology and Utopia* (Routledge, 1954).

MUSGROVE, F., *Youth and the Social Order* (Routledge, 1964).

MYRDAL, G., *Value in Social Theory* (Routledge, 1958).

NIBLETT, W. R. (ed.), *Moral Education in a Changing Society* (Faber, 1963).

OTTAWAY, A. K. C., *Education and Society* (Routledge, 1953; 2nd edition (revised) 1962; reprinted 1968), Chapter XI, 'Beyond Sociology', pp. 208–15.

PETERS, R. S., *Authority, Responsibility and Education* (Allen and Unwin, 1963).

PETERS, R. S., *Ethics and Education* (Allen and Unwin, 1965).

POPPER, K., *The Open Society and its Enemies* (Routledge, 1945).

REEVES, M., *Growing Up in a Modern Society* (Univ. of London Press, 1946).

RUSSELL, B., *Education and the Social Order* (Allen and Unwin, 1932; 6th impression 1961).

RUSSELL, B., *Authority and the Individual* (Allen and Unwin, 1949).

RUSSELL, B., *Impact of Science on Society* (Allen and Unwin, 1952).

RUSSELL, B., *Prospects of Industrial Civilization* (Allen and Unwin; 2nd edition 1959).

STREET, H., *Freedom, Society and the Individual* (Penguin Books; 2nd edition 1968).

WILSON, J. et al., *Introduction to Moral Education* (Penguin Books, 1967).

Name Index

Subject Index